CAN LIBERAL PLURALISM BE EXPORTED?

D1612468

Can Liberal Pluralism be Exported?

Western Political Theory and Ethnic Relations in Eastern Europe

Edited by

WILL KYMLICKA

and

MAGDA OPALSKI

OXFORD
UNIVERSITY PRESS

OXFORD

UNIVERSITY PRESS

Great Clarendon Street, Oxford OX2 6DP

Oxford University Press is a department of the University of Oxford.
It furthers the University's objective of excellence in research, scholarship,
and education by publishing worldwide in

Oxford New York

Athens Auckland Bangkok Bogotá Buenos Aires Cape Town
Chennai Dar es Salaam Delhi Florence Hong Kong Istanbul Karachi
Kolkata Kuala Lumpur Madrid Melbourne Mexico City Mumbai Nairobi
Paris São Paulo Shanghai Singapore Taipei Tokyo Toronto Warsaw

and associated companies in Berlin Ibadan

Oxford is a registered trade mark of Oxford University Press
in the UK and certain other countries

Published in the United States
by Oxford University Press Inc., New York

British Library Cataloguing in Publication Data

Data available

Library of Congress Cataloging in Publication Data

Can liberal pluralism be exported? : Western political theory and ethnic relations in
Eastern Europe / edited by Will Kymlicka and Magda Opalski.
p. cm.
1. Minorities—Civil rights—Europe, Eastern. 2. Minorities—Civil rights—Europe, Western.
3. Liberalism—Europe, Western. 4. Pluralism. 5. Europe, Eastern—Ethnic relations.
I. Kymlicka, Will. II. Opalski, Magdalena.
JC599.E92 C355 2001 323.1′47—dc21 2001033952

ISBN 0-19-924063-9
ISBN 0-19-924815-X (Pbk.)

1 3 5 7 9 10 8 6 4 2

Typeset by Best-set Typesetter Ltd., Hong Kong
Printed and bound in Great Britain by Biddles Ltd
www.biddles.co.uk

CONTENTS

NOTES ON CONTRIBUTORS

Will Kymlicka is the author of five books published by Oxford University Press: *Liberalism, Community, and Culture* (1989), *Contemporary Political Philosophy* (1990), *Multicultural Citizenship* (1995), *Finding Our Way: Rethinking Ethnocultural Relations in Canada* (1998), and *Politics in the Vernacular: Nationalism, Multiculturalism and Citizenship* (2001). He is also the editor of *The Rights of Minority Cultures* (OUP 1995), co-editor with Ian Shapiro of *Ethnicity and Group Rights* (NYU Press 1997), and co-editor with Wayne Norman of *Citizenship in Diverse Societies* (OUP 2000). He is currently a Professor of Philosophy at Queen's University, and a Recurrent Visiting Professor in the Nationalism Studies programme at the Central European University in Budapest.

Magda Opalski is a Professor of East European Studies at Carleton University in Ottawa and current director of Forum Eastern Europe, a Canadian-based international research group. She is the author of *Poles and Jews: A Failed Brotherhood* (Brandeis University Press 1993, co-authored with Israel Bartal), editor of *Ethnic Minority Rights in Central Eastern Europe* (Canadian Human Rights Foundation 1994), and *Managing Diversity in Plural Societies: Minorities, Migration and Nation-Building in Post-Communist Europe* (Forum Eastern Europe 1998), and co-editor of *Polin,* a journal of Polish-Jewish studies.

George Schöpflin is Jean Monnet Professor of Political Science and Director of the Centre for the Study of Nationalism at the School of Slavonic and East European Studies, University of London. He is the author of the influential *Politics in Eastern Europe: 1945–1992* (Blackwell 1993) and more recently of *Nations, Identity, Power: The New Politics of Europe* (Hurst 2000). He is also the co-editor of *Myths and Nationhood* (Hurst 1997) and of *State-Building in the Balkans* (Longo 1998). His principal area of research is the relationship between ethnicity, nationhood, and political power, with particular reference to post-Communist societies.

Urszula Doroszewska is a Warsaw-based sociologist and journalist specializing in political issues in the Caucasus and Ukraine. She is program director for the Foundation for Democracy in Eastern Europe (IDEE), and the author of its award-winning programs for the integration of the Crimean Tatars.

Tibor Várady is Professor of Law at the Central European University in Budapest, and at Emory University in Atlanta. A graduate from Harvard Law School, he taught law at Novi Sad University for more than 20 years. He briefly served as Yugoslavia's Justice Minister under Milan Panic (1992–93), and is currently serving as a legal adviser to President Kostunica. He is the author of many books and articles on law and ethnicity, and is editor in chief of the social science review *Létünk*.

Michael Walzer is a Professor at the Institute for Advanced Studies in Princeton. He is the author of *Just and Unjust Wars* (Penguin 1977), *Spheres of Justice: A Defense of Pluralism and Equality* (Blackwell 1983), *What It Means To Be An American* (Marsilio 1993), and *On Toleration* (Yale University Press 1997). With Mitchell Cohen, he is co-editor of *Dissent*, a magazine of the democratic left. He is currently working on a large collaborative project on Jewish political thought.

Boris Tsilevich is a member of the Latvian Parliament elected on the platform of the defense of minority rights, and is a member of the Parliamentary Assembly of the Council of Europe. A journalist, scholar, and political commentator he has written extensively on nation-building in multiethnic states, minority issues, and conflict prevention in post-Communist Europe. He is also the founder and moderator of MINELRES, a web site providing information on minorities and ethnopolitics in Eastern Europe, and co-founder of the Consortium on Minority Resources (COMIR).

Alexander Ossipov is a senior researcher at the Institute of Ethnology and Anthropology of the Russian Academy of Sciences, in Moscow. He is a leading expert on ethnic discrimination, minority protection, and ethnic relations in the Caucasus and southern Russia. His books in English include *Russian Experience of Ethnic Discrimination; Meskhetians in Krasnodar Region* (Moscow 2000) and *Discrimination on Ethnic and Residency Grounds in the Moscow Region* (Moscow 1999). He is also program director for the Memorial Human Rights Centre.

Panayote Dimitras is a founding member and spokesperson for Greek Helsinki Monitor, and a founding member of Minority Rights Group Greece, and principal organizer of the Balkan Human Rights web page. Trained in economics and politics, he has taught at various American and European universities. He has also served as a member of, or adviser to, several research groups on Balkan issues, including UNESCO's MOST group, the EU's Euromosaic and Mercator groups, and the International Commission on the Balkans.

Nafsika Papanikolatos is the Spokesperson for Minority Rights Group Greece and the coordinator of the Center for Documentation and Information on Minorities in South-East Europe (CEDIME-SE), and co-organizer of the Consortium on Minority Resources (COMIR). She has written several articles on human rights and minority rights in Southeast Europe.

Pål Kolstø is a Professor of Russian and East European Area Studies at the University of Oslo. His work in recent years has been devoted to ethnic relations and ethnopolitics in the former Soviet Union. He is the author of *Russians in the Former Soviet Republics* (Hurst 1995) and *Political Construction Sites: Nation-Building in Russia and the post-Soviet States* (Westview 2000), as well as editor and co-author of *Nation-Building and Ethnic Integration in Post-Soviet Societies: An Investigation of Latvia and Kazakhstan* (Westview 1999).

János Kis is Professor of Philosophy and Political Science at the Central European University in Budapest and a visiting professor at New York University. He is the author of two monographs and several articles in French, Hungarian, and English. In the early 1990s he served as a member of the Hungarian Parliament, before returning to academia in 1992.

Pavel Barša is an Associate Professor of Political Science at Masaryk University in Brno, Czech Republic. He is the author of three books in Czech: *Political Theory of Multiculturalism* (CDK 1999), *Nation-State and Ethnic Conflict* (CDK 1999, co-authored with M. Strimska), and *Introduction to Contemporary Anglo-American Philosophy* (KLP 2000).

Vello Pettai is a Lecturer at the Department of Political Science at Tartu University in Estonia. He is the author of several articles on ethnic politics in Estonia and Latvia. He has served as Advisor to

President Lennart Meri on minority issues and is actively involved in developing Estonia's new integration policy.

Gabriel Andreescu is the chair of the Romanian Helsinki Committee Center for Human Rights in Bucharest, and the author of several studies on the rights of the Hungarian minority in Romania. He is the founding editor of the bilingual English-Romanian journal *International Studies* and editor of *Romanian Review for Human Rights*.

Volodymyr Fesenko is a Professor of Sociology at Kharkiv State University, Ukraine. His academic research and publications deal with the emergence of new post-Communist elites, nation-building policies, and the impact of globalization on the transition process in Ukraine. He was also coordinator of the Renaissance Foundation (Soros Foundation) in Kharkov.

Aleksander Djumaev is a Professor of Central Asian cultural history currently teaching history of oriental music at Tashkent State Conservatory. In addition to music, he has written extensively about Islam, Soviet and post-Soviet cultural policies and ethnocultural problems in central Asia. He is program director for the Uzbek branch of the Open Society Institute (Soros Foundation), and co-editor of *Public Opinion*, a journal published in Uzbekistan, and of *Central Asia and Caucasus*, a sociopolitical academic journal based in Sweden.

LIST OF FIGURES

LIST OF TABLES

PREFACE AND ACKNOWLEDGEMENTS

WILL KYMLICKA

This book is a departure for me, in both content and format. Most of my previous work has focused on the status of ethnocultural minorities within Western democracies. In my 1995 book, *Multicultural Citizenship*, I tried to develop a normative theory for evaluating claims by minorities within the West for various kinds of cultural and political rights. In developing this theory, I took for granted the usual features of Western countries—that they are economically prosperous, politically stable democracies with liberal constitutions and market economies. My goal was to show how the claims of various kinds of ethnocultural groups, such as immigrants, national minorities and indigenous peoples, can be fairly accommodated within this context.

Until recently, I had not studied the issues of ethnocultural diversity in other parts of the world, such as the Middle East, Latin America, Africa, or the newly-democratizing countries in post-Communist Europe or Central Asia. However, in recent years I have received several requests to discuss the potential application of my theory in non-Western contexts, particularly in Eastern and Central Europe. Some of these requests have come from academics, NGOs, and governments in Eastern-Central Europe, looking to retool their minority policy on the basis of liberal-democratic rather than Communist premises. Other requests have come from Western organizations involved in the region, which have learned from painful experience that virtually all aspects of the transition from Communism to democracy—whether related to the economy, politics, law, education, environment, or media—have ethnocultural dimensions which cannot be ignored.

I was reluctant to take on this issue, since I have little familiarity with the history, demographics, or political economy of post-Communist countries. There are countless stories circulating in the region of Western 'experts' who make grand pronouncements about what freedom, democracy, and justice requires in Eastern Europe without any knowledge of the context, and whose recommendations have turned out to be unhelpful, if not counter-productive.

However, despite these reservations, I have decided to become involved in the debate on minority rights in Eastern Europe. One reason is my concern that many Western commentators writing about Eastern Europe are giving a misleading impression of ethnic relations, not only in Eastern Europe, but also in the West itself.

Western pronouncements in this debate have tended to take one of two disconnected forms. At a philosophical level, commentators describe the Western approach to ethnicity by invoking a series of abstract terms, such as civic nationalism, constitutional patriotism, common citizenship, non-discrimination, the separation of state and ethnicity, *laicité*, colour-blind constitutions, benign neglect, and so on. Eastern European countries are encouraged to adopt a constitutional philosophy grounded in these concepts.

At a more political level, Western states have been pushing Eastern European countries to adopt a number of very specific minority rights regarding the use of minority languages in schools, the media, public administration, and street signs, as well as rights regarding political representation and local self-government.

The problem is that these two levels of discourse do not neatly match up. The theory of liberal democracy presented at the philosophical level does not clearly defend, or even allow for, the sorts of minority rights being pushed at the political level.

Part of the difficulty here is that the three Western countries with the most intellectual influence in Eastern Europe are the United States, France, and Germany. They have been most active in promoting and funding democratization programmes in the region, and their experts are often consulted first in discussions of new political or judicial institutions or constitutions. Hence it is American models of colour-blind constitutions and non-discrimination, or French models of republican citizenship and *laicité*, or German models of constitutional patriotism, which are most influential and most actively promoted at the level of political philosophy.

Yet these models provide little guidance for thinking about minority rights in Eastern Europe. The United States, France, and Germany are—or think of themselves as—essentially monolingual nation-states. Citizens are assumed to share a common national identity and a common language, and if minority nationalisms exist they tend to be numerically marginal and geographically peripheral. Since most countries in Eastern Europe are not now, and are unlikely to become, monolingual nation-states, the people charged with the task of developing concrete recommendations on minority rights policies have tended to look to other Western examples for guidance, such as the official bilingualism or multilingualism policies in Switzerland, Belgium, Canada, or Spain, or the self-government regimes in Italy (South Tyrol), Finland (Åland Islands), or the United Kingdom (Scotland and Wales).

People in Eastern Europe are confronted, therefore, with somewhat contradictory demands from the West. They are told simultaneously to adopt models of the state developed in monolingual nation-states, and to adopt a series of minority rights developed in multilingual, multination states. Since the former are disconnected from the multilingual and multinational realities on the ground in Eastern Europe, they are not helpful. And since the latter are presented simply as political demands, disconnected from any theory or principles of liberal democracy, they are widely perceived in the region as arbitrary and selective.

When people in Eastern Europe express puzzlement about these contradictory demands, and when they fail to live up to one or other of them—as is unavoidable—they are then dismissed as politically immature, and not yet ready to rejoin civilized Europe. Their failure to live up to either our philosophical images of civic nationalism or our political demands for minority rights is then explained in terms of 'ancient ethnic hatreds', which allegedly make them unable to truly adopt liberal-democratic practices. Needless to say, this dismissive explanation is deeply resented in the region.

The process of transition in Eastern Europe is difficult enough without having to deal with incoherent and patronizing reactions from the West. So one of my motivations for this project is to provide a more accurate picture of how Western states in fact deal with ethnocultural diversity, and to explore what it would mean to adopt these practices in Eastern Europe. In my opening paper—Part 1 of the volume—I discuss how Western states have responded historically to ethnocultural diversity through a combination of majority nation-building and minority rights, and explain why models of civic nationalism and ethnocultural neutrality are a misleading description of these Western practices. Drawing on the work of several recent political theorists writing on liberal nationalism and minority rights, I offer an alternative theoretical model which shows how both majority nation-building and minority rights are related to deeper principles of freedom, equality, and democracy. The model I describe in this paper draws upon the ideas in *Multicultural Citizenship*, but offers a more systematic account of the relationship between nation-building and minority rights. I compare this model with existing practices in Eastern Europe, discuss what changes would be involved in adopting Western practices, and consider some of the most obvious difficulties in doing so. These difficulties are often serious, and in some cases insurmountable, at least in the short term, but their complexity and manageability are obscured by sweeping appeals to 'ancient ethnic hatreds'.

My concern is not so much to recommend that countries in Eastern Europe adopt these Western practices or models, although I think that some of them are indeed worth considering, but simply to explain what they actually involve. If it is true that many Western experts misunderstand the situation in Eastern Europe, it is equally true that many people in Eastern Europe have a distorted view of how Western democracies deal with these issues, and I hope to provide a more useful roadmap that clarifies the place of minority rights in both the theory and practice of liberal democracies.

My goal is to dispel some of the mutual misunderstandings that people in the West and East have about ethnic relations, so that we can have a more fruitful dialogue and more constructive co-operation. To this end, my co-editor, Magda Opalski, and I have invited several people from the region to comment on my paper, and to point out aspects of the situation in Eastern Europe which need to be kept in mind when thinking about minority rights. Several of these commentators discuss aspects of ethnic relations which apply generally in Eastern Europe, others focus on particular countries. These commentaries, as well as a few from Western experts on the region, comprise Part 2 of the volume.

In the concluding section—Part 3—I discuss some of the difficulties raised by the commentators concerning the application of Western models of minority rights in the region. I also suggest some ways in which Western organizations, like the Council of Europe or the Organization for Security and Co-operation in Europe (OSCE), could play a more constructive role in assisting countries in Eastern Europe to manage their ethnic conflicts in a fair and peaceful manner.

I hope this volume will be of interest to anyone who is concerned with the problems of ethnic conflict in Eastern Europe, whether as academics, activists, journalists, or simply as interested citizens. I hope it will also be of interest to people working on the more general question of whether Western liberal democracy can and should be promoted around the world. The issue of applying Western models of minority rights is a limited, but important, test case for this more general question about exporting Western political ideals and institutions. The contributions to this volume are written in non-technical language, and do not presuppose any detailed knowledge of either academic political theory or of ethnic relations in any particular country.

One final terminological point. As noted earlier, our focus is on the post-Communist countries of Eastern and Central Europe and the former Soviet Union. This is a very large and diverse region, extending from Central Europe to the Baltics, the Caucasus, the Balkans, and Central Asia. For ease of exposition, we will sometimes call this entire region Eastern Europe. This is obviously misleading, since it includes countries which may think of themselves as part of 'Central Europe' rather than Eastern Europe—such as Hungary—and others which are in fact part of Central Asia—such as Kazakhstan. But the alternative terms are cumbersome, and this is a handy short-form. In using this term, we do not mean to ignore or downplay the important variations within this region. On the contrary, we have sought out authors who are from, or who study, the diverse parts of this region, and these differences are an important theme in sections 2 and 3 of the book.

I have acquired many intellectual debts in this project. Until recently, I had only the sketchiest knowledge of minority rights issues in the context of Eastern Europe. It has been a steep learning curve, and I couldn't have achieved even my modest level of understanding without the help of many friends and colleagues. In particular, I would like to thank B. B. Kymlicka, Dejan Guzina, Levente Salat, Julie Bernier, Denise Roman, Nenad Miscevic, Eleanora Sandor, Rainer Bauböck, Charles Pentland, Zidas Daskalovski, John Hall, Rogers Brubaker, Nenad Dimitrijevic, John Packer, François Grin, Tamás Korhecz, John McGarry, Joseph Carens, Judy Young, Sue Donaldson, Cristiano Codagnone, Stephen Deets, and Stephen Holmes for their helpful comments and suggestions. I've benefited enormously from my annual trip to Budapest to teach an intensive course on minority nationalism in the Nationalism Studies Programme at the Central European University. I'm grateful to Mária Kovács for the invitation to teach at the CEU, and to my students there, whose constant questions have forced me to refine and revise many of my ideas.

I've presented some of the ideas in this volume in seminars or colloquiums at the politics department of the New School for Social Research, the Carnegie Council on Ethics and International Affairs, the working group on minority nationalism at the University of

Western Ontario; the School of Policy Studies at Queen's University, the philosophy department at the University of Victoria, the philosophy department at Loyola University, the Institute for Central European Studies in Budapest, the annual meeting of the Association for the Study of Nationalities, the politics department at McMaster University, and the Jaan Tönissoni Institute in Tallin, Estonia. Thanks to Ari Zolberg, Matthew Mattern, Michael Milde, Bob Wolfe, Colin Macleod, Paul Abela, Iván Gyurcsík, François Grin, Janet Ajzenstat, and Tänel Matlik for the invitations, and to the audience for their questions. I'd also like to thank Julie Bernier, Idil Boran and Sarah O'Leary for excellent research assistance. Thanks to George Perlin for inviting me to participate in the Ukraine Democratic Education Project at Queen's. I am grateful to the Rockefeller Foundation for inviting me to their magnificent Bellagio Study Center, where I completed the final draft of parts 1 and 3.

And, most importantly, thanks to Magda Opalski for introducing me to this entire topic, for many suggestions regarding topics and participants, for corresponding in several languages with our contributors, and for inviting me to participate in the activities of Forum Eastern Europe, particularly the workshops on 'managing diversity' held in Latvia and Ukraine. Those invitations were the original impetus for this project. It has been a delight to work with her.

Magda joins me in offering a special thanks to all the contributors to the volume, for their enthusiasm and willingness to participate in this experiment. Also to John Hannigan, whose careful editing work helped turn a melange of papers, originally written in various language and formats, into a single manuscript. Any project of this sort requires ongoing energy and enthusiasm—we would like to thank our respective spouses, Sue and Stefan, for sustaining us.

INTRODUCTION

WILL KYMLICKA AND MAGDA OPALSKI

The aim of this volume is to explore whether recent work by Western liberal theorists on issues of pluralism and minority rights is useful to understanding and evaluating ethnic conflicts in the post-Communist countries of Eastern Europe and the former Soviet Union. There has been a great deal of important work done recently by Western political theorists on the importance of accommodating ethnocultural, linguistic and religious pluralism in democratic societies— for example works by Charles Taylor, Will Kymlicka, Yael Tamir, David Miller, Jeff Spinner, Allen Buchanan, Rainer Bauböck, James Tully, Michael Walzer, and Iris Marion Young. These and other theorists have helped to define a new approach to ethnocultural diversity that argues that justice requires the public recognition and accommodation of diversity. This new position—we will call it the 'liberal pluralist' approach—differs significantly from the standard post-war liberal view—we will call it the 'orthodox liberal' view— that ethnocultural diversity should be relegated to the private sphere and not publicly supported in the form of minority rights or multiculturalism.

According to liberal pluralists, learning to live with the public expression and institutionalization of ethnocultural diversity is a key precondition for a stable and just democracy. This raises the obvious question: can the new Western models of liberal pluralism assist in the democratization and stabilization of post-Communist Europe?

Surprisingly, there has been very little written exploring this question. None of the major Western political theorists of liberal pluralism have themselves written extensively on Eastern Europe, although several have made brief discussions or comparisons between Western democracies and the post-Communist countries.[1] And, so far as we know, no Eastern European scholar has attempted to systematically apply any of these liberal pluralist theories to their own region, although here again several scholars have made passing references or citations to the works of Western theorists.

This is surprising since there is, in our experience, overwhelming interest in such a question amongst both Western and Eastern intellectuals and policy-makers. Many people in Eastern Europe are searching for (non-ideological) ways of conceptualizing their situation. There is no shortage of detailed descriptions and diagnoses of particular ethnic conflicts in particular countries, but very little in the way of general theorizing about the nature of minority rights or their relation to justice and democracy. As a result, proposals for resolving ethnic conflicts almost always appear as special pleading on behalf of this or that minority, rather than as the appropriate application of defensible moral principles. To avoid this perception that ethnic relations are nothing more than *ad hoc* compromises, there is interest amongst Eastern Europeans in determining whether Western theory provides useful ways to conceptualize minority rights in their region.

But the topic is also of great interest to many Western liberals. Western liberals are deeply interested in and committed to the democratization process in Eastern Europe, but are often confused by the role of ethnic conflict in this process. Indeed, recent events have shown that most Westerners have no clear how idea how they should respond to ethnic claims in the region.

Part of the explanation for this confusion, we believe, is that many Western discussions of the situation in Eastern Europe continue to reflect post-war 'orthodox liberal' assumptions about diversity. In particular, they tend to invoke stereotypical contrasts between the (peaceful, democratic, tolerant) 'civic nationalism' of the West and the (aggressive, authoritarian, xenophobic) 'ethnic nationalism' of the East; or between the (ethnically inclusive) 'constitutional patriotism' of the West and the (ethnically exclusive) 'Balkanization' of the East. In so far as Western liberals start with these dichotomies, they automatically interpret ethnic conflicts in Eastern Europe as relics of premodern and preliberal tribalisms that must be overcome if liberal democracy is to be achieved. These conflicts are seen as evidence that Eastern Europe is not ready for liberal democracy, rather than as conflicts which Western models of liberal democracy might help to resolve.

Recent theorists of liberal pluralism have disputed these conventional dichotomies between ethnic relations in Western democracies and Eastern Europe. The assumption that Western 'civic' nations have transcended all forms of ethnocultural particularism has been strongly challenged by recent liberal pluralists. By highlighting the extent to which issues of ethnocultural particularism remain salient to Western democracies, the liberal pluralist approach may have more relevance to Eastern Europe than is typically supposed.

Our main aims in this volume are thus two-fold: (a) to make available to Eastern Europeans recent work in Western political theory on ethnocultural pluralism, and to start a dialogue with Eastern Europeans on the ways in which this work may be relevant to the Eastern European context; and (b) to show to Western liberals that the conventional ways of distinguishing between ethnic relations in the West and East are unhelpful in understanding or responding to ethnic conflict in the post-Communist world, and to suggest an alternative framework to help Westerners in thinking about ethnic conflict in the democratization process.

The importance of this issue is obvious. The ability or inability of countries in Eastern Europe to resolve their ethnic conflicts has profoundly affected the process of democratization. While most countries without significant ethnic tensions have democratized successfully—for example Czech Republic, Poland, Hungary, Slovenia—those countries with major ethnic and linguistic cleavages are having a more difficult time consolidating democracy and civil society—for example Slovakia, Ukraine, Romania, Macedonia. At worst, these ethnic conflicts have led to civil wars that have shocked the world with their levels of brutality: Serbia, Croatia, Georgia, Azerbaijan, Chechnya. It is important to try to identify the relevant lessons and principles—if any—that the experience of Western democracies might offer to newly-democratizing countries struggling with these conflicts.

But the topic is urgent in another way. Several Western organizations have recently decided that respect for minority rights is one of the preconditions for post-Communist countries to 'rejoin Europe'. Countries which fail the test of respect for minority rights will not be allowed to join NATO and the European Union, and may lose their standing in the Organization for Security and Co-operation in Europe (OSCE) or the Council of Europe. Countries wishing to join these Western organizations must agree to allow detailed international monitoring of their treatment of minorities, and agree to abide by recently-established European norms on minority rights, such as the principles adopted by the OSCE on national minorities in 1990, or the Framework Convention for the Protection of National Minorities adopted by the Council of Europe in 1995. From the point of view of many Eastern European countries, Western countries are no longer simply offering models for possible consideration, but rather are imposing their own ideas of minority rights on Eastern Europe.

Many Eastern European countries have grave reservations about this process. And indeed there are many important questions to be asked about this decision to pressure Eastern European countries to respect pan-European standards on minority rights. But it is worth noting that this is in fact just one example of a much broader trend towards the codification of minority rights in international law. For example, the United Nations has adopted a declaration on the Rights of Persons Belonging to National or Ethnic, Religious and Linguistic Minorities (1992), and is debating a Draft Declaration on the Rights of Indigenous Peoples (1993). These may lead to much greater monitoring of the way countries around the world treat their minorities. The Inter-American Commission on Human Rights is also playing a role in formulating regional standards of minority rights in the Americas. Or consider the recent decision of the World Bank to include minority rights as one of the criteria for evaluating development projects around the world. There is even talk of trying to develop a 'universal declaration of minority rights', to supplement the 1948 universal declaration of human rights. In short, there is clear movement in the direction of *internationalizing* minority rights. The treatment of minorities is increasingly seen as a matter, not only of domestic politics, but also of legitimate international monitoring and perhaps even international intervention. As the OSCE puts it, minority rights 'are matters of legitimate international concern and consequently do not constitute exclusively an internal affair of the respective State'.[2]

This growing movement for the international codification and monitoring of minority rights presupposes that at least some minority provisions are not simply a matter of discretionary policies or pragmatic compromises but rather are a matter of fundamental justice. It implies that minority rights are indeed basic *rights*. This movement has primarily been advanced by Western organizations, NGOs and scholars, together with their allies in the rest of the world. And not surprisingly, their proposals typically involve codifying Western models as universal standards. There has been little input, and even less enthusiasm, from governments in Eastern Europe, Asia, or Africa, most of which tend to be very sceptical about the whole idea of internationalizing minority rights issues.

What is happening today in Eastern Europe, therefore, may be a harbinger of things to come elsewhere in the world. The decision of Western organizations to insist on respect for minority rights in Eastern European countries will be the first serious test case for the feasibility and desirability of 'exporting' Western minority rights standards to the rest of the world. For this reason, it is worthy of careful consideration by anyone interested in the issue of minority rights.

Given this background, there are two increasingly important tasks. First, we need to clarify the theoretical basis of Western models of minority rights, so as to distinguish the underlying principles from the myriad local variations in the way that these principles are institutionalized. As several commentators have noted, while Western organizations have decided to demand respect for minority rights standards, there remains considerable confusion about what these standards actually are, and it is far from clear that there is any consensus yet within the West on the precise nature of these principles. We need to distinguish the fundamental principles from the contingent practices, and to think carefully about the presuppositions and preconditions of these principles, and hence about the extent to which they are applicable elsewhere.

Second, we need to promote a dialogue with intellectuals and leaders from other parts of the world about issues of minority rights. Our aim in this volume is neither to support nor criticize recent moves to internationalize minority rights standards. But we do believe that any attempt to develop such international standards must be done in an inclusive way, with the active participation of non-Western countries, including representatives of both majority and minority groups. We need, in short, to start a transnational and intercultural dialogue on minority rights.[3] Many intellectuals and policy-makers in Eastern Europe have no clear idea of the principles underlying these Western standards. They are told that respect for minorities is an essential part of democratization, but are not told why minority rights are linked to democracy, or how these rights relate to principles of justice or freedom. Under these circumstances, it is essential to establish a genuine dialogue on this issue involving both Western and Eastern European scholars and practitioners.[4] We hope this volume will serve as a small step towards both of these goals.

Overview of the Volume

The volume has three main parts. It begins with a lengthy paper by Will Kymlicka entitled 'Western Political Theory and Ethnic Relations in Eastern Europe'. This paper has two main sections. The first half explores some of the interesting recent work done by Western political theorists on the management of ethnocultural diversity. It begins by rejecting what Kymlicka calls the myth of the 'eth-nocultural neutrality' of the liberal state, and offers instead an alter-native model of ethnic relations that several recent liberal pluralist theorists have developed. This alternative model defends the general principle that ethnocultural minorities can legitimately demand certain group-specific rights for the accommodation of their distinct identities, but argues that the precise nature of these rights depends on the nature of the minority group. He distinguishes six types of eth-nocultural groups found in Western democracies: national minorities and indigenous peoples; legal immigrants with the right to become citizens; illegal immigrants or guestworkers without the right to become citizens; racial caste groups; and isolationist ethnoreligious sects. He argues that each type of group has specific needs that require distinct rights.

He focuses in particular on the differences between the rights of immigrants and the rights of national minorities/indigenous peoples. He explores the sorts of accommodation rights claimed by immigrant groups, which lead to the familiar forms of immigrant 'multiculturalism' we see in Canada, Australia, Britain, the United States and increasingly other countries as well. He then contrasts this with the sort of self-government rights claimed by non-immigrant national minorities and indigenous peoples, of the sort which lead to familiar forms of regional autonomy or 'multination federalism' for national minorities—as in Quebec, Puerto Rico, Catalonia, and Scotland—and to forms of self-government for indigenous peoples—such as the American Indians, Inuit in Canada, Sami in Scandinavia, or Maori in New Zealand. Kymlicka argues that these forms of immi-grant multiculturalism and self-government for national minorities have worked well in the West, and promote liberal values of freedom and justice.

The second half then examines some of the possible applications of this model to Central and Eastern European countries. Kymlicka focuses in particular on two common objections to applying models of liberal pluralism in the region. The first objection states that the sorts of ethnocultural groups in Eastern/Central Europe are often very different from those in the West. For example, there is no group in the West that is quite like the Roma or 'gypsies' who are found throughout central and Eastern Europe; nor is there any clear paral-lel to the special situation of the ethnic Russians in the Baltics or Central Asia. Also, unlike in the West, many national minorities in Eastern Europe have a neighbouring kin state, which makes them potentially irredentist, rather than merely autonomy-seeking. And, unlike in the West, migration in Eastern Europe tends to be the result of forced migration rather than legal immigration. Given these profound differences in the nature of the minority groups themselves, Western models of immigrant multiculturalism or multination federalism may not be applicable to these groups. The second objection states that the very idea of liberal pluralism has little applicability to states in this region, which are rooted in very different political traditions, with their own distinct notions of nationhood and statehood. On this view, the absence of the appropriate traditions of either liberalism or democratic pluralism means that Western-style models will fail, and may indeed worsen the situation, promoting expectations that cannot be met and playing into the hands of dangerous ethnic entrepreneurs. Kymlicka concedes that there is some truth in both of these objections, but argues that Western experiences of the accommodation of ethnic differences can nonetheless be relevant for the region. Indeed, he suggests that there may be few viable alternatives to Western models of immigrant multiculturalism and multination federalism. Whatever the limits of these models, the alternatives may be even worse.

(2) The main paper is then followed by 15 replies and commentaries. Most of these are from scholars and writers in Eastern Europe: Urszula Doroszewska (Poland); Boris Tsilevich (Latvia); Alexander Ossipov (Russia); Aleksander Djumaev (Uzbekistan); Volodymyr Fesenko (Ukraine); János Kis (Hungary); Gabriel Andreescu (Romania); Tibor Várady (Serbia); Pavel Barša (Czech Republic); and Vello Pettai (Estonia). Five commentaries are by Western scholars who have written about Eastern Europe: Michael Walzer, George Schöpflin, Pål Kolstø, Magda Opalski, and Panayote Dimitras and Nafsika Papanikolatos. These authors represent a very wide range of countries, disciplines and professions, and political perspectives.

These commentaries address two types of issues. First, commentators directly respond to the theory developed in Kymlicka's paper, discussing whether the liberal pluralist approach is applicable in the region. While some of the authors express general sympathy with the approach, many identify distinctive features of the ethnopolitical situation that make it difficult or undesirable to apply liberal pluralism in the region. These factors include the legacy of Communism, the economic distress facing many countries, the history of empires and boundary-changes, the role of kin-states, the lack of political accountability for both state and minority élites, the inability of some states to implement policies and enforce the rule of law, and so on.

Second, commentators describe the existing terms and arguments used in the public discourse in their region, both at the élite and popular levels. It is clear that the sorts of concepts and terms used in Western political theory are not commonly used in many countries of Eastern Europe. To be sure, a certain discourse of human rights, tolerance, and respect for minorities has been adopted—or at least mimicked—widely in the region, particularly when international observers are present. However, this Western-style rhetoric co-exists with other forms of public discourse in Eastern Europe which are less liberal. The commentaries discuss, for example, the tendency of public discourse in some countries to draw on quasi-genetic arguments about national characteristics; the tendency to invoke the 'clash of civilizations' thesis or related views about the impossibility of peaceful ethnic co-existence; the pervasive discourse of loyalty and disloyalty; the role of stereotypes and historical memories, and so on. The authors discuss how these aspects of the existing public discourse assist or inhibit the accommodation of ethnocultural diversity, and how they affect the consideration of liberal pluralist models.

These commentaries provide rich insights into the nature of ethnocultural relations in post-Communist Europe, and the challenges facing any attempts to promote Western models of minority rights in the region.

The volume concludes with a reply by Will Kymlicka, which examines some of the specific issues raised in the commentaries, and also reflects on the more general issue about the exportability of Western political theory to newly-democratizing countries, and about the possible benefits/pitfalls of such comparative discussions. In particular, he focuses on what we could call the priority problem. Several authors argue that certain minority rights are unhelpful, and perhaps even dangerous, if they are adopted in an unstable or undemocratic context, without adequate legal and political safeguards. This suggests that priority should be given to consolidating democracy and the rule of law before attempting to deal with minority rights. The alternative view, often advanced by minority groups, is that the failure to manage ethnic conflicts properly is itself the cause of delayed democratization, and that giving priority to (central) state-building over issues of minority rights plays into the hands of authoritarian majority nationalists who are equally opposed to liberal democracy as to minority rights. Kymlicka considers these and other dilemmas associated with promoting ethnocultural justice under conditions of democratic and economic transition. He also discusses various difficulties in the role that Western organizations have played so far on issues of ethnic relations in the region, such as the lack of clear standards, the selective monitoring of ECE countries, and the vacillation between norms of justice and considerations of security as the basis for Western interventions. Kymlicka concludes by offering suggestions on how these organizations can play a more helpful and constructive role.

Although the volume mentions many cases of ethnic conflict in Eastern Europe, and many aspects of minority rights, it only scratches the surface of the topic. Our goal is not to provide a comprehensive survey of these issues, let alone to conclusively resolve any of them, but rather to give an indication of both the immense potential of, and the great need for, new work in this area. We hope to show that, despite the very great differences between the East and West in history, economic and political circumstances, academic training, and the vocabulary of public debate, we can learn from each other about these pressing issues of democracy and diversity.

NOTES

1. There are a few books by Western political theorists on Eastern Europe, but they have typically ignored or downplayed the issue of ethnic conflict—for example Ackerman (1992). There are a few shorter discussions by Western theorists on minority rights in Eastern Europe—for example a section in Michael Walzer's *On Toleration* (1997); and articles by Elizabeth Kiss (1995) and Graham Walker (1997). But these are isolated chapters in books that are generally focused on other topics or other regions of the world.
2. Report of the CSCE Meeting of Experts on National Minorities (Geneva, 1991).
3. Onuma Yasuaki has argued for an 'intercivilizational' approach to human rights (Onuma 1997), and there has indeed been a vibrant cross-cultural dialogue on human rights in the last decade (for example An-Na'im and Deng 1990; An-Na'im 1992; Bauer and Bell 1999). There has been much less of a cross-cultural dialogue on minority rights.
4. As André Leibich notes, even when Eastern European countries are members of these international organizations 'their voices are seldom listened to. They remain at the receiving end of these institutions' decisions, even in matters that concern them directly' (Liebich 1995: 317).

REFERENCES

Ackerman, Bruce (1992) *The Future of Liberal Revolution* (Yale University Press, New Haven, CT).

An-Na'im, Abdullah (ed) (1992) *Human Rights in Cross-Cultural Perspectives* (University of Pennsylvania Press, Philadelphia, PA).

——and Deng, Frances (eds) (1990) *Human Rights in Africa: Cross-Cultural Perspectives* (Washington).

Bauer, Joanne and Bell, Daniel (eds) (1999) *The East Asian Challenge for Human Rights* (Cambridge University Press, Cambridge).

Kiss, Elizabeth (1995) 'Is Nationalism Compatible with Human Rights? Reflections on East-Central Europe', in Austin Sarat and Thomas Kearn (eds) *Identities, Politics and Rights* (University of Michigan Press, Ann Arbor, MI), 367–402.

Kymlicka, Will (1995) *Multicultural Citizenship: A Liberal Theory of Minority Rights* (Oxford University Press, Oxford).

Liebich, André (1995) 'Nations, States and Minorities: Why is Eastern Europe Different?', *Dissent*, Summer 1995, 313–17.

Onuma, Yasuaki (1997) 'The Need for an Intercivilizational Approach to Evaluating Human Rights', *Human Rights Dialogue*, 10, 4–6.

Walker, Graham (1997) 'The Idea of Nonliberal Constitutionalism', in Will Kymlicka and Ian Shapiro (eds) *Ethnicity and Group Rights* (New York University Press, New York, NY), 154–84.

Walzer, Michael (1997) *On Toleration* (Yale University Press, New Haven, CT).

1

WESTERN POLITICAL THEORY AND ETHNIC RELATIONS IN EASTERN EUROPE

Will Kymlicka

WESTERN POLITICAL THEORY AND ETHNIC RELATIONS IN EASTERN EUROPE

WILL KYMLICKA

1. Introduction

The newly-democratizing states of Eastern and Central Europe sometimes look to the older Western democracies to see how various political issues have been handled. It is rarely possible or appropriate to simply transplant institutions or policies from one country to another, particularly when these countries have such different histories and economic conditions as those in Western and Eastern Europe. However, democratic reformers often want to at least understand the basic principles and ideals that underlie the operation of Western liberal democracies, and which have provided them with stability and legitimacy. Put another way, reformers often want to understand the *political theory* of Western democracies, even though the practical implementation of these underlying principles may differ substantially in Eastern and Central Europe (ECE).

In some areas, particularly with respect to basic individual civil and political rights, it is relatively easy to identify these basic principles. All Western democracies have the rule of law, freedom of the press, freedom of conscience, habeas corpus, free elections, universal adult suffrage etc., and there is a large and long-standing literature by Western legal and political theorists explaining why these are important values. Indeed, we can say that the protection of these rights and liberties is part of the very definition of a liberal democracy. And so the claim of ECE countries to be 'democratic' is measured by how well they accept and uphold these principles.

But when we turn to issues of ethnic relations, it is far more difficult to identify the principles guiding Western democracies. We can find a wide range of policies in the various Western democracies, and it is not clear what, if anything, they have in common. What then are the defining features of a liberal-democratic approach to managing ethnocultural diversity?

The problem is not just that various Western democracies have responded differently to issues of diversity, but also that the whole area of ethnocultural relations has been surprisingly neglected by Western political theorists. For most of the twentieth century, ethnicity was viewed by political theorists as a marginal phenomenon that would gradually disappear with modernization, and hence was not an important topic for forward-looking political theorists. As a result, even into the mid-1980s, there were very few political philosophers or political theorists working in the area. (Much the same can be said about many other academic disciplines, from sociology to geography to history.)

Today however, after decades of relative neglect, the question of the rights of ethnocultural groups has moved to the forefront of Western political theory. There are a number of reasons for this renewed interest in issues of ethnicity amongst Western political theorists. Paradoxically, the most important of these was probably the wave of ethnic conflict in ECE that arose during and after the collapse of Communism. Most Western theorists had assumed that liberal democracy would emerge smoothly from the ashes of Communism, and many theorists wanted to understand why issues of ethnicity and nationalism were able to derail this transition.

But there were many factors within Western democracies themselves which also pointed to the salience of ethnicity: the nativist backlash against immigrants and refugees in many Western countries—especially France, Britain, Germany, and the United States—the resurgence and political mobilization of indigenous peoples, resulting in the draft declaration of the rights of indigenous peoples at the United Nations; and the ongoing, even growing, threat of secession within some of the most flourishing Western democracies, from Quebec to Scotland, Flanders, and Catalonia.

All of these factors, which came to a head at the beginning of the 1990s, made it clear that Western liberal democracies had not in fact resolved or overcome the tensions which ethnocultural diversity can raise. It is not surprising, therefore, that political theorists have increasingly turned their attention to this issue. For example, the last few years have witnessed the first philosophical books in English in decades—perhaps ever—on the normative issues involved in secession, nationalism, immigration, multiculturalism, and indigenous rights.[1]

In this respect, democratic political theorists of ethnic relations in the West are not much farther advanced than those in ECE. Of course, most Western countries have a long—and sometimes bloody—history of dealing with ethnic diversity within a liberal-democratic constitutional framework. But until very recently, the lessons from this history have not been articulated into a well-defined theory, and so the actual principles and ideals which guide Western democracies remain obscure, often even to those who are involved in managing ethnic relations on a day-to-day basis. Moreover, as we will see, ethnic relations within many Western democracies are themselves in a state of flux, as old assumptions and policies are being tested and found wanting.

For all these reasons, Western political theory may have relatively little to offer to people in ECE struggling with ethnic conflicts. Compared to the literature on civil rights, we have only the beginnings of a theoretical literature on ethnic relations. Moreover, this literature is attempting to theorize about a rapidly changing reality. Whereas support for the constitutional and judicial protection of individual civil rights has never been higher in Western democracies, there is no similar consensus about managing ethnic diversity, and indeed virtually every aspect of ethnic relations in the West is subject to controversy.

My aim in this paper, therefore, is not to measure how well the current policies of ECE countries regarding ethnic relations conform to well-defined and long-standing Western principles, for there are no such principles. My aim, rather, is to outline some of the interesting recent work done by Western political theorists, and to see whether any of it is relevant to the debates discussed in this book. I think that these Western theories can help shed some light on the policy options in ECE, but I also think that the debates in Eastern and Central Europe can shed some light on the limitations of these newly-emerging theories.

One reason why Western theorists have failed to grapple satisfactorily with issues of ethnic diversity is that they have been blinded by what I will call the myth of 'ethnocultural neutrality'. It only became possible to develop a coherent liberal democratic theory of ethnic relations when this myth was set aside. So I will start this paper by exploring this myth (section 2), and then explaining the alternative model of ethnic relations which several recent liberal democratic theorists have developed (sections 3–4). I will conclude by examining some of the possible applications of this theory to ECE countries (sections 5 and 6).

2. *The Myth of Ethnocultural Neutrality*

As I noted earlier, Western theorists have had little explicit to say about how a democratic state should deal with ethnocultural diversity. But in so far as they had an answer at all, it was that the state should be 'neutral' with respect to ethnocultural differences. Liberal states should be 'neutral' with respect to the ethnocultural identities of their citizens, and indifferent to the ability of ethnocultural groups to reproduce themselves over time. On this view, liberal states treat culture in the same way as religion—that is, as something which people should be free to pursue in their private life, but which is not the concern of the state, so long as they respect the rights of others. Just as liberalism precludes the establishment of an official religion, so too there cannot be official cultures that have preferred status over other possible cultural allegiances.

For example, Michael Walzer argues that liberalism involves a 'sharp divorce of state and ethnicity'. The liberal state stands above all the various ethnic and national groups in the country, 'refusing to endorse or support their ways of life or to take an active interest in their social reproduction'. Instead, the state is 'neutral with reference to language, history, literature, calendar' of these groups. He says the clearest example of such a neutral liberal state is the United States, whose ethnocultural neutrality is reflected in the fact that it has no constitutionally recognized official language (Walzer 1992a: 100–1; cf. Walzer 1992b: 9).

Indeed, some theorists argue that this is precisely what distinguishes liberal 'civic nations' from illiberal 'ethnic nations'. Ethnic nations take the reproduction of a particular ethnonational culture and identity as one of their most important goals. Civic nations, by contrast, are neutral with respect to the ethnocultural identities of their citizens, and define national membership purely in terms of adherence to certain principles of democracy and justice (Pfaff 1993: 162; Ignatieff 1993).

This principle of ethnocultural neutrality has often been cited in the West as grounds for rejecting any claims by minorities for distinctive rights that go beyond the standard set of individual civil and political rights accorded to all citizens. Providing explicit recognition or rights to a minority group, on this view, is a radical departure from the traditional neutrality of the liberal state.

There is growing recognition, however, that this idea of ethnocultural neutrality is simply a myth. Indeed, the claim that liberal-democratic states—or 'civic nations'—are ethnoculturally neutral is manifestly false, both historically and conceptually. The religion model, with its strict separation of church and state, is altogether misleading as an account of the relationship between the liberal-democratic state and ethnocultural groups.

Consider the actual policies of the United States, which is the allegedly prototypically 'neutral' state. Firstly, it is a legal requirement for children to learn the English language in schools. Secondly, it is a legal requirement for immigrants over the age of 50 to learn the English language to acquire American citizenship. Thirdly, it is a *de facto* requirement for employment in or for government that the applicant speak English. Fourthly, decisions about the boundaries of state governments, and the timing of their admission into the federation, were deliberately made to ensure that anglophones would be a majority within each of the fifty states of the American federation.[2]

These decisions about the language of education and government employment, the requirements of citizenship, and the drawing of internal boundaries, are profoundly important. They are not isolated exceptions to some norm of ethnocultural neutrality. On the contrary, they are tightly interrelated, and together they have shaped the very structure of the American state, and the way the state structures society. They have played a pivotal role in determining which ethnolinguistic groups prosper, and which ones diminish.

One of the most important determinants of whether a culture survives is whether its language is a language of government—that is, whether its language is used in public schooling, courts, legislatures, welfare agencies, health services etc. Having publicly-funded education in one's mother tongue is crucial, since it guarantees the passing on of the language and its associated traditions to the next generation. And since governments account for 40–50 per cent of GNP in most Western countries, the language of government employment and contracts is also a major factor in determining which language groups prosper and which diminish. And in countries where military service is compulsory, the language of army units has played a similar role. Compulsory military service in French-language army units was pivotal in turning 'peasants into Frenchmen', as a famous study of French nationalism put it (Weber 1976), just as mandatory service in Hebrew-language army units remains an important tool of national integration in Israel today.

Given the spread of standardized and compulsory education, the high demands for literacy in work, and widespread interaction with government agencies, any language which is not a public language becomes so marginalized that it is likely to survive only amongst a small élite, or in a ritualized form, or in isolated rural areas, not as a living and developing language underlying a flourishing culture. Government decisions about the language of public schooling and public administration are in effect decisions about which language groups will survive.

In the United States, the result of these decisions was to establish the hegemony of English. Nor was this just an unintended or accidental by-product—it was the express aim of government decisions to establish this hegemony. These decisions were all made with the intention of promoting integration into what I call a 'societal culture'. By a societal culture, I mean a territorially-concentrated culture, centred on a shared language which is used in a wide range of societal institutions, in both public and private life—schools, media, law, economy, government, etc.—covering the full range of human activities, including social, educational, religious, recreational, and economic life. I call it a *societal* culture to emphasize that it involves a common language and social institutions, rather than common religious beliefs, family customs, or personal lifestyles. Societal cultures within a modern liberal democracy are inevitably pluralistic, containing Christians as well as Muslims, Jews, and atheists; heterosexuals as well as gays; urban professionals as well as rural farmers; conservatives as well as socialists. Such diversity is the inevitable result of the rights and freedoms guaranteed to liberal citizens—including freedom of conscience, association, speech, political dissent, and rights to privacy—particularly when combined with an ethnically diverse population.

The American government has deliberately promoted integration into such a societal culture—that is, it has encouraged citizens to view their life-chances as tied up with participation in common societal institutions that operate in the English language. All levels of American government—federal, state, and municipal—have insisted that there is a legitimate public interest in promoting a common language, and the Supreme Court has repeatedly affirmed that claim in upholding laws that mandate the teaching and use of English in schools and government functions.[3] Nor is the United States unique in this respect. Promoting integration into a societal culture is part of a 'nation-building' project that all liberal democracies have engaged in. Indeed, many other Western countries have been much more aggressive and coercive in their attempts at nation-building.

Obviously, the sense in which English-speaking Americans share a common 'culture' is a very thin one, since it does not preclude differences in religion, personal values, family relationships or lifestyle choices. Indeed, this use of the term 'culture' is in conflict with the way it is used in most academic disciplines, where culture is defined in a very thick, ethnographic sense, referring to the sharing of specific folk-customs, habits, and rituals. Citizens of a modern liberal state do not share a common culture in such a thick, ethnographic sense. But if we want to understand the nature of modern state-building, we need a very different, and thinner, conception of culture, which focuses on a common language and societal institutions. While this sort of common culture is thin, it is far from trivial. On the contrary, as I discuss below, attempts to integrate people into such a common societal culture have often been met with serious resistance. Although integration in this sense leaves a great deal of room for both the public and private expression of individual and collective differences, some groups have nonetheless vehemently rejected the idea that they should view their life-chances as tied up with the societal institutions conducted in the majority's language.

So we need to replace the idea of an 'ethnoculturally neutral' state with a new model of a liberal democratic state—what can be called the 'nation-building' model. While the idea of a culturally neutral state is a myth, this is not to say that governments can only promote one societal culture. It is possible for government policies to encourage the sustaining of two or more societal cultures within a single country—indeed, as I discuss below, this is precisely what characterizes multination states like Canada, Spain, Belgium, or Switzerland.

However, at one point or another, virtually all liberal democracies have attempted to diffuse a single societal culture throughout all of its territory. They have all engaged in this process of 'nation-building'— that is, a process of promoting a common language, and a sense of common membership in, and equal access to, the social institutions operating in that language.[4] Decisions regarding official languages, core curriculum in education, and the requirements for acquiring citizenship, have all been made with the express intention of diffusing a particular culture throughout society, and of promoting a particular national identity based on participation in that societal culture. Other common 'tools' of nation-building in the West have included the development of a national media, the adoption of national symbols and holidays, the renaming of streets, towns, and topographic features, such as rivers or mountains, in the majority language to memorialize majority heroes or events, and so on.[5]

Moreover, in some countries, these nation-building policies have been strikingly successful in extending a common societal culture throughout the entire territory of the state. Consider France or Italy. Who could have predicted in 1750 that virtually everyone within the current boundaries of France or Italy would share a common language and sense of nationhood? Other paradigmatic 'nation-states' in the West include Portugal, England, and Germany. There are other countries, as we'll see in the next section, where certain minorities have strongly and successfully resisted nation-building policies. But the quest to become a nation-state has been, and remains, a powerful one in most Western democracies.

Why has the implementation of liberal-democratic principles, and the consolidation of liberal-democratic states, been so closely tied historically to the promotion of a common national language and societal culture? This is a profoundly important question, yet it has been almost entirely ignored by liberal political theorists. None of the major figures in the liberal tradition has engaged in a sustained discussion of the justification or goals of nation-building policies, or of the limits on its permissible forms. For example, is it permissible for a liberal state to insist that immigrants learn the majority language as a condition of citizenship? One looks in vain for a discussion of this or other nation-building policies in Locke, Kant, Mill, Popper, Rawls, or Dworkin. This is a major gap in liberal theory, and much work remains to be done in filling it.[6]

One might think that this nation-building is purely a matter of cultural imperialism or ethnocentric prejudice. But many recent liberal theorists—known as 'liberal nationalists'—argue that this sort of nation-building serves a number of important and legitimate democratic goals.[7] For example, a modern economy requires a mobile, educated, and literate workforce. Standardized public education in a common language has often been seen as essential if all citizens are to have equal opportunity to work in this modern economy. Indeed, equal opportunity is often defined precisely in terms of equal access to mainstream institutions operating in the dominant language.

Also, participation in a common societal culture has often been seen as essential for generating solidarity within modern democratic states. The sort of solidarity required by a welfare state requires that citizens have a strong sense of common identity and membership, so that they will make sacrifices for each other, and this common identity is assumed to be facilitated by a common language. Moreover, a common language has been seen as essential to democracy—how can 'the people' govern together if they cannot understand one another? In short, promoting integration into a common societal culture has been seen as essential to social equality and political cohesion in modern states.

In these and other ways, nationhood can be seen, in Canovan's words, as 'the battery' which makes Western states run: the existence of a common national identity motivates citizens to act for common political goals (Canovan 1996: 80). Modern states need to be able to mobilize citizens in pursuit of a wide range of goals—as Cairns and Williams put it, 'what the state needs from the citizenry cannot be secured by coercion, but only cooperation and self-restraint in the exercise of private power' (Cairns and Williams 1985: 43)—and nationalism is one of the most effective means of mobilizing citizens. The 'battery' of nationalism can be used to promote liberal goals—such as social justice, democratization, equality of opportunity, economic development—or illiberal goals—chauvinism, xenophobia, militarism, and unjust conquest. The fact that the battery of nationalism can be used for so many functions helps to explain why it has been so ubiquitous. Liberal reformers invoke nationhood to mobilize citizens behind projects of social justice such as comprehensive health care or public schooling; illiberal authoritarians invoke nationhood to mobilize citizens behind attacks on alleged enemies of the nation, be they foreign countries or internal dissidents. This is why nation-building is just as common in authoritarian regimes in the West as in democracies. Consider Spain under Franco, or Greece or Latin America under the military dictators. Authoritarian regimes also need a 'battery' to help achieve public objectives in complex modern societies.

3. Towards Ethnocultural Justice: The Dialectic of Nation-Building and Minority Rights

While the role of nation-building in the operation of liberal democracies requires more study, it is already clear, I think, that this nation-building model requires us to radically rethink the issue of minority rights. The question is no longer how to justify departing from a norm of neutrality, but rather do majority efforts at nation-building create injustices for minorities? And do minority rights help protect against these injustices? Put another way, the standard for evaluating minority rights claims is no longer ethnocultural neutrality but ethnocultural justice.

Western political theorists are just beginning to rethink minority rights in this new way. This process of rethinking is complicated, since majority nation-building programmes impact differently on different types of groups. The sorts of minority rights being claimed, therefore, and the issues of justice they raise, vary from country to country, and from group to group. However, enough work has been done in the last few years to see the outlines of a new liberal theory of minority rights, which I will try to sketch in the rest of this section.

As Charles Taylor notes, the process of nation-building inescapably privileges members of the majority culture:

> If a modern society has an 'official' language, in the fullest sense of the term, that is, a state-sponsored, -inculcated, and -defined language and culture, in which both economy and state function, then it is obviously an immense advantage to people if this language and culture are theirs. Speakers of other languages are at a distinct disadvantage.   (Taylor 1997: 34).[8]

This means that members of minority cultures face a choice. If all public institutions are being run in another language, minorities face the danger of being marginalized from the major economic, academic, and political institutions of the society. Faced with this dilemma, minorities have—to oversimplify—four basic options:[9]

1. They can emigrate *en masse*, particularly if they have a prosperous and friendly state nearby that will take them in. This has rarely occurred in the recent history of the West, but is more important in Eastern Europe.
2. They can accept integration into the majority culture, although seek to negotiate better or fairer terms of integration.
3. They can seek the sorts of rights and powers of self-government needed to maintain their own societal culture—that is, to create their own economic, political, and educational institutions in their own language.
4. They can accept permanent marginalization, and seek only to be left alone on the margins of society.

Each of these reflects a different strategy that minorities can adopt in the face of state nation-building. To be successful, each of them—except emigration—requires certain accommodations from the state. These may take the form of multiculturalism policies, or self-government and language rights, or treaty rights and land claims, or legal exemptions. Different forms of minority rights reflect different strategies about how to respond to, and to limit, state nation-building pressures.

We can find some ethnocultural groups that fit each of these categories and other groups that are caught between them. For example, some immigrant groups choose permanent marginalization. This would seem to be true of the Hutterites in Canada or the Amish in the United States. But the option of accepting marginalization is only likely to be attractive to ethnoreligious groups whose theology requires them to avoid all contact with the modern world. The Hutterites and Amish are unconcerned about their marginalization from universities or legislatures, since they view such 'worldly' institutions as corrupt.

Virtually all other ethnocultural minorities, however, seek to participate in the modern world, and to do so, they must either integrate into the majority society or seek the self-government needed to create and sustain their own modern institutions. Faced with this choice, ethnocultural groups have responded in different ways. I will briefly discuss five types of ethnocultural groups that are found within Western democracies: national minorities, immigrants, isolationist ethnoreligious groups, metics, and racial caste groups. In each case, I will discuss how they have been affected by majority nation-building, what sorts of minority rights claims they have made in response to this nation-building, and how these claims relate to underlying liberal-democratic principles.

3.1 National Minorities

By national minorities, I mean groups that formed complete and functioning societies on their historic homeland prior to being incorporated into a larger state. National minorities can be subdivided into two categories: 'substate nations' and 'indigenous peoples'. Substate nations are nations which do not currently have a state in which they are a majority, but which may have had such a state in the past, or which may have sought such a state. They find themselves sharing a state with other nations for a variety of reasons. They may have been conquered or annexed by a larger state or empire in the past; ceded from one empire to another; or united with another kingdom through royal marriage. In a few cases, multination states arise from a more or less voluntary agreement between two or more national groups to form a mutually beneficial federation.

Indigenous peoples are peoples whose traditional lands have been overrun by settlers, and who have then been forcibly, or through treaties, incorporated into states run by people they regard as foreigners. While other minority nations dream of a status like nation-states, with similar economic and social institutions and achievements, indigenous peoples typically seek something rather different: the ability to maintain certain traditional ways of life and beliefs while nevertheless participating on their own terms in the modern world. In addition to the autonomy needed to work out that sort of project, indigenous peoples also typically require of the larger society a respect and recognition to begin to make amends for indignities they suffered for decades or centuries as second-class citizens—or even non-citizens or slaves.

The contrast between indigenous peoples and substate nations is not precise, and there is no universally agreed definition of 'indigenous peoples'. One way to distinguish substate nations from indigenous peoples in the Western context is that the former were contenders but losers in the process of European state-formation, whereas the latter were isolated from that process until recently, and so retained a premodern way of life until well into this century. Substate nations would have liked to form their own states, but lost in the struggle for political power, whereas indigenous peoples existed outside this system of European states. The Catalans, Basques, Flemish, Scots, Welsh, Corsicans, Puerto Ricans, and Québécois, then, are substate nations, whereas the Sami, Inuit, Maori, and American Indians are indigenous peoples. In both North America and Europe, the consequences of incorporation have been much more catastrophic for indigenous peoples than for other national minorities.[10]

However they were incorporated, both substate nations and indigenous peoples have typically resisted state nation-building, and have fought to maintain or regain their own self-governing institutions, often operating in their own language, so as to be able to live and work in their own culture. They demand to maintain or regain their own schools, courts, media, political institutions, and so on. To achieve this, they typically demand some form of autonomy. At the extreme, this may involve claims to outright secession, but more usually it involves some form of regional autonomy. And they typically mobilize along nationalist lines, using the language of 'nationhood' to describe and justify these demands for self-government.[11] While the ideology of nationalism has typically seen full-fledged independence as the 'normal' or 'natural' end-point, economic or demographic reasons may make this unfeasible for some national minorities. Moreover, it is increasingly clear that substantial forms of self-government can be achieved *within* the boundaries of a larger state, and so there is a growing interest in exploring these other forms of self-government, such as federalism.

In short, national minorities have typically responded to majority-nation-building by seeking greater autonomy which they use to engage in their own competing nation-building, so as to protect and diffuse their societal culture throughout their traditional territory. Indeed, they often seek to use the same tools that the majority uses to promote this nation-building—for example they seek control over the language and curriculum of schooling in their region of the country, the language of government employment, the requirements of immigration and naturalization, and the drawing of internal boundaries. We can see this clearly in the case of Flemish or Québécois nationalism, which have been concerned precisely with gaining and exercising these nation-building powers.

How should liberal democracies respond to such minority nationalisms? Historically, liberal democracies have tried to suppress minority nationalisms, often ruthlessly. At various points in the eighteenth and nineteenth centuries, for example, France banned the use of the Basque and Breton languages in schools or publications, and banned any political associations which aimed to promote minority nationalism; the British in Canada stripped the Québécois of their French-language rights and institutions, and redrew political boundaries so that the Québécois did not form a majority in any province; Canada also made it illegal for Aboriginals to form political associations to promote their national claims; and when the United States conquered the Southwest in the war with Mexico in 1848, it stripped the long-settled Hispanics of their Spanish-language rights and institutions, imposed literacy tests to make it difficult for them to vote, and encouraged massive immigration into the area so that the Hispanics would become outnumbered.

All of these measures were intended to disempower national minorities, and to eliminate any sense of possessing a distinct national identity. This was justified on the grounds that minorities that view themselves as distinct 'nations' would be disloyal, and potentially secessionist. And it was often claimed that minorities—particularly indigenous peoples—were backward and uncivilized, and that it was in their own interests to be incorporated—even against their will—into more civilized and progressive nations. National minorities, therefore, were often the first target of majority nation-building campaigns.[12]

But the attitude of liberal democracies towards minority nationalism has changed dramatically in this century. It is increasingly recognized that the suppression of minority nationalism was mistaken, for both empirical and normative reasons. Empirically, the evidence shows that pressuring national minorities to integrate into the dominant national group simply will not work. Western states badly misjudged the durability of minority national identities. The character of a national identity can change quickly—for example the heroes, myths, and traditional customs. But the identity itself—the sense of being a distinct nation, with its own national culture—is much more stable. Liberal-democratic governments have, at times, used all the tools at their disposal to destroy the sense of separate identity amongst their national minorities, from the prohibition of tribal customs to the banning of minority-language schools. But despite centuries of legal discrimination, social prejudice, and indifference, national minorities have maintained their sense of forming a distinct nation, and their desire for national autonomy.

As a result, when the state attacks the minority's sense of distinct nationhood, the result is often to promote rather than reduce the threat of disloyalty and secessionist movements. Indeed, recent surveys of ethnonationalist conflict around the world show that self-government arrangements diminish the likelihood of violent conflict, while refusing or rescinding self-government rights is likely to escalate the level of conflict (Gurr 1993, 2000; Hannum 1990; Lapidoth 1996). In the experience of Western democracies, the best way to ensure the loyalty of national minorities has been to accept, not attack, their sense of distinct nationality.

There was a time when eliminating this sense of nationhood amongst national minorities was a realistic possibility. After all, France was more or less successful in integrating the Basques and Bretons—but not the Corsicans—into the majority French national group in the nineteenth century. But this is no longer a realistic possibility for Western democracies. The evidence suggests that any national group that has survived into this century with its sense of national identity intact cannot be pressured into relinquishing its desire for national recognition and national autonomy. France was only successful in the nineteenth century because it employed a level of coercion against the Basques and Bretons that would be inconceivable now.[13] And even where a similar level of coercion has been employed in this century—for example against some indigenous peoples—it has failed to eliminate the minority's national identity. Few if any examples exist of recognized national groups in this century accepting integration into another culture, even though many have had significant economic incentives and political pressures to do so. As Anthony Smith notes, 'whenever and however a national identity is forged, once established, it becomes immensely difficult, if not impossible (short of total genocide) to eradicate'.[14]

So earlier attempts to suppress minority nationalism have been abandoned as unworkable and indeed counter-productive. But they have also been rejected as morally indefensible. After all, on what basis can liberal-democratic theory justify the suppression of minority nationalisms while allowing majority nation-building? The two seem on a par, morally speaking. If the majority can legitimately engage in nation-building, why not national minorities, particularly those which have been involuntarily incorporated into a larger state?

Liberal principles do, of course, set limits on *how* majority or minority national groups go about nation-building. Liberal principles will preclude any attempts at ethnic cleansing, or stripping people of their citizenship, or the violation of human rights. As I noted earlier, liberal-democracy is founded upon the principle of respect for individual civil and political rights. Moreover, liberal principles will also insist that any national group engaged in a project of nation-building must respect the right of other nations within its jurisdiction to protect and build their own national institutions. For example, the Québécois are entitled to assert national rights *vis-à-vis* the rest of Canada, but only if they respect the rights of Aboriginals within Quebec to assert national rights *vis-à-vis* the rest of Quebec.

These limits are important, but they still leave significant room, I believe, for legitimate forms of minority nationalism. Moreover, these limits are likely to be similar for both majority and minority nations. All else being equal, national minorities should have the same tools of nation-building available to them as the majority nation, *subject to the same liberal limitations.*

These limitations are sometimes described as a matter of 'balancing individual and group rights'. I don't think that the terminology of 'group rights' or 'collective rights' is helpful, for reasons I've explained elsewhere (Kymlicka 1995: ch. 3). But if we do talk about group rights, it is important to distinguish two kinds of rights that a minority group might claim. The first involves the right of a group against its own members, designed to protect the group from the destabilizing impact of internal dissent—for example the decision of individual members not to follow traditional practices or customs. The second kind involves the right of a group against the larger society, designed to protect the group from the impact of external pressures—for example the economic or political decisions of the larger society. I call the first 'internal restrictions', and the second 'external protections'. Given the commitment to individual autonomy, liberal pluralists oppose internal restrictions. Liberal pluralism rejects the idea that groups can legitimately restrict the basic civil or political rights of their own members in the name of preserving the purity or authenticity of the group's culture, traditions, or blood-lines. However, a liberal conception of minority rights can accord groups various rights against the larger society, in order to reduce the group's vulnerability to the economic or political power of the major-ity. Such 'external protections' are consistent with liberal principles, although they too become illegitimate if, rather than reducing a minority's vulnerability to the power of the larger society, they instead enable a minority to exercise economic or political dominance over some other group. To oversimplify, we can say that minority rights are consistent with liberal pluralism if they meet two condi-tions: they protect the freedom of individuals within the group: and they promote relations of equality (non-dominance) between groups.[15] Both state and substate nation-building should be con-strained by these principles.

What we need, in other words, is a consistent theory of permissible forms of nation-building within liberal democracies. I do not think that Western political theorists have yet developed such a theory. One of the many unfortunate side-effects of the dominance of the 'ethno-cultural neutrality' model of the liberal state is that liberal theorists have never explicitly confronted this question. Yet this is the key question we need to address. The question is not 'have national minorities given us a compelling reason to abandon the norm of eth-nocultural neutrality?', but rather 'why should national minorities not have the same powers of nation-building as the majority?'. This is the context within which minority nationalism must be evaluated—that is, as a response to majority nation-building, using the same tools of nation-building, subject to the same liberal limits. And the burden of proof rests on those who would deny national minorities the same powers of nation-building as those which the national majority takes for granted.

There is no guarantee that minority nationalisms will respect these boundaries of liberalism. In Flanders and the Basque Country, for example, there are radical wings of the nationalist movement that are illiberal. More generally, we can see an ongoing struggle within all minority nationalist movements between the liberal and illiberal ele-ments. The extent to which a particular form of minority nationalism is liberal or illiberal can only be determined by examining the facts, not by conceptual fiat or armchair speculation, and the clear trend throughout most Western democracies is towards a more open, liberal, and democratic conception of minority nationalism.[16] And I see no moral basis for majorities to reject the legitimacy of such liberal forms of minority nationalism.

For both prudential and moral reasons, therefore, an increasing number of Western democracies that contain national minorities accept that they are 'multination' states, rather than 'nation-states'. They accept that they contain two or more nations within their borders, and recognize that each constituent nation has an equally valid claim to the language rights and self-government powers necessary to maintain itself as a distinct societal culture. And this multinational character is typically manifested in some form of territorial autonomy for the national minority, and which may be explicitly affirmed in the country's laws and constitution.

In some countries, this shift to territorial autonomy has been achieved by adopting a federal system, since federalism allows the creation of regional political units, controlled by the national minority, with substantial and constitutionally protected powers of self-government. Countries that have adopted federalism to accommodate minority groups include Canada (for the Québécois), Belgium (for the Flemish), Spain (for the Catalans, Basques, and Galicians), and Switzerland (for the French-speaking and Italian-speaking minorities).[17]

It is important to distinguish these 'multination' federations from federal systems that were not designed as a response to ethnocultural pluralism—for example the United States, Australia, Germany, or Brazil. In these uninational federal systems, the federal units do not correspond in any way with distinct ethnocultural groups who desire to retain their self-government and cultural distinctiveness. In the United States, for example, a deliberate decision was made *not* to use federalism to accommodate the self-government rights of national minorities. Instead, it was decided that no territory would be accepted as a state unless national minorities were outnumbered within that state. In some cases, this was achieved by drawing boundaries so that Indian tribes or Hispanic groups were outnumbered (e.g. Florida). In other cases, it was achieved by delaying statehood until anglophone settlers swamped the older inhabitants (e.g. Hawaii; the Southwest). As a result, none of the fifty states can be seen as ensuring self-government for a national minority, the way that Quebec ensures self-government for the Québécois.[18]

We can call the American federal system a form of 'administrative-territorial' federalism, rather than 'multination' federalism. American federalism is a way of dividing powers on a territorial basis within a single national community, whose members are dominant within each of the subunits. It is not a way of accommodating minority self-government. The same is true in Brazil, Australia, or Germany. In multination federations, by contrast, the boundaries and powers of one or more subunits are defined with the intention of enabling a national minority to exercise self-government. This is the sort of federalism we see in Canada, Belgium, Spain, and to a lesser extent in Switzerland.[19]

In other countries, or for other national groups, there may be geographic or demographic reasons why federalism in the technical sense will not work. In these cases, we see the emergence of various *quasi-federal* forms of territorial autonomy. For example, Britain has recently adopted a quasi-federal system of devolution to Scotland and Wales, which now have their own legislative assemblies. And while Puerto Rico is not part of the American federal system—that is, it is not one of the fifty states—it has a special self-governing status within the United States as a 'Commonwealth'. Similarly, while Italy and Finland are not federations, they have adopted special forms of territorial autonomy for the German-speakers in South Tyrol; and for the Swedes in the Åland Islands. In all of these cases, territorial autonomy enables national minorities to establish and govern their own public institutions, often operating in their own language, including schools, universities, courts, and regional parliaments.

This trend towards quasi-federal forms of autonomy is even clearer in the context of indigenous peoples. Indigenous peoples in most Western democracies have demanded and increasingly acquired substantial forms of self-government over their lands. Indian tribes in the United States and Canada are recognized as having rights of self-government, and are acquiring—or reacquiring—control over education, heath care, policing, child welfare, natural resources, and so on. Similarly, the Scandinavian countries have created a Sami Parliament; the Maori in New Zealand have increased autonomy.[20]

Following Philip Resnick (1994), I will call these 'multination federations'. They are not all federations in the technical sense, but they all embody a model of the state in which national minorities are federated to the state through some form of territorial autonomy, and in which internal boundaries have been drawn, and powers distributed, in such a way as to ensure that each national group is able to maintain itself as a distinct and self-governing societal culture.

This trend towards multination federalism is very widespread in the West. Amongst the Western democracies with national minorities, only France and Greece have firmly rejected any notion of territorial autonomy for their historic minorities. Most national minorities have substantially more autonomy than they had 30 or 50 years ago, and few—if any?—national minorities have had their autonomy reduced over that period.

This trend is, I believe, one of the most important developments in Western democracies in this century. We talk a lot—and rightly so—about the role of the extension of the franchise to Blacks, women, and the working class in democratizing Western societies. But in its own way, this shift from suppressing to accommodating minority nationalisms has also played a vital role in consolidating and deepening democracy.[21] Indeed, it is important to stress that these multination federations are, by any reasonable criteria, successful. They have not only managed the conflicts arising from their competing national identities in a peaceful and democratic way, but have also secured a high degree of economic prosperity and individual freedom for their citizens. This is truly remarkable when one considers the immense power of nationalism in this century. Nationalism has torn apart colonial empires and Communist dictatorships, and redefined boundaries all over the world. Yet democratic multination federations have succeeded in taming the force of nationalism. Democratic federalism has domesticated and pacified nationalism, while respecting individual rights and freedoms. It is difficult to imagine any other political system that can make the same claim.

There is no guarantee that all of these Western multination federations will stay together in perpetuity. But we can safely say that many of these states would have either fallen apart or degenerated into authoritarian rule a long time ago had they not learned to accommodate minority nationalisms. We actually know very little about the sources of stability in multination states: this is a surprisingly neglected topic in both sociology and political theory. But the evidence in the West strongly suggests that democratic stability can only be achieved by recognizing, not suppressing, minority national identities.[22]

3.2 Immigrants

By immigrant groups, I mean groups formed by the decision of individuals and families to leave their original homeland and emigrate to another society, often leaving their friends and relatives behind. This decision is typically made for economic reasons, although sometimes also for political reasons, to move to a freer or more democratic country. Over time, and with the second and subsequent generations born in the new country of residence, they give rise to ethnic communities with varying degrees of internal cohesion and organization.

But it is essential to immediately distinguish two categories of immigrants—those who have the right to become citizens, and those who do not. Much confusion in the academic literature, and the wider public debate, has arisen from conflating these two cases. I will use the term 'immigrant group' only for the former case, and will discuss the latter case, which I will call 'metics', below.

Immigrants, then, are people who arrive under an immigration policy which gives them the right to become citizens after a relatively short period of time—say, 3–5 years—subject only to minimal conditions—such as learning the official language, and knowing something about the country's history and political institutions. This has been the traditional policy governing immigration in the three major 'countries of immigration'—namely, United States, Canada, and Australia.

Historically, immigrant groups have responded very differently to majority nation-building than national minorities. Unlike national minorities, the option of engaging in competing-nation building has not been either desirable or feasible for immigrant groups in Western democracies. They are typically too small and territorially dispersed to hope to recreate their original societal culture from scratch in a new country. Instead, they have traditionally accepted the expectation that they will integrate into the larger societal culture. Indeed, few immigrant groups have objected to the requirement that they must learn an official language as a condition of citizenship, or that their children must learn the official language in school. They have accepted the assumption that their life-chances, and even more the life-chances of their children, will be bound up with participation in mainstream institutions operating in the majority language.

Western democracies now have over 200 years of experience concerning how such groups integrate, and there is little evidence that legal immigrants with the right to become citizens pose any sort of threat to the unity or stability of a liberal democracy. There are few, if any, examples of immigrant groups mobilizing behind secessionist movements, or nationalist political parties, or supporting revolutionary movements to overthrow elected governments. Instead, they integrate into the existing political system, just as they integrate economically and socially.[23]

So immigrants have not resisted majority nation-building campaigns to integrate them into the mainstream society. However, what immigrants have tried to do is to renegotiate the terms of integration.

Indeed, recent debates over 'multiculturalism' in immigrant countries are precisely debates over renegotiating the terms of integration. Immigrants are demanding a more tolerant or 'multicultural' approach to integration that would allow and indeed support immigrants to maintain various aspects of their ethnic heritage even as they integrate into common institutions operating in the majority language. Immigrants insist that they should be free to maintain some of their old customs regarding food, dress, recreation, religion, and to associate with each other to maintain these practices. This should not be seen as unpatriotic or 'unAmerican'. Moreover, the institutions of the larger society should be adapted to provide greater recognition and accommodation of these ethnic identities—for example schools and other public institutions should accommodate their religious holidays, dress, dietary restrictions, and so on.

How should liberal democracies respond to such demands for immigrant multiculturalism? Here again, liberal democracies have historically resisted these demands. Until the 1960s, all three of the major immigrant countries adopted an 'Anglo-conformity' model of immigration. That is, immigrants were expected to assimilate to existing cultural norms, and, over time, become indistinguishable from native-born citizens in their speech, dress, leisure activities, cuisine, family size, identities, and so on. To be too visibly 'ethnic' in one's public behaviour was seen as unpatriotic. This strongly assimilationist policy was seen as necessary to ensure that immigrants became loyal and productive members of society.

However, beginning in the 1970s, it was increasingly recognized that this assimilationist model is unrealistic, unnecessary, and unjust. It is *unrealistic* because no matter how much pressure to assimilate is applied, immigrants never fully lose their distinctive identities and practices. The 'melting pot' image was never accurate. Immigrants do indeed integrate into common institutions and learn the dominant language, but they remain visibly, and proudly, distinctive in their ethnic identities and attachments. Pressuring immigrants to assimilate is also *unnecessary*, since the evidence shows that immigrants who maintain a strong sense of ethnic identity and pride can nonetheless be loyal and productive citizens. And, finally, pressuring assimilation is *unfair*, since it denies equal respect to immigrants, and turns integration into an oppressive process.

Immigrant demands for a more 'multicultural' model of integration are, I think, a fair response to majority nation-building. If liberal democracies are going to pressure immigrants to integrate into common institutions operating in the majority language, then we need to ensure that the terms of integration are fair. To my mind, this demand has two basic elements:

(a) we need to recognize that integration does not occur overnight, but is a difficult and long-term process which operates intergenerationally. This means that special accommodations are often required for immigrants on a transitional basis. For example, certain services should be available in the immigrants' mother tongue, and support should be provided for those organizations and groups within immigrant communities which assist in the settlement and integration process;

(b) we need to ensure that the common institutions into which immigrants are pressured to integrate provide the same degree of respect, recognition, and accommodation of the identities and practices of ethnocultural minorities as they traditionally provided for the dominant group. This requires a systematic exploration of our social institutions to see whether their rules, structures, and symbols disadvantage immigrants. For example, we need to examine dress codes, public holidays, or even height and weight restrictions to see whether they are biased against certain immigrant groups. We also need to examine the portrayal of minorities in school curricula or the media to see if they are stereotypical, or fail to recognize the contributions of ethnocultural groups to national history or world culture.

The move towards such a 'multicultural' model of immigrant integration is very widespread in the West. The first country to officially adopt such a 'multiculturalism' policy at the national level was Canada in 1971. But it has since been adopted in many other countries, from Australia and New Zealand to Sweden, Britain, and the Netherlands.[24] And while the United States does not have an official multiculturalism policy at the federal level, it too has implicitly adopted such an approach. One can find multiculturalism or 'diversity' policies at virtually all other levels of American government and in virtually all public institutions, from school boards and hospitals to the police and army. As Nathan Glazer puts it, 'we are all multiculturalists now' (Glazer 1997).

Some people worry that these immigrant multiculturalism demands do not just involve a renegotiation of the terms of integration, but in fact involve a rejection of the very idea of integration. According to critics, demands for multiculturalism are actually attempts by immigrants to avoid integrating into the mainstream society, and to avoid

having to participate in common institutions operating in the majority language.

But this is incorrect. It would be self-defeating for immigrants to
seek multiculturalism policies that would impede their integration.
After all, the overwhelming reason why people emigrate is for economic reasons—to get a better life for themselves and their children.
They have decided to leave their original society and culture, and
emigrate to another, more prosperous society, with the hope of
taking advantage of the greater educational and employment opportunities it provides. They make this decision knowing full well that
they can only take advantage of these opportunities if they are willing
to adapt to the new society, to learn its language and customs, and
integrate into its academic, economic, and political institutions. If they
valued cultural maintenance over economic gain, they would not have
come in the first place.[25] Given that the predominant motivation of
immigrants is economic, and given that they don't have the option of
trying to create a parallel society in their own language, it would only
make sense for immigrants to seek a sort of 'multiculturalism' which
is consistent with their socio-economic integration into the larger
society.

And indeed if we look at the actual demands pressed by immigrant
citizens, this is what we see. These demands are best understood as
revising the terms of integration, not abandoning the goal of integration (Kymlicka 1998: ch 2). Immigrants seek changes within mainstream institutions—schools, workplaces, courts, police forces, and
welfare agencies—so as to make it easier to participate within these
mainstream institutions. They want to reform these institutions so as
to provide greater recognition of their ethnocultural identities, and
greater accommodation of their ethnocultural practices, so that they
will feel more at home in these institutions. Thus they want schools
to provide more information about the immigrant experience; workplaces to accommodate their religious holidays or traditional dress;
government agencies to provide health care and welfare benefits in a
way that is culturally sensitive; and so on. Far from impeding integration, these policies assist it.

This suggests that concerns about the impact of multiculturalism
on integration are overstated. Having said that, there is no reason
to leave this to chance. It is appropriate, I think, for liberal states to
continue to expect immigrants to learn the dominant language as a
condition of gaining citizenship, as well as something about the
history and political institutions of their new society. Similarly, it is

appropriate for liberal democracies to continue to insist that the children of immigrants learn these things in school.

In fact, very few immigrants within Western democracies oppose these requirements. When immigrants demand multiculturalism, they are not rejecting the idea that they and their children have a responsibility to learn about the larger society, or that the larger society has an interest in instilling in children the sorts of knowledge and capacities needed for democratic citizenship.

In this sense, multiculturalism is not seen as competing with, or a substitute for, citizenship. Multiculturalism is rather the flip side of citizenship. It is recognition of the fact that the integration of new citizens is a two-way street. Just as immigrant citizens are expected to make a commitment to their new society, and to learn about its language, history, and institutions, so too the larger society must express a commitment to its immigrant citizens, and adapt its institutions to accommodate their identities and practices. Just as immigrant citizens are expected to make a new home in the receiving country, so the receiving country must make them feel at home.

I need to stress again that I am discussing the sort of multiculturalism that is sought by immigrant citizens. This is very different from the sort of 'multiculturalism' which is offered to metics, such as the multiculturalism policies which Germany formerly adopted towards its Turkish guestworkers, which I will discuss in section 3.4 below.

In my view, the vast majority of what is done under the heading of multiculturalism policy in Canada and Australia, not only at the federal level, but also at provincial and municipal levels, and indeed within school boards and private companies, can be defended as promoting fair terms of integration. These policies are not only justified in principle, but have been working well in practice to smooth the integration process for immigrants (Kymlicka 1998: chs. 1–7).

Others may disagree with the fairness of some of these policies. The requirements of fairness are not always obvious, particularly in the context of people who have chosen to enter a country. Here again, Western political theorists have not yet developed a fully satisfactory theory of fair terms of integration. But this is the relevant question we need to address. The question is not whether immigrants have given us a compelling reason to diverge from the norm of ethnocultural neutrality, but rather how can we ensure that state policies aimed at pressuring immigrants to integrate are fair?[26]

3.3 Isolationist Ethnoreligious Groups

Whereas most immigrants wish to participate in the larger society, there are some small immigrant groups which voluntarily isolate themselves from the larger society, and avoid participating in politics or civil society. As I noted earlier, this option of voluntary marginalization is only likely to be attractive to ethnoreligious groups whose theology requires them to avoid all contact with the modern world, such as Hutterites, Amish, or Hasidic Jews, all of whom emigrated to escape persecution for their religious beliefs. They are unconcerned about their marginalization from the larger society and polity, since they view its 'worldly' institutions as corrupt, and seek to maintain the same traditional way of life they had in their original homeland.

In order to avoid contact with the modern world, and to maintain their traditional way of life, these groups seek exemption from various laws. For example, they demand exemption from military service or jury duty, since these would implicate them in the operation of worldly governments. And they have demanded exemption from compulsory education laws, in order to ensure that their children are not exposed to corrupting influences—for example they seek the right to take their children out of school before the legal age of 16, and to be exempted from certain parts of the core curriculum which teach about the lifestyles of the modern world.

The response of these groups to majority nation-building is very different from that of either national minorities or immigrant groups. After all, nation-building aims to integrate citizens into a modern societal culture, with its common academic, economic, and political institutions, and this is precisely what ethnoreligious sects wish to avoid. Moreover, the sorts of laws from which these groups seek exemption are precisely the sorts of laws which lie at the heart of modern nation-building—for example, mass education.

How should liberal democracies respond to such demands to be exempted from majority nation-building? Perhaps surprisingly, many Western democracies have historically been quite accepting of these demands. This is surprising, since by their own admission these groups lack any loyalty to the state. Moreover, they are often organized internally in illiberal ways. They inhibit attempts by group members to question traditional practices or religious authorities—and indeed often try to prevent children from acquiring the capacity for such critical reflection—and may restrict women to the household. And they are not responsible citizens in the country as a whole, in the sense that they take no interest in trying to tackle problems in the larger society—for example they take no interest in how to solve the problems of urban poverty, pollution, or drug abuse.[27]

Jeff Spinner says that these groups want to be 'partial citizens', because they voluntarily waive both the rights and responsibilities of democratic citizenship (Spinner 1994). They do not exercise their right to vote and to hold office and their right to welfare benefits, but by the same token they also seek to evade their civic responsibility to help tackle the country's problems. Unlike most national minorities and immigrant groups, therefore, these ethnoreligious sects reject principles of state loyalty, liberal freedoms, and civic responsibility.

Why then were the demands of these groups accepted? Part of the reason, at least in the North American context, is that they arrived at a time when both the United States and Canada were desperately seeking immigrants to settle the western frontier, and were willing to make concessions to acquire large groups of immigrants with useful agricultural skills. It is not clear that liberal democracies today would be as willing to make the same concessions to newly-arriving ethnoreligious sects.

And indeed it is not clear whether it is appropriate, from the point of view of liberal-democratic principles, to offer such concessions. After all, these groups deny liberty to their own members, and avoid their civic obligations to the rest of society. For this reason, various attempts have been made over the years to take away these exemptions, and to force these groups to fulfil their civic duties—such as military service and jury duty—and force the children to attend the usual length of compulsory schooling, with the standard core curriculum, so that they learn to be competent democratic citizens capable of participating in the outside world.

However, in general, most democratic states continue to tolerate these groups, so long as they do not egregiously harm people inside the group—for example sexually abuse children—and so long as they do not attempt to impose their views on outsiders, and so long as members are legally free to leave. This toleration is typically justified either on the grounds of (a controversial view of) freedom of religion, or on the grounds that these groups were given specific promises of toleration when they entered the country—historical promises which were not given to other immigrants.[28]

These first three types of groups—national minorities, immigrants, and ethnoreligious sects—have all been the targets of majority nation-building programmes. As liberal states embarked on their projects of diffusing a common societal culture throughout the entire territory of the state, and encountered these types of groups, they sought to pressure them to integrate.

The final two types of groups I will discuss—namely, metics and racial caste groups, like the African-Americans—are very different. Not only were they not pressured to integrate into the majority culture, they were in fact prohibited from integrating. Whereas the first three types of groups were pressured to integrate, even if they wanted to remain apart, these last two groups were forcibly kept separate, even if they wanted to integrate. This history of exclusion continues to cause many difficulties for Western democracies.

3.4 Metics

While isolationist groups like the Amish voluntarily waive their citizenship, there are some migrants who are never given the opportunity to become citizens. This is actually a diverse category of people, including *irregular migrants*—for example those who entered the country illegally or overstayed their visa, and who are therefore not legally domiciled, such as many North Africans in Italy—and *temporary migrants*—for example those who entered as refugees seeking temporary protection or as 'guestworkers', such as Turks in Germany. When they entered the country, these people were not conceived of as future citizens, or even as long-term residents, and indeed they would not have been allowed to enter in the first place if they were seen as permanent residents and future citizens. However, despite the official rules, they have settled more or less permanently. In principle, and to some extent in practice, many face the threat of deportation if they are detected by the authorities, or if they are convicted of a crime. But they nonetheless form sizeable communities in certain countries, engage in some form of employment, legal or illegal, and may marry and form a family. This is true, for example, of Mexicans in California, Turks in Germany, or North Africans in Italy or Spain. Borrowing a term from Ancient Greece, Michael Walzer calls these groups 'metics'—that is, long-term residents who are nonetheless excluded from the polis (Walzer 1983). Since metics face enormous obstacles to integration—legal, political, economic, social, and psychological—they tend to exist in the margins of the larger society.

Generally speaking, the most basic claim of metics is to regularize their status as permanent residents, and to gain access to citizenship. They want, in effect, to be able to follow the immigrant path to integration into the mainstream society, even though they were not initially admitted as immigrants.

How should liberal democracies respond to this demand for access to citizenship? Historically, Western democracies have responded in different ways to these demands. Some countries—particularly the traditional immigrant countries—have grudgingly accepted these demands. Guestworkers who stay beyond their original contract are often able to gain permanent residence, and periodic amnesties are offered for illegal immigrants, so that over time they become similar to immigrants in their legal status and social opportunities.

But some countries—particularly those which do not think of themselves as immigrant countries—have resisted these demands. Not only did these countries not admit these particular individuals as immigrants, they do not admit any immigrants, and may have no established process or infrastructure for integrating immigrants. Moreover, many of these metics have either broken the law to enter the country (illegal immigrants), or broken their promise to return to their country of origin (guestworkers), and so are not viewed as worthy of citizenship. Moreover, countries with no tradition of accepting newcomers are often more xenophobic, and prone to view all foreigners as potential security threats, or as potentially disloyal, or simply as unalterably 'alien'. In these countries, of which Germany, Austria, and Switzerland are the best-known examples, the official policy has not been to try to integrate metics into the national community, but to get them to leave the country, either through expulsion or voluntary return.

We can see this policy reflected in the conception of 'multiculturalism' which has arisen for migrants who are denied access to citizenship—a conception which is very different from that in immigrant countries like Canada or Australia. In some German provinces (*lander*), for example, until the 1980s, the government kept Turkish children out of German classes, and instead set up separate classes for Turks, often taught in Turkish by teachers imported from Turkey, with a curriculum focused on preparing the children for life in Turkey. This was called 'multiculturalism', but unlike multiculturalism in Canada or Australia, it was not seen as a way of enriching or supplementing German citizenship. Rather, it was adopted precisely because these children weren't seen as German citizens. It was a way of saying that these children do not really belong here, that their true 'home' is in Turkey. It was a way of reaffirming that they are aliens, not citizens. Multiculturalism without the offer of citizenship is almost invariably a recipe for, and rationalization of, exclusion.[29]

In short, the hope was that if metics were denied citizenship, so that they only had a precarious legal status within the country, and if they were told repeatedly that their real home was in their country of origin, and that they were not wanted as members of the society, then they would eventually go home.

But it is increasingly recognized that this approach to metics is not viable, and is both morally and empirically flawed. Empirically, it has become clear that metics who have lived in a country for several years are highly unlikely to go home, even if they have only a precarious legal status. This is particularly true if the metics have married and had children in the country. At this point, it is their new country, not their country of origin, which has become their 'home'. Indeed, it may be the only home that the metics' children and grandchildren know. Once they have settled, founded a family, and started raising their children, nothing short of expulsion is likely to get metics to return to their country of origin.

So a policy based on the hope of voluntary return is simply unrealistic. Moreover, it endangers the larger society. For the likely result of such a policy is to create a permanently disenfranchised, alienated, and racially-defined underclass. Metics may develop an oppositional subculture in which the very idea of pursuing success in mainstream institutions is viewed with suspicion. The predictable consequences can involve some mixture of political alienation, criminality, and religious fundamentalism amongst the immigrants, particularly the second generation, which in turn leads to increased racial tensions, even violence, throughout the society.

To avoid this, there is an increasing trend in Western democracies, even in non-immigrant countries, towards adopting amnesty programs for illegal immigrants, and granting citizenship to guestworkers and their children. In effect, long-settled metics are increasingly viewed as if they were legal immigrants, and are allowed and encouraged to follow the immigrant path to integration.

This is not only prudent, but morally required. For it violates the very idea of a liberal democracy to have groups of long-term residents who have no right to become citizens. A liberal democratic system is a system in which those people who are subject to political authority have a right to participate in determining that authority. To have permanent residents who are subject to the state, but unable to vote, is to create a kind of caste-system which undermines the democratic credentials of the state (Bauböck 1994; Carens 1989; Walzer 1983; Rubio-Marin 2000).

These people arrived without any expectation or entitlement of becoming citizens, and may indeed have come illegally. But at some point, the original terms of admission become irrelevant. For all practical intents and purposes, this is now the metics' home, and they are *de facto* members of society who need the rights of citizenship.

So there are both prudential and moral reasons for offering citizenship to metics. Some democracies may strongly dislike the idea of naturalizing foreigners. If so, they must not allow foreigners to settle in the first place, by eliminating 'guestworker' programmes, and by preventing illegal immigration. Democracies have no obligation to admit would-be metics. But if a country allows a group of non-nationals to settle and become permanent residents, then liberal-democratic principles require that these metics be able to naturalize.

It might seem naïve to think that merely giving metics the right to become citizens will prevent the danger of a racially-defined underclass. Some people think that poor migrants from North Africa would form an underclass in Western European countries even if they were admitted with the right to naturalize. The cultural differences are too great, some people think, for such immigrants to integrate, no matter what the official immigration policy.

But the facts do not support this view. Studies show that wherever and whenever immigrants have been accepted as future citizens, cultural differences have not prevented integration. If we look at the experience of Poles in France, Nigerians in England, Iranians in Canada, Chinese in the United States, or the Vietnamese in Australia, integration has occurred despite enormous differences in culture. Integration has occurred whether they were Catholics, Protestants, Jews, Hindus, Sikhs, Buddhists, or Muslims; whether they came in small numbers or large; whether they came from democracies, military dictatorships, Communist countries, or theocracies; whether they were highly educated or illiterate; and so on. The speed of integration has of course varied for different groups in different countries, but the same basic pattern of social, economic, and political integration has repeatedly emerged. So long as these immigrants were given the right to become citizens, they invariably set off on the path to integration.

Various studies have shown that the key factor in determining the integration of immigrant groups in different countries is not the differences in culture between the country of origin and the receiving country, but rather the policy of the receiving country. Whether immigrants are integrated or excluded is not determined by cultural difference or education levels, but by state policies regarding settlement and citizenship (Castles and Miller 1993).

Nor should this surprise us. After all, immigrant citizens differ dramatically from illegal immigrants in their expectations, incentives, and opportunities regarding integration. Moreover, and equally importantly, the expectations and incentives of the host society regarding these groups differ dramatically.

A legal immigrant with a right to naturalize is seen as a future citizen. Indeed, the process of selecting such immigrants is seen precisely as a process of selecting future citizens. As a result, the host society has a large stake in the integration of these immigrants—they are expected to settle permanently, to naturalize and vote, and to have children who will themselves be undisputed citizens. Subsidizing the integration of immigrants is, therefore, a prudential investment on the part of the host society, reflected in such things as the language classes, citizenship classes, and job-training programmes which are typically offered to immigrants on a free or heavily-subsidized basis; in the funding of ethnic organizations which assist in immigrant settlement—for example housing, jobs, dealing with the government; as well in the insistence that the children of immigrants go to school, and in the careful attention paid to their progress in school. And having invested in these immigrants, the government then wishes to recoup its investment, by encouraging immigrants to in fact settle permanently and naturalize. This is reflected not only in explicit campaigns to encourage naturalization, but also in various other government policies, such as anti-discrimination legislation and affirmative action programmes.

By contrast, the host society has little or no incentive to invest in illegal immigrants. On the contrary, the government's official aim is to identify and deport them as quickly as possible. As a result, the illegal immigrant's strategy for remaining requires hiding from state authorities. He or she may succeed in escaping detection for many years, but only by avoiding precisely the sort of government-sponsored programmes which are created to assist the integration of immigrants. Indeed, illegal immigrants are often wary about registering their children for school, or about becoming actively involved in school affairs, for fear that this may lead to their being identified as illegal immigrants. Moreover, far from being protected against discrimination in employment, they are legally prohibited from taking up employment, and have no legal recourse if they are subject to discrimination in housing. In short, illegal immigrants are unable to take advantage of the programmes and institutions which assist the integration of immigrants.

There is a tendency amongst some postmodernist critics of liberal democracy to describe government programmes which promote the cultural integration of immigrants as 'oppressive', since they attempt to suppress difference in the name of a common national identity. But the situation of metics shows, I think, that it is actually exclusion from such nation-building programmes which is truly oppressive. Metics are exempted from majority pressure to integrate, but this is hardly grounds for celebration from a liberal-democratic point of view.

Access to citizenship also affects the incentive of immigrants to invest in the host society. Legal immigrants who have a right to work, settle permanently and naturalize have a much greater incentive to make the effort involved in integrating than do illegal immigrants who face the continuous threat of deportation. The legal immigrant is more likely to make the investment of time and money needed to learn the language properly upon arrival, to develop the job skills needed in the new society, to form or reunify their family, and more generally to set up a home and become involved in the local community. These sorts of investments often involve short-term economic costs, but have a long-term pay-off in the improved prospects for legal immigrants and their children. This sort of investment is only going to be made by people who have some reasonable security that they and their descendants will still be residing in the country in the long-term.

Integration is not just a matter of the decisions made by immigrants and the government. It is also influenced by the attitudes and reactions of the general public. And here again we can see a great gulf between the way legal and illegal immigrants are viewed. Many citizens bitterly resent illegal immigrants, partly because they are seen as exhibiting disrespect for the law, and partly because they are seen as jumping the queue—that is, taking away spaces which could have been allotted to more 'deserving' immigrants or refugees. This hostility is often picked up and reinforced by the government, which paints illegal immigrants as a threat to the country.

This government-fed hostility to illegal immigration is often hypocritical, since many governments know that their economy requires large numbers of illegal migrants, and so they turn a blind eye to it. And citizens who decry illegal immigration are more than happy to take advantage of the cheaper food or cheaper services which illegal immigrants make possible. But whether these attitudes are hypocritical or not, they surely affect the integration of immigrants. In countries where immigrants are selected as future citizens, the government actively defends the need for immigration, and encourages the public to view immigrants as future citizens. Some citizens will of course remain prejudiced against these legal immigrants, but the public rhetoric is one which encourages people to see immigrants as a beneficial part of national development. In countries which turn a blind eye to illegal immigration, by contrast, governments encourage their citizens to see illegal immigrants as a threat, rather than defending the necessity of immigration and the rights of immigrants.

In short, legal immigrants with a right to naturalize have the opportunity and incentive to integrate, and are encouraged in this expectation by the government, which actively defends immigration as part of the national interest. Illegal immigrants have fewer opportunities or incentives to integrate, and are stigmatized by the government, which actively identifies them as threats to the nation.

Whether or not immigrants have the right to become citizens, therefore, is not a trivial issue. It has enormous consequences, both for the immigrant and the larger society. And a liberal democracy, both for reasons of justice and for reasons of self-interest, must give all immigrants the right to become citizens.

3.5 African-Americans

One final group which has been very important in recent American theorizing about ethnic relations is the Blacks, or 'African-Americans' who are descended from the African slaves brought to the United States between the seventeenth and nineteenth centuries. Under slavery, Blacks were not seen as citizens, or even as 'persons', but simply as the property of the slave owner, alongside his buildings and livestock. Although slavery was abolished in the 1860s, and Blacks were granted citizenship, they were still subject to segregation laws which required that they attend separate schools, serve in separate army units, sit in separate train cars etc., until the 1950s and 1960s. And while such discriminatory laws have now been struck down, the evidence suggests that Blacks remain subject to pervasive informal discrimination in hiring and housing, and they remain disproportionately concentrated in the lower class, and in poor neighbourhoods.

African-Americans have a unique relationship to American nation-building. Like metics, they were historically excluded from becoming members of the nation. But unlike metics, the justification for this was not that they were citizens of some other nation to which they should return. Blacks in America can hardly be seen as 'foreigners' or 'aliens', since they have been in the US as long as the whites, and have no foreign citizenship. Instead, they were effectively denationalized—they were denied membership in the American nation, but nor were they viewed as belonging to some other nation.

African-Americans are unlike other ethnocultural groups in the West. They do not fit the voluntary immigrant pattern, not only because they were brought to America involuntarily as slaves, but also because they were prevented rather than encouraged from integrating into the institutions of the majority culture—for example racial segregation; laws against miscegenation and the teaching of literacy. Nor do they fit the national minority pattern, since they do not have a homeland in America or a common historical language. They came from a variety of African cultures, with different languages, and no attempt was made to keep together those with a common ethnic background. On the contrary, people from the same culture—even from the same family—were typically split up once in America. Moreover, before emancipation, they were legally prohibited from trying to recreate their own cultural structure—for example all forms of black association, except churches, were illegal. The situation of African-Americans, therefore, is virtually unique.

In light of these complex circumstances and tragic history, African-Americans have raised a complex, unique, and evolving set of demands. The civil rights movement in the United States in the 1950s and 1960s was seen by many of its proponents as enabling Blacks to follow the immigrant path of integration, through a more rigorous enforcement of anti-discrimination laws. Those African-Americans who were sceptical about the possibility of following the immigrant path to integration, however, have pursued the opposite tack of redefining Blacks as a 'nation', and promoting a form of Black nationalism. Much of the recent history of African-American political mobilization can be seen as a struggle between these two competing projects.

But neither of these is realistic. The legacy of centuries of slavery and segregation has created barriers to integration which immigrants simply do not face. As a result, despite the legal victories of the civil rights movement, Blacks remain disproportionately at the bottom of the economic ladder, even as more recent (non-white) immigrants such as Asian-Americans have integrated. But the territorial dispersion of Blacks has made the option of national separatism equally unrealistic. Even if they shared a common Black national identity, which they do not, there is no region of the United States where Blacks form a majority.

As a result, it is increasingly recognized that a *sui generis* approach will have to be worked out for African-Americans, involving a variety of measures. These may include historical compensation for past injustice, special assistance in integration (such as affirmative action), guaranteed political representation (for example through redrawing electoral boundaries to create black-majority districts), and support for various forms of Black self-organization (for example subsidies for historical black colleges, and for black-focused education). These different demands may seem to pull in different directions, since some promote integration while others seem to reinforce segregation, but each responds to a different part of the complex and contradictory reality which African-Americans find themselves in. The long-term aim is to promote the integration of African-Americans into the American nation, but it is recognized that this is a long-term process that can only work if existing Black communities and institutions are strengthened. A degree of short-term separateness and colour-consciousness is needed to achieve the long-term goal of an integrated and colour-blind society.[30]

It is difficult to specify precisely which principles should be used to evaluate these demands, all of which are controversial. As with most other groups, there are both moral and prudential factors to be considered. African-Americans suffer perhaps the greatest injustices of all ethnocultural groups, both in terms of their historical mistreatment and their current plight. Morally speaking, then, the American government has an urgent obligation to identify and remedy these injustices. Moreover, as with metics, the result of this ongoing exclusion has been the development of a separatist and oppositional subculture in which the very idea of pursuing success in 'white' institutions is viewed by many Blacks with suspicion. The costs of allowing such a subculture to arise are enormous, both for the Blacks themselves, who are condemned to lives of poverty, marginalization, and violence, and for society at large, in terms of the waste of human potential, and the escalation of racial conflict. Given these costs, it would seem both prudent and moral to adopt whatever reforms are needed to prevent such a situation.

4. The Emerging Dialectic of Nation-Building and Minority Rights

In the previous section, I have discussed five types of ethnocultural groups, and tried to show how their demands are best understood in relation to, and as a response to, majority nation-building. Each group's claims can be seen as specifying the injustices which majority nation-building has imposed or might impose on them, and as identifying the conditions under which majority nation-building would cease to be unjust. It is important to note that in all of these cases, minorities are not saying that nation-building programmes are inherently impermissible. But they do insist that nation-building programmes be subject to certain conditions and limitations. If we try to combine these different demands into a larger conception of ethnocultural justice, we can say that majority nation-building in a liberal democracy is legitimate under the following conditions:

1. No groups of long-term residents are permanently excluded from membership in the nation, such as metics or racial caste groups. Everyone living on the territory must be able to gain citizenship, and become an equal member of the nation if they wish to do so.
2. In so far as immigrants and other ethnocultural minorities are pressured to integrate into the nation, the sort of sociocultural integration which is required for membership in the nation should be understood in a 'thin' sense, primarily involving institutional and linguistic integration, not the adoption of any particular set of customs, religious beliefs, or lifestyles. Integration into common institutions operating in a common language should still leave maximal room for the expression of individual and collective differences, both in public and private, and public institutions should be adapted to accommodate the identity and practices of ethnocultural minorities. Put another way, the conception of national identity, and national integration, should be a pluralist and tolerant one.
3. National minorities are allowed to engage in their own nation-building, to enable them to maintain themselves as distinct societal cultures.

These three conditions have rarely been met historically within Western democracies, but we can see a clear trend within most democracies towards greater acceptance of them. This trend partly reflects prudential reasons: earlier policies to exclude metics, assimilate immigrants, and suppress minority nationalisms have simply failed to achieve their aims, and so new patterns of ethnic relations are being tested. But it also reflects a recognition that previous policies were morally illegitimate.

The patterns I have been discussing in this section are of course generalizations, not iron laws. Some metics, immigrant groups, and national minorities have not mobilized to demand minority rights, and even when they have, some Western democracies continue to resist these demands.[31] And even where these demands have been accepted, they often remain controversial, vulnerable to changes in popular opinion or governing party.[32]

Still, the general trend is clear: Western states today exhibit a complex pattern of nation-building constrained by minority rights. On the one hand, Western states remain 'nation-building' states. All Western states continue to adopt the sorts of nation-building policies I discussed in the American context, and no Western states have relinquished the right to adopt such policies. On the other hand, these policies are increasingly qualified and limited to accommodate the demands of minorities who feel threatened. Minorities have demanded, and increasingly been accorded, various rights which help ensure that nation-building does not exclude metics and racial caste groups, or coercively assimilate immigrants, or undermine the self-government of national minorities.

What we see in the 'real world of liberal democracies', therefore, is a complex dialectic of state nation-building (state demands on minorities) and minority rights (minority demands on the state). We can represent it this way:

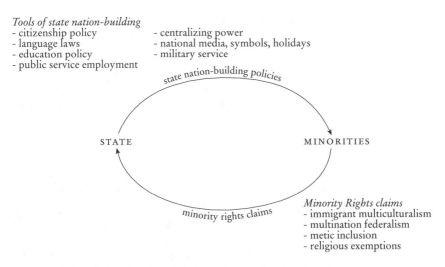

Fig. 1.1 The dialectic of nation-building and minority rights

In my view, it is essential to view both halves of this circle together. Too often in debates about minority rights, people simply look at the bottom half of the picture, and ask why pushy and aggressive minorities are asking for 'special status' or 'privileges'. What gives minorities the right to make such demands on the state? But if we look at the top half of the picture, it becomes clear that demands for minority rights must be seen in the context of, and as a response to, state nation-building. While minorities do make claims against the state, these must be understood as a response to the claims that the state makes against minorities.[33] Moreover, many of these minority rights claims are, I believe, legitimate. That is, the minority rights being claimed by metics, immigrants, racial caste groups, and national minorities really do serve to protect them from real or potential injustices that would otherwise arise as a result of state nation-building. There is growing recognition that such rights are needed to ensure justice in diverse societies.

If the presence of state nation-building policies helps to justify minority rights, one could also turn the equation around, and say that the adoption of minority rights has helped to justify state nation-building. After all, we cannot simply take for granted that it is legitimate for a liberal-democratic state to pressure minorities to integrate into institutions operating in the majority language. What gives the state the right to insist on common national languages, education systems, citizenship tests, and so on, and to impose such things on minorities? As I discussed earlier, liberal nationalists argue that there are certain valid purposes that are promoted by these nation-building policies, and I agree. But it is not legitimate to pursue these goals by assimilating, excluding, or disempowering minorities, or by imposing costs and burdens on groups that are often already disadvantaged. Unless supplemented and constrained by minority rights, state nation-building is likely to be oppressive and unjust. On the other hand, where these minority rights are in place, then state nation-building can serve a number of legitimate and important functions.

What we see, then, in the Western democracies, is a complex package of robust forms of nation-building combined and constrained by robust forms of minority rights. It is particularly complex in the case of multination federations, since the provision of self-government rights to national minorities means that the entire dialectic gets repeated at a *substate* level. As we've seen, national minorities use their self-governing powers to adopt their own nation-building policies within their federal subunit or autonomous territory, often using the same tools of nation-building as the central state, so as to diffuse their language and societal culture throughout the territory of their subunit—for example control over education, public service employment. This puts pressure on any 'internal minorities' within the self-governing territory—such as anglophones and indigenous peoples in Quebec; Castilians and North African immigrants in Catalonia. Confronted with this sort of substate nation-building, internal minorities obviously face the same limited set of options—do they accept integration into the national minority's societal culture, or do they fight to create or maintain their own self-governing institutions in their own language, or do they accept voluntary marginalization, or do they migrate elsewhere? And, in general, we see the same patterns of responses here as at the level of the larger state. For example, immigrants in Quebec typically choose integration into the francophone societal culture, whereas the indigenous peoples and long-settled anglophone community fight to maintain their own institutions. And each of these responses to substate nation-building involves making claims for minority rights against the government of the subunit or autonomous territory: immigrants seek a more multicultural form of integration in Quebec, while anglophones and indigenous peoples seek their own publicly-funded schooling, hospitals, media, universities. And just as central state nation-building is increasingly qualified by minority rights, so too we see a clear trends towards accepting internal minority rights as a constraint on substate nation-building.[34]

This means that there is a second-order dialectic of nation-building and minority rights in multination states at the substate level:

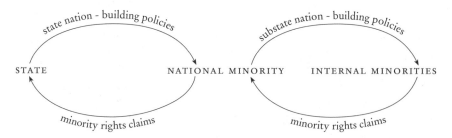

FIG. 1.2 Nation-building and minority rights in multination states

This second-order dialectic is unlikely in practice to be identical to the first. For example, few national minorities have control over naturalization policy or military service, which are two of the important tools of (central) state nation-building.[35] Still, in general we can say that in multination federations national minorities have many of the same powers of nation-building as the dominant nation, *subject to the same limitations*, including respect for the rights of (internal) minorities. Whether at the state or substate level, nation-building is illegitimate if it seeks to coercively assimilate immigrants, exclude metics, or suppress national minorities.

The resulting combination of state and substate nation-building, qualified by minority rights at both levels, may seem messy. But this is the real world of liberal democracy in multination states—a reality that is systematically ignored or obscured by the myth of a neutral state. Moreover, I believe that the particular package of nation-building and minority rights that we see emerging in Western democracies is in many respects working quite well. Of the five types of groups I've discussed, immigrants and national minorities are the most numerous in Western democracies, and, perhaps as a result, the most successfully accommodated. Liberal democracies have, over the years, learned a great deal about how to accommodate these two major forms of diversity. Both immigration and minority nationalisms continue to raise many conflicts and challenges for liberal democracies, but there are some well-established norms that help to regulate and manage these conflicts. We now have models of multination federalism and immigrant multiculturalism which have been tested over time, and which have proven relatively successful and stable.

There are of course many difficult issues left unresolved. There are many groups that are very far from achieving full equality: African-Americans in the United States, guestworkers in Austria, illegal immigrants in southern Europe, indigenous peoples in the Americas, Australasia, and Scandinavia. Moreover, even where policies are working well there is always the danger that some of these advances will be reversed. And the fact that these policies are working well is often more a matter of good luck than foresight and careful planning. This package has emerged in an *ad hoc* way, not guided by any theory or models, or any clear understanding of the underlying principles or long-term goals. As I've noted, liberal political theorists, until very recently, have had little or nothing to say about either state nation-building or minority rights, let alone the relationship between them. The existence of state nation-building and minority rights was ignored by liberal theorists, obscured by the myth of the ethnocultural neutrality of the state. Prior to the 1990s, one would be hard-pressed to find a single sustained discussion of either the legitimate goals or tools of state nation-building, or the legitimate forms of minority rights. Yet, in practice, liberal democracies have developed surprisingly successful forms of both.

So I believe there are grounds for cautious optimism that Western democracies really have made important steps in learning how to deal with ethnocultural diversity in a way that respects and promotes liberal values of freedom, justice and democracy. The particular package of state nation-building and minority rights that we see emerging in many Western democracies is better than earlier approaches to ethnocultural diversity, and better than the apparent alternatives.[36]

5. Relevance to ECE

So far, I have provided a thumbnail sketch of recent attempts to theorize about minority rights within Western democracies. To what extent, if any, is this relevant to ethnic conflicts in Eastern and Central Europe? Can we see a similar dialectic of state nation-building and minority rights in the region? I will start with nation-building, and then look at minority rights claims.

5.1 Nation-Building in ECE

It is obvious, I think, that the newly-democratizing countries of ECE are following the model of the 'nation-building' state. These countries are not, and do not pretend to be, ethnoculturally neutral, but are actively engaged in projects of nation-building, and of diffusing a common societal culture throughout the territory of the state (Pettai 1998). In doing so these countries are using many of the same nation-building tools Western democracies use. These include:[37]

(1) official language policies;[38]
(2) attempts to create a uniform system of national education;[39]
(3) migration and naturalization policies—that is, favouring co-ethnics in admissions decisions; requiring migrants to adopt a common national identity as a condition of naturalization;[40]
(4) the redrawing of administrative districts to dilute the weight of minorities in each of them.[41]
(5) the centralization of power, so that all decisions are made in a context where the dominant group forms a clear majority.[42]

Some Western commentators take these nation-building policies as evidence that newly-democratizing states in ECE are fundamentally different from Western 'civic' nations. But as we've seen, the use of nation-building is not, by itself, incompatible with Western liberal democracy. Liberal democracies have engaged in extensive campaigns of nation-building in an effort to diffuse a common set of institutions operating in a common language throughout the entire territory of the state, and thereby to promote a common national identity. Liberal democracies, as much as illiberal ones, attempt to give a distinctly 'national' character to public space.[43]

What then distinguishes liberal nation-building from illiberal nationalism? This is an interesting, and inadequately studied, question. I would highlight the following nine differences, all of which have implications for minority rights. If we examine nationalist movements along these nine dimensions, we should be able to get a good sense of how liberal they are. I should emphasize that these nine differences are all a matter of degree: nationalist movements fall along a continuum of liberalism in their nation-building projects, rather than being 'purely liberal' or 'purely illiberal'. Moreover, nationalist movements can be more liberal on some of these criteria and less liberal on others. Indeed, this is true of Western democracies as well as ECE countries, and many of my examples of illiberal nation-building are taken from the history of Western democracies. All real-world nationalisms are a complex mixture of liberal and illiberal elements, although the forms and depth of illiberalism vary enormously.

1. One difference between liberal and illiberal forms of nation-building is in the degree of coercion used to promote a common national identity. It wouldn't be true to say that liberal states only use voluntary means to promote nation-building. Historically, at least, liberal states have been quite willing to use coercion in the service of nation-building. There was nothing voluntary about the imposition of the French language on the Bretons after the Revolution, or the imposition of the English language on the Chicanos after the War with Mexico in 1848. And even today, there are coercive aspects to the way immigrants are pressured to integrate—for example language tests for naturalization. But it is generally true that liberal states impose fewer penalties or disadvantages on those who remain outside the dominant national group. For example, while a liberal state may not provide public funds to minority-language schools, they are unlikely to prohibit privately-funded minority schools.

2. This is related to a second difference—namely, that liberal states have a more restricted conception of the relevant 'public space' within which the dominant national identity should be expressed, and a more expansive conception of the 'private' sphere where differences are

tolerated. For example, parliamentary debates in a liberal state may be conducted exclusively in one language, but liberal states are unlikely to insist, as some ECE states do, that election posters and brochures be printed only in the dominant language, or that weddings be conducted in the dominant language. Liberal states may insist that the official language be used when filling in government-mandated health and safety reports in the workplace, but they are unlikely to insist that union meetings be conducted in the majority language.[44]

3. Third, liberal states are unlikely to prohibit forms of speech or political mobilization that challenge the privileging of a national identity. People who wish to give public space a different national character—perhaps by adopting a different official language, or even by seceding to form a separate state—are not forbidden from holding public office. Advocating such changes is not seen as disloyalty, or even if it is seen as disloyal, this is not viewed as sufficient grounds for restricting democratic rights. In Israel, by contrast, anyone who refuses to accept the principle that Israel is a 'Jewish state' is not allowed to run for political office.

4. Fourth, liberal states typically have a more open definition of the national community. Membership in the nation is not restricted to those of a particular race, ethnicity, or religion. Generally speaking, anyone can join the nation if they want to do so. When liberal states prohibited the public expression of a minority's national identity—as the French did with the Basques—they at least ensured that the minority could become full and equal members of the dominant nation. However coercive the French were towards the Basques, there was never any question that (assimilated) Basques could become Frenchmen. By contrast, in some countries, non-nationals are prevented from integrating into the dominant national group even as they are prohibited from expressing their own national identity. Bulgarian nationalism is currently undergoing major transformations, but until recently it used to be that to be a 'true' Bulgarian, one must have a Bulgarian surname, be descended from ethnic Bulgarians and be a member of the Orthodox church. Needless to say, it was very difficult for Turks living in Bulgaria to ever be accepted as members of the 'Bulgarian' nation, even if they wished to integrate.[45]

5. Partly as a result of this inclusiveness, liberal states exhibit a much thinner conception of national identity. In order to make it possible for people from different ethnocultural backgrounds to become full and equal members of the nation, and to allow for the maximum room for individual dissent, the terms of admission are relatively thin—for example learning the language, participating in common

public institutions, and perhaps expressing a commitment to the long-term survival of the nation. Joining the nation does not require one to abandon one's surname, or religion, or customs, or recreational practices, etc.

In so far as liberal nation-building involves diffusing a common national culture throughout the territory of the state, it is a very thin form of culture—what I've called a 'societal culture', centred on a shared language which is used in a wide range of societal institutions such as schools, media, law, economy, or government, rather than on common religious beliefs, family customs, or personal lifestyles. As I noted earlier, societal cultures within a modern liberal democracy are inevitably pluralistic, containing Christians as well as Muslims, Jews, and atheists; heterosexuals as well as gays; professional women as well as traditional homemakers; conservatives as well as socialists. In non-liberal states, by contrast, acquiring a national identity typically requires a much thicker form of cultural integration, involving not only a common language and public instituions, but also elements of religion, ritual, and lifestyle.[46]

6. Sixth, partly as a result of this cultural thinning, a liberal nationalism is less likely to view the nation as the supreme value. Illiberal nationalisms often see the nation as sacred, and as the ultimate value to which all else is subordinate and instrumental—for example defining women's role as the 'bearers of the nation'.[47] Liberal nationalism, by contrast, seeks to thin the content of the national identity and culture so that other areas of social life have room to flourish on their own terms—such as religion, family life, personal lifestyles, hobbies, and careers. These are not seen as subordinate and instrumental to the goal of national greatness or the achieving of a national destiny. Rather, they are accepted as having independent and intrinsic value. If anything, it is the nation which is seen as having instrumental value. The nation is primarily valuable, not in and of itself, but rather because it provides the context within which we pursue the things which truly matter to us as individuals—our family, faith, vocation, pastimes, and projects. As Jonathan Glover puts it, a useful maxim for liberal nationalists is: 'Always treat nations merely as means, and never as ends in themselves'.[48]

Of course, even in a liberal society, some individuals will view their nation as sacred, particularly if they subscribe to a religion which says that they are a chosen people who have made a covenant with God, and whose national destiny is ordained by God. A liberal society allows such views to exist, and to be expressed, as part of freedom of religion. But this is not the view of the state or of the constitution, and is not the basis for liberal nation-building programmes. In separating church and state, and in thinning the content of national identity, liberalism also desacralizes the nation, and makes room for other values to flourish on their own terms.

7. Seventh, and also a result of this cultural thinning and ethnic inclusiveness, liberal national cultures become more 'cosmopolitan'. I don't mean that citizens in a liberal nation adopt the *ideology* of cosmopolitanism. As an ideology, cosmopolitanism rejects all forms of nationalism, and opposes efforts by the state to protect national identities and cultures. It is clear that citizens of Western democracies are not 'cosmopolitan' in this sense: instead, they overwhelmingly accept that it is a legitimate function of the state to protect and express a particular national identity. But while liberal citizens remain committed to the principles and practice of nation-building, the actual substance of their day-to-day life is increasingly influenced by the beliefs, practices, and products of other parts of the world. This cultural interchange is the inevitable result of liberal freedoms, ethnic inclusiveness, and the thinning of the official national culture.

Put another way, in a liberal nation, the societal culture is an open and pluralistic one, which borrows whatever it finds worthwhile in other cultures, integrates it into its own practices, and passes it on to subsequent generations. Moreover, this sort of cultural interchange is seen as a good thing. Liberal nationalists reject a notion of culture that sees the process of interacting with and learning from other cultures as a threat to 'purity' or 'integrity', rather than as an opportunity for enrichment. In short, liberal nationalisms wish to become cosmopolitan in practice, in the sense of embracing cultural interchange, without accepting the cosmopolitan ideology which denies that people have any deep bond to their own language and cultural community.[49]

Illiberal nationalisms, by contrast, often aim to protect the 'purity' or 'authenticity' of their culture from 'corruption' by external influences. The claim of illiberal nationalists to be protecting their 'authentic' national culture is often a sham, since all forms of nationalism involve reshaping and modernizing traditional cultures. But even if just a pretence, this rhetoric of protecting cultural purity or authenticity can lead to xenophobic consequences, both in formal policies (for example prohibiting 'foreign' religions from proselytizing; prohibiting foreign ownership of land) and in public discourse (for example criticizing local NGOs for co-operating with international agencies).

8. Eighth, liberal nations are less likely to insist that national

identity must be exclusive. One can be a true 'Canadian' and also think of oneself as a member of the Irish or Vietnamese nation. Moreover, one can publicly express both of these national identities. Canadians of Irish descent can celebrate Irish national symbols and holidays as well as Canadian ones—there is no formal or informal prohibition on flying an Irish flag on one's property, or marching in a St Patrick's Day parade. By contrast, illiberal nationalisms tend to be more exclusive in their conception of national identity, and to insist that to be a true member of the nation one must renounce all other national identities. Here again, this difference is reflected both in formal rules—for example whether dual citizenship is legally permitted—but also in informal interactions—for example whether singing the anthem or flying the flag of another nation is seen as disloyal or provocative.[50]

This tolerance for dual nationality is obviously most relevant for immigrants, or for the children of mixed marriages. However, since increasing numbers of people fall into these categories, it is important that a nationalist movement can accommodate such people.

9. Finally, liberal nations accord public recognition to, and share public space with, those national minorities that consistently and democratically insist upon their national distinctiveness. Unlike France after the Revolution, or the United States in 1848, liberal states today recognize that territorially concentrated groups which were involuntarily incorporated into the state cannot and should not be forced to adopt the majority's national identity. If groups like the Québécois, Catalans, Flemish, Scots, or indigenous peoples see themselves as distinct nations within the larger state, then their national distinctiveness should be recognized in public life and public symbols, through such things as official language status, self-government rights, and recognition of their distinct legal traditions. In accepting the legitimacy of these minority nationalisms, states accept that they are the sort of 'multination' state that I discussed earlier.[51]

These nine differences are interconnected, and often mutually reinforcing. But it is possible for nationalist movements to be more liberal in some respects, and less liberal in others, and we should be aware of these nuances. It is also important to examine these nine issues both at the formal level of laws and constitutions and at the informal level of public discourse and attitudes. For example, it is possible for a country to have a liberal constitution that affirms equal rights for women, and yet an illiberal public discourse which says that women who exercise their rights are betraying their duties to the nation. Similarly, liberal naturalization rules can coexist with an illiberal discourse which denies that immigrants or children of mixed marriages are 'true' members of the nation. Removing illiberal, exclusionary, or discriminatory laws is obviously the first step, but nationalism can only become truly liberal if a wider public culture of tolerance develops. Liberal nationalism is not just about legal formalities, but also about the level of respect for dissent and diversity shown in everyday discourse and interaction amongst citizens.

There are undoubtedly many other ways in which liberal nation-building differs from illiberal nationalisms. But enough has been said already, I hope, to show that the issue is not *whether* states engage in nation-building, but rather what *kind* of nation-building, and also what *stage* of nation-building.[52] While liberal states see themselves as having the right to promote a particular national identity, and to try to diffuse it through the territory of the state, this nation-building project is a qualified and self-limiting one. Minorities are not seen as 'unnatural' blots on the nation's territory, but as full citizens whose interests must be given due concern, and not just weighed on the basis of how they affect the dominant national group. This means that any nation-building programmes must involve limited coercion; must leave ample room for the expression of differences in the private sphere; must allow non-members to become full and equal members of the nation if they choose; and must agree to share public space in cases where national minorities insist on maintaining their distinctiveness. In all of these ways, liberal democracies reject the view that the state belongs exclusively to the dominant national group.

Some commentators have attempted to summarize the differences between liberal and illiberal nationalism under the labels of 'civic' versus 'ethnic' nationalism. Civic nationalism, on this standard view, defines national membership purely in terms of adherence to democratic principles; whereas ethnic nationalism defines national membership in terms of a common language, culture, and ethnic descent. But this can be very misleading. Even in the most liberal of democracies, nation-building goes beyond the diffusion of political principles. It also involves the diffusion of a common language and national culture. What distinguishes liberal nation-building from illiberal nationalism is not the absence of any concern with language, culture, and national identity, but rather the content, scope, and inclusiveness of this national culture, and the modes of incorporation into it.[53] Moreover, there is not one distinction between liberal and illiberal nationalisms, but several. And each of these distinctions is a matter of degree. We cannot, therefore, divide real-world nationalist movements into two categories: 'liberal' and 'illiberal'. Rather, nationalist movements will turn out to be more liberal on some scales, and less liberal on others.[54]

5.2 Minority Rights Claims in ECE

So in terms of the first half of the nation-building/minority rights dialectic, we certainly see that states in ECE are using various tools of nation-building to protect and diffuse a dominant societal culture. In some cases, this state nation-building is more thick, coercive, or exclusionary than in Western democracies. How do minorities respond to state nation-building? As I noted earlier, minorities facing a nation-building state have limited options, ranging from integration to self-government to voluntary marginalization. Which of these options have minorities in ECE adopted? Do they respond by making similar sorts of claims as minorities in the West?

I have already mentioned one important difference in the response of minorities in ECE. Unlike the West, the option of mass emigration is a serious one for some groups. We can see several examples of minority flight. In some cases, virtually the entire minority population has left. For example, virtually all ethnic Germans and Jews have left Central Asia for Germany or Israel.[55] In other cases, there has been sizeable migration, sometimes into the hundreds of thousands. This is true of the ethnic Russians leaving Kazakhstan for Russia; ethnic Hungarians leaving Transylvania and Vojvodina for Hungary; or ethnic Greeks leaving southern Albania for Greece.[56] In all of these cases, there has been a sizeable migration, although most members of the minority group have stayed behind.

In most cases, however, the option of mass migration is neither feasible nor desirable for minorities. And where minorities are staying, we might expect that they respond to state nation-building policies by demanding various kinds of minority rights. And that indeed is what we see. In Moldova, for instance, both the demands of the Gagauz and of the Slavic community of Trans-Dniestr reflected, at least initially, a 'reactive nationalism', responding to the assertive nation-building policies of the Moldovan majority (Chinn and Roper 1995; Ethnobarometer 1999: 62–7; Kaiser 1994: 364–7; Thompson 1998). Most of the cases of minority separatism which emerged between the end of the 1980s and the beginning of the 1990s in the former Soviet Union—in Azerbaijan, Georgia, Moldova, and Ukraine—were initially a response to majority nation-building projects initiated in the republics (Ethnobarometer 1999: ch. 2). Similarly, the demands of the Turks in Bulgaria were a response to the pressure they faced to assimilate to the Bulgarian majority (Tomova 1998). Hungarians in Romania and Slovakia also reacted in the early 1990s to radical nationalizing policies (Ethnobarometer 1999: ch. 3). More generally, whenever a majority attempts to define the state as un- inational, national minorities have responded by demanding recognition as a 'distinct society' or 'constituent nation'.[57]

In all of these cases, claims for minority rights are not necessarily evidence that minorities have become aggressive and assertive, but rather can be seen as defensive responses to the threats posed by assertions of majority nation-building. In this sense, the basic framework which Western political theorists are now using to understand minority rights seems broadly applicable to ECE. That is, we should view minority rights as a response to actual or perceived injustices that arise in the course of majority nation-building.[58]

Of course, this is only a rather formal or abstract sort of similarity between the West and ECE, and doesn't tell us much about the actual content of minority rights. Is there any reason to think that states in ECE will (or should) adopt more specific Western-style models of minority rights such as immigrant multiculturalism or multination federalism? Will (or should) the West and ECE converge on similar principles of ethnocultural justice for the treatment of metics, immigrants, national minorities, or isolationist ethnoreligious groups and so on? I don't have the expertise to answer these questions in a definitive way. But let me make a few preliminary observations. I will start with the claims of national minorities (section 5.3), then migrant groups (5.4), then a few 'anomalous' cases that do not fit the usual categories, like the Roma, Russian settlers in the Near Abroad, or the Crimean Tatars (5.5).

5.3 National Minorities in ECE

So far as I can tell, the claims of territorially-concentrated national minorities in ECE are broadly similar to those of national minorities in the West, and it seems plausible that the same principles should apply in evaluating them. According to these principles, democratic countries should accept the claims of national minorities to national recognition and national autonomy, so that they can maintain themselves as viable and functioning societal cultures, with public institutions operating in their own language.

Indeed some of the same mechanisms used to accommodate minority nationalism in the West, such as federal or quasi-federal forms of territorial autonomy, could be used in ECE. Since multination federalism has worked to ensure peace, democracy, freedom, and prosperity for multination states like Spain, Canada, Belgium, Britain, and Switzerland, one might expect that there would be great interest in adopting it in ECE countries, most of which contain territorially-concentrated national minorities. And yet there is enormous resistance in virtually every ECE country to the idea of federalism or other forms of territorial autonomy for national minorities. Russia is the only country that voluntarily adopted a form of multination federalism that grants significant territorial autonomy to several national minorities.[59] But in all other countries, territorial autonomy has been strongly resisted.

In some cases, pre-existing forms of minority autonomy were scrapped: Serbia revoked the autonomy of Kosovo/Vojvodina; Georgia revoked the autonomy of Abkhazia and Ossetia; Azerbaijan revoked the autonomy of Ngorno-Karabakh. Indeed the revoking of minority autonomy was often one of the first things that these countries chose to do with their new-found freedom after the collapse of Communism.[60] In other cases, requests to restore historic forms of autonomy were rejected—Romania refused to restore the autonomy to Transylvania which had been revoked in 1956. In yet other cases, requests to create new forms of autonomy were dismissed—Estonia rejected a referendum supporting autonomy for Russian-dominated Narva; Kazakhstan rejected autonomy for ethnic Russians in the north; Ukraine rejected a referendum supporting autonomy for ethnic Romanian areas; Lithuania rejected requests for autonomy by ethnic Poles; Macedonia rejected a referendum for autonomy for Albanian-dominated Western Macedonia in 1992.[61] And in yet other cases, countries have redrawn boundaries to make it impossible for autonomy to be adopted in the future—Slovakia redrew its internal boundaries so that ethnic Hungarians would not form a majority within any of the internal administrative districts, and hence would have no platform to claim autonomy; Croatia redrew internal boundaries in Krajina and West Slavonia to dilute Serbian-populated areas.[62]

The only cases in ECE, outside Russia, where territorial autonomy has been accepted are cases where the national minority simply grabbed political power and established *de facto* autonomy without the consent of the central government. In these situations, the only alternative to recognizing *de facto* autonomy was military intervention and potential civil war. This was the situation in Trans-Dneister in Moldova; Abkhazia in Georgia; Krajina in Croatia; Crimea in Ukraine; and Ngorno-Karabakh in Armenia. Even here, most countries preferred civil war to negotiating autonomy, and only accepted autonomy if and when they weren't able to win militarily.[63]

This almost blind resistance to territorial autonomy is reflected in the recent history of Krajina, a Serbian-populated area of Croatia that has been the subject of a brutal civil war. Many commentators believe that autonomy for the Serbs was the only option that might have avoided this bloodshed (Vàrady 1997). However, Serb demands for territorial autonomy were considered too much for the Croats to accept after independence, and they offered only minimal forms of cultural autonomy without political self-government. So the local Serbs took up arms, backed by the Serbian-dominated Yugoslav army, and simply took over political power in the region. At this point, Croatia offered territorial autonomy to Krajina, but this was now considered too little by the Serbs, who would settle for nothing less than secession and incorporation into Serbia. When the Croat army retook Krajina, the Serbs reconsidered and accepted the Croat offer of autonomy, but by then the victorious Croats had withdrawn the offer of autonomy, and have proceeded to dispossess the local Serbs of their rights and property, and to resettle Bosnian Croats in areas of former Serb settlement. Both sides preferred civil war, secession, and ethnic cleansing to negotiating autonomy.

What explains this overwhelming resistance to the general principle of recognizing minority nationalism, and to the more specific idea of federalism, or other forms of minority autonomy?[64] These ideas are resisted for the same reasons they used to be rejected in West— for example fear of disloyalty and separatism. Yet most multination Western countries now see the attempt to suppress minority nationalism as counter-productive, and see federalism is a way of stabilizing multination states. Perhaps people in ECE may, in time, come to share that perception.

Indeed, this seems to be the evidence from the ECE as well. Compare the way Ukraine dealt with the Russian nationalists in Crimea, on the one hand, with the way Azerbaijan dealt with Nagorno-Karabakh, or Georgia dealt with Abkhazia and Ossetia, or Moldova dealt with Gagauz and Trans-Dniestr, or Serbia dealt with Kosovo, on the other hand. The latter four countries initially tried and failed to suppress minority nationalism. The result was armed conflict. They were later forced to offer concessions, but have not yet reached final settlements (Ethnobarometer 1999: ch. 2). By contrast, Ukraine continued to bargain with the Russians in Crimea, granted the peninsula the status of an autonomous republic, never undertook any repressive miltiary or police action, and thus avoided violence and maintained the dispute within the boundaries of peaceful politics. Ukraine and the Russians in Crimea have now reached what may be an enduring settlement (Ethnobarometer 1999: 67–71).[65]

In short, there is reason to believe that in ECE, as in the rest of the world, loyalty is best secured by encouraging, not suppressing, minority identities, and by enabling forms of minority self-government (Vàrady 1997: 47).[66] What Horowitz says internationally seems to apply to ECE: namely, that 'early, generous devolution is far more likely to avert than to abet ethnic separatism . . . Unfortunately, a good many governments have proceeded on the opposite assumption—that devolution feeds centrifugal forces' (Horowitz 1991: 224; cf. Hislope 1998).

However, the adoption of multination federalism in ECE countries is complicated by two factors not present in the West. First, there is the legacy of the pseudo-federalisms of the Communist regimes in Czechoslovakia, Yugoslavia, and the Soviet Union. The constitution of these federations contained a division of powers between the central and local levels of government, but in reality all power was centralized in the hands of the Communist Party which imposed its will on the subunits. As Dorff puts it, these countries were federal in 'structure', but entirely lacking in federalist 'procedures'—that is, lacking any tradition of partnership, negotiated co-operation and open bargaining concerning the accommodation of ethnic diversity (Dorff 1994: 100–1). Federalism of this sort was not adopted as a way of encouraging people to understand and accept the enduring diversity of interests and identities, but rather as a mechanism of centralized control over the expression of ethnicity, so as to remove any potential for any ethnic mobilization that was independent of the central state and Communist Party (Lynn and Novikov 1997: 187–8). The Party selected the homeland cadres, who then were given a monopoly over the mobilization of the relevant ethnic community. All other forms of ethnic mobilization were prohibited. This perverse form of pseudo-federalism, far from promoting practices of tolerance and inter-ethnic accommodation, laid the groundwork for the dissolution of all three federations (Dorff 1994: 102).[67] While there is very little in common between these federalisms under a Communist dictatorship and federalism in a liberal democracy (Linz 1996), the collapse of these three federations has dealt a 'severe setback' to the very idea of federalism in ECE (Liebich 1995: 317).

Second, and more important, many national minorities in ECE have a kin-state nearby that they might hope to join or rejoin, and so are potentially irredentist. This is quite different from national minorities in Western Europe, most of whom do not have a neighbouring kin-state. The Catalans, Basques, and Scots might occasionally entertain the thought of secession, but it would not be in order to join some larger state to which they feel tied by bonds of ethnicity. Similarly in North America, it's been at least a century since anyone seriously thought Puerto Rico might wish to rejoin Spain, or that Quebec might wish to rejoin France. And of course indigenous peoples in the Americas do not have a kin-state.

By contrast, many of the most difficult ethnic conflicts in ECE involve national minorities that have a neighbouring kin-state. The problem in such cases is not just that the minority may have a longing to rejoin their kin-state, but also the potential for political and even military intervention by the kin-state in order to 'protect' the interests of 'their' people. The paradigm example of this was the way the Nazis encouraged ethnic Germans in Czechoslovakia to lodge complaints about their treatment, and then used these complaints as grounds for invasion.

Many people in ECE fear that a similar situation may arise today. This fear arises in the context of ethnic Russians both in Crimea (Jaworsky 1998; Marples and Duke 1995) and in the Baltics (Pettai 1998; Mitrofanov 1998); the Russified Cossacks in Kazakhstan and the Northern Caucasus (Opalski 1998); the ethnic Hungarians in Slovakia and Romania (Mihalikova 1998; Nelson 1998; Andreescu 1997); the ethnic Albanians in Macedonia (Strazzari 1998); the ethnic Romanians in Ukraine (Jaworsky 1998); and the ethnic Serbs in Bosnia or Croatia (Crnobrnja 1998).

In some cases, the national minority may be willing to be guided by its kin-state. Jaworsky suggests this is true of the ethnic Romanians in Ukraine (Jaworsky 1998). But the problem of kin-state intervention exists even if the minorities themselves are not irredentist, and do not wish to join or rejoin their kin-state. For example, the evidence suggests that an increasing number of ethnic Russians in the Baltics not only reject the idea of rejoining Russia, but also think of themselves as having more in common with the local Latvians or Estonians than with ethnic Russians in Russia (Pettai 1998; Antane and Tsilevich 1998; Mitrofanov 1998). Yet this has not eliminated the danger that nationalists in Russia could use the existence of Russian minorities as grounds for intervention. As Pettai notes, Russia continues to speak in the name of ethnic Russians in the Baltic countries, and to adopt a confrontational attitude towards these countries, even though the local Russians themselves do not share Moscow's agenda. Similarly, Jaworsky notes that very few ethnic Russians in Ukraine—

outside of Crimea—think of themselves as a 'fifth-column' for Russia, yet some Russian nationalists in Moscow continue to assume that ethnic Russians do, and should, have supreme loyalty to Russia.

Finding a stable *modus vivendi* with a local national minority is difficult when a kin-state, with its own agenda, claims to speak for the minority. Many of the most difficult ethnic conflicts in ECE revolve around this triadic relationship between an ethnocultural minority, its host state, and its kin-state—other cases of this triadic relationship include ethnic Turks in Bulgaria and Greece, ethnic Poles in Lithuania, ethnic Tadjiks in Uzbekistan, ethnic Greeks in Albania, and ethnic Germans in the former Czechoslovakia.[68]

This kin-state phenomenon is an important aspect of ethnic conflict in Eastern Europe that is typically absent in Western democracies. But we can find analogous cases in the West. For example, Austria could be seen as a kin-state for the German-speaking minority in South Tyrol; France could be seen as a kin-state for the French-speaking Walloons in Belgium; Netherlands could be seen as a kin-state for the Flemish; Sweden could be seen as a kin-state for the Swedes on the Åland Islands. Yet in none of these do we talk about the problem of kin-states or the threat of irredentism. For some reason, apart from Northern Ireland and Cyprus, the presence of kin-states has not caused the same sort of problem in the West.[69]

It seems to me that there is a further factor at play here—namely, the historical relation between the minority and external powers. In many cases, minorities are seen, rightly or wrongly, as allies or collaborators with external powers that have historically oppressed the majority group. Hungarians in Romania and Slovakia are a relatively small and powerless minority—10–15 per cent of the population in each country—but Slovakians and Romanians perceive them as the embodiment of centuries of oppression under the Habsburgs. The Russians in Estonia and Latvia are not seen as a weak and disenfranchised minority group, but as a reminder and manifestation of former Soviet oppression. The Muslim Albanians in Serbia and Macedonia, or the Muslim Turks in Bulgaria, are seen as a reminder of centuries of oppression under the Muslim Ottomans.[70]

In short, the problem is not just that the minority has a kin-state, but rather the historical fact that the minority collaborated with this kin-state in oppressing the majority group. This, I think, is truly distinctive to Eastern Europe, not found in the West—except perhaps in Ireland and Cyprus.[71]

This and other factors have encouraged three interrelated assumptions which are now widely accepted by ECE countries: (a) that minorities are disloyal, not just in the sense that they lack loyalty to the state—that is equally true of secessionists in Quebec or Scotland—but in the stronger sense that they collaborated with former oppressors, and continue to collaborate with current enemies or potential enemies; (b) that a strong and stable state requires weak and disempowered minorities—put another way, ethnic relations are seen as a zero-sum game: anything that benefits the minority is seen as a threat to the majority; and (c) that the treatment of minorities is above all a question of national security.[72]

Where people accept one or more of these premises, there is little room for asking what package of minority rights would be fair or democratic. The whole question of what justice requires between majority and minority is submerged, since national security takes precedence over justice, and since disloyal minorities have no legitimate claims anyway. This helps to explain why there is little scholarly or public debate in ECE about what principles of justice should regulate the accommodation of ethnocultural diversity. Indeed, virtually the only reference to justice comes in the form of insisting that minorities pay for the historic injustices that the *majority* has suffered, and which the minority is perceived to be responsible for. Justice means that the majority should be compensated for the historic wrongs it has suffered; it does not mean that the state should seek to ensure a fairer distribution of power, rights, and resources between majority and minority.[73]

This pervasive rhetoric of loyalty/disloyalty is exacerbated in some countries by a local version of Samuel Huntington's 'clash of civilizations' thesis (Huntington 1996). On this view, the world is divided into distinct 'civilizations', grounded essentially in religion, that are in more or less inherent conflict. So the conflict between the Serbs and Albanians over Kosovo is not just a conflict between languages, cultures, or nations, but also between civilizations—an Orthodox Christian civilization and a Muslim civilization. Two civilizations cannot coexist as equal partners in a single state. One civilization must be dominant, and the other subordinate and hence prone to disloyalty. This clash of civilizations view is invoked, not only in conflicts between Christians and Muslims, but also between Orthodox and Catholics—for example in Romania, where there is said to be civilizational conflict between the Orthodox Romanian majority and the Catholic Hungarian minority—or between Protestants and Orthodox—for example in Estonia, where the majority Estonians are Protestant, and the minority Russians are Orthodox. Where people accept this premise about the clash of civilizations, there is again no room for questions about fairness or justice to minorities. Relations between conflicting civilizations are a matter of power and security, not justice.

Given these factors, the prospects for federalism in ECE are very slim, at least in the foreseeable future. Yet it is not clear to me what the alternative mechanisms are for accommodating minority nationalism. As Mihalikova notes, while majority Slovaks reject the idea of local autonomy for the ethnic Hungarians, they offer 'no coherent vision of the future' as an alternative. Indeed, she sees this lack of any long-term conception of ethnocultural justice as the 'biggest problem' in majority/minority relations in Slovakia (Mihalikova 1998). I think one could say the same thing about state policy in many other ECE countries, like Macedonia or Romania or Serbia. The resistance to federalism is clear and unmistakable; the preferred alternative is vague and secretive.

Of course, federal and quasi-federal forms of territorial autonomy are neither feasible nor desirable for many smaller and more dispersed national minorities, and for some groups subject to prolonged and severe assimilationist pressures—such as the Turks in Bulgaria. For such groups, some more creative alternatives are needed. For example, Russia adopted in 1996 a system of 'National Cultural Autonomy' for national minorities which cannot benefit from the Russian system of multination federalism—that is, groups which are too small or dispersed to form a local majority in a territorial subunit of the Russian federation, or for members of larger national minorities who live outside their self-governing homeland. The National Cultural Autonomy Act allows national groups, wherever they reside, to organize and administer their own publicly-funded schools in their mother tongue, to establish newspapers and media, and to address the organs of government. This Act remains a statement of aspirations—it has not yet been implemented in a meaningful way—but a generous interpretation would see this Act as a serious attempt to grapple with the needs of groups not well-served by usual models of territorial autonomy.[74] Similar systems of non-territorial cultural autonomy have been adopted in Hungary, and in parts of Ukraine—for the ethnic Russians in eastern Ukraine and the ethnic Hungarians in Transcarpathia.[75]

This conception of cultural autonomy—which echoes Otto Bauer's theory of non-territorial autonomy in the old Habsburg empire (Bauer 2000)—provides an interesting supplement to familiar Western models of minority rights. Unlike Western models of multination federalism, it does not involve territorial autonomy; but unlike Western models of immigrant multiculturalism, it involves a considerable degree of institutional separateness, self-administration, and extensive mother-tongue language rights.

This is an area where the ECE may have lessons for Western democracies. These emerging models of cultural autonomy may be relevant for those groups in the West which do not fit neatly into the categories of either territorially-concentrated nations or voluntary immigrants. Indeed, a recent Canadian government commission recommended what amounted in effect to a system of cultural autonomy for those Aboriginals who have moved off their self-governing reserves. This non-territorial system of cultural autonomy for off-reserve Indians would supplement the territorial autonomy exercised within Indian reservations (RCAP 1996).[76]

So it would be a mistake to suppose that territorial autonomy can work for all national minorities, no matter how small or dispersed. But I believe it would equally be a mistake to suppose that non-territorial forms of cultural autonomy can work for all national minorities, no matter how large or territorially concentrated. What works best for small and dispersed minorities does not work best for large, concentrated minorities, and vice versa.[77] Where national minorities form clear majorities in their historic homeland, and particularly where they have some prior history of self-government, it is not clear that there is any realistic alternative to territorial autonomy or multinational federalism.

As in the West, this sort of multinational federalism is not a magic formula for resolving all tensions or conflicts. As I noted earlier, there is no guarantee that federalism will not lead eventually to secession. And granting self-government to national minorities raises the danger that they will embark on their own illiberal forms of nation-building, restricting the rights of their own members or of other groups on the territory. There are all too many examples of this in the ethnorepublics of the Russian federation.[78]

It is an essential feature of a liberal-democratic conception of multination federalism that *all* governments—whether the central government or regional governments dominated by national minorities—be subject to constitutional restrictions that protect individual civil and political rights. As I noted earlier, justice requires that national minorities should have the same right to engage in nation-building as the majority, *subject to the same restrictions* of respect for the rights of others.

It may be difficult to achieve this sort of democratic multination federalism in ECE: majority nationalists too often resist granting self-government to national minorities; and minority nationalists too often exercise their self-government in illiberal and intolerant ways (Dimitras 1998). But to say it is difficult is not to say it is impossible. In any event, what is the alternative?

5.4 Immigrants/Metics in ECE

Let me shift now to ethnocultural justice for immigrants/metics. At first glance, these categories do not seem applicable to ECE, at least not in the same way that they apply in the West. ECE countries have not actively recruited immigrants, unlike the United States, Canada or Australia; nor have they recruited guestworkers, unlike Germany, Switzerland, or Austria; and nor, until very recently, have they been faced with large-scale illegal immigration, unlike many countries in Western Europe. It is only recently that significant numbers of migrants have entered the ECE. These 'transit migrants' often have the European Union as their final destination, but if they are kept out of 'Fortress Europe', some decide to settle in the ECE.

Despite these limits of applicability, it is worth briefly asking whether the Western model of immigrant integration is relevant to ECE. Should newcomers into ECE countries be seen as future citizens, and should the conception of national identity be 'thinned' so as to allow immigrants to maintain and express their ethnic identity while still integrating into the nation?

There are two standard objections to adopting this model in ECE. The first says that the very idea of immigrant integration is only viable for New World countries in which immigration is part of the founding myth of the nation, and cannot work in the more long-standing nations of the Old World. The second notes that migrants in ECE at the present time tend to be refugees or 'transit migrants' rather than immigrants, which makes the idea of integration more complicated. These are legitimate points, but I think they are often overstated.

The idea that immigrant integration can only occur in the traditional immigrant countries of the New World is often heard not only in ECE, but also in Western Europe. On this view, the fundamental divide is not between Western democracies and the ECE, but between New World democracies and Old World democracies. The North American/Australian model of immigrant integration cannot work in the Old World, it is said, because European nation-states are much older than New World states, and more culturally and ethnically homogenous. Immigration is one of the founding myths of New World states, promoting a receptive environment for succeeding waves of immigrants who have chosen a new nation for themselves. European states, however, are founded on myths of common origins, and on the belief that these common origins define a community of fate. Immigrants, on this view, can enter the national territory, but they can never really join the nation.

I am not persuaded of this view. There is considerable evidence that the sort of integration-based policies that characterize immigrant countries can work in Europe. After all, some West European countries have conceived of immigrants as future citizens—for example Britain and France—and these are precisely the countries where immigrants have historically integrated successfully.

Conversely, the success of many New World countries in integrating immigrants has nothing to do with their 'founding myths'. It is really only the United States that was founded on the idea of immigration. Most other New World countries were founded on the myth of being colonial outposts, reproducing the Old World culture in a new land. Countries like Canada and Australia aimed to be as British as possible, which meant, *inter alia*, as white and Protestant as possible. Large-scale immigration from non-British countries was therefore prohibited for a very long time, and is a relatively recent phenomenon compared to the United States. Indeed, until the 1960s, Australia defined itself as 'White Australia', and sought to be 'more British than the British'.

Yet the fact that Australia was not founded on the myth of openness to immigration has not prevented it from integrating its newcomers. On the contrary, in a relatively short period of time, it has completely redefined itself from a monocultural British country to a multicultural 'Asian' country. It now accepts more immigrants per capita than any other country in the world, most of them non-white and non-Christian. Although Australia was founded on a myth of British colonial settlement, not a myth of multiethnic immigration, it now very closely follows the model of older immigrant countries like the United States.

The fact is that this pattern of immigrant integration has worked in many different countries, for many different immigrant groups, despite long histories of prior exclusion. If Australia, one of the last bastions of British imperial culture, can adopt this model and make it work, why not Old World countries? Indeed, this is just what Sweden has recently done. It has adopted naturalization and multiculturalism policies that are quite similar to those of older immigrant countries, encouraging newcomers to think of themselves as future citizens. If Sweden, one of the most ethnically homogenous and tightly-knit societies, can adopt this policy and make it work, why not Germany, Italy, Ukraine, or Hungary?[79]

The New World-Old World dichotomy is too crude to be useful in thinking about the challenges of ethnocultural pluralism. There are differences between New World and Old World countries, of course, but they are often less significant than the differences between different types of groups *within* both Old World and New World countries. National minorities in the New World are completely unlike immigrant groups in the New World, in terms of their needs and aspirations, although they are very much like national minorities in the Old World. The Québécois in Canada have far more in common with the Catalans in Spain or the Hungarians in Romania than they do with recent immigrants to Canada. The same is true about the other categories of ethnocultural pluralism: Lapps in Sweden have little in common with immigrants in Sweden, although they have much in common with the indigenous peoples of North America or Siberia. Illegal immigrants in the United States have little in common with immigrant citizens in the United States, in terms of their social, political, and economic status, although they have much in common with illegal immigrants in the Netherlands. And so on.

So I see no reason to rule out the applicability of the Western model of immigrant integration in ECE.[80] But, as with national minorities, there are complicating factors in ECE that may make adoption of this model more difficult. In particular, most of the migrants in ECE countries today are *refugees* seeking asylum, rather than voluntary immigrants admitted under an immigration policy. This raises questions about the goal of integration.

Of course, Western democracies also accept many refugees. But in the West, it has been possible to treat refugees for all intents and purposes as if they were immigrants. Historically, the treatment of refugees within most Western democracies, in terms of their resettlement and integration, has been almost identical to that of immigrants. The government and general public expects that refugees, like immigrants, will settle permanently and take out citizenship in their new country, and this expectation has been borne out in practice.

This is changing, particularly in Western Europe, where several countries are moving towards a system of 'temporary protection' for refugees, rather than permanent resettlement (Zend 1998). But in the major immigrant countries of the West, the expectation remains that refugees will settle permanently and take out citizenship. One reason why this has been possible is that refugees in Western democracies tend to arrive in small numbers from great distances. Refugees in the

West do not come from a neighbouring state, but from another part of the world, and typically arrive as individuals or families rather than large groups. It is therefore easier for them to integrate, and more difficult for them to return to their country of origin. In the ECE, by contrast, refugees often come in great numbers from short distances, which makes integration more difficult, and the prospect of return more likely.

Under these conditions, it is not clear whether it is appropriate to expect or to encourage migrants to integrate, rather than simply providing safe asylum until things improve in their country of origin. This conflict between encouraging integration or providing temporary protection has arisen in Russia (Gavrilova 1998), Hungary (Zend 1998) and Yugoslvia (Crnobrnja 1998).

Both Zend and Crnobrnja suggest that temporary protection will remain the dominant aim of refugee policy in ECE. Yet even here, it is possible that ECE countries will gradually adopt the Western model of integration, except in cases where it is certain that the refugees will return quickly to their country of origin.[81] In most cases, refugees will be stuck in their new country for many years, and over time it will become their new home. Like the Turkish guestworkers, they may cling to the hope of returning to their country of origin. But if they have stayed long enough to get a job and to start raising a family in their new country, they are unlikely to leave. If so, then the only viable and just long-term solution is to allow and encourage their integration into the mainstream society. This is the only way to avoid the injustices and conflicts associated with the marginalization of metics. Adopting such a policy not only avoids the dangers of marginalization, but also allows a country to take maximal advantage of the skills and education of the refugees, so that they become a benefit to the country, not a drain (Gavrilova 1998; Ossipov 1998).

5.5 Hard Cases

In these two broad categories of national minorities and immigrants, therefore, I would say that the principles developing in Western democracies are potentially applicable to ECE, although the implementation of them is likely to be more difficult. But there are other more complicated cases in ECE for which there are no obvious analogues in Western experience, and for whom the West provides no useful models or principles. I will briefly discuss four such cases: the Roma, Russian settlers in the Baltics, the Crimean Tatars, and the Cossacks. This is a very selective list of such 'anomalous' cases. The long history of wars, imperialism, and the forced displacement of peoples has created many groups in ECE with complex relationships to the land, to neighbouring groups, and to the state. My aim in discussing these cases is not to provide a comprehensive survey of all such groups, let alone to try to offer a solution to their conflicts. My aim, rather, is to illustrate how the liberal pluralist might approach these complexities.

The Roma   The Roma are unlike immigrants or national minorities, since their 'homeland' is both everywhere and nowhere.[82] Some people have suggested that the situation of African-Americans is the closest parallel in the West, since they too lack territorial concentration, and are concentrated at the bottom of the social ladder wherever they live. Moreover, the Roma, like African-Americans, are divided over whether to seek integration as rapidly as possible, or whether to seek recognition as a distinct and separate culture (Mihalikova 1998). In both cases, we see some leaders promoting a civil-rights-oriented approach, which focuses on the elimination of discrimination and downplays issues of cultural diversity; while other leaders promote a more ethnocultural-oriented approach, which demands positive recognition and accommodation of difference. And in both cases, there appears to be a shift towards combining these two approaches, with an increased emphasis on cultural difference alongside issues of eliminating discrimination. As Gheorghe and Mirga put it, the Roma used to be seen as having no linguistic, cultural, or ethnic roots, but were instead seen only as a social category defined in terms of poverty, unemployment, criminality etc. Most Roma believe that the result was 'extremely negative', and so 'the present Romani political elites introduce into public discourse the language of ethnicity and cultural identity, of human and minority rights, and of nondiscrimination and equality' (Gheorghe and Mirga 1997: 15).[83] One can find similar statements about the need to view African-Americans as an ethnocultural group, not just a disadvantaged racial group (Cochran 1999; Valls 1999).

So there has been some interest in seeing whether any of the American policies towards Blacks might be appropriate for the Roma—for example affirmative action. But since these policies have not been very successful so far in improving the situation of Blacks, it is not clear how much we should expect from them in the case of the Roma. Moreover, the situation of Blacks is really quite different from that of the Roma. Blacks do not have a distinct language, and have always lived in settled communities in America. Moreover, despite the history of discrimination—and indeed partly because of the history of segregation—Blacks managed to build a wide-ranging set of social institutions, up to and including their own colleges and universities. This legacy of separate institutions is an ambivalent one for most Blacks, since segregated Black institutions only arose as a result of the exclusion of Blacks from white institutions. Yet the fact remains that, since the end of slavery, Blacks have had a high level of institutional completeness, and have many of the sort of modern institutions which the Roma have historically lacked. The issue for Blacks, therefore, is what to do with their inherited separate institutions, whereas for the Roma the question is whether to build such institutions in the first place.[84]

In answering this question, Roma leaders have recently been debating two models of minority rights. One option is to demand the same status as other national minorities within each ECE country. For example, the central organization of German Sinti says that they have a 600-year history in Germany, and so should have same rights as other 'domiciled' (national) minorities, such as the Danes and Sorbs. And indeed several countries have declared that the Roma are a 'national minority' for the purposes of the Council of Europe's Framework Convention for the Protection of National Minorities (eg., Germany, Hungary). Gaining this status of 'national minority' has provided certain benefits. For example, the Roma now have official recognition as a 'minority', and even parliamentary representation, either on nationwide party lists in Czech Republic, Bulgaria, and Hungary, or from their own party list in Romania. But this approach may not help the many Romani communities which are composed of recent asylum seekers, refugees, or stateless persons, and who cannot therefore claim to be a historic minority rooted in that country.[85] More generally, since they lack a territory, the Roma cannot benefit from many of the provisions that are typically demanded by national minorities. For this reason, Recommendation 1203 of the Council of Europe states that the Roma do not fit the definition of national minority, and so require a new status as a 'nonterritorial' minority.

This leads to the second option, which is to claim the status of a 'transnational' or 'European' minority, whose rights are protected by a European-wide charter, rather than by domestic legislation within each country. For example, the Romani National Congress argues that Romani are unique amongst Europe's legitimate nations, and so seeks a European Charter on Romani Rights, with a special status for Roma/Sinti 'as a nonterritorial (multistate-based or transnational) minority in Europe' (Gheorghe and Mirga 1997: 22). This approach would obviously help those Roma communities which have recently moved, or are still moving, between ECE countries, and reflects the long history of Roma migration. It would also eliminate any secessionist fears associated with the idea of claiming the status of a national minority. A tentative first step towards such a 'transnational minority' approach is reflected in the European Charter for Regional and Minority Languages (1992), which recognizes Romani, along with Yiddish, as a 'nonterritorial' language.

However, as Gheorghe and Mirga note, this idea of recognizing the Roma as a 'transnational' minority disconnected from citizenship in any particular country is feared by many states—and some Roma themselves—since it

does not fit the concepts and language of present-day international legal frameworks. It raises the question of loyalties and rights that would transcend those conferred by citizenship in a nation state and would inevitably lead individuals to experience conflicting loyalties and interests. It could also invite discrimination by the state against those who could be seen as not being fully a part of it.   (Gheorghe and Mirga 1997: 22)[86]

Moreover, most Roma are now sedentary, and have increasingly adjusted to the neighbouring cultures of their countries of residence, and so we see a growing divergence in Roma language use and customs from one country to another. And indeed attempts to organize or mobilize Roma on a transnational basis have proven very difficult. For better or worse, the Roma will probably have to negotiate a new status within each country, and this status may indeed differ dramatically depending on the size, history, internal diversity, and cultural retention of the various Romani communities within each country. There are no Western models for this complicated process.

Russians in the Baltics   Many ethnic Russians left Russia in the postwar period to move to other parts of the Soviet Union—that is, to parts of the Soviet Union where ethnic Russians formed a minority of the population. Yet these post-war Russians settlers in the Near Abroad did not think of themselves as a 'minority', or as 'immigrants' to another country. Instead, they saw themselves as moving around within a single country—a country in which Russians formed a majority throughout the country as a whole. Hence they expected to find, and did find, a full set of Russian-language institutions and services wherever they moved in the Soviet Union, and they increasingly came to see the whole of the Soviet Union as their 'homeland', not just Russia.[87]

At one point in the 1920s, Russian settlers in Central Asia were defined as a 'minority', but after 1933, this idea was rejected, and Russians were not supposed to feel like a minority anywhere in the Soviet Union. In every republic of the Soviet Union, they were told that they could live and work in their own institutions, schools, media and so on. This was described and justified, not as a form of Russian imperialism, but rather as a new Soviet internationalism, according to which Russians had the right to be monolingual throughout the Soviet Union, to travel freely, and to take new jobs anywhere without losing access to Russian schools or media (Laitin 1998: 69, 93; Druviete 1997: 181).[88]

However, they now find themselves as a minority within newly-independent and nationalizing states.[89] And while they are gradually accepting the fact that they are a 'minority', they still do not think of themselves as an *immigrant* minority.[90] Rather, they expect and demand to maintain the full set of Russian-language institutions that they are accustomed to. Hence they are demanding the sorts of rights which are typically demanded by national minorities—not just to citizenship, but also to the continued existence and funding of separate schools, institutions, and local autonomy.

For some members of the larger society, however, these settlers are more like illegal immigrants, who had no right to enter in the first place, since they came as a result of military occupation by the Red Army. As illegal immigrants, they have, at best, the right to gain citizenship only after proving their loyalty and willingness to integrate—for example by learning the local language. At worst, they can be permanently denied legal residence and citizenship, like illegal immigrants in other countries, in the hope that they will eventually return home. This indeed was a hope expressed by the original nationalist governments in Latvia and Estonia, who not only stripped the Russians of their citizenship, but also refused to provide them with permanent resident permits, and started a 'decolonization fund' to encourage them to move to Russia.[91]

It is difficult to imagine a more striking contrast in perceptions. Ethnic Russians emphatically reject the illegal immigrant label, since their migration was legal not only under the laws of the Soviet Union, but also under international law, which affirms a basic human right to move freely throughout one's country—it is important to remember, in this respect, that most countries recognized the boundaries of the Soviet Union, and so the UN Charter arguably did imply that ethnic Russians had a right to settle freely in any the Soviet republics. Nor do they see themselves as immigrants at all, since they had the expectation and assurance that they would have a full set of Russian-language institutions wherever they moved inside the Soviet Union, and would not have settled in the Near Abroad without this assurance.[92]

Despite this major gap in perceptions, there is some evidence that the two sides are converging on something like the immigrant model of integration, supplemented by some form of national cultural (non-territorial) autonomy.[93] Nationalists have given up the hope that denying citizenship to the ethnic Russians will encourage them to leave. As with the metics in Western Europe, it is increasingly recognized that the ethnic Russians are here to stay. Even if ethnic Russians in Latvia were unable to acquire citizenship, only a tiny fraction of them indicate that they would return to Russia (Antane and Tsilevich 1998). So nationalists in Latvia and Estonia have grudgingly accepted that the ethnic Russians must be offered citizenship and a chance to integrate. But the Baltic countries remain unwilling to view the ethnic Russians as a national minority, and continue to reduce the number of Russian-language institutions.[94] The nationalists now hope, in short, that the ethnic Russians will come to think of themselves as 'immigrants', and accept integration into the Latvian or Estonian societies, even though they had a very different self-conception when they moved to the Baltics. And it seems that many Russians are willing to accept this redefinition, at least in part, however grudgingly, so long as they feel there is a genuine prospect for integration for themselves and their children. Recent surveys show that a clear majority of Russians accept large parts of the 'nationalizing' programme of Baltic states, including the requirement to learn the titular language, and they now disavow any aspiration to territorial autonomy (Laitin 1998: 202).[95]

Russian settlers did not see themselves as immigrants, nor were they admitted by the host society as future citizens, but if both sides can rethink their attitudes, the immigrant model—supplemented with some forms of cultural autonomy—might yet work to achieve a stable arrangement.[96] It's important to emphasize that, as in the West, this approach will only work if the majority group enables the 'immigrant' group to integrate and succeed in mainstream institutions. And indeed the main concern of the Russians is that even when they learn the titular language and express loyalty to the state, they still are not accepted or welcome in public institutions.[97] This is partly a legacy of distrust, and partly the fact that many Balts still define group membership in terms of blood, so that no amount of cultural integration by Russians will lead to their acceptance (Laitin 1998: 126–7, 256). A crucial part of the recent 'integration policy' adopted by the Estonian government, therefore, is focused not only on encouraging Russians to accept integration, but also on persuading Estonians to allow the Russians to integrate, and to accept them as equal members of common Estonian-language institutions.[98] Should this effort fail, so that Russians become disillusioned about the prospects for successful immigrant-style integration, the potential exists for the Russian-speaking community to reorganize itself as a national minority and to mobilize for territorial and cultural autonomy.[99]

Crimean Tatars   The Crimean Tatars have adopted the label of 'indigenous peoples', and appealed in international forums to be recognized as such (Packer 1998: 315).[100] This, I think, differs from the usual use of the term 'indigenous peoples' in the West. As I noted earlier, in general usage in the West, what distinguishes national minorities from indigenous peoples is that the former were contenders but losers in the process of European-state-formation, whereas the latter were entirely isolated from this process until recently, and so retained a premodern way of life until well into this century. National minorities would have liked to form their own states, but lost in the struggle for political power, whereas indigenous peoples existed outside the system of European states. The Catalans and Québécois, then, are national minorities, whereas the Lapps and Inuit are indigenous peoples.

On this way of defining it, the Tatars are closer to national minorities than to indigenous peoples. The Tatar Khanate was an active contender in modern European politics, and had the balance of power differed slightly, it could easily have consolidated itself as an independent European state. But the Tatars lost, and now face many of the same issues as national minorities—such as fighting to regain language rights and some powers of self-government against the pressure of majority nation-building.

This is not to deny that, at least on some definitions, the Tatars qualify as 'indigenous peoples'. There is no universally agreed definition of 'indigenous peoples', and some of the extant definitions would indeed cover the Tatars.[101] But whatever terminology we use, it seems to me that the Tatars differ dramatically from most indigenous peoples in the West. What makes the case of the Tatars special is not that they are 'indigenous'—they are no more or less indigenous than the Hungarians in Transcarpathia—but rather that they suffered a horrendous wholesale communal deportation from the Crimea in World War II. This distinguishes the Tatars not only from national minorities in the West, but also from most indigenous peoples. Certainly, some indigenous peoples were subject to forced resettlement, often for similar reasons of national security. But this resettlement either happened so long ago that there is now no serious thought of returning—for example the Cherokee in the United States—or the people have been able to return to their old lands because no one else occupied them in their absence—for example the Inuit in Northern Canada. By contrast, the deportation of the Tatars was recent enough to make return a viable option, yet in the meantime all of their land and property has passed into the hands of settlers, for whom Crimea is now the only home they know.

The distinctive issue facing the Tatars, therefore, is how to deal with these issues of return from deportation, and compensation for historical injustice.[102] To my knowledge, there is nothing in the West, in theory or practice, to answer these questions.[103]

Cossacks Cossack groups have adopted the label of a 'nation', and have made familiar nationalist demands for territorial self-determination in those areas of Russia or the Near Abroad where they are concentrated. Yet, as Opalski notes, there are many puzzling features of the Cossack's self-conception of nationhood (Opalski 1998). For centuries, they formed a military caste *within* the Russian nation, found throughout the breadth of the Russian empire, rather than a separate nation rooted to its own territory existing apart from or alongside the Russian nation. Even today, Cossacks continue to see themselves as the carriers of 'true' Russianness, and as upholding Russian national culture from the threats posed by non-Slavic peoples and influences. There is something anomalous about the way Cossacks seek to protect Russia's national culture while simultaneously seeking to separate themselves from that culture, politically and territorially. The same schizophrenia is reflected in the way they determine who is a 'Cossack': in some contexts, the emphasis is placed on their different ethnic origins from Russians, in other contexts, the line between Cossack and ethnic Russian becomes blurred to the point of invisibility.

In any event, despite Cossack calls for territorial autonomy and recognition of a national homeland, there are no regions in Russia where they form a majority, and it is not clear whether the idea of a 'Cossack Republic' is feasible. Given the difficulty in clearly distinguishing their nationality from that of the Russians, and given their lack of territorial concentration, Cossacks have spent much of their political energies not on achieving national self-determination, but on two other more realistic goals: (a) 'rehabilitation' and official recognition after the many years in which any manifestation of Cossack identity was repressed by the Communists, as well as restitution or compensation for expropriated property; (b) gaining (or regaining) various group-specific rights within mainstream Russian institutions, such as the army, the economy, and parliament. These rights include tax credits, guaranteed political representation, and the equivalent of an affirmative action programme in the military.

These two goals may fit more comfortably with the current situation of the Cossacks, who are now inextricably intermingled with, and incorporated into, the majority Russian nation. Yet it is unlikely that the Cossacks will relinquish the rhetoric of nationhood in the near future, and so it is not clear whether these forms of rehabilitation and recognition will be used as a stepping-board for a more comprehensive form of separatism.

It is also unclear which of these various group-specific rights are defensible, from the point of view of liberal-democratic norms. While the Cossacks were singled out for repression under the Communists, and so are surely entitled to some form of rehabilitation and recognition, it appears as if many of the claims they are making would accord them an unfair share of power and resources. Put another way, it seems as if what the Cossacks are demanding is the restoration of unjust privileges, not simply fair compensation for past wrongs.

This is one component of a more general problem about the Cossack identity. It appears as if the right to rule over others has become part and parcel of the very idea of 'Cossack-ness'. As Opalski puts it, 'the key to the success and a central piece of Cossack ethos is dominance' (Opalski 1998). There is nothing unusual about ethnic or national groups defining themselves in opposition to other groups. But Cossacks define themselves, not only in opposition to other groups, but also as dominant over other groups. Indeed, it often seems as if this is the only way in which the Cossacks are able to maintain a coherent sense of distinct identity and group organization. Were this claim to dominance given up, it is not clear that Cossacks would have any basis or reason to distinguish themselves from other Russians, or to continue to mobilize for ethnic minority rights. In so far as this is true, it obviously makes it very difficult, if not impossible, to reconcile group-specific rights for the Cossacks with liberal-democratic norms. In any event, there is nothing in the Western experience that would tell us how to square this circle.

For all these cases, and many others that one could mention in ECE, we need completely new models of ethnocultural justice.

6. Conclusion

In this paper, I have tried to outline some recent work by Western political theorists on minority rights, and to identify some of the ways in which it might be relevant to ECE countries. Western countries have learned some hard lessons over the years about the management of ethnic relations in a democracy, and hopefully ECE countries can learn something from these mistakes, and so avoid some of the problems which have plagued Western democracies in the past. Yet there are many ways in which the problems in former Communist countries are unique, and for which the West offers no models or solutions.

But there is one more lesson which Western democracies have learned which I have not yet discussed, although it is perhaps the most important of all—namely, that controversies and conflicts over the management of ethnocultural diversity won't go away, or spontaneously resolve themselves. They are a permanent and enduring feature of liberal democracies that must be tackled head-on.

This is an important point, so I'd like to conclude by clarifying it. Until very recently, many Western liberals hoped and expected that ethnocultural cleavages would disappear, and they blamed the persistence of ethnocultural conflicts on temporary factors that they assumed would fade over time. Western liberals used to argue that ethnocultural conflict was really a by-product of some other, deeper problem, and would fade once this deeper problem was resolved.

For example, some liberals argued that the real problem was incomplete democratization and the rule of law, and that conflicts over these issues were displaced onto ethnocultural conflicts. On this view, once democratic rights and institutions were effectively established and accessible to all citizens, people would stop mobilizing on the basis of ethnocultural affiliation.

Other liberals argued that ethnocultural conflict was a substitute for modernization and economic well-being. On this view, the real problem was that some people felt left behind in the process of modernization, and once a certain level of economic development was achieved and accessible to all citizens, people would stop mobilizing on the basis of ethnocultural affiliation.

Yet other liberals argued that ethnocultural conflict was due to the persistence of irrational personal stereotypes and prejudices, based on ignorance of 'the other'. On this view, once people acquired and internalized democratic habits of tolerance and mutual respect, there would be no need to mobilize on the basis of ethnocultural affiliation.

Or, finally, some liberals argued that ethnocultural conflict was the result of foreign meddling in domestic politics, and the use of foreign *agents provocateurs* who spread lies and distortions to encourage otherwise satisfied minorities to complain about their treatment. On this view, once accurate information was available, and foreign interference was exposed, then ethnocultural mobilization would fade away.

All of these various explanations for ethnocultural conflict implied that once a prosperous democracy was firmly established, both institutionally and in terms of the larger public culture, then the strength and political mobilization of ethnocultural identities would disappear or at least substantially decrease.

But we now know that these predictions were wrong. There is not a shred of evidence from Western democracies that the achievement of democracy, economic prosperity, and personal tolerance will lead to an abatement of ethnocultural mobilization. On the contrary, ethnocultural demands have increased, not decreased, throughout the West even as these goals were being achieved. The achievement of democratization, prosperity, and tolerance has gone hand in hand with increased ethnocultural mobilization.

Consider relations between the French and English in Canada. Forty years ago, the Québécois were poor and politically quiescent, governed by autocratic political élites in collusion with the Catholic Church, and were subjected to great discrimination and prejudice from English-speaking Canadians. Today, they have the same standard of living as English-speaking Canadians, have a vibrant democracy within Quebec, and are more than proportionately represented in the federal government and bureaucracy. Public opinion polls show that English prejudice against the French has virtually disappeared— as has French prejudice against the English. On a personal level, there is virtually no animosity, dislike, or discomfort between members of the two groups. For example, the overwhelming majority of both groups would be happy if someone from the other group moved next door, or married into the family.

One might expect, then, that Québécois nationalism would have abated over the last forty years. In fact, just the opposite has occurred. Support for Quebec nationalism has grown steadily. This is not unique to Canada. We see the same phenomenon in Belgium, where democratization and economic development in Flanders have gone hand-in-hand with increased Flemish nationalism; and in Spain, where democratization and economic prosperity in Catalonia have been accompanied by increased Catalan nationalism. And we can see the same trend amongst many immigrant groups, which fight tenaciously for recognition of their ethnic identity even as they gain the same level of economic well-being and political representation as the majority group.

Democracy, economic prosperity, and personal tolerance are all great goods, of course—valuable in and of themselves. But they are not by themselves, or even when taken together, an answer to the issues of ethnocultural diversity. The accommodation of ethnocultural diversity will remain a powerful source of conflict—and may indeed increase in strength—even when all of these other goods are in place. This is the most important lesson that the West has had to learn. It was only when Western governments accepted this fact that they were able to begin learning about how to manage ethnocultural relations in a peaceful and democratic way, and to make the sort of progress which I discussed in sections 3 and 4.

I see no reason to think that ECE will differ in this respect. There are many people in ECE countries today who argue that ethnic conflicts are really just a substitute for, or displacement of, conflicts over incomplete democratization and inadequate economic development, and that we should therefore ignore the demands of ethnocultural groups and focus all our energies on the 'real' problem. They say that we can set aside the demands of the Albanians in Macedonia, for example, or of Hungarians in Slovakia, since these demands will fade once real democracy, economic development, and the rule of law are established. These demands are simply a by-product, not the 'real' issue.

This denial or denigration of the seriousness of ethnocultural identities is precisely the mistake which Western democracies have made again and again, often with terrible consequences. It is a mistake that I hope ECE countries will not repeat. If nothing else is learned from the Western experience with ethnocultural relations, I hope that ECE countries recognize the importance of tackling head-on issues of ethnocultural pluralism.

NOTES

1. Bauböck 1994; Buchanan 1991; Canovan 1996; Carens 2000; Kymlicka 1995; Miller 1995; Phillips 1995; Spinner 1994; Tamir 1993; Taylor 1992; Tully 1995; Walzer 1997; Young 1990; Levy 2000; Parekh 2000. I am not aware of full-length books written by philosophers in English on any of these topics predating 1990, with the exception of Plamenatz 1960. For a comprehensive bibliography of recent philosophical articles and edited collections on these issues, see Kymlicka and Norman 2000. For an account of the evolution of this debate over the last decade, see Kymlicka 2001: ch. 1.
2. For a more detailed discussion of these four points, see my 'Minority Nationalism and Multination Federalism' in Kymlicka 2001: ch. 5.
3. Gerald Johnson claims that 'It is one of history's little ironies that no polyglot empire of the old world has dared to be so ruthless in imposing a single language upon its whole population as was the liberal republic "dedicated to the proposition that all men are created equal"' (Johnson 1973: 119). But other Western republics have also been quite ruthless.
4. For the ubiquity of this process, see Gellner 1983; Anderson 1983; Calhoun 1997; Tilly 1975. So far as I know, Switzerland is the only country that never had this aim. It never made a serious attempt to pressure the French-speaking and Italian-speaking groups to integrate into majority German-language institutions.
5. They may even include policies to 'nationalize' people's surnames—see Scassa 1996.
6. See Norman 1999: 59–63 for a list of the kinds of nation-building policies that have been ignored by liberal theorists, despite their pivotal role in the creation of national identities: e.g., policies regarding education, media, military service, naturalization requirements, etc. As Calhoun notes, while many nineteenth-century liberals endorsed nationalism, they too 'failed to address the processes by which national identities came into being and by which the populations living in any one territory were encouraged (or forced) to adopt more or less similar identities, languages and lifestyles' (Calhoun 1997: 87).
7. For example Miller 1995; Tamir 1993; Canovan 1996; Margalit and Raz 1990; Taylor 1997. For a more detailed exposition and analysis of the arguments of these liberal nationalists, see Kymlicka 2001: chs. 11–12.
8. A comparable dilemma can arise even when the national groups share the same language—such as in Northern Ireland—if they have conflicting national identities, perhaps tied to different religious faiths, and if the majority insists that its identity, symbols, and values be privileged in public institutions. Such conflicts are often rooted in an earlier history of domination.
9. A fifth option would be to seek a military overthrow of the state, and to establish a minority-run dictatorship. This isn't on the cards in the West, but we can see examples in Africa—e.g., Rwanda—or Asia—e.g., Fiji.
10. On the distinction between indigenous peoples and other national minorities, and its relevance for rights claims, see my 'Theorizing Indigenous Rights', in Kymlicka 2001, ch. 6.
11. This is a long-standing aspect of minority nationalism by stateless nations, but it is also an increasingly dominant feature of indigenous mobilization. On the

increasing tendency of indigenous peoples in North America to adopt the language of 'nationhood', see Jenson 1993; Alfred 1995; RCAP 1996.

12. This raises the question captured nicely in the title of Walker Connor's famous
article: are nation-states 'Nation-Building or Nation-Destroying?' (Connor
1972). In truth, they are both. Nation-states have typically sought to build a
common nationhood by destroying any pre-existing sense of distinct nationhood on the part of national minorities.

13. David Laitin provides a nice example of how our views regarding state coercion
have changed over the centuries: 'It is said that in Spain during the Inquisition
gypsies who were found guilty of speaking their own language had their tongues
cut out. With policies of this sort, it is not difficult to understand why it was
possible, a few centuries later, to legislate Castillian as the sole official language.
But when Emperor Haile Selassie of Ethiopia pressed for policies promoting
Amharic, infinitely more benign than those of the Inquisition, speakers of
Tigray, Oromo, and Somali claimed that their groups were being oppressed, and
the international community was outraged. Nation-building policies available
to monarchs in the early modern period are not available to leaders of new states
today' (Laitin 1992: xi). Elsewhere, Laitin notes that the linguistic assimilation
of national minorities is unlikely to occur after the start of mass literacy (Laitin
1998: 42).

14. A. Smith 1993: 131; cf. Connor 1972: 350–1; 1973: 20. On the complete failure
of assimilationist policies towards Indians in Canada, see J. Miller 1991.
Schopflin cites Manx and Old Prussians as two examples of national minorities
that have accepted assimilation in modern times.

15. For a fuller explanation, see Kymlicka 1995: ch. 8.

16. For more on this, see Keating 1996; Hamilton 1999; Kymlicka 2001: chs. 12–16.

17. Swiss federalism is intimately concerned with the accommodation of linguistic
and religious differences, but it arose before the era of nationalism, and the
strong cantonal identities and protections which it engendered in fact obviated
the need for minorities to develop along specifically nationalist lines. Hence
many commentators deny that the francophone and italophone minorities
have mobilized as minority nationalisms, or that Switzerland constitutes a
'multination' federation, even though Swiss federalism is clearly closer to the
'multination' form than to the territorial/administrative form. See, e.g., Stepan
2000.

18. Indeed, far from helping national minorities, there is reason to believe that
American federalism has made them worse off. Throughout most of American
history, Chicanos, American Indian tribes, and native Hawaiians have received
better treatment from the federal government than from state governments.
State governments, controlled by colonizing settlers, have often seen national
minorities as an obstacle to greater settlement and resource development, and
so have pushed to strip minorities of their traditional political institutions,
undermine their treaty rights, and dispossess them of their historic homelands.
While the federal government has been complicit in much of the mistreatment,
it has often at least attempted to prevent the most severe abuses. We can see the
same dynamic in Brazil, where the federal government is fighting to protect the
rights of Indians in Amazonia against the predations of local state governments.
So too in Australia, where the federal government had to intervene and take
over jurisdiction regarding Aborigines from the brutal policies of the state
governments (Peterson and Sanders 1998: 11–16).

19. For a more detailed description of the theory and practice of multination federalism, and how it differs from American-style federalism, see Kymlicka 2001: ch. 5. Other multination federations around the world include Nigeria, Malaysia, India, Ethiopia, and Russia. For more on the Russian case, the only example of a multination federation in the ECE, see Part 3, note 33.

20. Even indigenous people in Latin America, who long faced the threat of coercive assimilation or even extinction, are now acquiring forms of territorial autonomy in some cases, for example in Colombia (Van Cott 2001).

21. The unwillingness to accommodate minority nationalism has played a role in the derailing of several attempts to establish liberal democracy. For example, the failure of liberal democrats in nineteenth-century Spain and in Russia after the February Revolution of 1917 has been blamed, in part, on the refusal of Spanish and Russian liberals to accept autonomy for national minorities—see, for example Rosenburg 1974.

22. And even if Quebec does secede from Canada at some point in the future, or Scotland from Britain, the fact that both majority and minority have learned to manage their conflicting national projects in a peaceful and democratic manner means that the secession is likely itself to take place in a peaceful and democratic manner. For more on the issue of secession, East and West, see my Reply, section 6.

23. It's worth noting that in the major immigrant countries, refugees granted asylum are included in this category of immigrants who have a right to become citizens. Indeed, government policy towards the resettlement and naturalization of refugees is virtually identical to the policy for immigrants, and historically refugees have followed the same pattern of integration as other more voluntary immigrants.

24. See the report of the Commission on the Future of Multiethnic Britain (the Parekh Report), released in October 2000, which reaffirms and seeks to strengthen Britain's multiculturalism policies (Commission on the Future of Multiethnic Britain 2000).

25. There are exceptions, of course. Some people emigrate to escape persecution in their homeland because of their religious beliefs or ethnocultural identity. But such people are more likely to be refugees than immigrants.

26. For discussions of the claims of immigrant groups, and their relation to liberal-democratic norms, see Carens 2000; Spinner 1994; Bauböck 1994; Parekh 2000.

27. They do of course accept strong responsibilities for attending to whatever problems arise within their own communities. But justice requires that we attend to problems beyond our immediate environment, even when we are not causally responsible for these wider problems.

28. For a good discussion of these groups, see Spinner 1994. The appeal to freedom of religion is controversial, because it privileges the freedom of the group to enforce its creed over the freedom of individual members to question and possibly revise their religious beliefs. It gives the group the right to live according to its traditions, even at the expense of restricting individual freedom of conscience. This is not the traditional liberal conception of freedom of religion, which views individual freedom of conscience as fundamental, and group autonomy as derivative. Or so I argue in Kymlicka 1995: ch. 8.

29. This earlier model has now been abandoned, and Germany is moving closer to what I call the immigrant model of multiculturalism.

30. For helpful discussions of the status and claims of African-Americans, and their connection to liberal-democratic norms, see Spinner 1994, Gutmann and Appiah 1996; Brooks 1996; Cochran 1999; and Kymlicka 2001: ch. 9.

31. In particular, France and Greece continue to resist any official recognition of either immigrant multiculturalism or multination federalism, and Switzerland and Austria continue to resist any serious move to integrate metics. But these countries are now the clear exceptions to the norms in the West. And France is *de facto* liberalizing its approach to both autonomy for Corsica and multiculturalism for immigrants.

32. It's worth noting, however, that no Western country has in fact reversed any of these major policy shifts—that is, no country which adopted multiculturalism has subsequently repudiated it; no country which federalized has subsequently recentralized; and so on.

33. The Prime Minister of Japan once expressed exasperation about the 'troublesome' minorities in his country. But behind every troublesome minority we are likely to find a troublesome state that has been putting pressure on minorities. This is certainly the case in Japan, which has systematically mistreated its indigenous minority (the Ainu) and its migrant groups—especially the Koreans. But it is true throughout the West as well.

34. For more on how national minorities deal with internal minorities in the West, see Kymlicka 2001: chs. 11–16.

35. However, even here, it's important to note that in Canada and Belgium, immigrants can naturalize in either of the two languages—French/English in Canada; Flemish/French in Belgium—and that the army has separate units for the two language groups. As a result, while naturalization policy and control of the military remain in the hands of the central government in both countries, they no longer operate to pressure the Québécois to integrate into English-language institutions, or to pressure the Flemish to integrate into French-speaking institutions. Hence they no longer operate as tools of nation-building *vis-à-vis* these groups—although they do operate as tools for pressuring immigrants into linguistic and institutional integration.

36. In principle, one could imagine three alternatives to the liberal pluralist position. The liberal pluralist view accepts that both nation-building and minority rights are legitimate within certain limits. To put it in the most schematic form, the three alternative views would be: (a) that nation-building is good, but minority rights are bad; (b) that both nation-building and minority rights are bad; (c) that nation-building is bad, but minority rights are good. Illiberal majority nationalists endorse the first; liberal cosmopolitans endorse the second; and some postmodernists endorse the third. We have lots of experience with the first alternative, both in the West and around the world. The second and third alternatives have not been tried in any countries, and it isn't even clear what it would mean to try to implement them. I defend the liberal pluralist position against all of these alternatives in Kymlicka 2001.

37. As in the West, many other tools of nation-building are also employed—for example national media, the nationalizing of toponomy and surnames.

38. See Mitrofanov 1998 for such policies in Latvia; Pettai 1998 for Estonia and Latvia; Ethnobarometer 1999: 219–21 and 243–5 for Romania and Slovakia; Jaworsky 1998 for Ukraine.

39. See Strazzari 1998 for Macedonia; Tomova 1998 for Bulgaria; Mitrofanov 1998 for Latvia.

40. See Antane and Tsilevich 1998 for Latvia and Estonia; Strazzari 1998 for Macedonia; Zend 1998 for Hungary; and Ossipov 1998 for Russia.
41. See Ethnobarometer 1999: 87–8 for such a policy in Slovakia.
42. Várady 1997: 46 for Serbia. In the case of Kosovo, Serbia also of course employed the most extreme nation-building tool—the murder and expulsion of the Albanians.
43. For the inconsistency in which the terms 'civic' and 'ethnic' are applied to Western and ECE countries, or indeed within the ECE, see Kuzio 1999.
44. See Tsilevich's commentary in Part 2 on 'designated areas' for minority culture. As he notes, the assumption in some ECE countries is not that minority languages can be used in social life unless there is a compelling public interest requiring language regulation. Rather the assumption is that the state language should be used in all social life, except in narrowly circumscribed 'designated areas'.
45. According to Kuzio, 'the overwhelming majority of states in post-communist Europe are inclusive and therefore civic, a trend which is increasing'. Indeed, he claims that some 'eastern' and 'nationalising' states are more 'civic' than their 'western', long-standing counterparts, since they offered automatic citizenship to all residents on their territory at independence, a practice not adopted in any Western state (Kuzio 1999: 24, 30). I think it would be more accurate to say that in the ECE, as in the West historically, the nation is open to some non-nationals but closed to others. For example, in interwar Poland, ethnic Ukrainians and Belarussians were welcomed in the Polish nation, but not Germans and Jews (Brubaker 1996). For much of this century, the US and Canada were open to European immigrants, but not to Asians. Today, the Czech Republic is inclusive of many people of non-Czech origin, but not for its Roma. As with the other criteria, this is not necessarily an all-or-nothing criterion.
46. In Germany, an Interior Ministry report says that the sort of integration required for naturalization includes not only knowing the German language, but also the 'renunciation of exaggerated national-religious behaviour'. Schmidt calls this and other conditions 'the equivalent of assimilation' (Schmidt 1999: 103). Similarly, in Greece, conversion to Greek Orthodoxy is considered a precondition for naturalization (MRG 1997: 157). Even in the United States there are those who argue for a 'thicker' conception of nationhood, such that immigrants should be taught 'American habits of mind and conduct' and 'the Protestant work ethic' as well as a common language and political principles (Pickus 1998: 14).
47. On the way in which illiberal nationalisms put pressure for conformity even in areas of sexuality, see Mosse 1985; Parker 1992. Indeed, dissent and diversity around issues of gender and sexuality within a national group are often seen as posing the same 'threat to the nation' as the presence of ethnic minorities.
48. Glover 1997: 29. For an example of this quasi-religious glorification of the nation, see the Croatian constitution.
49. For more on this distinction between cosmopolitanism as an ideology and as a reality of modern cultures, see my 'From Enlightenment Cosmopolitanism to Liberal Nationalism', in Kymlicka 2001: ch. 10.
50. Laws concerning flags are an interesting test here. In Macedonia, flying another national flag was only permissible alongside the Macedonian flag. In Romania, the 1995 Penal Code imposes a potential jail sentence for displaying the flag or insignia or playing the national anthem of another state. In Greece, students

have been charged with 'provocation of the national symbol' when they raised both Greek and Turkish flags as a way of promoting friendship.

51. Put another way, liberal nationalisms are universalistic, in the sense of according to other nations the same rights—subject to the same limitations—which they demand for themselves. They do not try to impose their national identity on other nations either within or outside their borders. Walzer calls this the test of the 'nation that comes next' (Walzer 1990). By contrast, illiberal nationalisms assert claims that cannot be universalized. For example the Yugoslav President Dobrica Cosic told the Bosnian Serb Assembly in 1993 that 'where Serbian houses are, wherever Serbian land is, and wherever the Serbian language is spoken, the Serbian state will exist' (quoted in Ramet 1997: 8). Cosic was obviously not intending that other nations could appeal to the same principle, such that wherever Albanian is spoken, the Albanian state will exist. Rather, the whole point of his comment was to say that this land is Serbian regardless of whether it is also a land in which Albanian or Croatian is spoken. Similarly, nineteenth-century German nationalists said that wherever German is spoken should be part of the German state, even if Germans are in a minority—such as in the Czech lands. This is illiberal ethnocentrism, not liberal nationalism. This sort of hypocrisy is rampant in nationalist discourse in the Balkans. Serbians refused to grant anything but a minimal cultural autonomy to Albanians in Kosovo while simultaneously saying that a similar offer of cultural autonomy to Serbians in Croatia was 'insulting' (Ramet 1997: 215, n. 64). Turkey vehemently protests the denial of linguistic and cultural rights to ethnic Turks in neighbouring countries, while suppressing the same rights of Kurds in Turkey. Greece protests that ethnic Greeks in Albania do not have adequate cultural rights, while simultaneously denying the very existence of Albanian and Macedonian minorities in Greece. Romania claims that ethnic Hungarian demands for 'collective rights' are immoral and illiberal, while demanding precisely the same sorts of rights for ethnic Romanians in Bukovina in Ukraine.

52. After a long period of nation-building, Western democracies now have well-established national institutions and symbols, and the language of the majority is accepted by most as a lingua franca. So they could be said to be in a 'nation-maintenance' mode, rather than a nation-building mode. And so most people—except for national minorities—may even forget that these institutions, symbols, and language are not neutral but that of the historically dominant group. By contrast, in most countries in ECE, this illusion is not possible since the institutions, symbols, and language laws are very recent, and the connection between the state and the majority is much clearer, and hence more conflictual.

53. As Michael Keating puts it, 'it is not the existence of language and culture policies which determine whether a nationalism is ethnic or civic, but the uses made of language and culture, whether to build a civic nation or to practice ethnic exclusion' (Keating 1996: 10).

54. For further discussion, see my 'Misunderstanding Nationalism', in Kymlicka 2001: ch. 12. Some people claim that if a nationalist movement scores high enough on all of these criteria, it is no longer nationalism at all, even if it is centrally concerned with maintaining a sense of (liberal) nationhood. I won't debate that semantic question here, except to say that (a) all nine of these criteria represent continua, and it seems quite arbitrary (to me) to say that at some point a movement magically goes from being nationalist to non-nationalist; (b) even if movements pass this magical threshold point, they can still give rise to serious

conflicts which will look to all and intents and purposes as 'nationalist' conflicts. Even if Québécois and Canadians, or Flemish and Walloons, are both fully liberalized in their nation-building, they would still disagree over many issues.

55. In the latter case, Israel is often simply the nominal or intermediary destination for people who really want to get to the United States or other Western countries.

56. For a detailed study of the option of flight, see Brubaker 1996: ch. 6. As he notes, the likelihood that a minority subject to nation-building pressures will migrate depends on various factors: the severity of the pressure, the attitude of the kin-state to which they might emigrate, the possibilities for successful political mobilization within their existing state, its rootedness and attachment to land, and so on—on the last factor, compare the attitudes of Hungarians in Transylvania, discussed in Andreescu's commentary below, with that of the Russians in Uzbekistan, discussed in Djumaev's commentary. This option of mass emigration is sometimes called 'forced migration'. But it's important to distinguish these cases of emigration from actual expulsions—for example of Kosovar Albanians by Serbia. Emigrating Germans, Jews, and Russians may feel subject to discrimination in the country, related to nation-building policies, but they are not forced or even encouraged to leave by the country. On the contrary, Kazakhstan, for example, has tried very hard to encourage its minorities to stay—see Open Society Institute 1998.

57. For discussions of these defensive assertions of minority rights, see Pettai 1998 (re Baltics); Mihalikova 1998 (re Slovakia); Thompson 1998 (re Moldova); Strazzari 1998 (re Macedonia); Ramet 1997: 172–3 (re Slovakia and Kosovo); Vàrady 1997 (re Serbia).

58. In ECE, as in the West, some minority leaders initially endorsed the idea of a purely 'civil state' based solely on universal principles of equal citizenship and individual freedom, in which there would be neither nation-building nor minority rights. But they have realized that this idea is unrealistic, given the centrality of nation-building to modern states, and they have concluded that, confronted with state nation-building, the only viable option is to demand minority rights (Gheorghe and Mirga 1997: 20).

59. It's an interesting question why Russia is an exception in this regard. For some speculation on this, see my Reply in Part 3, note 32. However, it's important to note that multination federalism is not in fact widely accepted in Russia. Most Russian leaders and intellectuals do not like what they call 'ethnic federalism', and would prefer to replace it with an American or German-style form of administrative/territorial federalism, in which national minorities would not exercise territorial self-government. Their acceptance of the existing system is almost entirely strategic and transitional. So Russia is not as different from other ECE countries as it first appears in its views of minority nationalism.

60. On the revoking of autonomy in Georgia, see Vasilyeva 1996; on Nagorno-Karabakh, see Dudwick 1996; on Kosovo, see Troebst 1998; Ramet 1997: 148–54.

61. For a detailed discussion of how various post-Soviet countries have approached issues of territorial autonomy, see Kolsto's commentary in Part 2. On the referendum in Estonia, see Laitin 1998: 95; on requests for autonomy in Ukraine see Solchanyk 1994.

62. On the gerrymandering in Slovakia, see Ramet 1997: 134; Hungarian Coalition

1997: 12, 22. Moldova proposed merging a predominantly Bulgarian district into a new larger county, but gave up after vigorous Bulgarian protest. Lithuania has proposed but not yet implemented a plan to redraw boundaries to incorporate Polish-majority districts into larger Lithuanian-majority districts (MINELRES 8 July 1999). There is a long history of such gerrymandering in the West, in the US, Canada, France, and Spain, particularly in the nineteenth-century. More recently, Italy redrew the borders of German-populated Bolzano after World War II to merge it with the Italian-dominated province of Trentino, so that Italians became a majority, although this policy was reversed in 1969 (Danspeckgruber 1997: 241). An even more extreme policy to forestall autonomy involves efforts to promote settlement of the majority group in the area of minority concentration, so as to swamp the national minority, and make it a minority even within its traditional territory, and hence incapable of exercising autonomy no matter how boundaries are drawn. There is a long history of this during the Communist era: for example in the 1980s, the Romanian dictator Ceauşescu was 'bulldozing Hungarian villages and colonizing Romanians in their place' (Cornwall 1996: 19; Ramet 1997: 69). More recently, Serbia tried to encourage massive Serbian 'recolonization' of Kosovo, by guaranteeing unemployed Serbs free land and higher wages if they moved to Kosovo (Miall 1999: 135; Ramet 1997: 33, 69, 149–54). Other historic examples in ECE include policies to promote Polish settlement in areas of ethnic Ukrainian concentration in Poland; ethnic Czech settlement in areas of Ruthene population in Czechoslovakia (Ramet 1997: 33). For a comprehensive discussion of such 'state-directed population movements', see McGarry 1998. As he notes, states encourage settlement of majority members in minority areas to act as 'demographic facts' to assert sovereignty, discourage external attack; intimidate local minorities and/or dilute/assimilate them by intermarriage. States encourage this sort of settlement through offers of free/cheap land, good jobs, tax breaks, and language rights. Here again there is a long history of such settlement policies in the West, particularly in the nineteenth century in the US and Canada. More recent examples include the financial inducements in 1967–74 for ethnic Greeks to settle in the Turkish-populated areas of Western Thrace, the resettling of Italians in German-populated areas of South Tyrol under Mussolini, and the French policy encouraging immigration to New Caledonia as a way of forestalling any demand by the natives for independence.

63. Ukraine was the only country that chose to accept autonomy rather than face civil war (Marples and Duke 1995), although even it threatened that the declaration of Russian autonomy in Crimea would lead to war (Laitin 1998: 100). The other four countries decided on military intervention. Georgia, Moldova, and Azerbaijan lost the war, and so are negotiating autonomy for Abkhazia, Trans-Dneister, and Ngorno-Karabakh. Croatia won their war against the Serbs in Krajina, and promptly expelled them, to make sure there would be no chance of Serbian autonomy in the future. The initial position of the Bosnian government of Alija Izetbegovic was also for a centralized unitary state, with no provisions for minority autonomy, and the current cantonal arrangements are the result of an inconclusive civil war.

64. As an official in the Office of the Prime Minister of Hungary put it, 'One of the most dreaded expressions in Central and Eastern Europe today is autonomy. In this region of Europe the fear of autonomy is too great, but without it

there can be no solution for the minority question' (quoted in Thornberry 1998: 115).

65. Ukraine was under great pressure from Russia and the OSCE to accommodate the desire for autonomy in Crimea, and couldn't afford to alienate the huge Russophone population in the east of Ukraine. Ukrainian acceptance of the Russians' desire for TA in Crimea has not extended to other groups seeking TA, such as the ethnic Romanians in Transcarpathia, or the Crimean Tatars. With respect to these groups, Ukraine follows the usual ECE model of strong resistance to TA. Indeed, one could argue that in its haste to accommodate the Russians' desire for autonomy, Ukraine accepted an arrangement in Crimea that fails to adequately address the more urgent needs of the Tatar population in Crimea.

66. Similarly, despite its unpopularity with Russia—see note 59 above—the system of multination federalism has almost certainly assisted in the democratization and cohesion of Russia. As James Hughes notes, multination federalism 'should be considered as an institutional bulwark against an ethnic Russian hegemonic state, and as part of the solution to a stable democratizing transition in Russia, not as part of the problem . . . [it] has performed the crucial functions of promoting political stability and institutionalizing elite bargaining in Russia's transition to democracy, factors that have been so problematic for democratic consolidation by their very absence in central politics. It is doubtful whether any other alternative institutional arrangement would be as stabilising for a transition to democracy where ethnic cleavages are territorialized as they are in the Russian federation, or indeed in any other deeply divided society' (Hughes 1999: 6, 15; cf. Solnick 1998: 58–9).

67. I am skipping lightly over a difficult and contested issue here. There is a major debate in the literature about how precisely these Communist federations simultaneously promoted and constrained ethnic identities, and about the unintended 'subversive' effects this had upon the collapse of Communism—see Bunce 1999 for a good overview. But whatever the correct acount is, it's clear that these Communist federations had a very different logic than that of Western democratic federations. As Linz emphasizes, the breakdown of nineteenth-century multination empires and twentieth-century multination Communist dictatorships tells us little about the future of democratic multination federations. On Communist federalism as a "licensing regime for ethnic sentiment", see Kagedan 1990: 164.

68. For a classic analysis of this triadic relationship, see Brubaker 1996. Some leaders in ECE say that the presence of a kin-state not only makes notions of self-government for a national minority more dangerous, but also morally illegitimate, on the grounds that the group's right of self-determination is already fulfilled by having a kin-state nearby. The right of Albanians to self-determination is exhausted by the existence of an Albanian state, so that any Albanians living outside that state have no basis for claiming self-government—even if the borders of Albania are completely arbitrary, and do not include areas of centuries-old Albanian settlement. Doroszewska suggests such an argument in her commentary in Part 2. I agree with Vàrady that this is a completely implausible position. The fact that one group of Albanians have rights of self-government does not diminish the right of other Albanians to self-government—see Vàrady 1997: 9–11.

69. Conversely, the fact that Russia's national minorities typically lack kin-states may explain Russia's willingness to accord them territorial autonomy. However, we can find several cases in ECE of national minorities that lack a kin-state yet were refused autonomy—the Abkhazians in Georgia; the Gagauz in Moldova; the Crimean Tatars in Ukraine. So it is quite misleading to suggest that ECE countries would have accorded autonomy to their minorities were it not for potential irredentism. The roots of the problem go deeper than that.

70. The flip side, of course, is that many of these 'post-imperial' minorities were once not just autonomous, but even privileged rulers over the majority group, and so have gone from privileged overlords to subordinate minorities. This has involved a dramatic reduction in status, as well as in rights and powers, which is not easy for them to accept.

71. As Grin notes, the task of maintaining unity in Switzerland is made easier because the French-speaking part of Switzerland 'has never, at any point of its history (bar a few years of Napoleonic rule with partial annexation) been part of France; the French-speaking Swiss are in no way descendents or cousins of the French . . . Similarly, German-speaking Switzerland has never been part of Germany, and Italian-speaking Switzerland has never been part of Italy' (Grin 1999: 5).

72. For examples and discussions of this disloyalty/security/fifth-column view, see Kamusella and Sullivan 1999: 179 (re Germans in Poland); Barcz 1992: 87; Andreescu 1997 (re Hungarians in Romania); Mihalikova 1998: 154–7 (re Hungarians in Slovakia); Nelson 1998; Solchanyk 1994 (re Russians in Ukraine); Offe 1993: 23–4; Strazzari 1998 (re Albanians in Macedonia); Pettai 1998 (re Russians in the Baltics).

73. See, for example, the 'Justification' section of the 1995 Law on the State Language in Slovakia, which consists mainly in recounting various Habsburg laws and policies from the nineteenth century which suppressed the use of Slovak and promoted Magyarization. There is no attempt to discuss what would be a fair accommodation of the diverse interests of the majority and minorities. (The Justification is translated into English and discussed in Minority Protection Association 1995).

74. There is also a more cynical interpretation of the Act. Some people think that the aim of the Act is to lay the groundwork for the elimination of multination federalism in Russia—that is, that the ultimate goal is to replace, rather than supplement, territorial autonomy. See Goble 2000.

75. For a detailed discussion of this system, see Codagnone 1998. As he notes, this system may also be appropriate for what he calls 'old settlers': groups whose migration dates back a century or two, and who were often invited to settle a particular region with the promise that they would have some form of cultural autonomy—for example, Germans in Russia and Ukraine.

76. Over 50% of Aboriginals in Canada no longer live on reservations.

77. This arguably is the main shortcoming of the recent Framework Convention for the Protection of National Minorities. It provides helpful guidelines for small and dispersed national minorities, but does not address the issues of territorial autonomy raised by larger minorities. For more on the limitations of non-territorial forms of autonomy, see my Reply, section 4.

78. On the undemocratic tendencies within some of Russia's ethnorepublics, see G. Smith 1996: 398; Vasilyeva 1995: 35; Stepan 2000.

79. Of course, the level of wealth affects the ability to offer some multicultural accommodations to newcomers. But offering citizenship is not itself a costly

measure, and can indeed reduce other social and economic costs created by the exclusion of metics.

80. I should note that contrasts between the Old and New Worlds are often used in a hypocritical and self-serving way on both sides of the Atlantic. In the Americas, the idea of being a 'New World' has been used to deny the rights, even the very existence, of indigenous peoples. Governments in both North and South America have consistently argued, first at the League of Nations and now at the UN, that because they are 'immigrant countries', therefore they have no 'minorities', and so the provisions of international agreements on the rights of minorities have no application to the Americas. This falsehood is rooted in the racist denial by European colonizers of the humanity of indigenous peoples, but has also been used to deny the rights of other long-settled groups that were involuntarily colonized or conquered—such as Puerto Ricans.

81. Or in cases where the refugees would affect the balance of power between the majority and a national minority already existing within the state. For example, ethnic Albanian refugees from Kosovo are unlikely to get citizenship in Macedonia, since that would strengthen the already-existing Albanian minority in Macedonia. The same applies to Albanian refugees into Greece. By contrast, Russians, Germans, and Jews leaving Central Asia for Russia, Germany, and Israel were immediately offered citizenship, since they strengthen the majority rather than the minority.

82. As Gheorghe and Mirga note, 'the Romani people have expressed similar attitudes toward the territories in which they live: it was not theirs: it always belonged to *Gadje* (non-Gypsies); and consequently the Roma were in some sense rootless' (Gheorghe and Mirga 1997: 23).

83. Also, as Gheorghe and Mirga note, the premise of the civil rights approach—namely, that there could be a purely (civil state) based solely on universal principles of equal citizenship and individual freedom ignores the reality of nationalizing states. Confronted with state nation-building, they note, the only viable option is to demand minority rights (Gheorghe and Mirga 1997: 20).

84. A similar problem arises with another possible comparison—namely, Jews in ECE before WWII. Like the Roma, pre-war Jews were not territorially concentrated, and were subject to extensive discrimination. And they too debated the options of assimilation, cultural autonomy, and proto-nationalism (political Zionism). But like the Blacks, and unlike the Roma, they had a much more differentiated set of institutions already established.

85. For example, most Roma in the Czech Republic are recent arrivals. See Barša's commentary in Part 2.

86. Gheorghe and Mirga are describing these fears, not endorsing them. To my mind, if these were the only objections to the transnational approach, they could be overcome.

87. On the institutional completeness of the Russian community throughout the Soviet Union, see Laitin 1998: 67–9. Whereas 80% of Georgians or Moldovans said that their homeland was Georgia or Moldova—not the entire Soviet Union—70% of Russians said their homeland was the Soviet Union—not just Russia. See Karklins 1994: 48.

88. This of course entailed that the local nationalities would have to become bilingual in order to interact with this increasing Russian presence. Hence the popular joke amongst the Balts that for the Soviets, someone who spoke two languages was a 'nationalist', while people who spoke only one language

(Russian) were 'internationalist'. Note that no other nationality group in the former Soviet Union had this privilege of taking their language rights with them as they moved throughout the Soviet Union. Ukrainians who left Ukraine for Russia had no right to Ukrainian language schools.

89. See Laitin's description of the 'double cataclysm' that hit the Russians in the Baltics: first the adoption of new language laws in 1989, which declared Latvian and Estonian as the sole official languages, and then independence in 1991 (Laitin 1998: 87).

90. It's important to emphasize that I am speaking of post-war Russian settlers. There are ethnic Russian communities in Ukraine, the Baltics, and Kazakhstan which date back two or more centuries. They are not viewed as immigrants either by themselves or by the majority.

91. 'In Estonia, the joint effort of legislators and civil servants was, as recently admitted, "to turn the life of Russians into hell" ', so as to encourage their emigration (Järve 2000: 8, quoting the former director of the Estonian Citizenship and Migration Board); cf. Laitin 1998: 94, 115, 166–7.

92. Indeed, the emigration of Russians to the Near Abroad stopped, and then reversed itself, as soon as these assurances were put in question in the late 1980s (Gavrilova 1998).

93. For the convergence in perceptions, see Pettai 1998; Antane and Tsilevich 1998; Laitin 1998: 159–60, 202.

94. As Laitin puts it, the Baltic countries endorsed the French model of a centralized nation-state over the Belgian model of a multination federation (Laitin 1998: 94).

95. It's important to note that this convergence is not taking place in Central Asia, where Russians continue to reject state pressure to integrate into institutions operating in the titular language, and many have decided to move to Russia rather than assimilate 'downward' to a Turkic language and culture (Laitin 1998: 175). Russians view the Balts as European peoples, with their own high culture and literature, and hence it is not an indignity to integrate into their society, whereas Kazakhs, Uzbeks, and Tajiks are seen as backward and Asian, and many Russian settlers in Central Asia view the idea of learning the titular languages as 'absurd' (Laitin 1998: 98, 121, 238).

96. In any event, it is difficult to think of any other model from the West that might be appropriate. Laitin suggests that partially analogous groups include the Palestinians after the establishment of the Israeli state, the English settlers in Rhodesia, and the French settlers in Algeria (Laitin 1998: ix).

97. Indeed, a recent survey in Latvia, taken in the summer of 1999, showed that Russian teenagers in Latvia are less likely to feel part of Latvia than their parents—even though all of the teenagers were born and raised there—and are less willing to speak Latvian than their parents—even though the teenagers have a better knowledge of it (MINELRES- Sept. 24, 1999). Most parents still hope or expect that learning the language will guarantee acceptance in the larger society; most teenagers no longer believe that. There is a similar decline in Estonia in the percentage of Russians people who believe that learning the titular language will ensure acceptance (Järve 2000: 13).

98. A January 1999 survey in Estonia showed that most Estonians thought integration was solely the responsibility of non-Estonians. Only 12% thought that it would require any effort or action on their part (Järve 2000: 14). The new integration policy is posted on the Estonian government website at: www.riik.ee/saks/ikomisjon/

99. On the potential of the Russian-speaking community to reorganize along nationalist lines, see Laitin 1998: 265, 296. As Laitin puts it, the Russians in the Near Abroad are 'consumed by the debate over what category of minority they belong to . . . Are they a people without a country (with passports from a defunct state), a legitimate minority within an equally legitimate nationalizing state, or a beached diaspora, awaiting high tide?' (Laitin 1998: 316–17). The relevant community includes not only ethnic Russians, but also other Russified settlers, such as Ukrainians, Belarussians, and Jews, who integrated into Russian-language institutions, and so many commentators prefer the term 'Russian-speakers' to 'Russians' (see Laitin 1998).

100. This choice might be influenced by Crimean Tatars' long exposure to the official Soviet doctrine and terminology concerning 'nationalities'. The national-ities which were accorded territorial autonomy in the 1920s and 1930s were defined by Soviet administrators both as 'titular' (*titul'nye*) and 'indigenous' (*korennye*). Crimean Tatars were therefore officially designated and recognized as the 'titular' and 'indigenous' nationality of the autonomous republic of Crimea which was created in 1924—and abolished in 1944, when the Tatars were deported *en masse*.

101. For a discussion of various definitions of indigenous peoples, and their rights in international law, see Anaya 1996.

102. This is not just an issue for Crimean Tatars. It applies in different ways to all of the 'deported peoples' of the USSR, including the Meshketian Turks, the Kalmyks, the Chechens, and Ingush. Some of these groups have had more success not only in returning to their homeland but also in regaining some forms of self-government—for example the Ingush and Kalmyks—others are still not allowed to return to their homeland—for example the Meshketian Turks, who are not allowed back to Georgia.

103. On any account of liberal-democratic principles, the Crimean Tatars who have returned should have their citizenship restored immediately. They should not be metics in the homeland from which they have been expelled. But there are no obvious Western models for addressing the other major issues facing the Tatars: property restitution, cultural autonomy, political representation in either the Crimean regional parliament or Ukrainian national parliament, and so on. It's important to note that the obstacle to the successful resolution of these issues is not necessarily or primarily the central Ukrainian government, but rather the regional Crimean government, dominated by ethnic Russians. Russians have demanded and received territorial autonomy in the Crimea, but are exercising this autonomy in a way which violates the rights of the Tatar minority in Crimea. This case illustrates the need to ensure that self-governing minorities respect the rights of other groups within the territory.

REFERENCES

Alfred, Gerald (1995) *Heeding the Voices of our Ancestors: Kahnawake Mohawk Politics and the Rise of Native Nationalism* (Oxford University Press, Toronto).

Anaya, S. James (1996) *Indigenous Peoples in International Law* (Oxford University Press, New York, NY).

Anderson, Benedict (1983) *Imagined Communities: Reflections on the Origin and Spread of Nationalism* (New Left Books, London).

Andreescu, Gabriel (1997) 'Recommendation 1201 and a Security (Stability) Network in Central and Eastern Europe', *International Studies* (Bucharest), 3, 50–63.

Antane, Aina and Tsilevich, Boris (1998), 'The Problem of Citizenship in Latvia', in Opalski (ed), 33–50.

Barcz, Jan (1992) 'European Standards for the Protection of National Minorities', in Arie Bloed and Wilco de Jonge (eds) *Legal Aspects of a New European Infrastructure* (Europa Instituut, Utrecht), 87–99.

Bauböck, Rainer (1994) *Transnational Citizenship: Membership and Rights in International Migration* (Edward Elgar, Aldershot).

Bauer, Otto (2000) *The Question of Nationalities and Social Democracy*, with an introduction by Ephraim Nimni (University of Minnesota Press, Minneapolis, MN).

Brooks, Roy (1996) *Separation or Integration? A Strategy for Racial Equality* (Harvard University Press, Cambridge, MA).

Brubaker, Rogers (1996) *Nationalism Reframed: Nationhood and the National Question in the New Europe* (Cambridge University Press, Cambridge).

Buchanan, Allen (1991) *Secession: The Legitimacy of Political Divorce* (Westview Press, Boulder, CO).

Bunce, Valerie (1999) *Subversive Institutions: The Design and the Destruction of Socialism and the State* (Cambridge University Press, Cambridge).

Cairns, Alan and Williams, Cynthia (1985) *Constitutionalism, Citizenship and Society in Canada* (University of Toronto Press, Toronto).

Calhoun, Craig (1997) *Nationalism* (University of Minnesota Press, Minneapolis, MN).

Canovan, Margaret (1996) *Nationhood and Political Theory* (Edward Elgar, Cheltenham).

Carens, Joseph (1989) 'Membership and Morality: Admission to Citizenship in Liberal Democratic States', in W. Brubaker (ed) *Immigration and the Politics of Citizenship in Europe and North America* (University Press of American, Lanham, MD).

——(1994) 'Cultural Adaptation and Integration: Is Quebec A Model for Europe?', in Rainer Bauböck (ed) *From Aliens to Citizens* (Avebury, Aldershot), 149–86. An expanded version appears in Joseph Carens (ed) *Is Quebec Nationalism Just?* (McGill-Queen's University Press, 1995), 20–81.

——(2000) *Culture, Citizenship and Community* (Oxford University Press, Oxford).

Castles, Stephen and Miller, Mark (1993) *The Age of Migration: International Population Movements in the Modern World* (Macmillan, London).

Chinn, Jeff and Roper, Steven (1995) 'Ethnic mobilisation and reactive nationalism: The case of Moldova', *Nationalities Papers*, 23 (2), 291–326.

Cochran, David Carroll (1999) *The Color of Freedom: Race and Contemporary American Liberalism* (State University of New York Press, Albany, NY).

Codagnone, Cristiano (1998) 'New Migration in Russia in the 1990s', in Khalid Khoser and Helma Lutz (eds) *New Migration in Europe: Social Constructions and Social Realities* (Macmillan, London), 39–59.

Commission on the Future of Multiethnic Britain (2000) *The Future of Multiethnic Britain* (Profile Books, London).

Connor, Walker (1972) 'Nation-Building or Nation-Destroying', *World Politics* 24, 319–55.

——(1973) 'The Politics of Ethnonationalism', *Journal of International Affairs* 27/1, 1–21.

——(1984) *The National Question in Marxist-Leninist Theory and Strategy* (Princeton University Press, Princeton, NJ).

——(1999) 'National Self-Determination and Tomorrow's Political Map', in Alan Cairns, John Courtney, Peter Mackinnon, and David Smith (eds) *Citizenship, Diversity and Pluralism: Canadian and Comparative Perspectives* (McGill-Queen's University Press, Montreal), 163–76.

Coppieters, Bruno Darchiashvili, David and Akaba, Natella (eds) (2000) *Federal Practice: Exploring Alternatives for Georgia and Abkhazia* (VUB University Press, Brussels).

Cornwall, Mark (1996) 'Minority Rights and Wrongs in Eastern Europe in the Twentieth Century', *The Historian*, 50, 16–20.

Crnobrnja, Mihailo (1998) 'Politics of Refugee Resettlement in the Former Yugoslavia', in Opalski (ed), 191–207.

Danspeckgruber, Wolfgang (1997) 'Self-Determination, Subsidiarity and Regionalization in Contemporary Western Europe', in Wolfgang Danspeckgruber and Arthur Watts (eds) *Self-Determination and Self-Administration: A Sourcebooks* (Lynne Rienner, Boulder, CO), 221–48.

Dimitras, Panayote (1998) 'The Minority Rights Paradox', *War Report*, 58 (February–March 1998).

Dorff, Robert (1994) 'Federalism in Eastern Europe: Part of the Solution or Part of the Problem?' *Publius*, 24, 99–114.

Druviete, Ina (1997) 'Linguistic Human Rights in the Baltic States', *International Journal of the Sociology of Language*, 127, 161–85.

Dudwick, Nora (1996) 'Nagorno Karabakh and the Politics of Sovereignty', in Ronald Suny (ed) *Transcaucasia, Nationalism and Social Change*, Rev edn. (University of Michigan Press, Ann Arbor, MI).

Ethnobarometer Programme (1999) *Ethnic Conflict and Migration in Europe: First Report on the Ethnobarometer Programme* (Consiglio Italiano per le Scienze Sociali, Rome).

Frideres, James (1997) 'Edging into the Mainstream: Immigrant Adult and their Children', in Wsevelod Isajiw (ed) *Comparative Perspectives on Interethnic Relations and Social Incorporation in Europe and North America* (Canadian Scholars Press, Toronto), 537–62.

Gavrilova, Irina (1998) 'Does Russia Have a Migration Policy?', in Opalski (ed), 51–74.

Gellner, Ernest (1983) *Nations and Nationalism* (Blackwell, Oxford).

Gheorghe, Nicolae and Mirga, Andrej (1997) *The Roma in the Twenty-First Century: A Position Paper* (Project on Ethnic Relations, Princeton, NJ).

Glazer, Nathan (1997) *We Are All Multiculturalists Now* (Harvard University Press, Cambridge, MA).

Glover, Jonathan (1997) 'Nations, Identity and Conflict', in Jeff McMahan and Robert McKim (eds) *The Morality of Nationalism* (Oxford University Press, New York, NY) 11–30.

Goble, Paul (2000) 'A New Kind of Autonomy', *RFE/RL Russian Federation Report*: 2/17 (May 10, 2000).

Greenfeld, Liah (1992) *Nationalism: Five Roads to Modernity* (Harvard University Press, Cambridge, MA).

Grin, François (1999) *Language Policy in Multilingual Switzerland: Overview and Recent Developments*, (ECMI Brief #2, European Centre for Minority Issues, Flensburg).

Gurr, Ted (1993) *Minorities at Risk: A Global View of Ethnopolitical Conflict* (Institute of Peace Press, Washington, DC).

——(2000) 'Ethnic Warfare on the Wane' *Foreign Affair*, 79/3, 52–64.

Gutmann, Amy and Appiah, Anthony (1996) *Color Conscious* (Princeton University Press, Princeton, NJ).

Hamilton, Paul (1999) 'The Scottish National Paradox: The Scottish National Party's Lack of Ethnic Character', *Canadian Review of Studies in Nationalism* 26, 17–36.

Hannikainen, Lauri (1996) 'The Status of Minorities, Indigenous Peoples and Immigrant and Refugee Groups in Four Nordic States', *Nordic Journal of International Law*, 65, 1–71.

Hannum, Hurst (1990) *Autonomy, Sovereignty, and Self-Determination: The Adjudication of Conflicting Rights* (University of Pennsylvania Press, Philadelphia, PA).

Harles, John (1993) *Politics in the Lifeboat: Immigrants and the American Democratic Order* (Westview Press, Boulder, CO).

Hislope, Robert (1998) 'Ethnic Conflict and the Generosity Moment', *Journal of Democracy* 9, 140–53.

Horowitz, Donald (1991) *A Democratic South Africa: Constitutional Engineering in a Divided Society* (University of California Press, Berkeley, CA).

Hughes, James (1999) 'Institutional Responses to Separatism: Federalism and Transition to Democracy in Russia', paper presented to Association for the Study of Nationalities Annual Convention, New York, May 1999.

Hungarian Coalition in Slovakia (1997) *The Hungarians in Slovakia* (Information Centre of the Hungarian Coalition in Slovakia, Bratislava).

Huntington, Samuel (1996) *The Clash of Civilizations and the Remaking of World Order* (Simon and Schuster, New York, NY).

Ignatieff, Michael (1993) *Blood and Belonging: journeys into the new nationalism* (Farrar, Straus and Giroux, New York, NY).

Järve, Priit (2000) "Language Legislation in the Baltic States: Changes of Rationale", presented to annual meeting of the Association for the Study of Nationalities, New York.

Jaworsky, John (1998) 'Nationalities Policy and Potential for Interethnic Conflict in Ukraine', in Opalski (ed), 104–27.

Jenson, Jane (1993) 'Naming Nations: Making Nationalist Claims in Canadian Public Discourse', *Canadian Review of Sociology and Anthropology* 30/3, 337–57.

Johnson, Gerald (1973) *Our English Heritage* (Greenwood Press, Westport, CT).

Kagedan, Allan (1990) "Territorial Units as Nationality Policy", in Henry Huttenbach (ed) *Soviet Nationality Policies* (Mansell, New York).

Kaiser, Robert (1994) *The Geography of Nationalism in Russia and the USSR* (Princeton University Press, Princeton, NJ).

Kamusella, Tomasz and Sullivan, Terry (1999) 'The Germans of Upper Silesia: the struggle for recognition', in Karl Cordell (ed) *Ethnicity and Democratisation in the New Europe* (Routledge, London), 169–82.

Karklins, Rasma (1994) *Ethnopolitics and Transition to Democracy: The Collapse of the USSR and Latvia* (Woodrow Wilson Center Press, Washington D.C.).

——(2000) 'Ethnopluralism: Panacea for East Central Europe?', *Nationalities Papers*, 28/2, 219–41.

Keating, Michael (1996) *Nations Against the State: The New Politics of Nationalism in Quebec, Catalonia and Scotland* (Macmillan, London).

Kuzio, Taras (1999) 'Nationalising States or Nation-Building? A Critical Review of the Theoretical Literature and Empirical Evidence', paper presented for the annual convention of the Association for the Study of Nationalities, New York, April 1999.

——and Noldberg, Marc (1999) 'Nation and State Building, Historical Legacies and National Identities in Belarus and Ukraine', *Canadian Review of Studies in Nationalism* 26, 69–90.

Kymlicka, Will (1995) *Multicultural Citizenship: A Liberal Theory of Minority Rights* (Oxford University Press, Oxford).

——(1998) *Finding Our Way: Rethinking Ethnocultural Relations in Canada* (Oxford University Press, Toronto).

——(2001) *Politics in the Vernacular: Nationalism, Multiculturalism and Citizenship* (Oxford University Press, Oxford).

——and Norman, Wayne (eds) (2000) *Citizenship in Diverse Societies* (Oxford University Press, Oxford).

Laitin, David (1992) *Language Repertoires and State Construction in Africa* (Cambridge University Press, Cambridge).

——(1998) *Identity in Formation: The Russian-Speaking Populations in the Near Abroad* (Cornell University Press, Ithaca, NY).

Lapidoth, Ruth (1996) *Autonomy: Flexible Solutions to Ethnic Conflicts* (US Institute of Peace Press, Washington, DC).

Levy, Jacob (2000) *The Multiculturalism of Fear* (Oxford University Press, Oxford).

Liebich, André (1995) 'Nations, States and Minorities: Why is Eastern Europe Different?' *Dissent*, Summer 1995, 313–17.

Linz, Juan (1996) *Problems of Democratic Transition and Consolidation* (Johns Hopkins University Press, Baltimore).

Lynn, Nicholas and Novikov, Alexei (1997) 'Refederalizing Russia: Debates on the idea of federalism in Russia', *Publius* 27/2, 187–203.

Margalit, Avishai and Raz, Joseph (1990) 'National Self-Determination', *Journal of Philosophy* 87/9, 439–61.

Marples, David and Duke, David (1995) 'Ukraine, Russia and the Question of Crimea', *Nationalities Papers*, 23/2, 261–89.

McGarry, John (1998) 'Demographic Engineering: the state-directed movement of ethnic groups as a technique of conflict regulation', *Ethnic and Racial Studies*, 21/4, 615–38.

Miall, Hugh (1999) 'The Albanian communities in the post-communist transition', in Karl Cordell (ed) *Ethnicity and Democratisation in the New Europe* (Routledge, London), 131–44.

Mihalikova, Silvia (1998) 'The Hungarian Minority in Slovakia: Conflict Over Autonomy', in Opalski (ed), 148–64.

Miller, David (1995) *On Nationality* (Oxford University Press, Oxford).

Miller, J. R. (1991) *Skyscrapers Hide the Heavens: A History of Indian-White Relations in Canada* (University of Toronto Press, Toronto).

MINELRES (Electronic Resources of Minority Rights in Eastern Europe): daily messages are archived at http://www.riga.lv/minelres

Minority Protection Association (1995) *The Slovak State Language Law and the Minorities: Critical Analyses and Remarks* (Minority Protection Association, Budapest).

MRG (Minority Rights Group) (1997) *World Directory of Minorities* (Minority Rights Group, London).

Mitrofanov, Miroslav (1998) 'Language in a Multicultural Community: The Case of Daugavpils', in Opalski (ed), 51–74.

Mosse, George (1985) *Nationalism and Sexuality: Middle-Class Morality and Sexual Norms in Modern Europe* (University of Wisconsin Press, Madison, WI).

Nelson, Daniel (1998) 'Hungary and its Neighbours: Security and Ethnic Minorities', *Nationalities Papers*, 26/2, 314–30.

Norman, Wayne (1999), 'Theorizing Nationalism (Normatively): The First Steps', in Ronald Beiner (ed) *Theorizing Nationalism* (SUNY Press, Albany, NY), 51–66.

Offe, Claus (1993) 'Ethnic Politics in East European Transitions', in Jody Jensen and Ferenc Miszlivetz (eds) *Paradoxes of Transition* (Savaria University Press, Szombathely), 11–40.

Opalski, Magda (1998) 'The Cossack Revival: Rebuilding an Old Identity in a New Russia', in Magda Opalski (ed) *Managing Diversity in Plural Societies: Minorities, Migration and Nation-Building in Post-Communist Europe* (Forum Eastern Europe, Ottawa), 75–103.

Open Society Institute (1998) *Kazakhstan: Forced Migration and Nation-Building* (Forced Migration Project, Open Society Institute, New York, NY).

Ossipov, Alexander (1998) 'Krasnodar Krai: Migration, Nationalism and Regionalist Rhetoric', in Opalski (ed), 260–74.

Packer, John (1998) 'Autonomy within the OSCE: The Case of Crimea', in Markku Suksi (ed) *Autonomy: Applications and Implications* (Kluwer, The Hague), 295–316.

Parekh, Bhikhu (2000) *Rethinking Multiculturalism: Cultural Diversity and Political Theory* (Harvard University Press, Cambridge, MA).

Parker, Andrew, Russo, Mary, Sommer, Doris, and Yeager, Patricia (eds) (1992) *Nationalisms and Sexualities* (Routledge, New York, NY).

Payton, Philip (1999) 'Ethnicity in Western Democracy Today', in Karl Cordell (ed) *Ethnicity and Democratisation in the New Europe* (Routledge, London), 24–36.

Peterson, Nicholas and Sanders, Will (eds) (1998) *Citizenship and Indigenous Australians: Changing Conceptions and Possibilities* (Cambridge University Press, Cambridge).

Pettai, Vello (1998) 'Emerging Ethnic Democracy in Estonia and Latvia', in Opalski (ed), 15–32.

Pfaff, William (1993) *The Wrath of Nations: Civilization and the Furies of Nationalism* (Simon and Schuster, New York, NY).

Phillips, Anne (1995) *The Politics of Presence: Issues in Democracy and Group Representation* (Oxford University Press, Oxford).

Pickus, Noah (ed) (1998) *Becoming American/American Becoming: Final Report* (Duke University Workshop on Immigration and Citizenship, Durham, NC).

Plamenatz, John (1960) *On Alien Rule and Self-Government* (Longman, London).

Poulton, Hugh (1998) *Minorities in Southeast Europe: Inclusion and Exclusion* (Minority Rights Group, London).

Ramet, Sabrina (1997) *Whose Democracy? Nationalism, Religion, and the Doctrine of Collective Rights in Post-1989 Eastern Europe* (Rowman and Littlefield, London).

RCAP—Royal Commission on Aboriginal Peoples (1996) *Report of the Royal Commission on Aborignial Peoples. Volume 2: Restructuring the Relationship* (Ottawa).

Resler, Tamara (1997) 'Dilemmas of Democratisation: Safeguarding Minorities in Russia, Ukraine and Lithuania', *Europe-Asia Studies*, 49/1, 89–106.

Resnick, Philip (1994) 'Toward a Multination Federalism', in *Seeking a New*

Canadian Partnership: Asymmetrical and Confederal Options, ed. Leslie Seidle (Institute for Research on Public Policy, Montreal), 71–90.

Rosenberg, William (1974) *Liberals in the Russian Revolution* (Princeton University Press, Princeton, NJ).

Rubio-Marin, Ruth (2000) *Immigration as a Democratic Challenge: Citizenship and Inclusion in Germany and the United States* (Cambridge University Press, Cambridge).

Scassa, Teresa (1996) 'National Identity, Ethnic Surnames and the State', *Canadian Journal of Law and Society* 11/2, 167–91.

Schmidt, Sandra (1999) 'Immigration Policy and new ethnic minorities in contemporary Germany', in Karl Cordell (ed) *Ethnicity and Democratisation in the New Europe* (Routledge, London), 91–105.

Smith, Anthony (1993) 'A Europe of Nations—Or the Nation of Europe?', *Journal of Peace Research* 30/2, 129–35.

Smith, Graham (1996) 'Russia, ethnoregionalism and the politics of federation', *Ethnic and Racial Studies*, 19/2, 391–410.

Solchanyk, Roman (1994) 'The Politics of State-Building: Centre-Periphery Relations in Post-Soviet Ukraine', *Europe-Asia Studies*, 46/1, 47–68.

Solnick, Steven (1998) 'Will Russia Survive? Center and Periphery in the Russian Federation', in Barnett Rubin and Jack Snyder (eds) *Post-Soviet Political Order: Conflict and State-Building* (Routledge, London), 58–80.

Spinner, Jeff (1994) *The Boundaries of Citizenship: Race, Ethnicity and Nationality in the Liberal State* (Johns Hopkins University Press, Baltimore, MD).

Stanley, F. G. (1961) *The Birth of Western Canada: A History of the Riel Rebellions* (University of Toronto Press, Toronto).

Stepan, Alfred (2000) 'Russian Federalism in Comparative Perspective', *Post-Soviet Affairs* 16/2, 133–76.

Strazzari, Francesco (1998) 'Macedonia: State and Identity in an Unstable Regional Environment', in Opalski (ed), 165–90.

Tamir, Yael (1993) *Liberal Nationalism* (Princeton University Press, Princeton, NJ).

Taylor, Charles (1992) 'The Politics of Recognition', in Amy Gutmann (ed) *Multiculturalism and the 'Politics of Recognition'* (Princeton University Press, Princeton, NJ), 25–73.

——(1997) 'Nationalism and Modernity', in R. McKim and J. McMahan (eds), *The Morality of Nationalism* (Oxford University Press, New York), 31–55.

Thompson, Paula (1998) 'The Gagauz in Moldova and Their Road to Autonomy', in Opalski (ed), 128–47.

Thornberry, Patrick (1998) 'Images of Autonomy and Individual and Collective Rights in International Instruments on the Rights of Minorities', in Markku Suksi (ed) *Autonomy: Applications and Implications* (Kluwer, The Hague), 97–124.

Tilly, Charles (1975) 'Reflections on the History of European State-Making', in Charles Tilly (ed) *The Formation of National States in Western Europe* (Princeton University Press, Princeton, NJ), 3–83.

Tomova, Ilona (1998) 'The Migration Process in Bulgaria', in Opalski (ed), 229–39.

Troebst, Stefan (1998) *Conflict in Kosovo: Failure of Prevention* (European Centre for Minority Issues, Flensburg).

Tully, James (1995) *Strange Multiplicity: Constitutionalism in an Age of Diversity* (Cambridge University Press, Cambridge).

Valls, Andrew (1999) 'Reconsidering Black Nationalism', paper presented at conference on 'Nationalism, Identity and Minority Rights', Bristol, September 1999.

Van Cott, Donna Lee (2001) "Explaining Ethnic Autonomy Regimes in Latin America", *Studies in Comparative International Development* 35/4. 30–58.

Vàrady, Tibor (1997) 'Majorities, Minorities, Law and Ethnicity: Reflections on the Yugoslav Case', *Human Rights Quarterly*, 19, 9–54.

Varennes, Fernand de (1997) 'Ethnic Conflicts and Language in Eastern Europe and Central Asian States: Can Human Rights Help Prevent Them?', *International Journal on Minority and Group Rights* 5, 153–74.

Vasilyeva, Olga (1995) 'Has Ethnic Federalism a Future in Russia?', *New Times*, March 1995, 34–7.

——(1996) *The Foreign Policy Orientation of Georgia* (Stiftung Wissenchaft und Politik, Ebenhausen).

Waever, Ole (1995) 'Securitization and Desecuritization', in Ronnie Lipschutz (ed) *On Security* (Columbia University Press, New York, NY), 46–86.

Walzer, Michael (1983) *Spheres of Justice* (Basic Books, New York, NY).

——(1990) 'Nation and Universe', in Grethe Peterson (ed) *Tanner Lectures on Human Values* Volume 11 (University of Utah Press, Salt Lake City, UT), 532–56.

——(1992a) 'Comment', in Amy Gutmann (ed) *Multiculturalism and the 'Politics of Recognition'* (Princeton University Press, Princeton, NJ), 99–103.

——(1992b) *What it Means to be an American* (Marsilio, New York, NY).

——(1997) *On Toleration* (Yale University Press, New Haven, CT).

Weber, Eugene (1976) *Peasants into Frenchmen: The Modernization of Rural France* (Chatto and Windus, London).

Young, Iris Marion (1990) *Justice and the Politics of Difference* (Princeton University Press, Princeton, NJ).

Zend, Natalie (1998) 'Hungary's Migration Policy 1987–1996: External Influences and Domestic Imperatives', in Opalski (ed), 208–28.

2

COMMENTARIES

GEORGE SCHÖPFLIN

URSZULA DOROSZEWSKA

TIBOR VÀRADY

MICHAEL WALZER

BORIS TSILEVICH

ALEXANDER OSSIPOV

PANAYOTE DIMITRAS
AND NAFSIKA PAPANIKOLATOS

PÅL KOLSTØ

JÁNOS KIS

PAVEL BARŠA

VELLO PETTAI

GABRIEL ANDREESCU

VOLODYMYR FESENKO

MAGDA OPALSKI

ALEKSANDER DJUMAEV

2.1

Liberal Pluralism and Post-Communism

George Schöpflin

The principles of liberal pluralism in Central and South-Eastern Europe have several sources, the most important of which has been the reception of liberal democratic forms of government and legitimation after 1989. Pre-Communist elements of liberalism did, indeed, exist, even if practice was markedly illiberal in various spheres. The introduction of liberal democracy after 1989 was most clearly evidenced in the adoption of relatively liberal constitutions, parliamentary government, separation of spheres and, in many cases, fairly powerful constitutional adjudication through strong constitutional courts.

The reasons underlying this reception can be found in the contingent circumstances of the collapse of communism, which also explain the weaknesses of liberal pluralism. Communism collapsed, in effect, because its internal functioning, its capacity to sustain coherence, had become blocked. It was no longer capable of self-reproduction, it had lost its capacity for legitimation and pivotally as far as the rulers were concerned, self-legitimation. In sum, the élites had lost their will to rule.

An implosion of this kind would not necessarily have been enough to produce collapse. The existence of a vibrant, visible, nearby alternative was also needed to ensure that, if Communism were to disappear, there would be something else—something seen as better—to replace it. The Communist system was not only no longer exemplary and binding, but liberal democracy—in its Communist period reading—had become so, albeit in a mythic and symbolic sense.

One of the consequences of the post-1989 reception was that the West (Western Europe, North America) was brought actively to underpin the newly fledged democratic systems of Central and South-Eastern Europe, an engagement that persisted and was strengthened with the passage of time. But the non-symbolic Europe of the West was very different from the myth and symbolic 'Europe' which had had such an impact in the 1980s; in effect 'Europe' existed as a twofold aim—as cultural aspiration and as EU membership, as a set of institutions, practices, procedures of which the post-Communist countries were largely ignorant and saw as irrelevant to their needs. The integration of Central and South-Eastern Europe into Europe, through eastward enlargement of the European Union and the undeviating adherence by the EU to the Copenhagen criteria, created benchmarks that the post-Communist states had no alternative but to accept if their commitment to democracy was to be taken seriously. The cases of Slovakia under Meciar, Belarus, Croatia under Tudjman, and Serbia demonstrated the nature of other options. The upshot of eastward enlargement was that on both sides of the West–East divide, the overt goal was the far-reaching reconstruction of post-Communist systems into an ideal-typical European democracy.

However, the principles of liberal democracy and democratic pluralism would only function if they matched existing political, sociological, and cultural realities. Crucially, the transformation process—widely, but somewhat misleadingly termed 'transition'—raised a generally undiagnosed difficulty, the distinction between consent to the exercise of power and democracy itself. In sum, post-communist systems were consensual, a consent that was expressed regularly in elections and through other institutions, but were not democratic in as much as democratic values were only sporadically to be observed. In particular, there was a marked lack of self-limitation, moderation, responsibility, and commitment to the procedures and process on the part of political actors.[1]

In this respect, there was a clear gap between form and content as far as these systems were concerned. The open and unanswered question was the pace and success of form and content in finding some of kind of a match. Clearly this was to be a time-consuming and arduous process, involving a thoroughgoing shift in institutional cultures. From this perspective, a proper understanding of the sociology and cultural norms of the region, including both short-term and longue duree legacies of the past, would help to account for the shortcomings and failures that have been evident in the reconciliation of form and content and the corresponding move towards democratic values. The broad cultural matrix within which power moves, in which interests are understood, in which language is used, and in which thought-styles are born and reproduced is an essential aspect of the problematic of liberal pluralism in Central and South-Eastern Europe.

It is vital to recognize two further factors here. The first is that Anglo-Saxon analyses of post-Communism are frequently, persistently, and understandably hampered by the analysts' own cultural baggage, their doxa,[2] the term that Bourdieu uses to describe the tacit assumptions that we make about the world in which we live, in this instance the nature of democratic best-practice, and which they elevate to immanent yardsticks for the measurement of the success and failure of democracy under post-Communism.

They cannot and do not understand that the Anglo-Saxon concept of democracy which they privilege is only one possible form of democracy among many and that the traditions of the region often make for a poor match with the legacies of English parliamentarism, say, with all the consequent grounds for misunderstanding, something that is greatly exacerbated by the current prestige and power of the United States and its inclination to regard its own values and practices as the axiom of best-practice and, maybe, sole model, an inclination that has led it—not necessarily consciously—to impose its ideas and institutional forms on very different political cultures. Anglo-Saxon analysts have more time for reflection than politicians and less excuse for not scrutinizing their implicit success and failure criteria. In much of the Anglo-Saxon analysis, one can discern a reluctance to approach post-communism reflectively and, for that matter, reflexively; instead there is a readiness to see the patterns of Anglo-Saxony as universal and universally applicable.

Second, it is vital to recognize in this connection that Europe has generated a very wide set of practices and concepts of democracy, all of which are acceptably democratic—compare Norway and Portugal—and, indeed, that certain political practices in the United States are not acceptable by European criteria, like the death penalty or the lack of limitation on election expenditure. Central Europe and South-Eastern Europe will certainly come to generate their own democratic norms, concepts, and patterns which will be different and democratic. All the foregoing demands a much deeper and much more thoughtful assessment of the success and failure criteria of democracy than Anglo-Saxon analysis tends to offer.

The central tension in the context of liberal pluralism is the relationship between individual and collective identities and the reluctance to recognize that both exist, both have authenticity, and both are the source of moral values. There is a line of thought that is prejudiced, to put it no more strongly, against the idea that liberal pluralism and the rights and obligations that flow from it, can or should be extended to ethnic collectivities. It should be noted that this bias is overwhelmingly Anglo-Saxon and French—'French' here includes all the inheritors and practitioners of the Jacobin tradition wherever they may be. In terms of historical reality, a liberal pluralism that seeks to balance collective and individual identities in the context of ethnicity has several antecedents. These include the Austro-Marxist ideas of Bauer and Renner and their implementation in interwar Estonia, the Moravian compromise of 1905, its Bukovinan and Galician counterparts of 1910 and 1914 respectively, the Dutch agreement, the Swiss and Finnish settlements, the South Tyrol package etc. All of these can be brought under the general heading of consociationalism, the term used by Arendt Lijphart to describe the successful political systems that accept that liberal theories of citizenship will not in themselves provide for ethnic security.[3]

The point to understand here is that collective identities—based on shared meanings, values, a sense of shared past and future, shared myths and symbols—may delimit individual choice and be coercive in terms of cognitions, but are universal in structure, even if their content varies enormously. Paradoxically, the universalist assumptions of the Anglo-Saxon and French liberal thought-world are similarly coloured by what are directly or ultimately ethnic assumptions. This is inescapable. We all have ethnicity, we are all affected by ethnic belonging and the rules of this ethnic community influence our beliefs, our implicit assumptions, our sense of right and wrong, our thought-styles, and our ways of structuring the past and the future. In the modern world, ethnicity is a powerful plausibility structure[4]—the term used by Peter Berger to describe the set of beliefs that each and every collectivity relies on to secure itself—and we are deceiving ourselves if we pretend otherwise.

All this is perfectly legitimate; what is not is the denial of this ethnic legacy, of the ethnic underpinning of our plausibility structures, as universalists tend to do and then to take the next step, which is to equate their own particularisms with universal norms and then to impose these on other cultures. What takes place in these situations is an illicit conversion of the particular into the universal and in the post-Enlightenment hierarchy of values, the universal is in a higher position than the particular, regardless of the damage that is done to other cultures and to the poor fit between this pseudo-universalism and particular forms of knowledge. From this perspective, the acceptance of certain collective identities as legitimate in the Anglo-Saxon world—it has still to happen in France—is no more than a catching up with the established practice of the rest of Europe.

There is a problem here, however. Given the cultural prestige of the United States and the weakness of the post-Communist states, there is a certain readiness on the part of local élites that describe themselves as 'liberal' to import Anglo-Saxon liberalism wholesale and to disregard the cultural context in which those ideas came to fruition. The currently fashionable discourse of multiculturalism is a case in point. The details of US-style multiculturalism arguably make sense in the strongly particularistic context of US politics and society. Simply adopting this discourse and its practices without further thought, a pattern unthinkingly encouraged and even imposed by NGOs or aid donors, is bound to result in poor outcomes: poor by the criteria of democratic values.

The acceptance of collective identities—ethnic groups of various kinds—as legitimate political actors requires investigation of the nature of ethnicity. Ethnicity can take various forms. Ethnicity refers to a collective identity group that makes a claim to define its own TimeSpace—the term used by Koselleck and others to signify the particular quality attributed to the temporality and spatiality of events, that is, how events in the past are understood in different periods, their speed, locus, identification with places and people, and is thus a key constituent of memory—its own boundaries, boundary markers and control of the boundary traffic, its own group solidarity and coherence, moral worth, collective representation of self and of others and be engaged in cultural reproduction.[5] When a group so defined makes claims on political power, and in the modern world this is all but inescapable, we are dealing with the phenomenon of ethnonationality, because the collectivity in question, once it has embarked on the process of claiming political power, will look to secure its cultural reproduction by condensing power—concentrating capacities, effectiveness, and legitimacy—and delegitimating competing reality-defining agencies. Note here that ethnonationality is not an escalator to independent statehood. What is particularly noteworthy in Europe at the Millennium is that statehood is one option for ethnonational groups, but not necessarily the only one, as long as consociational solutions are on the agenda.

To ethnonational groups may be added ethnoreligious groups, which define themselves by religion as a badge of identity, when other raw materials like language are lacking, but are otherwise identical with ethnonationality. Ethnofolkloric groups exist but are without significant access to political power and lack the capacity to condense it—the Sorbs in Germany or the Kashubs in Poland are illustrations of this point. In ethnoregionalism, loyalty to the region is or is said to be the strongest marker of identity. In general, the region in question must also have a degree of political autonomy on the basis of which it can condense sufficient power to make ethnoregional identities superordinate, persistent and pervasive, indeed exemplary and binding, otherwise the identities involved may be captured by other groups. Switzerland illustrates this process, in as much as in the nineteenth century, its francophones and alemannophones were exposed to the powerful attractions of France and Germany, but the Swiss state had already acquired a sufficient organic solidarity, the sense of being members of a single community of feeling, shared identity, and history, to be able to withstand the cultural blandishments of language. But this is rare in Europe. For the most part, attempts to condense organic solidarities on the basis of geography and, maybe, history have been less successful than those that used language, the state, and other elements.

The next question, then, is why, after the best part of two centuries of persistent denigration and delegitimation by liberals—and Marxists, of course, who have somewhat better excuses—have ethnic identities endured? What is the purposiveness of ethnicity, what are its roles and functions in the contemporary world? If we accept that they do have a purposiveness, then it follows that ethnicity also generates its own rationality and that too requires definition.

The core of ethnicity is that each and every collectivity seeks to create coherence, to make cosmos from chaos.[6] Without coherence individuals are lost, they have no way of assigning meanings to the world in which they live, of making sense of the manifold experiences that they undergo, so that they would be at the mercy of a myriad sensory inputs and impressions, thereby making it impossible to conceptualize present, past, and future. TimeSpace would not come into being; nor would language. The world would be a set of arbitrary signs. Further, collectivities are a source of moral regulation, a set of bounded and ordered rules, creating the consistency and predictability by which individuals narrate and explain their lives and sustain a shared existence.

Moral regulation legitimates collective existence and condenses power over the past and the future. Beyond that, collective existence as identity defines internal boundaries of what is proper and improper, what conduct attracts reward and punishment, what accounts for success and failure; in effect, ontology is grounded in shared identity. The dynamic of collective identities is the maintenance and adaptation of this system of moral regulation and boundaries. To ensure that the system is not questioned, for questioning would erode or damage coherence, the foundations of the system are sacralized and placed into the implicit world of doxa by the use of myth, symbol, and ritual.[7] This is the process of cultural reproduction, and cultural reproduction, as already suggested, establishes its own overriding rationality, one that competes with liberal individualism.

Collectivities will go to extreme lengths to protect their collective identities and existence and to secure their reproduction. Clearly a collective which has no implicit world or only a very limited one will tend to have a weak commitment to its own future and may well choose—by default, possibly—to abandon its cultural reproduction. This was not unknown in the premodern era, and there are several instances like the Etruscans or the Cumanians. In the modern period it is very rare. Manx and the Old Prussians[8] are two examples that come to mind. There is a further point that has to be made here. If we accept that identity axiomatically creates boundaries, then it follows that identity requires alterity, others against whom we define our 'we-ness'. If we accept this as axiomatic, then the problem of multi-ethnicity is not ethnicity as such, but the means of dealing with inter-ethnic contact or conflict.

This last point is significant in another context, that of hetero-representation, that only members of a collectivity are entitled to speak about themselves and their experiences, whereas outsiders may not as that constitutes an illicit exercise of power.[9] There is a certain line of argument in some academic enterprise that hetero-representation is either inherently wrong or at any rate, it is morally reprehensible when two unequal groups are involved and the stronger of the two uses its superior power to impose its negative stereotypes on the weaker.[10] It follows logically from the above, from the nature of alterity, that hetero-representation is an inescapable aspect of ethnicity, and rather than seek to prohibit it, it is a preferable strategy to control it instead. Banning it will drive it underground, into covert and coded areas of communication or, even worse, into doxa, where it becomes a basic part of the implicit assumptions of the community and no amount of post-modern unmasking will shift it.

Next, it is important to look at the role of political institutions and cultural reproduction. In the modern period, the central such institution is the state. The word 'modern' is vital, because the nature of the state was fundamentally transformed from the sixteenth to seventeenth centuries onwards, with the rise of new forms of knowledge and new technologies endowing the state with a new and far greater power of ordering and rationalization.[11] The consequence of this radical shift of power in favour of the state was that the state began to play a greatly increased role as an identity-forming process, so that while in the premodern period state-driven, etatic identities were relatively unimportant and the central nexus of political power was feudal regulation, dynastic loyalty based on the hierarchy of birth—to a lesser extent attainment—or religion, the modern state maintains itself by accepting that power is most effectively exercised when it is consensual. Non-consensual modes of exercising power have been tried repeatedly and while some of them appear to promise high yields in terms of mobilization and planning, they have failed a la longue because they have been unable to respond to the mounting complexity that is the central characteristic of modernity. When placed in this perspective, it becomes evident that the state is the key agency in enabling liberal pluralism and conversely needs the liberal pluralism of civil society to help it avoid the bureaucratic stultification that follows from a monopoly of power.

Consensual rule, however, demands different relationships between rulers and ruled to premodern patterns and non-consensualism, a key feature of which is that the ruled should accept the superior rationality of state as a part of their doxa, of the 'natural order', so that its existence may not be questioned. Lack of consent, in reality, erodes state capacity, which is essential for sustaining coherence. To curtail a longer argument at this point, the most effective means of achieving this is to base consent to state power on a shared culture, sustaining its characteristics, shaping it and fostering it, in order to create and secure an organic, cohesive relationship between rulers and ruled—in a word, base it on ethnicity. Inevitably, this creates problems with multi-ethnic states, which means practically every state in Europe. In such instances, multi-ethnicity was overcome, or reduced as a political obstacle, by downgrading the saliency of the competing ethnic identities—for example, the Occitans in France; in others, multiethnicity was accepted and became the (new) foundation for the state—for example, Finland; in yet others, multi-ethnicity was ignored or marginalized with a few low-level concessions—for example, Scotland until the 1960s.[12]

It should be evident from the foregoing that the state, as an instrument for creating coherence, acquires a vested interest in its own reproduction and will not readily make concessions to what it regards as competing or centrifugal forces. This helps to explain the reluctance of even the liberal state to accept demands legitimated by reference to ethnic identities other than those of the dominant ethnic groups. By ostensible liberal criteria, the maintenance of the state is only rational as long as its citizens so believe, and if a group of citizens consistently and over time demand exit, the liberal state should readily accede to this. As we know from the evidence, states deeply dislike the idea of secession.

The potential for disruption and thus for state failure, an intolerable prospect as a deeply felt threat of incoherence, comes to be seen as too high. Nevertheless, the modern European state is more contingent than it likes to pretend. It is a product of history, it is privileged on pragmatic grounds of stability even when this no longer serves stability and pivotally it has been subjected to failure far more frequently than might appear at first sight. By strict criteria, only one state in Europe—Switzerland—escaped some form of state failure in the twentieth century. These criteria are disappearance—Austria-Hungary, Montenegro, the GDR, the Soviet Union; loss or addition of territory, both profoundly disruptive—the United Kingdom, Germany, France to name but a few; decolonization; and conquest with foreign occupation.

The implication of the frequency of state failure in Europe is that fission or territorial cession has been an accepted feature of the political landscape in the twentieth century and was only made to seem intolerable because of the extraordinary stability brought about by the Cold War, so that it was the 1945–89 period that was exceptional in freezing existing state frontiers. But the stability of the Cold War was time-bound and contingent. The outcome is much greater pressure on the frontiers that were hastily and in many cases contradictorily drawn at the Paris Peace Settlement of 1918–20. The Kosovo war of 1999 was a case in point.

In Western Europe, the post-1945 state was the beneficiary of several conjunctural trends that permitted it to evolve to a fairly high capacity on a consensual basis. The trends included the shock and trauma of the Great European Civil War (1914–45) and the determination on the part of post-1945 élites that it should never be allowed to happen again. There was the ironic stability of the Cold War; an unprecedented period of prosperity; the creation of a wholly new state of affairs, where by the 1980s roughly four-fifths of the population had escaped primary poverty and the welfare state ensured that the remainder did not have to starve—something that had not been true in the interwar years; the definitive end of peasant agriculture and the growth of urban cultures, including literacy, political sophistication, and socio-economic complexity. The post-war era saw an initial revulsion against ethnonational identities as a factor of political power, seen as they were as the cause of two World Wars,[13] European integration as both a goal and a method—see below—and a near universal acceptance of democracy as the best (morally, pragmatically) political system, coupled with the growing confidence derived from 45 years of success. The extension of democracy to non-democratic, right-wing authoritarian regimes only added to this confidence.

In Central and South-Eastern Europe, on the other hand, the situation was very different indeed, qualitatively so in a number of respects. First, the historical legacy of state-building as a contest between local élites and ruling empires had given birth to rather low capacity states, which experienced greater difficulty than their counterparts in the West in generating consent and, generally, a sense that modernization had failed, democracy had not worked, and modernity had eluded these polities.[14] The imposition of Communism proved to be yet another failure, in essence, because its concept of modernity was non-consensual, simplistic to the point of reductionism, and perceived as alien. By and large, Communism worked against the grain of existing cultures, thereby being quite incapable of mobilizing either state or social capacity, even while it did create a kind of distorted and unwilled modernity, together with complexity, but was necessarily prevented by its ideology from developing the cognitive and institutional instruments to negotiate that complexity. Crucially, Communism could not and did not create the means for resolving the conflicts that derived from modernity—the normal contest of ideas, interests, institutions—because it insisted on a very high level of ideologically determined homogeneity and thus could not provide the cognitive and concrete instruments for resolving the problems of complexity that it had created.[15]

All this is barren ground for liberal pluralism; but there is worse to follow. When Communism collapsed, it was not—as many thought at the time—a matter of the death of an ideology that could be relatively easily replaced. Rather, seeing that Communism had sought to bring into being its own model of modernity and particular type of all-embracing state, not to mention its own reality-definition and exclusive plausibility structure, the disappearance of Communism necessarily meant the failure of the Communist state. Consequently, the post-Communist state is a low capacity, low prestige agency, which is required to preside over a massive transformation of structures, practices, belief systems, moral regulation, attitudes, values, and aspirations. Simultaneously, Communism had largely destroyed the rather weak civil societies that had existed at the time of takeover, so that unlike in Western political communities, ethnicity was effectively the sole source of coherence in the public sphere, the pre-eminent meaningful narrative of collectivity, the only principle of cohesion, solidarity, criteria of success and failure and so on, to command general support.

The new states of Central and South-Eastern Europe—in this sense they are all new, even if some are significantly newer than others: the states of the Yugoslav space, the Baltic states, Slovakia—are rebuilding from the bottom up, using somewhat low-grade top down resources to complete a modernization towards which they have long aspired, but which demands painful adjustment. The weakness of the state makes it extremely difficult to establish and enforce the rule of law, which in turn undermines trust and thereby erodes the potential for liberalism.

Much has been written about civil society and its function in sustaining liberal pluralism. In the post-Communist world, civil society has been endowed with a democratizing responsibility that is not really being discharged. This requires an explanation. In effect, although these civil-social entities have the appearance of being the bearers of democratic values; in reality they are something else. By and large, they tend to be weakly rooted, not least because these societies lack the material resources to support well-established lobbies and similar group activity. But in some ways more importantly, they are in reality at best semi-civil, in as much as they tend to operate within a partial view of society as a whole, see themselves as representing an ideological and thus a party-ideological interest, and not operate invariably in accordance with democratic values.

Furthermore, civil society in the post-Communist world cannot function in ways that its Western counterpart does because of the weakness of the state. At this point, a deeper analysis is called for. The underlying conception of democracy in the post-Communist world was heavily influenced by the thinking of the democratic opposition that had challenged Communist Party rule in the years before 1989. The perception of the democratic opposition was primarily governed by two broad principles. One of these was that the state was the Communist state, which it was inclined to see in moralistic terms as inherently negative and thus condemned the public sphere to function without the strong legal framing of state regulation. The other was the propensity—the other end of the polarity—to regard society and the private sphere as the reservoir of virtue.

The democratic opposition had no clear theory of the vital separation between public and private and, may be even more gravely, had no theory of the state, other than as a source of oppression.[16] This was in many ways understandable, given where the democratic opposition was coming from politically, but the absence of a clear understanding of institutional and procedural rules and of the key role of the state as the guardian of legality has contributed to the hybrid that post-Communism has become—large but weak states, attempting to fulfil far-reaching undertakings, like their own dismantling through the redistribution of state assets, but without any clear central concept of what the state is, what a just society might be, what are necessary rules and what are superfluous, and the like.[17]

It follows from the foregoing that those making direct comparisons between the established democratic state and the post-Communist state are doing something rather useless, because the underlying culture and value systems between the two are so divergent. At the journalistic level, the comparison can become fertile ground for moralizing rhetoric—'these East Europeans are inherently unde-mocratic'—with racist overtones—'they are predisposed to undemo-cratic behaviour, irrationality, enmity etc by descent'. This is a classic example of reliance on a natural metaphor, a practice that usually harbours hidden agendas.

The problem is much deeper and more intractable. The states and political communities of Western Europe have been able to evolve liberal practices not through some kind of genetic endowment, but because of real historical and sociological reasons, the absence of alien, imperial rule being among the most important. This experience of native rule was enormously influential in the construction of the modern high capacity state that could generate consent among the governed. At the same time, it also meant that élites had extensive cul-tural capital to draw on in government and the corresponding self-legitimation and self-confidence when it came to the distribution of power. This dynamic has been one of the crucial underpinnings of liberalism, in as much as modernity implies continuously growing complexity and that in turn requires provision for the access to power for new political actors.

Furthermore, Western European élites have been much better placed in the grounding of the first and second order rules that govern the exercise of power.[18] First order rules include the formal regulation by which every system operates, like the constitution, laws govern-ing elections, procedures for the settlement of conflict and the like. Second order rules are the informal, tacit rules of the game that are internalized as a part of doxa, and this necessarily means that all the political actors accept the others as insiders to the political com-munity and that they will abide by the same set of rules. In sum, whereas in well-established democracies, second order rules function smoothly, in the post-Communist world they do not. In effect, the different political contestants under post-Communism begin from the assumption that they are the possessors of the single truth and hence that other political actors, who represent a different single truth— the logical contradiction is deliberate—are motivated by ill-will or worse. This makes compromise extremely difficult to bring about, seeing that policy differences are understood as ontological differences. This cleavage extends to the nature of democracy itself, which is consistently regarded as an ideology and a teleology, rather than as a set of broadly accepted values and procedures that are universally binding.

The absence or weakness of second order rules means that the key democratic values of self-limitation, feedback, moderation, commitment, responsibility, the recognition of the value of competing, multiple rationalities cannot function adequately, given that other political actors—potentially all other political actors—are seen as enemies and not as opponents. In effect, political parties in the post-Communist world tend to see themselves, though this is denied, as if they were or should be Communist parties, possessors of a single, ideologically determined truth.

Hence, unlike in the West, there is a real fear that the loss of power through defeat at the polls can mean destruction of one's attainments because the other political actors seek wholly to transform the system. From this perspective, ruling parties cannot afford to be liberal and tolerant, they are impelled to maximize their political gains and make them irreversible. And it should be made very clear that in this framework behaviour of this kind is completely rational. Thus it is erroneous to see post-Communist systems as post-modern; on the contrary in many ways they should be seen as a destructive but rational variant of modernity. The outcome of this is that the discourse of liberalism remains stuck at the level of rhetoric, not least because it is claimed by one particular political current as its exclusive, monopoly possession. In such systems, trust is very hard to enroot. Trust in institutions and procedures is based not only on respect for overt regulation, but equally on the deeper, implicit values of organic solidarity.

The foregoing applies to intra-ethnic politics. Matters are worse when it comes to inter-ethnicity, because dealing with ethnic others is burdened by infinitely greater problems of lack of trust, of solidarity and absence of shared codes of informal communication. Different ethnic groups differ not least because they have different doxic baggage. They make the world differently and believe that theirs is the best and only morally legitimate way of doing so. In this light, the formal provisions of citizenship are little more than a step in the right direction, a point of entry into the political system for members of ethnic minorities, but there is no guarantee at all that they will be able to move very far beyond that point of entry. The outcome is perfectly logical and sticks in the craw of Western multiculturalists—and their local allies—the existence of parallel societies, which have a minimum of overlap and are engaged primarily in producing and reproducing their own thought-worlds and thought-styles without paying much attention to other groups.

Note that this can and does happen within the same physical space, not least in urban areas. Members of different ethnic groups meet at the surface level, go through ritual courtesies and leave it that. There is no deeper communication or understanding, let alone 'the sharing' so beloved of multiculturalists. The cases of the Hungarians in Transylvania or the Russians in Estonia illustrate these processes very well. Contact between Hungarians and Romanians is minimal, polite, and superficial; this even applies to the one area where one might have expected more intense contact, the University of Cluj, where teaching takes place in Hungarian as well as in Romanian.[19] By the same token, Russians in Estonia, two-thirds of whom had citizenship by the end of the 1990s, rarely mix with Estonians, have separate cultural institutions and lives, and seem more concerned with cultural reproduction than with multiculturalism.[20]

Viewed against this background of a poor fit between institutions, values and cultural norms, the record of the post-Communist states with respect to liberal pluralism is rather better than is assumed to be. Despite sensationalist stories of 'fascism', 'ancient hatreds' and something that approaches an assumption of a genetic inheritance of violence and intolerance, the post-Communist states have avoided inter-ethnic war—with the exception of Yugoslavia, where a very special set of avoidable circumstances produced full state collapse with no agreed alternative. There are countless tensions, but these have found political solutions. Likewise, the pattern of evolution in the political system pointed towards democracy, though with serious shortcomings where democratic values were concerned. Numerous changes of government had taken place as the outcome of democratically conducted elections and only one state, Belarus, was sliding towards authoritarianism. Nudged by the West, the integration of inter-ethnic relations into something like a democratic framework, while far from ideal, was broadly moving towards the often reluctant acceptance of alterity both inter-ethnically and intra-ethnically, though the Kosovo war of 1999 was a prominent exception.

Time, however, posed a different problem. All the states of the region were determined to 'rejoin Europe' and this meant not only accepting the rules by which Western Europe governed itself but respecting them in practice. Whereas in the early years of post-Communism, it was a common enough response on the part of nationalists and others uneasy with diversity, that democracy in the region was not significantly different from that in the West, stricter monitoring and insistence on the Copenhagen criteria, particularly during accession negotiations to the European Union, created a new and much tighter conditionality than before. To what extent the European Union would overlook deviations was unclear, but it seems a reasonably good guess that inter-ethnic relations would be much more stringently scrutinized than intra-ethnic tensions.

At the end of the day, the problems of Central and South-Eastern Europe with the absorption of democracy as both consent and values would always involve greater difficulty than most people anticipated and the liminality that governed the political systems of the region would endure.[21] But the question that many in the post-Communist asked was this: was post-Communist democracy treated as of being of a lower quality than the systems of the West? Something of an answer was given in 1999, when Haider's *Freiheitliche Partei* (FPÖ) in Austria, which stood well to the right of the Western European mainstream, received well over a quarter of the votes in the elections. This caused little more than raised eyebrows at the time, though some commented that if any of Haider's counterparts in any of the post-communist states had done as well, an OSCE mission would have arrived in that country within 24 hours.

However, when the FPÖ was actually included in the coalition, the other members of the EU opted to boycott the new Austrian government. The question of double standards had been raised in a dramatic fashion, but not answered in any principled way in the political realm. There is a clear evidence that with respect to inter-national law on human rights, especially the law on the protection of minorities, the difference between West and East in Europe was one of degree and not of kind,[22] but the Central and South-East Europeans remained concerned that human rights enforcement was treated as automatic in the West, but something to be monitored in the post-Communist world. In this sense, a double standard was in existence.

Furthermore, the Haider boycott, and for that matter the demand

for the extradition of Pinochet, raised another unanswered question—
if the FPÖ and the Chilean dictator were unacceptable because of
their fascistoid qualities, then how should Europe deal with their
communist counterparts? Crimes against humanity were, after all,
single and seamless, but the issue has remained buried for the time
being. This was unfortunate from the perspective of the Central and
South-Eastern Europeans, because it implied that their history and
memory were regarded by the West as less significant. In other words,
another double standard was creeping into existence.

It may be that the application of these double standards was legitimate. The burdens of the short- and long-term past, the negative
practices of post-Communism itself, the dangers of spillover from
the interface between democracy and authoritarian systems—like
Serbia—all implied that greater vigilance was needed. To that extent,
democracy and liberalism could be taken for granted in Western
Europe, whereas in Central and South-Eastern Europe it could not.
But whatever the argument, it would always be difficult actually to
assess when liberal pluralism had, in fact, reached consolidation in the
region, because of the undiagnosed diversity of local political cultures
and differences in establishing the necessary success and failure criteria that this generated.

NOTES

1. These values are derived from Weber, Max 'Politik als Beruf' *Gesammelte Poli-
tische Schriften*, 2nd edition, (Tübingen: Mohr Verlag, 1958), 493–548.
2. Bourdieu, Pierre *The Field of Cultural Production* (Cambridge: Polity, 1993).
3. Lijphart, Arendt *The Politics of Accommodation* (Berkeley, CA: University
of California Press, 1968); Macartney, C.A. *The Habsburg Empire 1790–1918*
(London: Weidenfeld and Nicolson, 1968).
4. The term is taken from Berger, Peter *The Sacred Canopy: Elements of a Sociological Theory of Religion* (New York, NY: Doubleday, 1967).
5. On TimeSpace, see Koselleck, Reinhart, 'The Temporalisation of Concepts',
Finnish Yearbook of Political Thought Vol.1 (Jyväskylä: SoPhi, 1997), 16–24:
and Boyarin, Jonathan (ed.) *Remapping Memory: the Politics of TimeSpace*
(Minneapolis, MN: University of Minneapolis Press, 1994). On boundaries, see
Barth, Fredrik (ed.) *Ethnic Groups and Boundaries: the Social Organisation of
Culture Difference* (Bergen/Oslo, CA: Universitetsforlaget, 1969). On moral
worth, see Horowitz, Donald, *Ethnic Groups in Conflict* (Berkeley, CA: Uni-
versity of California Press, 1985).
6. Eliade, Mircea *The Myth of the Eternal Return: Cosmos and History* (London:
Penguin, 1954).

7. Kertzer, David I. *Ritual, Politics and Power* (New Haven, CT: Yale University Press, 1988).

8. Bojtár, Endre *Bevezetés a baltisztikába: a balti kultúra régiségben* (Budapest: Osiris, 1997).

9. Heller, Agnes *Az idegen* (New York and Budapest: Múlt es Jövö, 1997).

10. Said, Edward, *Orientalism* (London: Penguin, 1978).

11. Mann, Michael *The Sources of Power: The Rise of Class and Nation-States 1760–1914* (Cambridge: Cambridge University Press, 1993); Scott, James C., *Seeing like a State: How Certain Schemes to Improve the Human Condition Have Failed* (New Haven, CT: Yale University Press, 1998).

12. Schöpflin, George *Nations, Identity, Power: the New Politics of Europe* (London: Hurst, 2000).

13. McCrone, David *The Sociology of Nationalism* (London: Routledge, 1998).

14. Glenny, Misha, *The Balkans 1804–1999: Nationalism, War and the Great Powers* (London: Granta, 1999).

15. Schöpflin, George *Politics in Eastern Europe 1945–1992* (Oxford: Blackwell, 1993).

16. Havel, Vaclav et al. *The Power of the Powerless* (London: Hutchinson, 1985).

17. Mastnak, Tomaz, 'Fascists, Liberals and Anti-Nationalism' in Richard Caplan and John Feffer, *Europe's New Nationalism: States and Minorities in Conflict* (Oxford: Oxford University Press, 1996), 59–74; Sztompka, Piotr 'The Intangibles and Imponderables of the Transition to Democracy' *Studies in Comparative Communism* 24:3 (September 1991).

18. Offe, Claus, 'Agenda, Agency and Aims of Central East European Transitions', in Stefano Bianchini and George Schöpflin (eds.), *State Building in the Balkans: Dilemmas on the Eve of the 21st Century* (Ravenna: Longo, 1998); and Offe, Claus *Modernity and the State: East, West* (Cambridge: Polity, 1996).

19. KAM, *Valtozásban? Elemzések a romániai magyar társadalomról* (Csikszereda/ Miercurea-Ciuc: ProPrint, 1995); remarks on the University of Cluj are based personal observation over two visits, in 1998 and 1999.

20. Interview in Tallinn, July 1999. See also Marju Lauristin and Peeter Vihalemm, *Return to the Western World: Cultural and Political Perspectives on the Estonian Post-communist Transition* (Tartu: Tartu University Press, 1997).

21. Bauman, Zygmunt 'After the Patronage State: a Model in Search of Class Interests', in Christopher Bryant and Edmund Mokrzycki (eds.), *The New Great Transformation* (London: Routledge, 1994), 14–35.

22. Biró, Anna-Mária, 'Westward Enlargement—Law and Enforcement: A Minority Rights Perspective from Central and Eastern Europe', in George Schöpflin (ed.), *The Westward Enlargement of Central Europe* (London: School of Slavonic and Eastern European Studies Occasional Paper No.43, 2000), 13–23.

Rethinking the State, Minorities, and National Security

Urszula Doroszewska

The topic of ethnic relations continues to attract students of East European and post-Soviet politics and fuel lively academic debates. Ethnic conflict, on which these discussions typically focus, may indeed be the most visible, and perhaps the most 'colourful' of problems facing the region. However, not enough attention in this debate has been devoted to the general context in which national tensions arise in the post-Soviet political space and, in particular, to the nature of the post-Soviet state.

Will Kymlicka's theoretical propositions are based on the premise that these post-Soviet states function in the same way other European states do, that is, they have the political will to solve problems resulting from their ethnocultural diversity; there exists some kind of national 'majority' which defines the state's policy toward national 'minority'; and the state has a vision of what this policy should or should not be, and makes the appropriate decisions to meet these objectives. In my view, this assumption, which the author never fully articulates, is unwarranted. To substantiate this claim, I examine the nature of the state, national security, and the identification of a national minority in the post-Soviet context, and then look at the specific example of the Crimean Tatars.

The Existence of the State

Before addressing the question of minority policy in the former USSR, one should examine the power structure in post-Soviet successor states by asking a few basic questions. If political entities which emerged from the ruins of the USSR are real states, in whose name are they governed? Where are their power centres located and who is responsible for the decision-making process? One does not have to be a learned Sovietologist to see that most post-Soviet states are controlled by organized crime groups who have succeeded in privatizing national economies, and whose direct interest in governance rarely goes beyond the taxation system and foreign trade. At best, decisions in these states are made by the executive power. More frequently, however, the actual decision-makers are large economic organizations linked to oil and weapons trade, while the role of parliaments is reduced to that of discussion clubs. Ruling élites show little interest in other aspects of social life such as education, health care, and minority issues unless minorities are seen as a security threat. Due to a passivity learned under the Communist system, the public at large does not object to this state of affairs.

Even if some elements of state policy toward national minorities are defined, rarely is there one single power centre responsible for its implementation. Sometimes, as in the case of Russia's policy in the North Caucasus, there are several power centres enforcing diametrically opposed policies. Due to the limited and selective interest of the ruling élites in the affairs of the state, in several areas of state activity no policy decisions are being made let alone implemented. Take the example of education. To assess the shape of minority education one should see how the educational needs of the 'majority' are met by the state. In the countries of the former Soviet Union the state is in the process of winding down its activities in the field of education. No financing for the state-owned institutions of higher learning is available, so steep tuition fees are being introduced on a massive scale. Primary schools do not receive funding for the maintenance of school buildings or the supply of teaching material. Teachers go unpaid for months and no new textbooks are published. If the state fails to address the most elementary needs of education in the state language, one can hardly expect it to successfully run an educational system for minority groups or even bother to work out a concept of minority education.

The governments of the successor states to the USSR do not regulate social life, do not collect taxes, and do not fight crime. Social change occurs spontaneously. In all the new post-Soviet states minority groups strengthen their positions. It is clear that their rising aspirations and escalation of demands cannot be stopped because the state is too weak to control the process. In any case, the return to a model in which minorities were unconditionally subordinated to majorities appears unlikely. Therefore the multination model becomes more realistic—but we should not misunderstand the nature of this change. It occurs spontaneously as a result of weakness, and not as a result of any consciously planned activities of the state apparatus.

The weakness of the post-Soviet state cannot be explained entirely through the difficulties of transition to a market economy, the psychological resistance of the élites to change, and its inability to make political decisions. This weakness also results from a lack of vision about the direction in which the state should be moving: toward European integration, market economy, and NATO, or toward integration with Russia and a return to Communism? Ukraine offers a good example of a state at the crossroads. Pro-Russian and pro-Communist forces are not sufficiently strong to impose their vision of Ukrainian statehood that would block reforms necessary to move Ukraine in the alternative direction. 'Pro-Russian Communists' and their 'democratic' opponents take diametrically opposed positions on national minorities issues. Pro-Russian Communists, who see the German, Polish, Jewish, and Tatar minorities in Ukraine as allies of Western capitalism and a potential security threat, are determined to prevent any strengthening of their position. Their Communist worldview has no understanding of, and is fundamentally hostile to, diversity. On the other hand, the democratic and pro-Western camp is free of minority bias and seeks to solve minority issues in a civilized fashion. However, it is too weak to translate them into an official policy of the state.

National Security Issues

Theories of multiculturalism proposed by Western scholars are based on the experience of Western European and American societies, which for at least a couple of decades have enjoyed stable democracy. National minorities of Western Europe share with other nations of the region a number of common values. They include the convictions that: (1) law constitutes the basis of social life; (2) a multi-party system and parliamentary democracy constitute a superior way of political participation to the mono-party and Communist system; (3) the market economy is superior to the planned economy as the basis for economic development; and (4) NATO represents a more reliable ally in security matters than, say, Iran and Libya. Such understandings are universally shared by the citizens of those Central and East European countries recently admitted to NATO membership—Poland, the Czech Republic, and Hungary—including national minorities residing on their territories.

Even if the most radical wishes of national minorities were realized, such as the emergence of a Basque state, an independent Corsica, or the break-up of Belgium along national lines, this would not pose a serious threat to European security, and the new states would not rush to conclude military alliances with Russia, Iran, or China. In Western Europe, national minority issues concern culture, education, political representation, and social equality. They are not issues of special interest to military intelligence.

It would be naïve, however, to apply some of these generalizations to minority problems in the former USSR. Minorities in post-Soviet states often assume diametrically opposed geopolitical positions to the majorities. For example, the Armenian minority in Georgia actively seeks Russia's political support and opposes the withdrawal of Russian troops from the territory of Georgia. In Ukraine, the Russian national minority in Crimea supports Communism—that is a system incompatible with parliamentary democracy. In the parliamentary elections conducted in April 1988 in the Autonomous Republic of Crimea, the ethnic Russian vote allowed the Communists to capture as much as 40 per cent of the seats—much more than in other parts of Ukraine. An overwhelming majority of Crimea's Russian population supports the idea of the re-annexation of Crimea by Russia and opposes integration with the West, as sought by independent Ukraine. Also in Crimea, the Crimean Tatars, who do not have a single representative in the parliament of the Autonomous Republic display a strong anti-Communist bias, want Ukraine to join NATO, and actively support integration with the West and Turkey.

Over the last few years Russia has consistently tried to undermine the new independent states by fostering minority separatism and arming separatist forces. In such a way, some of the movements for greater minority autonomy degenerated into regular wars of secession that claimed thousands of victims. Such was the case in the bloody confrontation between the Abkhaz and the Georgians, in which the Abkhaz nation of fewer than 100,000 people defeated the regular army of the Georgian state, whose population is 5 million. With Russian military assistance, the Abkhaz separatists succeeded in detaching from Georgia a vast chunk of territory. Likewise, the

200,000-strong Armenian community in Nagorno-Karabakh, which initially called for cultural autonomy within Azerbaijan, within a couple of years had defeated the regular army of Azerbaijan (population 7 million) and claimed one-fifth of its territory. Both Abkhazia and Nagorno-Karabakh remain to this day under the control of armed military formations that prevent the return of refugees or a form of international control.

The two examples of Abkhazia and Nagorno-Karabakh demonstrate that the question of national minorities in the former USSR is much more directly tied to national security concerns than is the case in Western Europe or Canada. The security of nations of the Caucasus and Crimea can only be guaranteed if Russia refrains from exploiting minority issues in the region, and accepts 'western' standards of political conduct.

Who Is a 'National Minority'?

Terminological questions—who is and who is not a nation or a national minority—in the rapidly changing political conditions of the former USSR acquire a political dimension. Everyone familiar with central and eastern Ukraine is aware of the fact that the border between Russians and Ukrainians is fluid—regardless of how this border is defined by political élites in Russia and Ukraine. The region is inhabited by millions of people who cannot clearly answer the question of who they are: Russian or Ukrainian. The question itself strikes them as absurd. They know from school the standards of literary Russian and in everyday life use Russian, albeit with a 'southern accent' and borrowings from Ukrainian. To call these people 'Russians', and to claim that Ukraine is 'home to a many-million-strong Russian minority', amounts to a political declaration.

In the last couple of years one can observe the growing acceptance of the idea of Ukrainian statehood among these 'Russians', a concept they originally found awkward and hard to comprehend. Recent developments—such as the war in Chechnya—which claimed the lives of many Russian conscripts, and the economic chaos in Russia—seem to have further weakened the Russian ethnic identity of this population. It may therefore be more precise to describe this group as 'Russian-speaking citizens of Ukraine' rather than 'Russians'. On the other hand, the Russian population of Crimea is distinctly Russian in terms of its ethnic and political identity, and can legitimately be called a Russian national minority in Ukraine.

Choosing a Model for the Crimean Tatars

Will Kymlicka questions the appropriateness of the Crimean Tatars' self-definition as an 'indigenous nation'. Let me briefly explain how the Crimean Tatars themselves understand this label. They regard Crimea as their only homeland to which they have rightfully returned after several decades of forced exile, and from which they now have no intention of leaving.[1] In this respect, their situation in Ukraine differs significantly from that of Poles, Germans, Russians, Armenians, Romanians, and other national groups that have their states (ethnic homelands) outside Ukraine's borders. Kin-states can to some extent meet the social and cultural needs of these minorities, and offer them refuge in an emergency—as currently is the case for Poles, Germans, Czechs, and Russians repatriated from Central Asia or the Caucasus.

Crimean Tatars see themselves as a nation, not an 'ethnic group' or a 'national minority'.[2] Much of the confusion regarding their status in Crimea comes from the term 'Tatar', which has been used historically by Russians to refer to all Muslims regardless of their ethnic origins and geographic roots, be it the Caucasus, the Urals, or the Volga valley. For example, the Turkic-speaking population of Azerbaijan was traditionally referred to as the 'Caucasian Tatars'. Turkophone Muslims of Crimea, on the other hand, describe themselves as *Kyrymyly*, best translated simply as 'Crimeans'. The term 'Crimean Tatars', applied to them by others, may be misleading as it implies that the Muslim inhabitants of Crimea are not a separate nation but part of a large and vaguely defined Tatar 'ethnos', at home somewhere in the steppes of Asia. Therefore, many Russians still see the Crimean Tatars as immigrants from Asia rather than rightful citizens of Crimea. Soviet authorities did their best to preserve and reinforce the negative stereotype of 'Tatars' in the minds of the Slavs who moved to Crimea in the 1960s and 1970s, and who today represent a large majority of the peninsula's population. Many of them continue to hold the view that the deportation of the Crimean Tatars was an act of historical justice and that the Tatars should have stayed in Central Asia. It is precisely in order to counter the stereotype of 'savages from Asia' and to emphasize their ties to the Crimean soil that the Crimean Tatars insist on being an 'indigenous nation' of the peninsula.

Crimean Tatars have a 600-year old tradition of statehood in Crimea—the Crimean Khanate—in addition to rich literary, architectural, and musical traditions. Moreover, they have a tradition of conducting their own state policy, which included military and diplomatic relations with other European nations. Conquered in the late eighteenth century and absorbed into the Russian empire, the Crimean Tatar state was revived after 1917 as an autonomous Soviet republic. The Crimean ASSR became the first Muslim country to grant all citizens, including women, full voting rights. The republic was eventually abolished by the Bolsheviks who moved to destroy finally the Crimean Tatar nation by deporting the entire population to Central Asia in 1944.[3]

In the 1960s and 1970s the Crimean Tatars created in the places of their resettlement the largest civil rights movement in the former USSR. Thousands of Crimean Tatars signed letters of protest to Khrushchev and organized demonstrations to demand the right to return to their Crimean homeland.[4] Their massive return to Crimea in the late 1980s was superbly organized.[5] A self-governing body, the majlis, was established in every Tatar settlement. The majlis system functions at three levels: village majlises elect regional majlises, which in turn elect their delegates to Kurultay, the national assembly. Milli Majlis, the highest representative organ of the Crimean Tatars is elected by the Kurultay. Unfortunately, Ukrainian authorities do not recognize this efficient and well-run system of self-government. The majlis system, in fact, is a state-like organism without the actual political power of a state. Crimean Tatars have no state of their own and their self-government functions within the *de facto* purely Russian political environment of the Crimean Autonomous Republic.

In direct conflict with the Russian administration of Crimea and in compliance with Ukrainian laws, but without any outside support, Crimean Tatars are currently building their system of national education. It is noteworthy that the Majlis enjoys great respect among the Crimean Tatar population. There are still individuals who, under very harsh economic and sociopolitical conditions, are willing to assume the responsibility for the well-being of the Crimean Tatar community. It is also interesting that many local Russians indirectly recognize the legality of the Majlis by turning to it—rather than to local police—in the case of conflicts with the Tatar population.

Crimean Tatars, who number 260,000 and make up 12 per cent of the peninsula's population, have no representation in the parliament of the Autonomous Republic of Crimea. However, they have two seats in the Ukrainian parliament in Kiev. They are incomparably more active, socially and politically, than the Slavic population of

Crimea. They demand supplementary elections to compete for seats in the Crimean parliament, recognition of the Majlis, and settlement of the citizenship problem by Ukraine.

That these legitimate demands of the Crimean Tatars have not been met in independent Ukraine is explained by the weakness of the Ukrainian state and the resulting inability to develop and implement a consistent minority policy.[6] This situation is further reinforced by the political deadlock in which pro-Western democrats and anti-Western Communists, with their respective visions of Ukraine's future, effectively neutralize each other. Hostile to the Tatars, the Communists oppose their political demands. Against this, the Tatars have consistently voiced distinctly anti-Communist views, and supported independent Ukraine, within its current borders, and its pro-democratic camp.[7] In the last parliamentary elections, Mustafa Dzimilev and Refat Chubarov, the only Crimean Tatar members of the Ukrainian parliament, ran as candidates of the Rukh movement. In the media, Crimean Tatar leaders have consistently articulated a vision of a modern and capitalist Ukraine, allied with Western Europe and Turkey. This defines the position of the Crimean Tatars in the political landscape of independent Ukraine. In Crimea, they represent the only pro-democratic political force. Although cornered and isolated, they are by far the most effective and best organized political group in regional politics. This makes them a convenient target of attacks by the anti-Western and pro-Communist majority in Crimea—and provides one more reason why they need protection.

In the long run, I believe the Crimean Tatar question would be best solved by a model of the two-nation state, despite the huge disproportion in the populations of the Ukrainian (60 million) and Crimean Tatar nations. In the last few years the Tatars have demonstrated their capacity to establish and maintain a political system based on democratic representation. Their interests are strongly tied to Crimea and not to those of any other state. The establishment of a Crimean Tatar Autonomous Republic in Ukraine would, of course, require that the interests of other minorities residing in Crimea are taken into consideration. The model of 'two nations in one state' would pose no security threat to Ukraine, which is home to many other national minorities. For the Crimean Tatars, it would offer generous compensation for their historical misfortunes, adequate to their political aspirations and capacity for effective self-government.

NOTES

1. Deklaratsia o natsional'nom suverenitete krymskotatarskogo naroda, *Dokumenty kurultaya krymskotatarskogo naroda 1991–1998*, Simferopol 1999.
2. *Ibid.*
3. *The Tatars of Crimea. Return to Homeland*, Edward A. Allworth (ed.) London 1988, 180.
4. 'Krymskie Tatary v *Khronike Tekushchikh Sobytii*,' *Crimean Studies*, 5–6, September–November 2000, Kyiv; Alan Fisher, *The Crimean Tatars*, Stanford 1987, 165–201.
5. Urszula Doroszewska, 'Crimea—whose country?' *Uncaptive Minds*, 3, 1992, 39.
6. Alexander Piskun, 'Crimean Tatar People's Integration into Ukrainian Society: Problems of Political-Legal Regulation,' *Crimean Studies*, 1, January 2000, 79.
7. 'We Prefer Ukraine' An Interview with Nadir Bekirov, by Urszula Doroszewska, *Uncaptive Minds*, 2, 1995, 55.

On the Chances of Ethnocultural Justice in East Central Europe

Tibor Várady

Introductory Remarks

In his insightful and bitter essay 'The Failure of the Elite', Milovan Danojlic says:

The defeat is complete. The winner is post-communism with a nationalist face. What we proposed turned out to be lukewarm, unconvincing, and abstract. We failed to offer anywhere near satisfactory answers to any of the painful questions raised by the break-up of Yugoslavia. 'Democracy solves everything' is what we kept repeating, and each time we were less and less convinced of what we were saying. How can you bring to democracy tribes that hate each other? How can you find harmony between the principle of the sovereignty of the new states and the duty to respect minorities? And who would, anyway, accept today the status of a minority? Only those who have no choice. (Milovan Danojlic, *Muka duhu (Trouble with the Soul)*, (Belgrade, 1996), 404.)

Milovan Danojlic is one of the very best Serbian writers of our time. He has not been engaged in politics. During the last decade he spent most of his time in Paris. Yet as an intellectual, he felt co-responsible for failing to offer anything beyond traditional liberal arguments.

Will Kymlicka, in summarizing those liberal arguments, points to their underlying premise that '... once democratic rights and institutions were effectively established and accessible to all citizens, people would stop mobilizing on the basis of ethnocultural affiliation.'[1] He cites another example of the traditional liberal argument: '... ethnocultural conflict was a substitute for modernization and economic well-being. On this view, the real problem was that some people felt left behind in the process of modernization, and once a certain level of economic development was achieved and accessible to all citizens, people would stop mobilizing on the basis of ethnocultural affiliation.'[2] The chain of events in the former Yugoslavia has certainly not proved this contention. Admittedly it has not been refuted either, since the desired level of modernization and economic well-being—which could arguably stop mobilization on the basis of ethnic affiliation—has not been achieved, and is nowhere in sight.

Kymlicka's own view, however, is that, 'There is not a shred of evidence from Western democracies that the achievement of democracy, economic prosperity, and personal tolerance will lead to an abatement of ethnocultural mobilization.'[3] It is not likely that Yugoslavia, or the rest of East Central Europe (ECE) would provide the missing evidence. Even allowing for the benefit of the doubt, the events of the last ten years in Yugoslavia have shown the simple fact that without recognizing the importance of ethnocultural justice, and without basic arrangements that would assure some balance among ethnic aspirations, the process of modernization cannot start to unfold. The society might very well wish economic well-being but will remain unable to make purposeful and concerted efforts to achieve it. Whether modernization and economic well-being, on the one hand, and the decrease of ethnic tensions, on the other, are correlated remains questionable. Even if they were, the sequencing must be reversed, or maybe intertwined.

It is important to note that the 'democracy solves everything' slogan resonates better with majority aspirations. Believers in ethnocultural neutrality and group-neutral regulation—and who are proponents of a majority perspective—would usually stop at the 'one man, one vote' principle, asserting that liberal tenets only require us to make sure that 'one man' means any man (or at least any citizen) irrespective of his/her ethnic background, race, or religion. From a minority perspective, the requirements of fairness and equality confront us with additional issues. To mention a simple one, it is important to know in which language(s) electoral ballots will be printed. A more difficult question arises in societies which, to a greater or lesser extent, possess the characteristics of 'ethnic societies',[4] that is, environments where a history of unchecked ethnic rivalry often translates into an ethnic vote. In such circumstances, fairness and equality might require regulation which would yield adequate, or at least some, minority representation in spite of existing ethnic undercurrents.

Is Ethnocultural Justice a Novelty in ECE Countries?

The key question put before the contributors to this volume is whether new Western models of ethnocultural justice might assist post-Communist countries in finding a democratic approach to ethnic diversity. To better understand this issue one must probe a prior question: are concepts of ethnocultural justice, public recognition, and accommodation of diversity, novelties in ECE countries? My short answer to this latter question is a simple no. Various societies, states, and their successor states, as well as social thinkers in ECE countries whom one could label 'liberal' within the given social context, were well aware of the fact that ethnocultural neutrality cannot yield social justice and harmony. To mention just one author, Oszkár Jászi, a leading Hungarian sociologist prior to World War I—a time when Hungary was concerned with large groups of non-Hungarians within its borders rather than with large groups of Hungarians outside its borders—stresses: 'One can summarise a minimal program with the following words: people need good schools, good public administration, and a good judiciary. There is only one way towards good schools, good public administration and a good judiciary, which is more important than any technical or institutional perfection, and which can shortly and simply be defined the following way: we shall only have good schools, good public administration, and a good judiciary if people get these in their own language.'[5] This line of reasoning was not an isolated case.

Granted, thoughts of liberal sociologists in ECE countries or elsewhere have rarely been fully translated into political action and legal norms. But rulers, or even dictators, were aware of the fact that ethnocultural neutrality simply does not work in countries where national minorities make up a considerable segment of the population. Rulers may not have been guided by liberal ideas of social justice, but they were aware that the lack of group-sensitive attitudes and regulation could undermine stability. Assuring loyalty to the state is difficult. But it is practically impossible to expect loyalty to a common state and common cause from those whose cherished identity is excluded from common concepts. It is easier to envisage a country as my country if I can refer to it in my language, and if the cultures and languages of that country are reflected in the public domain. During centuries of Ottoman rule in the Balkans, Turkish invaders prudently avoided any temptation to impose one language and one religion.

Lenin spoke often in favour of maintaining diversity—although he opposed the idea of cultural autonomy. He argued that Russian should not be imposed as the only official language in Russia, or later in the Soviet Union. He viewed Switzerland's three official languages positively, noting that 70 per cent of the Swiss population was German, while in Russia only 43 per cent was Russian.[6]

Tito was also well aware that stability in a multicultural country—even under a one-party system—could only be achieved through constant attention to ethnic diversity and balance.[7] Since Tito did not belong to the majority nation in Yugoslavia, for him the option of imposing the majority culture was hardly possible. He was therefore personally limited in his choices for accommodating ethnic and cultural rivalries, and creating a society that is capable of functioning in spite of these rivalries. The remaining option was the difficult task of forging a balance.

The point here is that the reverberations of 'liberal-pluralist' thinking will hardly represent a revelation in the Balkans and ECE countries. They simply confirm what was known in better periods of the history of these countries. And yet, the expansion and growing authority of 'liberal-pluralist' concepts in Western political thinking may have two highly important practical consequences in ECE countries.

First, at a time when the West and Western precepts are clearly regarded in ECE countries as models—and sometimes given more credit than they actually merit—classical liberal teaching that bespeaks ethnocultural neutrality might present a stepping-stone to majority aspirations and demagoguery; and liberal canons, whose perception of equality does not include the right to be different, might justify concepts that equate the majority with normalcy. Using Western-style discourse is a clear rhetorical advantage at a moment in history when practically all ECE countries are aiming at membership in the European Union and NATO and, consistent with this endeavour, are trying to appear as 'euroconforming' as possible. It is material, therefore, to appreciate which principles can be postulated as 'Western' and 'liberal'.

Second, while providing an authoritative justification for a return to the practical wisdom of seeking stability through ethnocultural justice, 'liberal-pluralist' concepts might also help in finding ways of implementing a policy of ethnocultural justice within the context of modern democracies. In Tito's Yugoslavia, in spite of many imperfections and the lack of genuine democracy, a viable accommodation of ethnic identities was achieved. I do not fully see the point of those critics who say that in Yugoslavia the ethnic problem was just brushed under the carpet, not solved. The problem of ethnic differences can never be solved. It needs constant attention—and this applies to Serbs, Croats, Bosnians, Albanians, and Hungarians, just as it applies to ethnic groups in Spain, Belgium, Switzerland, Italy, Finland, and Canada. Tito's recipe for implementation was a blend of culture and party discipline—in some cases more culture, in other cases more party muscle. During the years of break-up, transition, and civil war, both ingredients have practically vanished. What is badly needed now is some guidance on how to achieve ethnocultural justice without traditional devices, and how to build a new culture without party discipline.

On Three Facets of Ethnocultural Justice

I submit that one can identify three facets of ethnocultural justice, albeit distinguished in different societies by their relative values, different tools for implementation, and different levels of recognition. The first facet requires some separate space for minorities. Ethnocultural justice clearly supposes a sphere or space where minorities can organize themselves, at least for cultural interaction. Communist regimes did not recognize the legitimacy of this facet because of their adherence to an inflated notion of public space. Minority demands for a self-reliant network of cultural organizations, or some other form of cultural autonomy, were greeted with the same suspicion as requests for autonomy of the university, or attempts to organize another political party.

The second facet concerns an equitable sharing of public space. On this account, some ECE countries did a much better job under Communism than they did with the first facet. For example, in the former Yugoslavia, within the large sphere of state activities and competencies, more languages were recognized as official, road signs and street names were multilingual, documents were issued and accepted in more than one language, and the state subsidized cultural institutions and media in both majority and minority languages.

The most difficult and most controversial facet of ethnocultural justice is the search for a counterweight which would neutralize ethnic undercurrents and biases, and which would prevent the transformation of the 'one man, one vote' principle into an ethnic monopoly of the majority over the minorities.

Further Thoughts on Neutralizing Ethnic
Undercurrents and Biases

I remember the incident—and the discomfort I felt—when I was a second year law student and a professor of constitutional law explained to us that 'nations' and 'nationalities' in Yugoslavia were entitled to adequate representation in state authorities. I asked him what 'adequate' was, and he responded that proportional representation is usually adequate, but it need not be so. My next question was, 'By what means was this being implemented?' This proved to be politically incorrect. I got an icy response. According to the professor, my query showed that I was lacking optimism and confidence, and although I may have had good intentions, I was in danger of falling under the influence of 'reactionary objectivism'.

During the decades that followed, I never learned what 'reactionary objectivism' actually was, but I got a pretty good idea about what was wrong with my question. Having lived for decades in post-World War II Yugoslavia, I had ample opportunity to observe the concern for adequate ethnic representation in decision-making bodies at all levels. Being a lawyer, I also knew that this was not the consequence of legal rules. This was the 'party line'. In the Autonomous Province of Vojvodina, it was unthinkable not to have Hungarians, Croats, Romanians, Slovaks, and Ruthenians—in addition to Serbs—in the Vojvodina Parliament, local assemblies, executive bodies, and committees of the Communist Party.

The Province of Vojvodina, which became part of Yugoslavia after World War I, has always had a most complex ethnic landscape. (Actually, I have to be careful with the word 'always'. In Central and Eastern Europe—and probably elsewhere as well—national aspirations are sometimes based on events which took place many centuries or even a millennium ago, and I do not really know much about the ethnic structure of Vojvodina, let us say, 900 years ago. I am certain, however, that it has been a most diverse multiethnic region within at least the last 300 years.) Until recently, no ethnic group had an absolute majority in Vojvodina. The Serbs first passed this threshold in 1948, when they reached 50.42 per cent,[8] compared with 26.13 per cent Hungarian and 8 per cent Croat. According to the latest (1991) census, the Autonomous Province of Vojvodina has 2,013,889 inhabitants, of which 56.8 per cent are Serbs (1,143,723) and 16.9 per cent are Hungarians (340,946). The third group is comprised of 168,859 Yugoslavs,[9] or 8.6 per cent. Croats make up 3.7 per cent, Slovaks 3.1 per cent (63,545), and Romanians 1.9 per cent (38,809).[10] Demographic statistics in Vojvodina also include Montenegrins, Gypsies (Roma), Ruthenians, Macedonians, Ukrainians, Moslems, Albanians, and Slovenians. Two minorities which used to play an important role in the economic and cultural life of Vojvodina but have, practically, disappeared since World War II are the Germans, the third largest group before the war, and the Jews.

To bring to life the atmosphere in Vojvodina, and in Yugoslavia, during the first decades after World War II, I will relate an event from my high school days. I remember the consternation when we elected the board of the swimming club in my home town and, as it turned out, all chosen board members were Serbs. The coach and some older members of the club—those who had some political experience—said that this outcome was unacceptable. Most of us, who were in our teens, did not really care about who was on the board. We felt that the outcome was somehow odd, but since we wanted to terminate the boring meeting in the shabby building, some of us argued that one should not interfere with democracy. The president of the club— a former swimmer and later a 'socio-political worker'—explained, however, that democratic elections need not yield democratic results. (Forty years later, I heard almost the same words pronounced by Richard Holbrooke, who had a crucial role in the negotiations to end the war in Bosnia. Waiting for the first post-war election in Bosnia and being wary of its possible outcome, Holbrooke said in an interview to ITN News, 'Democratic elections might bring an undemocratic result'.)[11] The president and coach then approached almost all non-Serbs—there were quite a few Hungarians on the team, one Romanian, and one Jew—and pressured us to become candidates to fill an additional position on the board. At the end of the day, we had a board which was not ethnically homogeneous.

In this case, the reason behind the self-styled affirmative action was not even the endeavour to offset possible ethnic bias. People simply felt that it was wrong—one might say dangerous—to have an ethnically homogeneous leadership in a multi-ethnic environment. Aware of right and wrong patterns, people felt that the right pattern needed to be followed, even in a completely innocuous, and pointless situation. This attitude was rooted in the experience which taught us that ethnic biases do exist, that they might come to the fore if the position at stake were more consequential, and that it is hardly possible to structure a stable multi-ethnic society in ECE countries without a balancing mechanism. Awareness of the real danger posed by an ethnic undercurrent and of the paramount importance of patterns of balance might explain Holbrooke's unexpected turn of phrase—and implied doubt in a Western axiom. In this situation, there was a real danger that elections might simply yield a result that reinforced existing ethnic inequalities in Bosnia.

I learned in Tito's Yugoslavia that law was not the main instrument for the implementation of patterns of balance. More oblique, flexible methods were used, imposing fewer restrictions on those who were in a decision-making position. In line with the one-party system, informal 'consultations' were much more important than elections, and chosen minority representatives were not necessarily people who had the confidence of a minority—the same often applied to representatives of the majority as well. Patterns of balance have also become, to a considerable extent, a matter of culture, and they were often followed, particularly at the local level, without arm twisting or 'consultations'.

One can also question whether law is, indeed, the tool best suited to implement patterns of ethnic balance. To illustrate the problem, suppose my background and experience lead me to the conclusion that it was neither a coincidence nor a result of choices based on merits that the judges in both O. J. Simpson trials—criminal and civil—were from Japanese origin. I accordingly conclude that these were choices based on the wisdom that in a case accompanied by racial tensions and divisions between blacks and whites, the most appropriate judge is someone who is neither black nor white. But this is hardly possible to lay down as a legal rule.

After the disappearance of Tito's mechanisms of power and authority, and after years in which politicians were using and abusing ethnic stereotypes to create a new basis of authority, it became difficult to avoid law as an instrument for accommodating ethnic interests and balance. After the ascension of Milošević to power, the election of judges was one of the first big debates in the Serbian Parliament. The issue was tainted by the Kosovo problem, and the balancing of ethnic undercurrents had to be posed as a legal question. Serbian Members of Parliament argued that judges, including lay judges, should be elected by the Serbian Parliament, rather than locally. The Serbian Parliament had a comfortable Serbian ethnic majority, while local elections in Kosovo could have been influenced—and determined— by the Albanian majority in Kosovo. 'Consultations' were not an available option. In post-Communist countries, elections can no longer be reduced to irrelevance.[12] Unfortunately, the problem was perceived by the Serbian Parliament as an 'either-or' issue, and the result was, predictably, a complete centralization of the election and dismissal of judges and lay judges.[13] Possible compromises—such as quotas, or multilevel elections that would allow some of the judges to be elected by the Serbian Parliament and the remainder by local constituencies—were outside the prevalent range and mode of thinking. A pattern was set in the wrong direction.

There are several ways in which legal regulation might offset ethnic undercurrents. One option is decentralization, that is, territorial and/or personal autonomy. Minorities could be allowed, for example, to organize their own schools. Financing could be arranged by a relatively simple regulation. If all schools were private, minorities should finance their schools with their own money. If schools are state schools, as they are in Yugoslavia, and financed by taxpayers' money, minority schools should receive at least the amount which corresponds to the input of minority taxpayers. On this basis, Hungarian schools in Vojvodina would receive 16.9 per cent of the total amount devoted to schools.[14] In some instances, a blend of decentralization and centralization might be needed. Albanians in Kosovo might get protection through far-reaching territorial autonomy, but in this case, Serbs in Kosovo need either strong protection from Serbian authorities, or some kind of autonomy of their own, or both.

Another avenue of legal remedy is detailed regulation. I shall try to indicate the thrust of the problem through an example. Article 14(2) of the Council of Europe's Framework Convention for the Protection of National Minorities states: 'In areas inhabited by persons belonging to national minorities traditionally or in substantial numbers, if there is sufficient demand, the Parties shall endeavour to ensure, as far as possible and within the framework of their education systems, that persons belonging to those minorities have adequate opportunities for being taught the minority language or for receiving instruction in this language.' This is fine, but it leaves practically everything to interpretation, which is in the hands of state authorities, that is, the majority. Terms like 'adequate', 'as far as possible', or 'shall endeavour', are hardly sufficient shields against biases. More guarantees will be provided by rules such as s.43 of the 1993 Hungarian Act on National and Ethnic Minorities, which states that the state is obliged to start and maintain a minority language class if this is requested by not less than eight parents belonging to the same minority.

Various types of autonomy, interlocking patterns of decentralization and centralization, as well as detailed regulation may pose difficult drafting problems, but these are hardly avoidable in a multicultural society where rivalries persist.

A Missed Opportunity for the Creative Application of Western Precepts of Ethnocultural Justice on ECE Ground— The Dayton Agreement

In 1991, the Serbian Parliament lacked experience in finding ethnocultural balance in an environment where elections—rather than 'consultations'—were expected to determine political results. Liberal-pluralist Western political theory may have represented a source of inspiration, but it was not turned to. Less than five years later, an opportunity arose to employ Western precepts of ethnocultural justice on ECE ground. The circumstances were unusual, and difficult to evaluate. Years of tragic ethnic bloodshed in Bosnia were first accompanied by years of Western hesitation and growing but always less-than-necessary involvement,[15] until finally a decisive Western effort was made—including NATO bombing of Serbian positions—which paved the road towards the Dayton Agreement. In the ensuing situation, leaders of the warring factions and Western diplomats met at a US military base, which they did not leave until they had signed an agreement.

The present Constitution of Bosnia and Herzegovina emerged as Annex IV of the Dayton Agreement. The documents accepted are quite voluminous, and it may not be easy to establish who exactly authored them. It seems to be common ground, however, that American and other Western experts had a considerable role in drafting the documents—just as Western politicians had a considerable role in seeing to their acceptance. The Dayton environment may not have presented a desirable set of circumstances for a creative transfer of Western political theory, yet an opportunity for the exercise of Western influence did exist. The outcome has also created an occasion for critical evaluations.

While venturing into a criticism of the Dayton Agreement, one has to be aware of the fact that it did lay down a framework for a very difficult peace. The balance is delicate and still precarious. Removing elements of its construction—even if this is done with the intention of making improvements—might jeopardize the still uneasy truce. And yet, the Dayton rules will have to be further developed sooner or later, and this necessitates some criticism.

One of the most difficult questions which the drafters of the Dayton Agreement had to face was the relationship between the rights of citizens on the one hand, and the rights of nations and ethnic groups on the other. The roots of both war and peace may lie under this issue. The reader of this Constitution infers that it was drafted by authors belonging to a culture that tends to deny the legal relevance of difference, rather than to a culture in which difference is observed within the domain of legal regulation. Those who conceived the rules of the Constitution probably did not have much experience with group-sensitive regulation, nor with complex structures that aim to provide adequate representation, including access to power-sharing, to groups and persons belonging to ethnic groups. At the same time, these people must have known—and obviously did know—that in Bosnia and Herzegovina, access to decision-making cannot be safeguarded by the 'one man, one vote' principle, and that issues, such as the question of official languages, must not be decided by majority vote.

The problem faced by the drafters was an extremely difficult one. The rules of conduct, which were used to provide an acceptable *modus vivendi* in Bosnia, were only in part a legal regulation. After 1989, essential parts of the solution had lost their main pillars: the pre-eminence of the Communist Party, and a culture of tolerance, which was all but destroyed during the years of war. In the emerging situation, law had to assume a greater and more pervasive role in social regulation, in blending together group-neutral and group-sensitive norms. Models were scarce, and not completely fitting. Given the conceptual predicament—coupled with the time constraint—the drafters had powerful excuses for not doing a perfect job. But even if one makes all of these allowances, the result is somewhat disappointing. In some instances, the problem was simply avoided, while in other places ethnic affiliation is observed with a brutal straightforwardness. One has the feeling that those confronted with the task of incorporating the components of group affiliation into the document lacked empathy towards both the problem itself and group-sensitive regulation as such, perceiving them as an imposition. Some of the rules, as drafted, seem to carry an implicit 'if that's what you want, that's what you will get' message.

An example of avoidance is Article II of the Constitution of Bosnia and Herzegovina, devoted to human rights and fundamental freedoms. This article offers a simple and correct catalogue of traditional individual human rights. It lacks, however, any direct reference—let alone elaboration—of those rights which represent the *differentia specifica* of the Bosnian problem, that is, cultural rights, language rights, and political rights that would endeavour to achieve a balance and sense of justice among the ethnic groups and individual citizens of Bosnia and Herzegovina.

The last paragraph of the Preamble of the Constitution of Bosnia and Herzegovina stresses that: 'Bosniacs, Croats, and Serbs, as constituent peoples (along with Others) and citizens of Bosnia and Herzegovina hereby determine that the Constitution of Bosnia and Herzegovina is as follows...'. This sentence may not be strictly speaking factual, and the inclusion of the people as framers of the Constitution may be nothing more than rhetorical generosity. Yet, at the same time, it identifies the core of the problem. There are three nations which claim—and probably deserve—a special position in all settlements, there are 'Others' who must not be left without rights, and all of them are citizens entitled to civil rights. These rights and claims are not easy to reconcile—and have not been reconciled.

The notion of 'constituent people' has not been clarified, but a number of articles recognize special group rights of Bosniacs, Serbs, and Croats. Completely missing, however, is any attempt to harmonize these rights with the principle of non-discrimination among equal citizens. The Constitution has simply juxtaposed principles and declarations, reaching some sort of a rhetorical balance, but stopping short of real accommodation. Speaking of non-discrimination, Article II (4), states that enjoyment of rights and freedoms 'shall be secured to all persons in Bosnia and Herzegovina without discrimination on any ground such as sex, race, colour, language, religion, political or other opinion, national or social origin, association with a national minority, property, birth or other status.' After this, however, Article IV(1) states that the House of Peoples shall comprise fifteen delegates, specifying that this will include five Croats, five Bosniacs, and five Serbs. Article V is equally direct and brusque: 'The Presidency of Bosnia and Herzegovina shall consist of three members: one Bosniac and one Croat, each directly from the territory of the Federation, and one Serb directly elected from the territory of the Republika Srpska.' This juxtaposition of mutually exclusive precepts threatens to transmute legal norms into empty slogans. How can one believe in the principle of non-discrimination when a Serb from the Federation, or a Bosniac or Croat from the Republika Srpska, do not even have a theoretical chance of being elected to the House of Peoples, or becoming a member of the Presidency, and when citizens who are neither Bosniacs, Serbs, nor Croats—but, let us say, Jews, Hungarians, Ukrainians, or Roma—can simply not be elected to any of these authorities within the country of which they are, in principle, equal citizens with equal rights.

It is plain that the viability of Bosnia is unthinkable without some constitutional guarantees that would strike a balance among the three nations that represent the backbone of Bosnia—and of the conflicts within Bosnia. But there are more subtle methods which would not fly into the face of other constitutional principles, and which could provide some room for the idea of equal citizens. Defining constituencies—instead of predetermining the outcome of elections—could yield acceptable results. It could be quite sufficient to say, for example, that the Republika Srpska elects five members of the House of Peoples, and one member of the Presidency. There is absolutely no reason to add that these people have to be Serbs. They will probably be Serbs, considering the ethnic structure of the voters; opening a chance to non-Serbs would not jeopardize the interests of the Republika Srpska. The situation is somewhat more complicated within the Federation, but even here, a solution is possible. One could, for example, identify cantons with a Bosniac or Croat majority as voting units, and allocate the desired number of slots to cantons or groups of cantons.

To give another example, it is difficult to understand why it was necessary to pronounce in Article VII that the first Governing Board of the Central Bank shall include, in addition to members nominated by the IMF, three members nominated by the Presidency, one Bosniac, one Croat, and one from the Republika Srpska. Again the balance among the 'three constituent peoples' could have been achieved in a more subtle way, allowing, for example, each member of the Presidency to nominate one member of the Governing Board of the Central Bank. It is quite likely that for a while, political realities would yield choices that mirror the ethnic composition of the Presidency, but there is no reason to cement this into a constitutional norm, which is clearly contrary to the principle of non-discrimination underlined in Article II of this very same Constitution. Moreover, even on the grounds of the present realities, one can well imagine that some of the members of the Presidency would have been ready to nominate a trusted expert who belonged, let us say, to the 'Others'.

Conclusion

I would like to reiterate that experience in ECE countries has shown that ethnocultural neutrality and group-neutral regulation cannot accommodate cultural pluralism, and cannot guarantee stability and peace between ethnic majorities and minorities. Traditional liberal attitudes lack empathy towards maintaining diversity, and cannot provide solutions in traditionally multicultural environments where equality presumes an equal right to maintain one's distinct identity. When forced under the same roof with hard facts of ethnic pluralism and rivalry, traditional liberal precepts are unable to find viable models of accommodation and cohabitation.

The search for a solution is facilitated by the following circumstance: ideas of ethnocultural justice have some roots in ECE countries. Furthermore, a new receptiveness in these countries towards Western ideas and principles means an openness towards liberal-pluralist precepts as well. Yet the task remains ponderous. Democratic processes in post-Communist countries do not automatically provide for a just accommodation of ethnic and cultural diversity. The new 'euroconforming' structures are simply creating a new set of opportunities and constraints that need to be reckoned with in the process of discovering, or rediscovering, patterns of ethnic balance within a new political environment.

NOTES

1. See Will Kymlicka in Part 1 of this volume, 'Western Political Theory and Ethnic Relations in Eastern Europe', 82.
2. Ibid., 82–3.
3. Ibid., 83.
4. For a discussion of ethnic societies, see Tibor Várady, 'Minorities, Majorities, Law and Ethnicity: Reflections of the Yugoslav Case', *Human Rights Quarterly*, 19, 1997, 42–53.
5. Oszkár Jászi, 'A nemzetiségi kérdés és Magyarország jövöje (The Nationality Issue and the Future of Hungary)', lecture for the January 28, 1911 meeting of the Galilei Circle (Budapest: Galilei Circle, 1911), 12.
6. Lenin's data on the national structure of Switzerland and Russia are from 1913. A compilation of Lenin's texts, with commentaries, on the nationality issue can be found in Lászlo Rehák and Tibor Várady, *V.I. Lenin a nemzetiségi kérdésröl (Lenin on the Nationality Question)*, Novi Sad, Forum, 1970, 53 and, in particular, 66–8.
7. Várady, 'Minorities, Majorities', 17–23.
8. *Vojvodina u brojkama (Vojvodina in Figures)*, (Novi Sad: Vojvodina Institute of Statistics, 1985); Antal Biacsi, *Kis délvidéki demográfia (Little Demography of the Southern Region)*, (Szabadka: életjel, 1994), 130.
9. All of the 2 million residents of Vojvodina registered in the census were Yugoslav citizens. Everyone had the option of choosing a 'nationality', meaning national or ethnic background, rather than citizenship. A growing number of citizens—particularly those from mixed marriages—had been giving Yugoslav as their 'nationality'. In the 1990s, this trend has stopped.
10. See Biacsi, *Little Demography*, 135 and Milan Lucic, *A kisebbségek helyzete és*

jogai Vajdaságban (The Position and Rights of Minorities in Vojvodina), (Novi Sad, Forum, 1994) 11.

11. ITN News, September 6, 1996, 7:00 am.
12. Undue influence or even the outright forgery of election results is still conceivable, but the irrelevance of elections has gone with the demise of Communism.
13. Zakon o sudovima (Act on Courts), *Sluzbeni glasnik Republike Srbije*, No 46, 1991. See in particular Articles 3, 40, and 45.
14. If there were differences among ethnic groups regarding their economic strength or attitude towards paying taxes, then an ethnic group's share of the population might not be the best indicator of its tax input. Within Vojvodina, however, there are no meaningful differences.
15. See Tibor Várady, 'The Predicament of Peacekeeping in Bosnia', *Cornell International Law Journal*, 28, 1995, 701–7.

Nation-States and Immigrant Societies

MICHAEL WALZER

Will Kymlicka's paper is an excellent account of the current debates
about ethnic relations and immigration, and I find myself mostly
agreeing with his policy argument. But there are different ways of
organizing the argument, different ways of distinguishing the states
and groups that are its subjects—and these differences may have consequences for policy-making. I want to defend a modest alternative
to Kymlicka's way. He marks off five 'types of ethnocultural groups'
and then considers the different forms of integration or accommodation appropriate to each one in democratic states. The groups are carefully differentiated; the states are not. The states are, at least ideally,
of the same sort, though in practice they obviously pursue different
policies, which Kymlicka distinguishes as liberal or illiberal—or some
complex combination of the two. It is crucial to his programme
to reject all efforts to distinguish different types of states—hence his
critique of the old world/new world distinction in the last part of
his paper.

But one version of this latter distinction, which marks off nation-
states and immigrant societies, seems to me analytically useful. Of
course, the differences between these two are not absolute, and they
are probably declining in importance in the contemporary world.
Perhaps they can no longer be invoked, as I am inclined to invoke
them, to justify a range—rather than a set—of policies. Still, it is worth
insisting that there are different types of states, even of liberal democratic states, and the differences need to be described before we can
argue about what their consequences ought to be.

I will try to cast my description in Kymlicka's terms. Nation-states
engage in a very strong version of what he calls 'nation-building'. He
sees that project as pretty much universal, at least in the modern
world. Nonetheless, it can take very different forms. Describing its

American form, Kymlicka recognizes that the national culture that is being 'built' is very thin; he contrasts it with culture in the 'thick ethnographic sense'. That contrast seems to me important; thinness is a feature of immigrant societies, where the state, even if it fosters a culture of its own, is neutral among the various thick cultures sustained by different groups of immigrants. Nation-states, by contrast, aim precisely to foster a thick culture; they are engines of cultural reproduction in a very strong sense. They do not encourage the kind of hyphenated identities that are possible, and widely accepted, in the United States.

Kymlicka is right to stress the nationalizing pressures of American life. In my own work, I have probably underestimated those pressures, in part because of my experience as an American Jew, living in what is surely the best of all host societies in the long history of the Jewish diaspora. Of course, American Jews have had to learn English, and most of us have forgotten the Yiddish of our ancestors and have given up Hebrew except as a liturgical language. We are very much *American* Jews. On the other hand, we are clearly not Anglo-Americans. What has always struck me as the most remarkable feature of American history, impossible to imagine in any 'old world' nation-state, is that the Anglo-Americans allowed themselves to become a minority in—what they must have imagined to be—*their* country. They did indeed establish a national culture in their own image, into which the rest of us have been pressured to assimilate; it is a mistake not to acknowledge the assimilative power of this culture—but also its capacity to change, to adapt to what it assimilates. On the other hand, it is a thin culture, in both its original and its transformed versions, as Kymlicka says, and it leaves a lot of room for thickness elsewhere. By contrast, the culture of European nation-states, France being the classic example, is (or was) much thicker, the assimilative pressures even stronger, and there is (or was) less room for alternative versions of thickness. France is far more French than America is Anglo-American. And, though France was and is an immigrant society, the French will never become a minority in *their* country, not even a minority among thoroughly assimilated and entirely francophone East and South European and North African immigrants.

What difference does this difference make? I do not want to argue for some radical alternative to Kymlicka's proposals; these are matters of more or less. Still, multiculturalism is more problematic and difficult in France, say, than it is in the United States, and this fact suggests an argument of roughly the following sort: the thicker the 'national' culture, the more likely it is that large groups of immigrants—such as North African Muslims in France—will have to be accommodated as national minorities rather than as hyphenated nationals. Or, alternatively, multiculturalism may have to take a more corporatist form when the dominant culture is strongly supported by the state. For in that case, defenders of the other cultures will insist on similar if lesser support, and their insistence will be justified. In practice, what they will ask for is some sort of state funding and functional autonomy for their institutions. And this obviously approaches what a territorially-based national minority, in Kymlicka's sense, is entitled to.

When the national culture is thinner, it is plausible to say that immigrant groups are less in need of subsidy and autonomy—and so have a lesser title to it. They have to accept the cultural risks that immigration entails and sustain their own thick culture, if they can, through voluntary association and communal self-taxation. But culture, Kymlicka argues, depends upon language, and if the dominant national culture, however thin, requires linguistic assimilation, as in the American case, then thick and thin make little difference: the immigrants are in as much need as they would be if they were under heavy pressure to become, say, French men and women. There are, however, counter-examples to this claim. Kymlicka sustains it only by sharply separating ethnicity and religion, which is a strange thing to do, especially with regard to the United States, where religious affiliation is such a crucial marker of identity. The groups that have been most successful in sustaining their culture and cohesion in the United States are ethnic-religious combinations: German and Scandinavian Lutherans, Irish and Italian Catholics, Jews, Black Baptists, and so on. Perhaps shared belief substitutes for a lost language in these cases— it is also possible, of course, that the substitution will prove to be only temporarily successful. In any case, groups of this sort have so far survived with some state subsidies but without extensive corporatist arrangements. But they do not have to pit themselves against a dominant culture of the same sort as their own. For 'American' national culture does not have this ethnic-religious form. It has its origin, indeed, in White Anglo-Saxon Protestantism, but there are few WASPs who would recognize its present version as authentically, let alone exclusively, theirs.

North African Muslims are a group similar to American immigrant communities, and they could probably survive and prosper in France exactly as American Jews have survived and prospered in the United States—if Frenchness were as undemanding as Americanism is. But faced with a culture that is so strongly French, and so alien to themselves, immigrant Muslims are likely to look for something more like an alternative than an added (hyphenated) identity. And if I am right to say that becoming French involves a greater loss of older cultural forms than becoming American does, and if France is to remain a democratic and liberal society, then a way must be provided to sustain that alternative, which means becoming French citizens without becoming French in that strong sense. The protections of citizenship will have be to be disentangled from (some of) the cultural baggage which once went along with them, unless all the world is to become like America, where cultural baggage was always lighter than in the 'old world'. And there is no reason to think that that is happening or should happen.

Ancient, territorially-based national cultures are not going to disappear; nor are those among them that have achieved nation-statehood going to give it up. Nor will or should those nation-states cease to aim at the reproduction of a thick national culture. But they will increasingly have to make room for other sorts of thickness, and this will have to be room of a sort appropriate to the nation-state formation—with the same furnishings, so to speak, as are provided for the national majority.

This is the crucial point that follows from acknowledging that there are different sorts of states: in countries like the United States, groups that originally were or incipiently are national minorities—like the Chicanos—can perhaps be dealt with as if they were immigrants. In countries more like France, groups that are in fact immigrants may have to be dealt with as if they were national minorities.

2.5

New Democracies in the Old World: Remarks on Will Kymlicka's Approach to Nation-building in Post-Communist Europe

BORIS TSILEVICH

The transition to liberal democracies and market economies in East Central Europe (ECE) seems to be accompanied by widespread illusions. After the collapse of the Communist empire—whose stability had been greatly exaggerated—the expectations for fast and successful democratic transformations in the newly independent European countries were unreasonably optimistic. The difficulties encountered in re-establishing democratic structures and civil societies turned out to be greatly underestimated. The capabilities of many of these states to handle emerging ethnic controversies and minority-related issues appeared particularly weak. As a result, various ethnic conflicts erupted in post-Communist Europe.

Liberal-democratic philosophy does not offer clear rules for handling ethnocultural diversity. Neither is it a panacea. As Will Kymlicka correctly states, 'controversies and conflicts over the management of ethnocultural diversity will not go away, or spontaneously resolve themselves'. Liberal-democratic values do, however, provide some clear markers for acceptable approaches to minorities policies, something that is lacking in ECE countries.

Peculiarities of Minority Related Conflicts in ECE

Similarities and Differences between Old and New Democracies

Why are the states that have clearly declared, albeit recently, adherence to basic liberal values so different from 'old' democracies in their tackling of ethnocultural diversity? The explanation, in my view, is twofold.

First, cultural differences have been predetermined by the historical peculiarities of the nation-building process in the region—the Balkans give the most salient evidence of these differences. 'Ethnic nationalism has always been a dominant political philosophy in Eastern Europe.'[1] Historically, statehood was understood in ethnic rather than civic terms. Pål Kolstø has identified two interrelated historical factors to explain this: the conspicuous absence of the national bourgeoisie and a more prolonged dominance of an imperial, dynastic state.[2]

Second, the long-term consequences of the decades-long existence of East European nations under authoritarian Communist rule are yet to be fully realized. The distorted nature of intra-societal ties, the lack of civil society, and permanent ideological pressure, particularly against 'alien, capitalist' liberal values, greatly reinforced the dominance of ethnic over civic allegiances. Ethnic solidarity prevails over any other societal ties.

Nationalism of the Communist Kind

The legacy of the Communist concept of the so-called 'national question', with the 'ethnic' right to self-determination as a cornerstone, is a particularly important factor. This right was understood in a way similar to E. Gellner's definition of nationalism: the 'ethno-nation' was considered the right-holder, and self-determination implied the establishment of 'statehood'.[3] As a rule, though, this 'statehood' existed only in the decorative form of 'Soviet Socialist Republic', autonomous unit, or satellite.

A complicated, multilevel, ethnonational hierarchy had been elaborated. Communist federations 'were based on a sophisticated system of regionalisation based on nationality and ethnicity. In the USSR, different ethnic groups (nations or nationalities) were given status by being titular nationals of union republics, or autonomous republics, krais and okrugs. . . . In reality, power remained within the centralised Communist party. The territorial division was not filled with democratic content but with status allocations. An elaborate arrangement involving selected representatives of the titular nationalities in the bureaucracies, the nomenklatura, gave the impression of ethnic and national power, which was fictitious.'[4]

Even after the Communist ideology as such lost its popularity—to the extent that the regeneration and recruitment of effective political élites capable of keeping control over the states appeared impossible—the belief that the republics or autonomies 'belonged' to the titular ethnic group remained widespread. The switch to liberal values was understood by post-Communist ethnic groups not as the abandonment of Communist-type 'self-determination' and ethnonational hierarchy in favour of inclusive, non-ethnically-based democracy, but as the genuine implementation of nationalistic principles which had been hypocritically declared and not implemented by Communist leaders. Instead of perceiving newly independent and newly democratic states 'as a framework within which to build an inclusive democracy, involving all inhabitants residing there on an equal level, it has led to an exceptionally strong process of ethnic identification in many of the republics and the sub-units, with the corresponding quests for secession by those ethnic groups which did not belong to the dominant ethnos.'[5]

Dualism of Values

Adherence to liberal-democratic values by the world community came largely as a result of the horrors of World War II. An international legal framework based on the elaboration and adoption of a broad range of international human rights conventions started to take shape immediately after the end of the war. The nations of East Central Europe, which were then under Communist rule, did not participate in this process. Only in the late 1980s did they acquire these 'ready-made' legal instruments, as well as the basic values that lay behind them. Post-Communist nations were consumers, rather than co-authors, of this modern and generally accepted liberal-democratic political philosophy. As it happens, these new users were insufficiently qualified and did not always apply the obtained mechanisms in full compliance with the original objectives. Nor did they make full use of the opportunities provided.

There is, therefore, a fundamental dualism of values in the reconstructed and newly constructed post-Communist societies of East Central Europe. Declared liberal-democratic values are eclectically combined with more authoritarian ones that are archaic in terms of liberal philosophy. In particular, substantively individual liberal values in a bizarre way coexist with strong nationalistic feelings that are based on the presumption of the predominance of one ethnic group.

This dualism of values is reflected in the emerging social and political frameworks. Generally recognized democratic procedures are often combined with formal or informal mechanisms of an authoritarian, tribal, or criminal nature. Examples of deviations from the liberal nature of political systems include the overt denial of some basic principles of democratic government (as in Belarus), systematic violations of electoral procedures (in Kazakhstan), the coalescence with clan hierarchy (in Central Asia and the Caucasus), and rampant corruption. In other words, a visible gap often emerges between the rhetoric and practice. A frequent pattern that emerges is the declaration of liberal laws but the implementation of contradictory government regulations and the lack of efficient enforcement mechanisms.

The Role of Élites

The role of new political élites is of particular importance in the transition to liberal-democratic societies. Each of the post-Communist states has its peculiar and complex process for establishing new political élites. Common to most post-Communist states, however, is that the new élites broadly and effectively exploit nationalistic rhetoric to win over and mobilize their constituencies. In this respect, 'recirculated' old Communist élites are often more extreme and militant than the new ones. Their emphasis on ethnic solidarity and 'the rights of a nation' allowed them, in some sense, to justify their Communist past. Alignment with ethnic values is to a considerable extent a means of remaining in power. In any event, belonging to—or at least articulating one's loyalty to—the titular groups, the 'masters of their lands', seems to be a necessary prerequisite for becoming part of the new political élites in most of the post-Communist countries.[6] Instead of playing a role as the avant-garde of liberal principles, the new élites often stir up nationalistic emotions within their constituencies in order to stay on top of the nationalistic wave.

Of course, nationalist parties and political leaders enjoy popularity in 'old democracies' too. The difference, however, lies in the methods considered to be permissible, and the limits on expressions of nationalistic ideas. In Canada, for example, a popular premier of the province of Quebec had to resign immediately after his emotional speech, made in frustration after closely losing a referendum on sovereignty, wherein some statements were seen as insulting for some ethnic groups. In post-Communist countries, such a speech would only have enhanced a politician's popularity.

Minorities as 'Reversed Majorities'

It should be understood clearly that minorities themselves also act within the same distorted system of values as the titular nations. 'In spite of the growth of a culture of minority rights in society as a whole, there is virtually no minority rights-based political culture within the minorities themselves',[7] a prominent expert from the Balkans wrote. Indeed, claims of the 'post-Communist minorities' are rarely expressed in terms of non-discrimination or a modern approach to minority rights. They rely instead on an ethnic understanding of self-determination.

All these factors predetermine the strong politicization of ethnicity. Unlike in 'old democracies', the nation-building projects in post-Communist East Central Europe are, as a rule, of an 'ethnic' nature. Political leaders do not strive to turn 'peasants into Frenchmen', but rather aim to secure proper territory for the 'nation'—that is, ethnic group—which, in their view, already exists and for which possession of a certain, 'historically granted' piece of land is a necessary precondition for socio-economic development or even survival.

As Will Kymlicka rightfully points out, in the West, minority nationalism has been opposed when seen as running contrary to liberal-democratic principles or endangering 'societal culture'. In post-Communist East Central Europe, on the other hand, minority nationalism is perceived as a danger to the very existence of the state. Indeed, claims to retain a separate identity are viewed as a threat to nation-building. Political rhetoric to maintain a minority group's separate identity is seen as the first step along the road to secession—and not always groundlessly.

'Designated Areas' for Alternative Societal Cultures

As a result of the dualism of values mentioned above, a peculiar political system has emerged in post-Communist East Central Europe. Graham Smith defined post-Communist political regimes in Estonia and Latvia as 'ethnic democracies',[8] the model originally developed for Israel. It seems that this notion can be, to a greater or lesser extent, applied to many post-Communist ECE states. The essence of the 'ethnic democracy' model is a combination of certain principles of general democracy with elements of ethnic favouritism.

The peculiar feature of such regimes is that the general recognition of minority rights is accompanied with the identification of some 'designated areas' for minority cultures. As a rule, there are three such areas.

1. *Religious practices.* The political leadership of 'nationalizing' states tolerates the religious activities of 'traditional' faiths and, although it keeps an eye on them, does not actively interfere unless they become a real threat to the dominance of a titular group.
2. *Special ethnic cultural associations.* These are often not only tolerated but even promoted and financially supported. This may include the establishment of NGOs, although these may be more for form's sake. 'Acceptable' minority associations must explicitly limit their activities to singing ethnic folk songs, celebrating traditional holidays, maintaining Sunday schools, etc.
3. *The private sphere, but understood in a very restricted sense.* The controversy over what is private and what is public is clearly illustrated by the debates over language legislation in Latvia and Estonia. Legislatures insist that they have a legitimate right to prescribe the language to be used in private companies, NGOs, and at public gatherings, for example, as these venues are not considered to be only private.

These examples comply with the dominant model that outlines 'the correct behaviour' for minority groups in post-Communist states. It reflects the dualism of values: minorities should not be denied the right of enjoying their culture and using their language, but it must only be within their 'own', isolated environments. Everyone must have the right to sing his or her songs and to dance traditional dances, but at the public level everyone must fully accept the societal culture of the majority. This is neither a completely assimilationist model nor a 'two-way integration model' characteristic, as Will Kymlicka writes, of liberal democracies.

The Applicability of Will Kymlicka's Concept to ECE

The peculiarities of post-Communist societies necessitate a reconsideration of the ways to accommodate ethnocultural diversity as practised in 'old democracies'.

Controversies of Federalism and Autonomy

Federalism and territorial autonomy, proven to be successful in many Western countries, are perceived with great suspicion in post-

Communist ECE countries. This is not only because, as Kymlicka notes, 'federalism has become tainted with the abuses of Communism'. Under post-Communist circumstances, regional autonomous élites, as well as existing political and economic structures, can be easily and rapidly mobilized to serve a minority's secessionist attempts. Virtually all successful secessionist movements in the former Soviet Union—Nagorno-Karabakh, Transdniestria, Abkhazia, South Ossetia, and Chechnya—were based on some existing autonomous structures.

The abolition of autonomy, however, is not an answer. Instead of removing the separatist threats, it sharply escalates the conflict, as happened in all the cases just mentioned, as well as in Kosovo—the most recent, bloody, and large-scale conflict in post-Communist ECE. In this respect, the 'new democracies' seem not to differ much from the 'old' ones.

In principle, federalist arrangements can be at least as effective in ECE countries as they are in 'old democracies'. In some cases, establishment of federal arrangements appeared extremely efficient. For example, establishment of the Gagauz autonomy in Moldova practically removed the threat of violent conflict in this region—in sharp contrast with the situation in another part of the same state, Transdniestria, where prospects for peaceful settlement still remain very unclear.

The question is whether societies of the ECE countries will take advantage of the strong points of federal models, and refrain from abusing them. This is true for both ruling titular political élites and minorities. One can assume that federalism and autonomy will become more and more effective with the liberal-democratic development of the ECE societies. In the meantime, the premature introduction of these principles might discredit them.

Mobilization and Self-Assertion of Post-Communist Minorities

As Will Kymlicka mentions, many post-Communist minorities are potentially irredentist. Indeed, minorities with a neighbouring kin-state might be expected to cause the most 'trouble' for the new European democracies. In such cases, a triangular model—nationalizing states/national minorities/ethnic homeland—suggested by Rogers Brubaker[9] can be used to explain the development of the situation, although the lines along which a potential conflict might evolve vary significantly. In this model, the notion of diaspora is sometimes more appropriate than minority or, as a rule, the groups can be defined as post-imperial minorities.

Hungarian minorities in Romania and Slovakia are usually mentioned as an example of a mobilized diaspora. Given the ramification of a strong framework of social, cultural, and political organizations, stable and active ties to the kin-state are typical of this minority. A consistent and persistent strategy of the well-organized political parties of the Hungarian minorities finally resulted in their joining ruling coalitions in both Romania and Slovakia. Of course, in no way can one declare that this fact alone resolved all problems related to these minorities. Nevertheless, the methods in which these problems are tackled—that is, through institutionalized dialogue with political parties representing minorities—seem to be efficient, despite reasonable doubts about the democratic nature of the ethnically-based political parties.

In contrast, Serbian minorities in the states of former Yugoslavia present a scary and tragic pattern of ethnocultural self-assertion. These groups, which strongly relied on the kin-state, in fact found themselves to be merely a tool for the implementation of aggressive nationalism by its political leadership.

Russian-speaking communities in the newly independent states of the former USSR represent another example. Not surprisingly, this issue in particular enjoyed the attention of political analysts. If these groups were to choose 'the Serbian pattern', it might undermine the stability of Europe. So far this does not seem to be the case.[10] Russian communities in the 'near abroad'—a characterization that is clearly disliked by the countries so labelled—are still in flux, and their methods of self-assertion are only in the process of taking shape.

The existence of a powerful 'external patron' able to effectively back the nationalistic aspirations of a minority increases the chances that separatist and/or irredentist claims will succeed. But the patron need not be the kin-state. It may instead be linked to the separatist group through religious, linguistic, or even commercial ties. Abkhazia, Transdniestria, and Chechnya are good examples of successful separatism without the presence of 'formal' kin-states.

Different Minorities—Different Rights?

The classification of minorities suggested by Will Kymlicka, as well as his propositions on the effective rights these groups can legitimately claim, are no doubt well-reasoned and persuasive. Nevertheless, it is difficult to imagine how the distinction between, for example, 'national minority' and 'immigrant minority' can be established at the level of national or international law. Procedural difficulties—for example, the length of time an immigrant group must reside in a country to claim the status of national minority—are also very perplexing. In addition, the problem of discrimination persists. As soon as a person acquires citizenship, any differences between this person's and a native citizen's guarantees of human rights can be regarded as discriminatory. In the meantime, minority rights are definitely viewed as a part of human rights. However, an attempt to assign different status to different minority groups, with attendant minority rights, may appear as a breach of the basic principle of non-discrimination.

Virtually every Western democracy treats its national minorities differently from its immigrant groups, typically granting language rights and/or self-government rights to the former that are not granted to the latter. However, none of the Western democracies explicity assigns different categories to different minority groups in the law—that is, Western laws and constitutions do not define the terms 'national minority' and 'immigrant group', or list which groups which fall into which category. (Declarations made during ratification of the Framework Conventon for the Protection of National Minorities are the only exception, an issue discussed below). The question is whether this approach can also be effective in the ECE countries.

In my view, one should be rather cautious in extending this approach to post-Communist ECE states. As a rule, immigrant minorities in 'old democracies' are formed by people who consciously left their home countries for Western states—regardless of whether they immigrated legally or not. They were aware of the 'rules of the game' in advance, and arguably their decision to immigrate was based upon acceptance of these rules, including acceptance of the new societal cultures, and a readiness to integrate into their new societies. By contrast, typical immigrant minorities in the ECE countries found themselves in their countries of residence due to the collapse of empires, change of borders, involuntary population movements as a result of wars, etc. No doubt some immigrant minorities in the post-Communist countries—for example Vietnamese, Korean, Chinese minorities, and people from Arabic and African countries—also came in more 'traditional' ways. However, these groups—much less numerous than other minorities in the region—practically never demand recognition of their cultural and linguistic rights, or any form of officially recognized self-government. Thus, these groups behave rather like immigrant minorities in Western countries.

Another threat concerns the peculiarities of the perception of nation-building and the dual nature of the basic values of the new political élites, as mentioned above. In 'old democracies', when the status of a minority is determined, the view of that minority is taken into account to a greater or lesser extent. By contrast, in the ECE countries, minority groups are often perceived as a threat to nation-building projects. Titular political élites tend to exclude minorities, and are inclined to classify minorities into 'national' (traditional) and immigrant groups on the basis of arbitrary—ideological and politi-cized—criteria. In other words, this classification may appear as a dis-tinction between 'good' and 'bad' minorities from the point of view of the current political regime, regardless of how rooted they are in the society and other objective factors.

Granted and Demanded Rights

It is difficult to claim that there are clear, formal standards in the field of implementation of minority rights. However, there are some clear, basic principles derived from liberal theory and included into basic international instruments on minority rights: non-discrimina-tion, the right to preserve one's identity, and prohibition of forced assimilation. These goals can be achieved in different ways in differ-ent countries.

Some documents—first of all, the European Framework Con-vention for the Protection of National Minorities—were criticized for overly vague provisions. Many articles of this Convention contain numerous reservations—such as 'where appropriate', 'if necessary', or 'if there is a real demand'. However, this vagueness reflects a very important feature of minority rights, which makes them different from the rest of human rights. The crucial aspect is whether there is a real demand for minority rights, as well as an objective opportunity to meet these demands.

For example, there is little sense in financing a school to provide instruction in a minority language if the minority does not want their children to receive education in this language—this is the case for most Belorussian minorities in the former USSR. Besides, peculia-rities of this or that minority should be taken into account. For example, the Jewish identity is based primarily on religion, while language is of much lesser importance. This is why Jewish schools usually adopt a state's official language as the language of instruction for all subjects not directly connected with Jewish religion or history. In contrast, language is at the core of the Russian minorities' distinct identity, while religion is much less important. Russian minorities are therefore very sensitive to linguistic limitations and prescriptions. Because different minority rights are of varying importance to different minorities, demands are also diverse.

To sum up, Will Kymlicka's classification of national and immigrant minorities, which proved to be appropriate in practically all 'old democracies' can also, in principle, be applied in the ECE countries. However, because of the low level of development of civil society and democratic traditions, the lack of effective mechanisms of dialogue between titular élites and minorities, and the tendency to perceive minorities as a threat to nation-building and to exclude them from this process, there is a high probability that this model will be applied in an abusive way. Thus, this approach may be dangerous. The formal recognition and legitimization of some minorities, while denying others, can even aggravate conflicts, instead of ameliorating them.

Values of Liberal Democracy and the International Legal Framework

The Impact of the 'Old Democracies'

Nation-building in post-Communist East Central Europe can not be adequately understood without taking into account external factors, the first of which is the attitudes and activities of what we call the international community. The (re)construction of democratic institutions in post-Communist Europe is often described as a 'return to the civilized world community'. New political élites articulately express their adherence to international norms and standards. In addition to some pragmatic considerations—such as access to loans and financial assistance—this attitude seems to have a highly symbolic value for newly democratic European countries. Post-Communist political élites want to be, or at least to appear as, 'good pupils'. This goal is difficult to achieve, however, if the lessons are worded in a vague and ambiguous manner. In this regard, the point made by Will Kymlicka about the lack of clear-cut rules and practices for handling ethnocultural diversity and the claims of non-dominant groups is of particular importance.

The lack of clarity in 'old' liberal democracies regarding the treatment of minorities is not a crucial problem for them. As a rule, customary traditions, experiences, and precedents, based on a broad consensus of the spirit of liberal values, allow these societies to find solutions to conflict on a case-by-case basis. In contrast, for the 'new democracies', the ambiguity represents a serious impediment to the 'return to the civilized world'.

The broad diversity of practices in 'old' democracies—all of which used to be recognized as legitimate and corresponding to liberal-democratic standards—creates confusion for those diligently working to build ethnic policies in accordance with 'civilized Western patterns'. Ironically, it also provides radical nationalists with good pretexts for avoiding the fair treatment of minorities. They often ridicule those in the West for being mere proselytizers, and tend to challenge the West: 'Why don't you take these aliens and treat them as you admonish us to do?' In fact, though, minority activists easily find much more generous practices in the West—for example full bilingualism in Finland, or 'dual monolingualism' in Belgium. Thus, both sides use references to the 'experience of old democracies' in a broad sense, and often speculatively, to meet their own needs.

Values and Policies: the Case of Asylum Seekers

In terms of its role as a model for new democracies, the dilemma the West faces can be described as 'moralizing vs. burden-sharing'. The policies of most West European states towards asylum seekers illustrate this dilemma. On the moralizing side, these countries declare full adherence to the obligations of international conventions and urge the newly democratic states of East Central Europe to undertake similar obligations as soon as possible. With a policy objective of burden-sharing, the Western countries also want the new democracies to accept as many refugees as they can.

Meanwhile, the old democracies are in the process of strengthening 'fortress Europe' and implementing increasingly restrictive policies towards asylum seekers.[11] In these circumstances, even honest attempts to share good practices can understandably be perceived by the newly democratic European states as a way to make the poorer ECE countries accept refugees whom the West itself is trying to get rid of. Thus, one might claim, the Western countries are preserving their 'societal cultures', using Kymlicka's term, and defending them from culturally different asylum seekers, while denying the same possibility to ECE countries.

International Legal Instruments and Institutions

The vague nature of liberal standards of minority treatment is clearly reflected at the level of international legal instruments. In fact, prior to the collapse of the Communist system, neither the United Nations nor the Council of Europe had adopted special conventions aimed at the protection of minorities. Although the inclusion of minority rights provisions had been discussed in the context of the *Universal Declaration of Human Rights*, the proposition was finally rejected. Instead, the General Assembly adopted a special resolution saying that while the United Nations cannot remain indifferent to the fate of minorities, 'it is difficult to adopt a uniform solution of this complex and delicate question, which has special aspects in each State in which it arises' and therefore 'decides not to deal in a specific provision with the question of minorities in the text of this Declaration'.[12]

Article 27 of the *International Covenant on Civil and Political Rights* does oblige the state parties, in a very general form, to respect the minorities' right 'to enjoy their own culture, to profess and practice their own religion, or to use their own language.' This provision says nothing about how this right must be practically guaranteed, or which implementing institutions and arrangements must be created. Although the UN Human Rights Committee has occasionally handled individual complaints related to alleged violations of Article 27, and although the Committee's judgements are meaningful as precedents, one can hardly claim that implementation of the Covenant has established clear 'rules of the game'.

In 1992, the United Nations adopted the *Declaration on the Rights of Persons belonging to Ethnic, National, Religious or Linguistic Minorities*. Although the Declaration defines much more clearly a set of provisions regarding what minorities can claim, it is not a legally binding document, and does not provide for monitoring mechanisms. As a result, it cannot be effectively applied.

Only in the 1990s did the Council of Europe adopt two basic legal instruments related to minority rights. The *European Charter for Regional and Minority Languages* was opened for signature in 1992 and the *Framework Convention for the Protection of National Minorities* in February 1995. The former instrument entered into force on 1 March 1998 and the latter on 1 February 1998. Some experts believe that the Charter, elaborated before the eastward expansion of the Council of Europe, was based predominantly on the experience of Western states. Nevertheless, it recognizes different practices for handling ethnocultural diversity. The so-called 'à la carte' principle allows state parties to choose different options, ranging from 'weak' to 'strong', from the list of provisions.

The *Framework Convention* took into account situations typical of the new ECE member states of the Council of Europe. Although heavily criticized by human rights lawyers for its numerous reservations, vague nature and possibilities for the broad interpretation of its provisions, the *Framework Convention*, as 'a document of principles', sets forth a range of standards on the rights of minorities. In particular, for the first time in history the *Framework Convention* overtly prohibits the forced assimilation of minorities. It remains to be seen whether a special body—the Advisory Committee for monitoring the implementation of the *Framework Convention*—will be effective.

In the meantime, several attempts to add a special minority rights protocol to the *European Convention of Human Rights*— thus enabling minority representatives to bring individual complaints of minority rights violations before the European Court of Human Rights—have so far been unsuccessful. A recommendation of the Parliamentary Assembly[13] of the Council of Europe was in fact suspended.

Somewhat paradoxically, the most efficient mechanism for handling minority issues in Europe has been created not within the Council of Europe, which claims to be a leading European institution to protect human rights, but within the Organization of Security and Co-operation in Europe (OSCE). Officially, the mandate of the OSCE High Commissioner on National Minorities has little to do with human rights, *per se*, focusing instead on diplomatic and political methods for the early warning and prevention of conflict. This is why important recommendations, elaborated in recent years under the auspices of the High Commissioner,[14] have no legal force and are not binding. This means that the High Commissioner must intervene when a real threat of violent conflict emerges, but not in all cases when the rights of minorities are neglected.

With this mandate in mind, one can claim that for minorities 'bad behaviour is rewarded'. For example, when municipalities in the north-east of Estonia, inhabited predominantly by ethnic Russians, organized a referendum on *de facto* secession, the High Commissioner, backed by the Council of Europe, put considerable pressure on Estonian central authorities to make them reconsider the *Law on Aliens*, the main cause of the Russian minority's dissatisfaction. It is not obvious that if Russians had used only 'fully legitimate' means, the efforts to protect their interests would have been as forceful.

To sum up, two main trends are evident in the elaboration of international legal standards for handling ethnic diversity. First, since the 1990s new instruments on minority rights have been and are being elaborated. On the other hand, the 'old' and 'new' democracies only half-heartedly embrace this effort. To put it simply, nation-states realize the urgency of acting on these issues, but are clearly not eager to undertake serious obligations towards their minorities. The old democracies react, if at all, to the potential for a proliferation of ethnic-related violence rather than to violations of liberal principles in the treatment of minorities.

The Definition of a Minority

Problems related to the classification of minorities—see the preceding section on 'Different Minorities—Different Rights?'—are probably the main reason why there is still no universally accepted juridical definition of a minority. Somewhat surprisingly, the working definition adopted within the framework of the United Nations[15] is much broader and more generous than the one informally—though not legally—accepted by the Council of Europe in the above-noted Recommendation 1201 of the Parliamentary Assembly.

Indigenous peoples are the only group explicitly singled out in international law. However, an obvious trend emerged in elaborating international instruments to determine the rights of indigenous peoples: these instruments are not included in the general framework of instruments on minority rights but are dealt with separately. In other words, the rights of indigenous peoples make up a separate area of human rights law, and are considered as substantially different from 'common' minority rights.

As already mentioned, the state parties of the Framework Convention are free to determine the groups to which they will grant the minority rights enshrined in the Convention. For example, some states—Germany, Denmark, Slovenia, Former Yugoslav Republic of Macedonia—list the groups eligible for those minority rights guaranteed by the Convention. Many other state parties have adopted very restrictive definitions. For example, to claim minority rights in Estonia and Switzerland, persons must, in addition to possessing citizenship of the state, also 'maintain longstanding, firm and lasting ties' with that state. In Luxemburg, persons must have 'settled for numerous generations on its territory'. Others, such as Liechtenstein and

Malta, when ratifying the Framework Convention, overtly declared that there are no minorities at all within their territories.[16]

Conclusions

Conflicts over the handling of ethnocultural diversity are no doubt the main threat to the peaceful and democratic development in East Central Europe. In the event of a large-scale explosion, the West will hardly be able to hide behind a new 'iron curtain'. Thus, the problems of the 'new democracies' pertain, in essence, to the 'old democracies' too. The West's vital interests in elaborating effective rules and mechanisms to cope with these threats are motivated by 'selfish reasons', not out of pure humanism. So far, 'the international community's reaction [has] oscillated between persistent under-reaction (like in Chechnya and Bosnia) and belated overreaction (like in Kosovo).'[17] Accordingly, greater understanding of the peculiarities of post-Communist nation-building is of pivotal importance. The approach developed by Will Kymlicka offers an appropriate foundation for this understanding. Transferring the basic principles and values of liberal democracy into legal provisions and enforcement mechanisms must be the next—and perhaps much more complicated—step.

NOTES

1. Richard Rose, 'Rights and obligations of individuals in the Baltic states', *East European Constitutional Review*, 1, Winter 1997, 35–43.
2. Pål Kolstø, 'Nations and Nation-Building in Eastern Europe', in *Nation-Building and Ethnic Integration in Post-Soviet Societies. An Investigation of Latvia and Kazakhstan* (Boulder, CO: Westview Press, 1999) 56.
3. See, for example, Ernest Gellner, *Nations and Nationalism*, Basil Blackwell, 1983.
4. Asbjorn Eide, 'Minorities in a Decentralized Environment', in *The New Yalta: Commemorating the 50th Anniversary of the Declaration of Human Rights in the RBEC Region* (New York, NY: Regional Bureau for Europe and the CIS of the UN Development Programme, 1998) 55–67.
5. Ibid., 59
6. On the formation of new élites in the Baltic states, see Anton Steen, 'The new elites in the Baltic states: Recirculation and exchange', *Scandinavian Political Studies*, 20/1, 1997, 91–112. The actual merger of pro-Communist and nationalistic political groups in Russia is also revealing.
7. Panayote Elias Dimitras, 'The Minority Rights Paradox', *WarReport*, 58, 1998, 64–66.

8. Graham Smith, 'The Ethnic Democracy Thesis and the Citizenship Question in Estonia and Latvia', *Nationalities Papers*, 24/2, 1996, 199–216.
9. Rogers Brubaker, *Nationalism Reframed. Nationhood and the National Question in the New Europe* (Cambridge: Cambridge University Press, 1996).
10. Anatol Lieven suggests an interesting explanation for the low level of mobilization among the 'new' Russian minorities. Anatol Lieven, 'The Weakness of Russian Nationalism', *Survival*, 41/2, 1999, 53–70.
11. For a detailed discussion of this problem, see Natalie Zend, 'Hungary's Migration Policy, 1987–1996. External Influences and Domestic Imperatives', in Magda Opalski (ed.) *Managing Diversity in Plural Societies. Minorities, Migration and Nation-Building in Post-Communist Europe* (Ottawa: Forum Eastern Europe, 1998) 208–28. See also Boris Cilevics, 'Restrictions on asylum in the member states of the Council of Europe and the European Union', Doc. 8598, Report to the Parliamentary Assembly of the Council of Europe on behalf of the Committee on Migration, Refugees and Demography, 1999 (http://stars.coe.fr/doc/doc99/edoc8598.htm).
12. 'Fate of minorities', UN General Assembly Resolution 217 C (III), 1948.
13. 'On the additional protocol on the rights of minorities to the European Convention on Human Rights', Parliamentary Assembly of the Council of Europe Recommendation 1201, 1993.
14. *The Hague Recommendations Regarding the Education Rights of National Minorties*, 1996, and *The Oslo Recommendations Regarding the Linguistic Rights of National Minorities*, 1998.
15. UN Human Rights Committee, *The rights of minorities* (Article 27: General comment 23) 4 August 1994.
16. The list of ratifications, as well as reservations and declarations made by the state parties, are available at http://www.coe.int/tablconv/157t.htm.
17. Panayote Elias Dimitras, 'The Minority Question in Europe', *Speaking about Rights* (Canadian Human Rights Foundation Newsletter, Montreal), 14/2, 1999, 2.

Some Doubts about 'Ethnocultural Justice'

ALEXANDER OSSIPOV

Many of Kymlicka's ideas on 'ethnocultural justice' and its application in post-Communist countries are welcome, while several components can and must be criticized. I will concentrate on the latter, even though critiquing articles that are written in the genre of social prescription is not an easy task. Arguments, whether pro or con, seem disputable and weak. Conclusions are tenuous because the practical experiences needed for substantiation are scarce and only marginally comparable. Apart from the problem of determining what is negative and positive, it is not clear how to evaluate the overall balance of positive and negative outcomes when criteria are ambiguous and subjective. But even when the nature of the discussion is largely unquantifiable, unclear, or arbitrary, one can still debate the article's underlying assumptions, deconstruct its language and, speculatively, or by using analogies, try to anticipate risks and unexpected outcomes.

The easiest way to proceed would be to demonstrate that many of Kymlicka's suggestions do not apply to the realities of the former Soviet Union, and Russia in particular. To my mind, however, the issue must be put in a broader social and geographic context, as concerns about the applicability of Kymlicka's approach could be valid outside the post-Communist countries. In my view, there are several fundamental problems: some of Kymlicka's basic assumptions are arbitrary and disputable, the internal logic seems contradictory, potential gains are overestimated, and some potentially undesirable effects are not taken into consideration.

Assumptions and Terminology: Is an Ethnic Group a Social Actor?

Kymlicka offers some perfect examples of the type of language that is used in the discourse on ethnocultural justice: 'the question of the rights of ethnocultural groups'; 'which language groups will survive'; 'the issue of minority rights'; 'minorities . . . seek to participate . . .'; ' . . . create and sustain their own modern institutions'; 'any national group engaged in a project of nation-building must respect the right of other nations . . .'; and 'national minorities would have liked to form their own states'. Criticizing some of the language of the (ethno)nationalist discourse should not be equated with a criticism of liberal pluralism, although there are some common elements and parallels that do raise concerns.

Over the last forty or more years, debates on discrimination, protection of minorities, nationalism and ethnicity have occupied not only the academic community. International organizations and politicians have also been working in the area, with anti-discriminatory laws or legislation for the protection of minorities. Despite all the differences among schools, disciplines, and countries, a common language—often described as nationalistic—has emerged and spread so widely that it has even appeared in the documents of some international organizations.

With some reservations, this language reflects a perception of a group—such as 'nation', ethnic community, people, or minority—as a cultural and social entity, a developing system or 'social organism', and a social actor possessing interests, free will, and an ability to make decisions and choices. As such, an ethnic group possesses rights in a legal sense and, in a more radical sense, universal values that need special protection for its 'survival'.

These types of views on ethnic groups, social actors, and rights are usually presented as axiomatic. They are postulated, not proved, are not clearly articulated, and, regretfully, rarely become a subject of reflection.

Why is an ethnic group perceived as an entity when it has vague and movable boundaries and embraces various linguistic and cultural preferences? Why is an ethnic group—in a symbolic or statistical sense[1]—considered to be a social and even quasi-legal subject? Why is it that a number of activists, who put themselves forward as representatives, are perceived as the 'embodiment' of the group, rather than a voluntary association or political movement? Why should an outside observer automatically accept the language of self-representation, characteristic of ethnonationalist movements? Why should one assume that such movements rest on some natural, or basic, interests or needs of the group? Why does one not say that the term 'group interests' has been invented and developed by the persons and organizations that claim representative status?

In a democratic society, many organizations of various types claim to represent some group interests through electoral campaigning and lobbying activity.[2] If they are successful at the polls, nobody would challenge their 'democratic accountability'.[3] If a voluntary association or ethnically-based party is comprised of almost all of the people who belong to a certain ethnic group, this is one thing. If, however, a government prescribes and declares that it will deal only with a single 'lawful representative' of an ethnic group, this would be a quite different matter. Is there anything liberal in the latter approach? Surely it is strange to equate a representative organization with the entire group to be represented, assess it in terms of its capacity to mobilize, and insist that it be a type of political subsystem and collective actor.

Why should ethnically-based organizations or movements benefit from a special status in comparison with purely civil and political ones? Why must minority associations or ethnic parties be treated differently from other non-governmental organizations that play the same social role? I can find only two reasons for this discriminatory approach that favours ethnic associations. The first is the traditional stereotype of perceiving an ethnic group as a 'collective individual'.[4] The second concerns the political correctness of ethnic leaders and activists who usually protest against treating ethnic groups in any way other than as quasi-nations with specific group rights. Both of these reasons seem completely irrelevant. One should simply eliminate atavistic stereotypes; and the opinions of nationalist activists, which may be appropriate in terms of political bargaining, should not enter into academic debates.

Can a society be interpreted as a combination of ethnic communities? If a community is to be defined as an ethnic group, bound by its internal structure, common ideology (solidarity), and membership, then there were no communities in the former Soviet Union, and I suppose not in many other countries. If, on the other hand, a community is a non-governmental voluntary association, then each ethnic group in Russia—that is, people with the same nationality, as it appears in their passports—consists of dozens of communities.

Russia, for instance, can hardly be described in terms of an ethnically-segmented or divided society. Persons of various ethnic backgrounds attend schools with the same curricula, work together at the same enterprises, and watch the same television programmes. Cultural institutions, associations, and media for ethnic minorities attract relatively little interest from their intended audience. In spite of the many nationalist parties that profess to speak on behalf of an ethnic majority or minorities, their candidates regularly lose in national and regional elections. Inhabitants of the republics within Russia vote at the national level for federal parties, and in regional elections for authoritarian republican leaders who combine moderate local nationalism with regionalist rhetoric. Voters across Russia demonstrate the same model of behaviour regardless of their ethnic affiliation. Voting patterns along more ethnic lines are isolated cases, arise out of violent confrontations, such as the Ingush–Ossetian conflict, and can hardly be considered a result of a fair and free choice.

Hence, in Russian society, it is a considered opinion that minorities are integrated into the mainstream. At the same time, though, people belonging to minorities retain an identity in terms of their ethnicity, and have many modes of behaviour to express that identity. They do not simply choose between autonomy and integrating into the majority. Granted, Russian society is not ethnically blind or ethnically tolerant; the nationalist discourse affects many spheres of social life. This does not mean, however, that ethnic relations are characterized by one majority 'community' and a number of minority 'collective individuals'.

Does Minority Protection Require Group Rights?

In his argumentation, Kymlicka opts for the language of group rights. One can argue against this approach. The possible institutional arrangements do not necessarily require this kind of justification. Moreover, many ideas should be seen in terms of individual solutions and not normative principles or requirements: they may work properly in one circumstance but not in another.

If a government supports *institutions* that promote minority cultures and languages, this does not mean that *persons* belonging to a minority group enjoy special status, are being treated preferentially, or have more possibilities to exercise their rights. First of all, access to schools where a minority language is being taught is not restricted to minority members. Those who attend these schools can not be equated with a minority group. Second, resources from public funds and state budgets are regularly distributed disproportionately in favour of some categories of the population, such as special allowances and benefits for the unemployed and disabled, and regional development programmes. In many places, cultural institutions such as theatres and museums, as well as municipal transport, are not self-sufficient and therefore have to be financed from public funds. Not everybody uses city buses or underground transit, and few people attend museums. Nevertheless, nobody talks about affirmative action, special rights or group rights of those who benefit from such facilities.

Any public support to institutions that address specific needs of persons belonging to minorities can be justified in terms of individual rights. In general, existing legislation already does this, especially within the contexts of welfare or social partnership. In any event, it is still not obvious that everything in this area can or should be reflected in terms of rights. There are other grounds on which to base actions that protect minorities.

In general, the word 'right' is not suitable in this context. It would be better, and more practical, to speak in terms of governmental obligations under international standards and national legislation. The government of a country where 100 languages are spoken can hardly be expected, even if it had the resources and goodwill, to open, within a short time, schools where those 100 languages would be taught. To describe this situation as a violation of somebody's rights or as inequitable treatment would be strange.

Members of a society who belong to minorities do have legitimate interests, such as the use of their language in public institutions and instruction in their mother tongue. If members of the majority can teach their children in their mother tongue, persons belonging to minorities should be able to do the same. These interests must be met by the state. A real problem, however, is determining the degree to which such minority interests can feasibly be developed. Providing minority language instruction at the level of the primary school is not a problem. But what about higher education? Who would take responsibility for the employment prospects of its graduates? In such matters, universal prescriptions cannot and do not exist. The actual approaches have to be specific to the circumstances. Strongly-worded universal declarations of group rights in the cultural area, which actually define obligations of the state, are unlikely to offer suitable solutions. They would be more likely to lead to the artificial creation of groups of persons who did not previously consider their rights to be violated. This process would risk bringing nothing more than increased tensions and intolerance.

It is not obvious that group or special rights offer an effective instrument for governments to protect minorities. As a practitioner, I do not believe in the miraculous force of a piece of paper. A law or treaty is nothing more than a well-meaning wish unless the government and society respect it. Relying on the goodwill of government and the cultural majority is cold comfort, but we really have nothing else. Moreover, the whole idea of the rule of law is based on voluntary self-restriction and goodwill. If the political culture is not compatible with the ideas of the rule of law, there is little prospect for either the protection of human rights or non-violent conflict resolution. Cyprus, Iraq, Sudan, Serbia, and some post-Soviet states such as Georgia, illustrate this.

Governments have good reasons for not suppressing minorities and for undertaking positive measures in their favour. A responsible government is always seeking ways to avoid social unrest and destabilization. Affirmative action in the United States is not guaranteed by autonomous institutions dominated by non-Whites. Minorities are always dependent on majorities and disadvantaged groups are reliant on the institutions controlled by the dominant classes. That is inevitable; acceptable alternatives just do not exist.

If a government plays fair and implements deep reforms, including territorial autonomy for minorities, it does not need a universal normative requirement along the lines of group rights. Even if there were such a normative requirement, a government that rigidly opposes the idea of an ethnically-based territorial division of the state would simply ignore it. And on the flip side, a minority nationalist movement claiming territorial autonomy or secession would do so regardless of existing international standards.

In the final analysis, there are more moderate, less provocative alternatives to the language of group rights used in some international instruments. Two good examples are the Framework Convention for the Protection of National Minorities, and the European Charter for Regional or Minority Languages. Alternative language is also provided in the recommendations of some international organizations such as The Hague and Oslo Recommendations of the High Commissioner for National Minorities of the Organization for Security and Co-operation in Europe.

What is Just and Unjust in Ethnic Relations?

Kymlicka actually equates the so-called structural inequality among people belonging to different ethnic groups with deliberate exclusion and discrimination, and finds both outcomes unjust. He also finds the differentiation in the social standing of the mainstream or societal culture and language, on the one hand, and minority cultures and languages, on the other, unjust. Is this vision of the boundary between just and unjust consistent and realistic?

Deliberate discrimination must be condemned from the legal, religious, and (theoretical) liberal standpoints. In a modern society, people belonging to the cultural mainstream generally possess more advantages in social terms than people belonging to minorities, even if there are no deliberate practices of minority deprivation or exclusion. Is this situation of social inequality unique? No. As a rule, the rural population in modern countries is structurally disadvantaged, that is, they have fewer social opportunities in comparison with urban dwellers. The same might be said in comparisons of blue collar workers with white collars, inhabitants of mountainous areas with those living in fertile plains, females with males, or persons who inherit a fortune with those who inherit nothing. Few people seriously interpret social outcomes of this kind in terms of discrimination or violation of rights. A modern state may not be ethnically and culturally neutral, but it is also not neutral in terms of gender, age, class, or geography. Many social actors work toward reducing social inequality but, as far as I know, few support the granting of special rights to disadvantaged persons without recognizing others.

Is it possible to equate social and ethnic categories? A negative answer presumes that ethnic groups constitute or must constitute something different and isolated from the mainstream, like quasi-nations. In other words, the norm must be a segmented society. But this is neither a starting point for social engineering nor, from the liberal viewpoint, a goal of such engineering.

Mainstream and marginal languages and cultures cannot occupy the same ground and have the same functions within a given society. Thus, the promotion of a minority culture has some objective limits. For example, while the government of the Czech Republic may contribute much to the education of the Roma minority, and may even grant official status to the Roma language within some municipalities, the Roma language will never compete with Czech in the entire society. Similarly, the Armenian language will never have the same functions of instruction and communication as Russian does in the southern part of Russia—Rostov, Krasnodar, Stavropol—even though many Armenians live there.

If this kind of inequality is unjust, then justice must mean the elevation of marginal languages and cultures into the mainstream. In most cases, though, this could be achieved only by severe administrative pressure and the implementation of harsh restrictions and prescriptions. Such active governmental interference and the potential limitation on individual autonomy have little in common with liberalism. If restrictions were placed on the 'dominant' majority for some abstract ideological purposes, would this be just?

Regrettably, few theorists assess the official ethnic policies of societies in transition. How would liberal theory evaluate the bans and restrictions on certain languages, and their speakers, that have been implemented in some autonomous regions or newly independent states as a way to protect or ensure the survival of 'native languages'? Latvia and Ukraine are fighting against Russian, even to the point of interfering in the private domain, and Slovakia restricts the use of Hungarian and Czech, as does Quebec with English. Can these restrictions be justified within liberal theory? My opinion on this matter is definitely negative.

Double Standards: Ethnic Statehood vs. Ethnic Autonomy

Liberals criticize the idea of the nation-state in so far as it exclusively 'belongs' to a certain ethnic or cultural community. Some of them, however, approve of territorial autonomy for minorities, or 'ethnic federalism'. But this is really the same model and similar ideology to that of the nation-state: a certain territory and power structures for the titular ethnic group and at least a symbolic exclusion of others.[5] Saying that a certain ethnic group has territorial autonomy or statehood automatically means that inhabitants of the same territory who belong to different ethnic groups live outside their own statehood. In practice, such restrictions and prescriptions based on this assumption might be even more rigid than in a nation-state—for example Quebec, Åland Islands, or constituent regions of Belgium. If a liberal theorist rejects the exclusion of groups at the nationwide level—that is, the idea that a state belongs to a certain ethno-nation—the same conclusion should hold at the subnational level. Otherwise, we have a double standard.

In Kymlicka's argumentation, it appears that exclusion at the national level in favour of ethnonation A could be tolerated if minority group B were allowed to have its own autonomy that was probably territorially based and perhaps even exclusive. This could be tolerated and justified if a group C within B's autonomy were allowed to occupy its own room—probably a municipality—and this in turn could be tolerated if the same rights were granted to D, for example an ex-territorial corporation. In this case, the double standard would not necessarily apply, although the model would not be easy to implement without neglecting the rights and interests of individuals.

Nevertheless, why is such an approach needed when it is simply possible to do without it? Territories with a significant minority population could acquire special status and establish a specific linguistic regime, the objectives of which would be to help individuals belonging to minorities participate more effectively in politics and administration, and to improve their social and cultural life. If a certain group constitutes a majority whose language is strong enough to be the main means of communication, the others could be relatively disadvantaged, but this is not the same as symbolic and procedural exclusion.

Double Standards: Hosts and Guests

Kymlicka's classification of ethnic groups in the West is based in part on the division between 'national minorities' (traditionally settled groups, or hosts) and immigrants (guests). In some cases, distinguishing between these two categories is clear and reasonable, but the distinction can also appear arbitrary, particularly when we analyse Eastern Europe and the former Soviet Union. For instance, according to the 1989 USSR Census, 81.5 per cent of the population of the Russian Federation were ethnic Russians. Of the remaining 18.5 per cent, made up of many ethnic groups, only 6.7 per cent lived within 'their' ethnic states or autonomies. Most of the remaining population of national minorities were persons belonging to the 'internal diaspora', that is, ethnic groups such as Tatars, Bashkirs, and Chuvash who had their own 'titular state' within Russia but who lived outside of it. In addition, there are many Russians who live in the autonomous republics within Russia, as well as in the former union republics. Are these people considered to be immigrants, even though they never crossed an internationally recognized border? How many years or generations must a family reside in a certain place before losing the status of immigrant? Are immigrants only those people who shift from one independent country to another one? Moreover, are the many Jews, Germans, Koreans, Poles, and Turks who have lived in Russia for centuries considered to be immigrants? In legal terms, and according to common sense, they are not. In the context of the nationalist discourse, however, they are, because they live outside of their 'ethnic homeland'. But what exactly is an ethnic homeland?

In Russia, some national minorities are referred to as indigenous populations or constituent nations. Their languages and cultures, however, remain marginal. They constitute a numerical minority within the territories they inhabit and live and work side-by-side with people of other ethnic affiliations. In many cases, these groups do not constitute a distinct society, and instead integrate into the cultural mainstream, which is usually Russian. How does one refer to these people?

Many ethnic groups in Russia, as in many other countries, consist of persons of diverse origin. For example, among the Armenians who live in Krasnodar province in southern Russia, one can find descendants of immigrants from the Ottoman Empire and Crimea dating back to the eighteenth and nineteenth centuries, Soviet-period migrants from Armenia, Georgia, and Central Asia, and refugees from conflicts in Abkhazia and Azerbaijan in the late 1980s and early 1990s. A similar situation holds for the Tatars, who reside in Samara province—83 per cent Russian—which is located in the Middle Volga region and borders Tatarstan. Some of the Tatars have lived there for centuries, some are nineteenth-century or Soviet-period migrants, while others are forced migrants from Central Asia, arriving during the last decade. This list can be extended. Who within such groups are immigrants and who are minorities? How can they be separated? Even the use of the term 'migrants' in the post-Soviet context is disputable. For instance, Russians in the former Soviet Union did not move from their state; rather, the state 'moved' from them.

In any event, why must persons belonging to these types of groups be treated in different ways, while the actual differences between them are conditional and elusive? If one presumes the equal dignity, rights, and needs of all individuals, why should the claims of one culturally distinct group be considered less legitimate than similar claims of another? Why are some categories considered more equal than others? One could say that an immigrant chooses integration into an alien society, but such an assertion can hardly be made with regard to the second or third generations. Moreover, what is the practical meaning of this kind of division? Should regional authorities in Krasnodar and Samara prohibit pupils whose grandparents are not local natives from attending publicly funded schools that offer instruction in, respectively, the Armenian and Tatar languages?

In accordance with contemporary international legal norms, minority protection can be divided, in general terms, into three elements:

symbolic recognition, 'protective' rights—meaning freedom from discrimination, and from any prohibition or restriction on the maintenance and expression of cultural identity—and positive measures, such as funding minority cultural institutions. A number of international covenants, as well as the national legislation of almost all countries, contain anti-discriminatory provisions. For example, all citizens are equal before the law and authorities, and non-nationals must not be discriminated against on the grounds of origin, ethnicity, or race. Any division in official discourse into 'more equal', or 'more respectful', or 'more valuable' ethnic groups is incompatible with the objectives of anti-discriminatory legislation.

Authorities may set priorities for the financing of institutions that serve minority cultures, taking into consideration public opinion, the size of a group, and available resources. These preferences can be and must be justified by practical, not ideological, reasons. Can a responsible and liberally-oriented government challenge an ethnic group on the pretext that it is not indigenous enough? Would it be reasonable to have a negative attitude towards them and increase tension by creating socially and culturally deprived categories?

A clear division between 'hosts' and 'guests', and treating the latter as a potential threat to the development, identity, or even survival of the former are cornerstones of ethnonationalism. This type of attitude is widely spread, but there is nothing liberal about it. Why, therefore, should a liberal theorist follow these views or support them directly or indirectly? Politicians might arbitrarily make the distinction for political purposes, but it is not clear why theoreticians must follow the same logic. The power structures and political movements acting on behalf of native groups in many cases appear to have more resources and capability to impose their vision of the situation than the pressure groups acting on behalf of migrants. In any event, political pressure is an argument of a different type, and one should not confuse principle and fact. *Ad hoc* decisions may go beyond some standard requirements, but they should not automatically alter the principle itself.

The Risks

In assessing the potential outcomes of Kymlicka's model of 'ethnocultural justice', the symbolic reality that encompasses the issue of ethnic relations must not be neglected. The notions of hosts and guests, people living in or outside a state of their own, and the special rights of minorities, are much more than words. The language of group rights defines a symbolic space, predetermining the perception of the reality, agenda, and mode of behaviour of many people, including those who participate in decision-making. Even if such symbols do not find their way into policy prescriptions, they still have an impact. The language of this approach towards ethnic groups has some inherent risks in so far as certain outcomes can contradict initially declared goals.

The first risk lies in the constant indoctrination of the public consciousness with the idea that a society is a sum of 'collective individuals' possessing a set of rights and interests. This leads to social relations being recast as inter-ethnic—that is, intergroup—relations. The second risk stems from the influence of external agents on the creation and strengthening of intergroup boundaries and divisions. Such boundaries are always being established by ethnic leaders and activists, in many cases in competition with one another. When governments, the academic community, international organizations, and foreign experts become involved in this process, the divisive effect is more far-reaching. It is, therefore, far from clear that drawing and strengthening inter-ethnic boundaries matches the objective of liberal theoreticians of an open and internally integrated society.

All arguments in favour of preferential treatment for minorities can be used to justify the protection of an ethnic majority, as it can also be described as a non-dominant community whose culture is at risk of alien influences and requires defensive measures. Russia offers a good example. At the end of the 1980s and beginning of the 1990s, the arguments for protecting 'minority peoples' and 'minorities' prevailed in public debates. Subsequently, the same arguments and underlying motives have been widely used for justifying the protection of Russians within and outside Russia, in so far as they are a disadvantaged people in an unfavourable position.

Territorial autonomy, or any other type of special status for an ethnic group, is usually justified by the need to protect a certain group from external cultural and linguistic influences. Discrimination is justified as a necessary protective measure on behalf of weak groups. Group rights for autonomous political institutions, a form of 'the peoples' right to self-determination', promotes the idea of unilateral actions in the name of some collective entity, in any circumstance regardless of the context. But this is based on the logic of revolution. Political segmentation of a culturally heterogeneous society along the lines of group rights denies the legitimacy of almost any state. This leads to situations where, for example, Hungarians in Serbia or

Armenians in Georgia are regarded not as vulnerable groups, but as agents of external powers.

If the notion of group rights through territorial autonomy, or any other model of segmentation, were internationally declared, it would deepen the existing internal conflict rather than lead to conciliation. When a subversive movement operates in accordance with some international standards, it understands that it will have support for a more radical and uncompromising position. Declaring a winner in advance and providing a 'liberation' movement with additional symbolic capital is not a good strategy in terms of law, human rights, and international security.

If countries were subjected to external coercion in their internal affairs on the basis of some strongly-worded 'universal' requirements, it would be a direct route to the destruction of the existing international system, which is based on state sovereignty. Violation of the principle of state sovereignty, including any form of support to 'liberation' movements, is unlikely to be compatible with international regulations. The case of Kosovo is an obvious example. Although a model under which the international community—that is, the US and NATO—decides which ethnic group is entitled to territorial autonomy and which to secession is feasible in technical terms, it is unlikely to be viable. Countries whose state sovereignty is threatened would cease their co-operation with international institutions, resulting in the fragmentation of the international community.

Concluding Remarks

I completely agree that the area of ethnic relations should not be neglected by liberal theory. Such issues as minority protection, the prevention and elimination of discrimination, conflict resolution, multiculturalism, and immigration policies contain a set of controversies and puzzles worthy of the deepest attention. As many of these issues are of crucial practical importance, attempts to put forward new normative guidelines or models based on liberal principles are very useful and welcome.

Nevertheless, my opinion regarding Kymlicka's initiative is that it appears unsuccessful, for the following reasons. Although Kymlicka addresses some of the problems that are created or aggravated by ethnonationalist doctrines or policies, his proposals for a solution are themselves based on the same or similar logic and language. The author also misuses generalizations and adheres to some disputable interpretations. Not everything, particularly in the area of 'ethnic relations', happens by virtue of some normative requirements; many things should be considered a matter of fact and not of principle. In some spheres, such as ethnic relations, universal or stereotypical prescriptions and solutions appear to be invalid too often. To my mind, such attempts would be fruitful only under certain preconditions, some of which I have tried to formulate in this paper.

In addition, one should not advocate a transition from position A to position B when the outcome of the transition is doubtful or its cost is knowingly higher than the benefits of position B. Is it useful to call the marginal position of minority languages and cultures an injustice when inequality is a permanent feature of each society and granting status to another minority language is impossible? One might criticize the popular model of multiculturalism—that is, the mainstream culture in the public domain and marginal cultures in the private sphere—but the model is honest and realistic. What is wrong with solving concrete problems, such as making the life of people belonging to minority cultures more socially, culturally, and psychologically comfortable, instead of misleading people?

When confronted with several solutions, one should opt for that one which is most flexible and does not potentially exclude other options. Imagine two completely different strategies. One selects some 'non-state nations' from a variety of culturally distinct groups and grants them a privileged status that raises their languages and cultures to the societal level. The other provides persons belonging to minorities more comfortable living conditions within a common society. If the first strategy is put forward as a normative requirement, it would lead to confrontation, making any positive output doubtful. The second strategy, however, does not exclude the development of a marginal language into a societal one under suitable conditions and with the consensus of the parties involved.

NOTES

1. An ethnic group is seen in statistical terms by governments, which institutionalize the groups through such mechanisms as censuses and registers.
2. An anthropologist might say that such organizations simultaneously construct these interests.
3. Democratic choice by the grassroots is not completely free and fair. It depends on the institutional framework within which elections are held and the ways in which the agenda was set.

4. This term was first used by Anthony Smith. See his *Theories of Nationalism* (London: Duckworth, 1983, 2nd edn) 64.

5. According to the 1989 USSR Census, the so-called 'titular nationalities' of the autonomous republics in Russia had, on average, a 42% share of those republics' population. (There are 21 such republics in the Russian Federation.) Russians constituted another 42% and the other ethnic groups accounted for 16%. Is it possible for a liberal theorist, not to mention a pragmatic politician, to talk about the autonomous regions as the 'property' of their titular nations? None of the local languages—the only probable exception being Tatar—is developed enough to substitute in the short term for Russian without violence, administrative coercion, and harsh restrictions.

Reflections on Minority Rights Politics for East Central European Countries

PANAYOTE DIMITRAS AND
NAFSIKA PAPANIKOLATOS

The new 'liberal pluralist' or 'liberal nationalist' approach to ethno-cultural diversity can provide a framework to reinterpret reality so that old concepts, nowadays considered obsolete, acquire different meanings, compatible with modernity. In this way East Central European (ECE) countries may be able to redefine many concepts overburdened by the weight of the region's history. Concepts such as nation, nationalism, ethnicity, nationality, kin-states, and minorities have to date been interpreted through signifiers which make them incompatible if not opposed to concepts such as democracy, diversity, pluralism, democratic republic, civil rights, minority rights, self-government, or federalism. Conditions must now be developed to provide for a framework that will make the notions of minorities, nations, national identities, and so on part of the democratic consol-idation. This is a long-term process requiring the development of a liberal and democratic political culture in these countries. It includes adapting constitutions to a multicultural notion of society, and estab-lishing stable, integral political institutions that respect and promote both pluralism and democracy. Most importantly, the process must enhance an autonomous civil society, which embraces all parts of society and guarantees that no particular ethnic, national, religious, linguistic, economic, or political majority and/or minority can dom-inate over individuals or minorities and limit their rights. By follow-ing this path progressively, ECE countries may create conditions unfavourable to illiberal ethnic nations and favourable to liberal civic nations. This certainly will not eliminate ethnocultural diversity and antagonisms. It will nevertheless provide the basis for acknowledging that conflicting relations are endemic to the liberal-democratic process. Therefore, inventing ways of managing them, rather than pretending neutrality or seeking to abolish them, is the way to secure stability and progress.

Today most ECE societies are very reluctant, if not hostile, to apply the liberal and democratic approach because they seem unable to overcome the burden of an authoritarian tradition. Formally, they may have become what are generally referred to as democracies in transition. In reality, this democratic process is immobilized in many instances by the transformation of one authoritarian model based on a socio-economic ideology to another authoritarian model based on the explosion of an aggressive nationalism of the majority versus minorities and neighbouring peoples. As long as each ECE state continues to cultivate the myth of belonging to the founding historic nations, whose primacy is a vital element for its survival, the evolution to 'multination' or 'multicultural' states to accommodate ethnocultural diversity will be perceived as tantamount to undermining the foundations of these nations.

The dismantling of former Yugoslavia and especially the case of Kosovo are very instructive, however tragic, examples supporting this argument. At the beginning of the crisis, the northern Yugoslav republics of Slovenia and Croatia were not so keen for independence, looking instead for a looser federal system. Had Belgrade acquiesced, a confederal Yugoslavia might still exist and millions of people's lives would not have been so tragically affected. As well, had Serbia maintained the autonomy introduced in Kosovo in 1974, this province would still have been part of the Federal Republic of Yugoslavia (FRY), perhaps as a republic. This was achievable as recently as 1998, but no longer is. Montenegro, weary of the suicidal tendencies of Miloševic-led serbia, started slowly but steadily seceding in 1999. Serbia's democratization, after October 2000, came probably too late to help the FRY survive. So Montenegro, backed by the international community, will end up formally severing its links with Serbia, and a distinct Montenegrin national identity and separate language, both already being elaborated, will be formally recognized.

Another supposedly less intolerant version of the reluctance to accommodate ethnocultural diversity asserts that granting minorities equal status with majorities would only invite, in the end, calls for the secession of territory to the benefit of some adjacent 'kin-state(s)'. This version, usually developed in foreign ministries, adds that the full enjoyment of individual rights, including self-identification, provides sufficient respect for prevailing international norms. In contrast, political, not to mention constitutional, collective recognition of ethnonational minorities would open Pandora's box. This line of argument would use abundant real or fabricated evidence from the recent or distant past when ethnonational minorities had secessionist agendas and/or were used by neighbouring countries' revisionist policies with potential or actual destabilizing results. Such minorities, even if they have never stated any autonomous or secessionist claims in the last one or two generations, continue, conveniently, to be perceived as latent Trojan horses.

In a context where cultural purity and authenticity predominate, national identities are exclusive and coercive, cultivating racism and xenophobia and promoting a monocultural society and nation-state that has become the property of only the dominant national group. The question is how the idea of respect for national identities or the right of nation-building can be rid of the semantics of exclusion and authenticity with which they have been historically impregnated in the ECE countries. How can they become compatible with the idea of liberal pluralist, open and democratic societies, in order for minority rights to be respected and multiculturalism to become the model for ECE countries, as it has become for the West, regardless of the degree of actual progress in the latter?

Some terms, usually perceived as innocuous in the West, tend to have a negative connotation in ECE countries, particularly in the Balkans. For example, the concept of 'minority' is most often perceived as pejorative. Ethnonational groups in successor states of the former Yugoslavia, which used to be officially called 'nations' or 'nationalities' and may have had in some cases near or real constituent status at the federal republican if not the federation level, resent being called minorities. They feel that this is a pejorative term and that it would deny them some of the rights they are claiming. Thus, Albanians in Macedonia and in Kosovo who have been fighting, respectively, for constituent nation status and outright independence perceive being 'relegated' to minorities as incompatible with their demands. In Greece, most Roma or members of the various Christian religious or linguistic minorities—Catholics, Protestants, Aromanians (speaking a neo-Latin language akin to Romanian) or Arberor (speaking a form of Tosk Albanian)—also loathe the term, but for different reasons. It is taken to mean only (ethno)national minority, thus implicitly denying them the right to feel, and be proud of being, ethnic Greeks.

Another example, which Kymlicka correctly raises, is that the examples of the Yugoslav, Czechoslovak and Soviet states gave a bad reputation to the concept of federalism in ECE countries. But the reluctance, if not suspicion, towards accepting such a concept also reflects the prevailing idea that a nation-state cannot grant equal status to another nation even at the substate level. Such a solution would be tantamount to granting ethnonationally-based autonomy. In the Balkans, *all* states started as autonomous units within the Ottoman Empire and, when the opportunity arose and/or when the Great Powers saw it in their interest, they were proclaimed independent: autonomy is therefore perceived as a first step to independence. This was also one of the main psychological stumbling blocks in the efforts to find a workable solution in Cyprus after 1974. Even today, many Greeks and Greek-Cypriots criticize as an act of submissiveness the 1977 acceptance, in principle, of a federal model by then President Makarios.

A sketchy doomsday scenario that is very popular, in public opinion as well as among opinion-makers, in all Balkan countries is the following. First a cultural group tries to achieve an ethnonational minority status identifiable to a kin-state. Once successful, it seeks territorial autonomy or federal status. Then, when the time is ripe or when major powers unsympathetic to the host state so decide, autonomy will turn into secession followed by annexation by the kin-state. This can be better understood by considering that in most ECE countries, national minorities were formed at the same time as national majorities, which sometimes was *after* the establishment of nation-states. In some cases, nations or proto-nations were formed and populations developed national identities only a considerable time after states in their region were established. This led to the emergence of new (proto-)nations, with their related national minorities whose legitimacy is no less than that of long-established identities. Kurds, Macedonians, and Muslims/Bosniacs are such cases.

In that light, in ECE countries, but also in most Western liberal democratic nation-states, one must speak of four and not three options for minorities. The first option for minorities is permanent *marginalization*, which characterizes the Roma community in many countries. *Assimilation* is the second option and the prevailing principle in ECE nation-states. Minorities practically merge culturally with majorities and cease to be identifiable by any cultural distinctiveness. This is distinct from *integration*, the third option, where minorities acquire some of the characteristics of the majority's societal culture but also keep many of their own distinct cultural characteristics. This is why integration is a 'two-way process': it must involve both majorities and minorities, educating majorities to be tolerant to differences and assuming a societal culture that does not address only mainstream citizens.[1]

There are, however, two types of integration. The first is achieved through what Kymlicka refers to as 'competing nation-building' founded on separate economic, political, and educational institutions in the minority's language: in this case a minority has achieved *de jure* or *de facto autonomy*, usually on a territorial basis. Another form of integration is *personal cultural autonomy*: within the dominant culture, minority members can keep and develop some of their own cultural characteristics without, or with only partially, resorting to parallel institutions, and hardly ever with a territorial basis. For example, they can receive bilingual rather than only minority-language education and have their own cultural institutions but participate in the majority-language-based economy, as in North America or Australia. This latter form of integration is hardly possible in cases of minorities that have just come out of protracted and/or atrocious conflicts with the majority, as in Cyprus, Kosovo, and Bosnia. There, parallel institutions are the only solution, with the hope that this separation will in the long-term vanish, after sustained reconciliation and efforts to join the globalized society or at least a European Union without borders.

ECE states have mostly tried to limit their minorities to the first two options of marginalization and assimilation—when they did not succeed in ethnically cleansing them. International norms, however, nowadays direct states to offer minorities one of the two options of integration, depending on the circumstances. The comprehensive Framework Convention for the Protection of National Minorities, for example, specifically prohibits 'assimilation' and encourages 'integration'. In both cases of integration, however, it is necessary to define what is and what is not permissible, not only concerning the external protection that states must grant minorities but also the internal restrictions they may be allowed to impose.

One of the most 'insecure' countries on issues of minority rights is Greece, which has repeatedly stated that it recognizes a religious minority, that of the Muslims, but no ethnic, national, or linguistic ones. Greek public opinion and the intellectual community have been profoundly conditioned to think in these 'nationally correct' terms. They not only strongly deny the existence of any other ethnonational group within Greece—let alone any related discrimination or other human rights violation—but go as far as denying the ethnonational identity of some minorities in neighbouring countries even though the latter are officially recognized therein. The 1999 Kosovo crisis gave ample evidence that, for all Greek media and politicians, the majority of the region's population was made up of 'albanophones' rather than 'Albanians'. Even when translating speeches of foreigners, including Miloševic, the media used 'albanophones' instead of 'Albanians'. Bulgaria may have recognized a Turkish community on its territory, but many in Greece prefer to refer to it in the Greek way, as 'Muslims'. Bulgaria, though, is a separate example. It officially claims that it has no 'minorities', just 'minority groups'. They believe that this semantic difference will ward off the issue of potential secessionism. 'Naturally', Macedonians are not among these groups, just as Bulgarians are not among the officially recognized minorities in Macedonia.

Greece may not be a post-Communist country in democratic transition, but it shares most of the ethnocultural, diversity-related problems of the other ECE and especially Balkan countries. It is the only ECE country that does not recognize the presence of an ethnonational minority or minority group on its territory. Although Greece has been, for almost two decades, a signatory and member of most international conventions and institutions addressing human and minority rights issues, its political culture remains quite distant from these principles. Undoubtedly, it enjoys the stability and progress provided by liberal-democratic institutions in modern Western states. Nevertheless, this transformation has so far remained fundamentally formal. Greek society still lacks a civic culture guaranteeing the rule of law. For a very long period, Greece appeared to follow a pattern more consistent with illiberal ethnic nations than liberal civic nations. Moreover, Greece is the only ECE country with a substantial immigrant/metic population, although it is similar to most EU countries in this respect.

Greece has had a thick, culturally sensitive policy of citizenship. Applicants not only had to reside in the country for some period, but they had to show they had assimilated Greek culture. The latter was perceived to include a Greek surname, a Greek mother tongue, at least formal adhesion to Orthodox Christianity and, usually, Greek parentage. Those coming from sensitive neighbouring countries—Albania, Macedonia, Turkey—as well as Muslims were practically excluded from naturalization. Faced with a flood of over half a million metics in the 1990s, as well as a declining population, Greece eventually launched a legalization process in 1998 and was considering in July 1999 to change its citizenship requirements towards a thinner, more open concept.

In late July 1999, suddenly and for the first time in modern Greek history, there was a debate on the modernization of the country's minority and citizenship policies. Under the impetus of Foreign Minister George Papandreou, then considered a supporter of multiculturalism, the public was informed that Greece was possibly moving towards the application of some principles of what Kymlicka would call 'ethnocultural justice'. In repeated interviews, the Minister said that the country had nothing to fear from the right of self-identification of its minority citizens: 'If the borders are not challenged,' he argued, 'it concerns me little if someone calls himself a Turk, a Bulgarian or a Pomak.'[2] Elsewhere he explained, 'Greece has nothing to fear from whoever feels he has such a [Macedonian] origin, and I want to stress that this is not just my thoughts. It is a well-established practice that allows the integration of minorities throughout Europe, as well as in other countries like Canada, Australia, and the USA. Such an attitude defuses whatever problems might have existed, allows the real blossoming of democratic institutions, as well as gives these people the feeling that they too are citizens of this country.'[3]

Coincidentally, a few days before Foreign Minister Papandreou's statements, all three Turkish minority deputies, along with thirteen Macedonian, Turkish, and human rights NGOs, made a public appeal for the recognition of Macedonian and Turkish minorities, the unconditional ratification by Parliament of the Council of Europe's Framework Convention for the Protection of National Minorities, and respect of these minorities' rights. At the same time, the Ministry of the Interior leaked to the media a plan that would radically change the citizenship policy to allow immigrants, after some years of residence, to qualify for citizenship. The new plan would not exclude, as has been the case until now, those from neighbouring countries or of a Muslim faith. Even the thorny issue of allowing the return of ethnic Macedonian political refugees, who fled as a result of the civil war in the late 1940s, was to be finally settled.

The reaction to these three proposed changes to minority and citizenship policies showed how in Greece, and probably everywhere else in the Balkans, public opinion as well as opinion leaders consider such policies inapplicable or undesirable. First, there was a near unanimous, verbally violent reaction to the appeal, enriched with xenophobic and other malevolent speech, and even some defamatory personal attacks against the signatories. The Foreign Minister's statements, as well as the coverage of the attempts to change the citizenship policy, were met with similarly harsh reactions, including those of some leading politicians and even from the government party, calling for his resignation. The reputedly authoritative morning dailies, in their editorials, called the statements 'a lapse'[4] and referred to an attitude of 'submissiveness'.[5] The newspaper *To Vima* elaborated further: 'There could not be even one Greek citizen, however conciliatory, ready to even discuss the presence of racial [*sic*] minorities. The Greek people is one and indivisible, with various religious beliefs that do not, however, affect the unity of the whole population. The government should immediately rectify a lapse, even involuntary, that gestates obvious and less obvious dangers.'[6] A column in the newspaper *Kathimerini*, by Stavros Lygeros, on 'The Sorcerer's Apprentices' revealed clearly the weight of history on many of the concepts raised in the discussion. Some people in the government of Costas Simitis (PASOK), we read,

with parochial fanaticism are trying to apply the model of the multicultural society in a national state. Yet Greece is not a country that was created by immigrants, like the United States and Australia, nor is it a former empire, like Britain, which incorporated some of its former subjects. After all, these countries don't recognize minorities. Greece is the country of an historic nation, which lives in a region full of ethnic prejudices and disputes and which has to face direct threats. That's why it can't afford to have sorcerer's apprentices at the helm.   (Stavros Lygeros, in *Kathimerini*, 30 July 1999, 1)

As a consequence of these reactions, the Greek government abandoned its reforms, and intolerance towards minorities remained unaffected. Greece demonstrates how difficult it is, even for a state integrated into the European framework of liberal pluralist and democratic institutions, to free itself from the weight of the regional historical dramatization of reality; it continues to interpret the present through the prejudicial, intolerant, and exclusionist policies inherited from the past.

Yet, majority aggressive nationalism, which excludes the 'others', and minority defensive nationalism, which employs similar means to defend itself in an unfavourable environment, go hand in hand. In both cases what is clearly lacking is an integral human rights culture that includes minority rights or a minority rights culture emerging from a human rights culture. In other words, a liberal pluralist and democratic approach to the question of minorities and minority rights is lacking. Surely, one can easily argue that, the culture of minority rights has developed to an unprecedented extent. This is far from an 'Era of Human Rights' for minorities, however. The apparently widespread interest in human and minority rights is rarely devoid of ulterior motives and thus subjected to ensuing limitations. It would be naive to believe that any country views respect for civil rights as a priority at home and abroad, and does not subjugate them to stability or narrow-minded national interests. Nevertheless, this absence of sincere commitment to human and minority rights is not the main reason why minorities cannot expect a brighter future. In spite of the growth of a culture of minority rights in society as a whole, there is virtually no minority rights-based political culture within the minorities themselves. This is the 'minority rights paradox'. (Panayote Elias Dimitras, 'The Minority Rights Paradox', *War Report*, 58 (February–March 1998) 64–5). Minority organizations and the leaders who articulate minority agendas appear to be driven mostly by ethnonational aspirations rather than by any deep-rooted respect for civic rights. To them, human rights are often just a tool for the achievement of their aims, as they are for most states. The Kurdistan Workers' Party (PKK) is an extreme but very eloquent example of this tendency: its ruthless and repressive methods are a mirror image of those used by the Turkish armed forces.

Minorities' unwillingness to see each other's demands as similar and thus work together to achieve them is a further obstacle to progress. Even formally trans-minority parties, like those in Albania and Bulgaria, function more as vehicles for the interest of one minority, as is the case with Greeks in Albania and Turks in Bulgaria. In both cases, Greek and Turkish minority leaders have stated that there is no Macedonian nation and no Macedonian minority in Greece and Bulgaria, thereby aligning themselves with Greek and Bulgarian hegemonic nationalism. Minority groups in Greece also hope that by accepting the country's intolerant nationalism they will improve their own situation within Greece. To this end Greek Catholics and Greek Jews have sent appeals to their fellow believers around the world stressing the 'historical' Greek character of Macedonia; the Jews even based their arguments on their ancient holy books. For their part, Aromanians (Vlachs) and Arberor (Arvanites) refuse to join forces with Macedonians (and Turks) to enable Greece, like all other EU countries, to support the establishment of a national office of the European Bureau for Lesser-Used Languages. Even the Roma, much despised by the Greek state, have rallied to the struggle with among other things lyrical contributions on the Greekness of Macedonia. They are also reluctant to work with international Romany organizations which, they have been led to believe, are suspect and potentially 'anti-Greek'.

There appear to be three reasons for such a paradox. First, minorities unfortunately tend to ape the behaviour of their oppressors: to the host state's hegemonic and aggressive nationalism, minorities usually respond with various sorts of defensive and peripheral, if not parochial, nationalism, equally exclusive and intolerant. One explanation for this tendency is that, in most cases, minorities in the Balkans, being less educated than majorities, lack the necessary knowledge to help them address their problems politically. It is also true that political leaders of both majorities and minorities find it easier and more convenient to rally their followers round illiberal nationalist policies than to elaborate liberal and rights-oriented ones.

A second reason is that most minorities simply ape the behaviour of their kin-state, of their corresponding 'mother' nation. All Balkan states are products of illiberal nation-building with a considerable degree of intolerance towards their domestic minorities. It is therefore almost instinctive that 'kin minorities', usually trained, if not educated, in the 'mother nation's' cultural and/or political institutions, would share the same illiberal values, and would refrain from criticizing minority rights violations in their 'mother nation-state'. This association with the kin-state, moreover, makes minorities easy targets for charges of separatism, and possibly of acting as foreign agents. It is, for example, no secret that the Turkish minority's policy in Greek Thrace is influenced, if not shaped by, the local Turkish Consulate, just as the Greek minority's policy in Albania is focused on the Greek embassy in Tirana and the consulate in Gjirokastra. Similar ties, albeit to a lesser extent, exist between Macedonia's Albanians and political forces, sometimes even the government, in Albania. Bulgaria's Turks have a somewhat comparable relationship with Turkey. Only Macedonia appears to have shied away from such privileged relations with her minorities in neighbouring countries—and is consequently accused of 'betrayal' by the Macedonian diaspora.

The absence of links between a minority and its homeland does not automatically make these minorities more realistic or devoid of nationalist leanings, however. The Macedonian political movement in Bulgaria is often separatist and maximalist, a position that has not helped them make substantial inroads into Bulgarian society. Greece's Macedonian activists represent a wide range of beliefs, from convinced pro-Europeans to fundamentalist nationalists. Luckily for them, the pro-European voices have been predominant and so many Greeks have come to sympathize with their struggle, indeed to accept what is otherwise a 'national taboo', that is, the existence of such a minority. In turn, Greece's Macedonian problems get wider international attention than those of their counterparts in Bulgaria, even though the latter suffer a worse form of repression.

A third reason for the 'minority paradox' is the absence in the region of civil societies that are worthy of that name. In well-developed democracies, non-governmental organizations and intellectuals from the majority help minorities acquire the necessary tools to defend their rights; they also tend to defend minority rights with vigour as they perceive such an attitude as a necessary component of their struggle for more integral and stable democracies. In the post-Communist countries, on the other hand, civil society is only now emerging. Its development is usually slow, if not distorted, due to the lack of a democratic culture in society. There is a prevailing tendency for the large majority of the NGOs and the intellectuals to adopt 'nationally correct' attitudes and thus accept their being used as instruments in the illiberal nation-building of their ethnonational group.

The lack of an independent and organized civil society also characterizes Greece, which has not been through a long-term authoritarian regime, although almost all governments prior to the colonels' dictatorship (1967–74) were characterized by a kind of 'paternalist democracy' where parliament was unable to function independently of the arbitrary interventions by the military and the crown. Thus, it is understandable that civil society could not have flourished, and the last twenty-five years of consolidating democracy have revealed a deficiency in liberal pluralist and democratic culture in society and the political world.

It is a 'paradox of the minority paradox'—or an exception that confirms the rule—that Hungarian minorities in Southeast Europe tend to be much less nationalistic than other minorities, although they live in rather or very intolerant countries—Romania and present-day Yugoslavia are the respective examples. In fact, this differentiation of Hungarian minorities may simply reflect the fact that their kin-state, Hungary, has chosen to be a strong supporter of minority rights: its political élite has correctly evaluated that such a strategy is more beneficial to a country with hardly any major domestic national minority problems but a considerable number of kin minorities in half-a-dozen countries around it. Already by 2000, the new Hungarian government's more nationalistic approach to Hungarian minorities is held by some responsible for the hardening of the attitude of some Hungarian minority leaders, in particular Vojvodina.

One can safely state that when the minority paradox is eclipsed, minorities will stand a fair chance of recognition of, and respect for, their rights. At the same time, however, majority nation-building in their corresponding nation-states will have to overcome those coercive practices, hegemonic methods, restrictive policies, and exclusivist agendas that only lead to ethnocultural conflicts. To reach such a goal, the liberal nation-building model is very useful because it is based on the reconciliation of nationalism with liberal pluralism and democracy. In this way, nation-building becomes a respected rather than a reactionary concept, for both majorities and minorities. Only its limits need be defined in ways that would also make it consistent both internally and externally. Democratic consolidation and respect for human rights can become fully effective only if elaborated transnationally. The key norm is that each nation-building project should respect all other such projects.

For example, Greeks have the right to defend their nation-state and the rights of Greeks in Albania and Turkey, but should at the same time also respect the rights of those citizens of Greece who identify with the nation-building processes of the Macedonian and Turkish nations. This argument was aptly used by Foreign Minister Papandreou in the July 1999 debate: 'Imagine if they told a Greek of Albania or in America that you cannot call yourself a Greek, because you are classified as Ottoman or Orthodox, but you are not a Greek, what the reaction of that Greek will be.'[7] Conversely, Turks have the right to ask for the respect of their nation as well as for the various Turkish minorities in the Balkans; but they should also be expected to respect competing nation-building processes in Turkey, the Kurdish example being the most obvious. At the same time, Turkish as well as Albanian minorities should also respect the rights of other Muslims in the Southern Balkans to assert non-Turkish identities, be they Pomak, Bulgarian, Macedonian, Torbesh, Gorani, etc. Likewise, Greeks should respect the right of many Aromanians (Vlachs)—mostly outside Greece—not to identify as Greeks, just as Albania should not limit the territory within which an Albanian citizen can claim a Greek or Macedonian identity. Bulgarians and Macedonians have to overcome the mutual lack of respect that makes these minorities in each other's nation-states 'taboos'.

This primordial principle should also extend beyond ethnonational minorities. In dozens of East and West European countries, traditional religions are showing varying degrees of intolerance towards 'New Religious Movements'—the use of the term 'sect' is demeaning and should be avoided—as if these traditional religions were not once new religious movements themselves. Many ethnonational cultures also contain elements at odds with gender equality or respect for sexual orientation.

Indeed, as Kymlicka notes, 'national minorities should have the same tools of nation-building available to them as the majority nation, subject to the same liberal limitations'. It is the latter condition, however, which appears to be lacking in the Balkans. The developments in Kosovo after the end of the 1999 NATO strikes on the FRY indicate that, unfortunately, under the very eyes of the international community, the former, and atrociously oppressed, Albanian minority oppresses and cleanses Kosovo of the Serbs and Roma who remained there. Thus, the Serb ethnic cleansing project is being reproduced or aped by the very community against which it was originally directed. The paradox seems to persist as respect for human and minority rights becomes more and more a distant vision in that region.

Western experience shows that what are often perceived as shocking assimilatory practices in the late twentieth century Balkans, aimed at strengthening the position of the dominant nations in their states, are often repetitions of what Western countries did one or two centuries ago, when the ruthlessness of these methods was not considered unacceptable. Assimilation via a highly centralized state apparatus, which was controlled by the privileged ethnocultural majority, was a legitimate practice of the time and in some cases continues to this day. This should not serve as an excuse for a modern imitation but as a way to show that, in fact, there are no exceptions, and that nation-building has followed similar methods regardless of the geographic location of the nation-states. 'Multination' states and policies of multiculturalism have been applied slowly, involving often painful struggles and many debates. Including ethnocultural diversity as a fundamental political right for the realization of modern liberal and democratic nation-states has not been an unconditional principle for any nation-state.

In the past two centuries all emerging liberal democratic nation-states struggled to guarantee participation in the governmental institutions and an autonomous civil society. At the same time, however, they had to secure the nation from ethnocultural diversity. Economic progress in the past century has allowed the assimilation and/or integration of various groups. Yet, even cases of voluntary integration and involuntary assimilation were rarely accompanied by deep-rooted political liberties arising from the recognition of minority rights. Thus, whenever an economic crisis marginalized again all those without real political rights—including minorities—the deficiency of a culture of political liberty, that is, the right of identity in liberal democracies, became apparent.

One need not feel surprised at the new rise of racism and xeno-phobia in the European Union and elsewhere. The new immigrants, refugees, and metics entering the Schengen fortress of a liberal demo-cratic European Union are confronted daily with the exclusionist and intolerant political culture of European societies and governments. Minority rights, whatever their identity, are political rights, and their effective exclusion from the map of fundamental rights calls for the questioning of the nature of our political systems. The debate over minority rights is far from a debate that concerns only ECE coun-tries. It is a wider one, which should involve, equally, old Western liberal democracies and new emerging ones. Both can learn from their respective experience. The former can learn that rights should be assigned to all, irrespective of identity, rather than treating them as privileges reserved only for majorities, and the latter that liberal democracies need not fear minority rights, since most examples demonstrate that promoting them has led to stability and progress for minorities as well as majorities.

NOTES

1. Will Kymlicka, *Multicultural Citizenship: A Liberal Theory of Minority Rights* (Oxford: Clarendon Press) 1995, 96.
2. *Klik*, July 1999 (interview available at: http://www.papandreou.ge/july99/synklik27799.html.
3. 29 July 1999, radio station *Flash* (interview available at: http://www.papendreou.ge/july99/synklik27799.html) web site address correct as of March 2001.
4. *Kathimerini*, 30 July 1999, 2.
5. *To Vima*, 30 July 1999, 1.
6. Ibid.
7. *Flash* interview. (see note 3 above).

Territorial Autonomy as a Minority Rights Regime in Post-Communist Societies

PÅL KOLSTØ

The vast majority of the new states that were established in 1991 on the territory of the former Soviet Union have proclaimed themselves as 'nation-states', the term by which democratic states in the Western world are designated. Among former Soviet citizens transition to national statehood is often regarded as inseparable from democratization and de-Communization. Instead of the Communist dictatorship they have suffered for most of the twentieth century, their country shall now be ruled by the people itself, by the 'nation'.

A major problem with this kind of reasoning, however, is that the concept of 'nation' is ambiguous. While it may indeed be conceived as synonymous with 'the people itself', the *demos*, in Eastern Europe the nation is at the same time very often seen as identical with 'the ethnic community'. In ethnically homogeneous countries like Iceland such an ambiguity would have few practical consequences, but hardly any states in Eastern Europe belong to this category—which is the exception rather than the rule among the states of the world. At the time of the collapse of the USSR, all of the former Soviet republics except Armenia had sizeable ethnic minorities among their population—between 17 and 60 per cent.[1] When political independence was proclaimed in the name of the 'people' and 'the principle of national self-determination', the status of these minorities was unclear. In some documents and declarations, in particular those that were designed for an international audience, they were spoken of as full-fledged members of the nation. When it came to practical policies, however, the situation was somewhat different. Nation-building—that is, the actual policies that are pursued to bring about the desired nation-state—took the language, culture, and traditions of the majority population as its starting point.[2]

Up to a point, this was hardly avoidable. As Will Kymlicka has pointed out, a state may well tolerate a plethora of religions and other cultural identities among the population, but when it comes to such a crucial matter as language, it can hardly remain completely neutral. It is impractical and costly to institutionalize more than one language for government business—the 'state language' or 'official language'.[3] In the vast majority of states there is only one official language, which is also the language of the majority population.[4] With the exception of Belarus, all former Soviet republics conform to this pattern.[5] In addition, nation-building is also geared towards the identity and interests of the titular nation in a number of areas in which ethnically neutral solutions could have been found.

Given the lack of congruity between *demos* and nation in post-Communist states, there is an in-built tension between what Juan Linz and Alfred Stepan have called the 'conflicting logics of democracy and nation state.'[6] One possible way to address this problem is to allow the minorities to pursue, as it were, their own nation-building on a smaller scale within the larger nation-state. A cultural group that constitutes a minority in the total population of the state will often form a majority in certain areas. Such areas may be designated as the 'homeland', and given a status as 'their' autonomous unit. If they cannot expect to hear their language spoken from the rostrum of the national parliament, they may be given a legislative assembly of their own within this autonomous territory, in which the traditional language of their group is the working language. This assembly could be invested with jurisdiction over such matters as education, language policy, and other issues that may be decided locally.

In international political science literature, territorial autonomy (TA) has been put forward by a number of experts as one possible conflict-reducing mechanism, among others.[7] IGOs have been more cautious in recommending this device, but in 1990 the Copenhagen meeting of the Conference of the Human Rights Dimension of the CSCE pointed to 'appropriate local or autonomous administrations corresponding to the specific historical and territorial circumstances' as a way of protecting or promoting the ethnic, cultural, linguistic, or religious identity of 'certain national minorities.'[8] This resolution, however, was not followed up by the Council of Europe when it adopted the Framework Convention for the Protection of National

Minorities in 1995, which has been described as 'unusual, to say the least, in the field of minority protection.'[9]

Even so, an increasing number of West European states are adopting TA as a part of their minority protection repertoire. In addition to the long-established Swiss federation a number of other states are evolving towards an ethno-federal model—the prime examples being Spain, Belgium and, most recently, the United Kingdom. The time when the prototypical Western democratic state was based on the centralized, unitary model—the Republic of France being the modular case—seems to have passed.

In the post-Soviet space and in post-Communist Eastern Europe, demands for TA have been set forth by a number of ethnic minority leaders but they have rarely been met. The political authorities in the new states usually aver that they are willing to go to great lengths to accommodate their minorities, but they draw an absolute line at territorial autonomy. The very mention of these two words by a minority leader is often taken as a sign of his or her untrustworthiness and disloyalty towards the state. Two main reasons are given for this total rejection. First, territorial autonomy is seen as a stepping stone to secession. Any concession of this kind will jeopardize the territorial integrity of the newly-established nation-state. TA is rejected as contrary to *raison d'état*.

Second, it is pointed out that, as a rule, the putative minority homeland is no more culturally homogeneous than is the state as a whole. Sometimes it is populated by a second-order minority, other times by sizeable groups of the majority population, or by both. These groups will not feel comfortable with a TA arrangement designed to cater to the needs of one particular ethnic group. For second-order minorities it might mean, for instance, that they have to learn not two but three languages—their own, the state language, and the official language of the autonomous unit in which they are living. Thus, the entire problem of minority discrimination, which TA is supposed to remedy, is reproduced and perhaps even magnified by this political device. TA, then, may be dismissed not only by *raison d'état* but also by human rights arguments.

In this chapter I will discuss the validity of these two objections to TA in the post-Soviet states against the background of the history of TA in the Soviet Union and the actual experiences with TA in the successor states. People's attitudes and perceptions towards TA will inevitably be coloured by their previous experiences with this arrangement. These attitudes and perceptions will to a large degree determine how well TA might work at present.

The Soviet Legacy

Vladimir Lenin, the founder of the Soviet state, was a staunch believer in the unitary nature of the state. As he saw it, reasons of control and efficiency dictated the need for strong centralization. Territorial autonomy would pander to nationalist sentiments in the population and be detrimental to the building of socialism. It is true that in 1903 he had insisted that the Bolshevik party should include in its programme a clause guaranteeing the right of the nations to self-determination, but this should not be interpreted as an acceptance of TA. Rather, it was a promise that those nations in the multinational Russian empire that did not want to remain in the state after the revolution, which he was determined to bring about, should be granted the right to secede altogether. But this promise was not made in good faith. Rather it was a sop thrown to the disgruntled minorities in the Russian empire to harness them to the cause of a Bolshevik revolution.[10]

Lenin, however, was very much a pragmatist willing to bend his principles to the contingencies of the day. During the first years of Soviet power he became convinced that TA needed to be granted to the major non-Russian minorities to quell dissent and win them over to the cause of Bolshevism. Thus, when the Soviet Union was established in 1922, this state was given a federal structure after all. Lenin and his advisors reasoned that nothing much was lost by that: real power in the Soviet Union rested not with the state structures anyhow, but with the Communist Party, which remained strictly centralized.

The Soviet federation was an extremely complex structure, with no less than four levels of autonomous units. At the top were the union republics, followed by autonomous republics, autonomous oblasts (counties), and national, later renamed autonomous, okrugs (districts). Each category had its own set of prerogatives and rights, fewer the further down in the hierarchy one descended. In the West there was a strong tendency among Soviet nationality experts to dismiss these rights as fictitious, and indeed they were far less wide-ranging in real life than on paper. Each union republic had its own legislative assembly, government, legal code, state insignia, and even a constitutional right to secede, but they were still in many respects treated as ordinary administrative regions ruled from Moscow. This was particularly true with regard to economic policy.

At the same time, it seems clear that during some periods this federal framework was filled with a certain amount of real content.

This was the case during the so-called *korenizatsiia* or 'indigenization' period in the 1920s, when decentralization took place by design, and again in the late Brezhnev era, when decentralization took place by decay. During those periods the local élites were able to influence life in the republics in three policy areas in particular: language, education, and recruitment to top positions in the party and state apparatus. In all three areas the members of the titular ethnic group and their culture were given preferential treatment.[11]

While the Soviet population censuses listed more than one hundred ethnic groups, only some fifty had an autonomous unit of their own.[12] Indeed, many ethnic groups in the USSR were so small that the establishment of a separate autonomy for them was out of the question but, importantly, some larger groups also had to do without their own homeland. These were the diasporas, such as Poles, Koreans, Bulgarians, and Greeks. In most cases these diaspora groups did not live on a compact territory, but were dispersed.[13] Besides, these groups belonged to nations that had their own separate nation-states elsewhere, such as Poland, Korea, and Bulgaria. It was felt that nobody could be entitled to more than one homeland.

The 'internal Soviet diasporas'—Ukrainians outside Ukraine, Tatars living outside Tataria, and so on—enjoyed no cultural protection or linguistic rights.[14] The only exception to this rule was the 25 million Russians living outside the RSFSR. They could read Russian-language newspapers, send their children to Russian-language schools, and so on, but this was not the result of any special minority rights protection. Rather it followed from the fact that Russian was the dominating culture in the Soviet Union and Russian was *de facto*—but not *de jure*—the official language of this state.[15]

Contrary to received opinion, it seems fair to say that for long periods more ethnic groups enjoyed more linguistic and cultural rights in the Soviet Union than in most multinational states in the modern world.[16] (The fact that the Soviet Union was a non-democratic state in which all citizens were denied basic political rights has tended to obscure this circumstance). The Soviet nationality model was also exported to some, but not all, states in the Eastern bloc. *In casu*, the Yugoslav federation was closely patterned on the Soviet model and was filled with even more substance than its prototype after Tito's break with Stalin. Romania, under its leader Gheorghe Gheorghiu-Dej, introduced a separate autonomous district for the Székelys (ethnic Hungarians) of Transylvania but this arrangement was scrapped under Nicolae Ceauşescu. Czechoslovakia remained a strongly centralized state under the Stalinist regime of

Antonin Novotny, but was partially federalized in 1969 as the only lasting result of the Prague Spring.[17] The Soviet minority model was even exported to some Communist countries outside Europe, and can still be found in adapted versions in the state structure of Vietnam and the People's Republic of China.[18]

Thus, all across the Communist bloc minority rights were given a territorial form. This is one important reason why TA has been high on the list of demands of national minorities in both the former Soviet Union and former Eastern Europe after the fall of Communism. TA is simply the only kind of minority rights regime with which they have any experience. Minority leaders fully recognize that even if they are granted TA this may well turn out to be just another 'Potemkin village', sheer tokenism, as was the case during high Stalinism. Still, they reason, all alternative arrangements will give them even fewer guarantees against assimilatory or marginalizing policies in the new nationalizing states.

Territorial Autonomy in the Soviet Successor States

While all the new states in Eurasia share a common Soviet legacy of nationality policy, their preconditions for minority rights regimes in general and for TA in particular differ in many other respects: in terms of the number and size of the minorities; the degree to which the minorities live in compact groups or are dispersed all over the territory of the state; and so on. As we have seen, the Soviet legacy did not affect all the ethnic groups in a uniform way. There were different kinds of TA arrangements, and some groups had no TA at all. Furthermore, some post-Soviet minority groups seem to have a strong sense of common identity and strongly nationalist leaders. They have made vocal demands for TA, and are even prepared to fight for it with weapon in hand, while others are not. Finally, the reactions of the authorities in the new states have also varied considerably, both between states and over time, from complete rejection of TA to various degrees of accommodation and compromise. The few TA arrangements that have been offered have different content and structure.

All this makes it extremely difficult to generalize about TA as a conflict-reducing and justice-promoting mechanism in the Soviet successor states. In order to introduce some simplicity and structure in the below presentation, I will arrange them according to two binary variables: TA versus no TA, and before versus now. This gives us a four-fold typology:

	Had TA in the USSR	Did not have TA in the USSR
Has TA today	1	3
Does not have TA today	2	4

Group 1

The highest number of TA arrangements—in the Soviet period and today—are found in the Russian Republic. Russia is the only Soviet successor state that is formally proclaimed as a federation, and ethnicity is a basic structuring element in its federal structure. No ethnic group that enjoyed the status as titular nationality in an autonomous republic, autonomous oblast, or autonomous okrug in Soviet Russia has been deprived of this status after the fall of Communism—and no new groups have been granted this status either. This, however, does not mean that the federal arrangement in Russia has been static. On the contrary, there has been a constant tug-of-war over the prerogatives the autonomous units, the so-called subjects of the Federation, shall enjoy. This struggle had already started under perestroika when all autonomous republics in Russia, as well as most of the autonomous oblasts, unilaterally upgraded their status to 'republic'. This unilateralism was grudgingly accepted by the central authorities and this is the status these units enjoy in the current Russian constitution.

In addition to the constitutional provisions regulating the relationship between central authorities and the republics in Russia, Moscow has concluded bilateral treaties with a large number of federation subjects, in which different degrees of rights and prerogatives have been enshrined.[19] As a result, more minority groups enjoy more rights in Russia than in any other Soviet successor state. Some Russian politicians believe that these rights are excessive and want to trim them down, even to the point of abolishing the federal structure of the state altogether. This latter solution, however, is simply not feasible under current conditions, and no responsible politician in Russia is seriously advocating it. The structure of the Russian federation is still in the process of being negotiated but it is clearly here to stay.[20] Most Western experts seem to agree that TA arrangements in Russia have played a stabilizing role in transition politics in Russia—the major exception to this is of course Chechnya.[21]

Uzbekistan, Tajikistan, and Georgia have also inherited TA arrangements from the Soviet period that continue to exist: Karakalpakia, Gorno-Badakhshan, and Ajaria, respectively. In Uzbekistan, this arrangement seems to have as much of a pro forma character today as it had under Communism; in Tajikistan, the Gorno-Badakhshan autonomous oblast is the home of a number of Ishmaelite mountain tribes and became one of the strongholds of the Islamist opposition in the civil war that ravaged the country in 1992–5.[22] This TA arrangement appears to have been one factor that increased the mobilizational possibilities of the opposition and has thus arguably contributed to the fragmentation of the state. Ajaria is the home of Georgian-speaking Muslims and is today the only one of three TA arrangements in Georgia that is still functioning.

Group 2

Besides Ajaria, Georgia inherited from the Soviet period the autonomous oblast of South Ossetia and the autonomous republic of Abkhazia, both of which have been abolished by central authorities in Tbilisi. The autonomous status of South Ossetia was repealed in December 1990 under the erratic Georgian President Zviad Gamsakhurdia, an act that immediately unleashed a civil war.[23] The autonomous status of Abkhazia disappeared from the constitutional arrangement of Georgia when the Georgian national assembly in February 1992 decided to re-enact the pre-Communist constitution of 1921 that assigned no formal status to Abkhazia. Abkhazia reacted in July the same year by reinstating the 1925 constitution for Soviet Abkhazia, which gave Abkhazia the status of a Soviet union republic outside Georgia. Civil war in Abkhazia broke out the next month.[24] The Abkhazians won with Russian military support. Both Abkhazia and South Ossetia are today *de facto* independent under Russian protection.[25]

Group 3

In three instances TA arrangements have been granted to groups in a former Soviet republic that did not previously enjoy them. These are Crimea in Ukraine, and the republics of Gagauzia and Dniestria, both in Moldova. Crimea had enjoyed an autonomous status within the Russian Federation between 1921 and 1944 but when this predominantly Russian-populated peninsula was transferred from the jurisdiction of the RSFSR to the Ukrainian Soviet Republic in 1954 it had already been downgraded to an ordinary oblast (county). In January 1991, local Crimean authorities arranged a referendum on autonomy, a motion that received overwhelming support from the local population. Ukrainian authorities accepted the results of this referendum, and the republic of Crimea was established as a constituent part of Ukraine.

Crimean autonomy politics, however, have not been plain sailing. In the protracted and complicated tug-of-war over the delineation of prerogatives between Crimean and Ukrainian authorities, both parties have occasionally tried to pull the rug from under the other party. In May 1992, Kiev unilaterally reduced the competence of Crimean organs of power, an act to which the Crimean Supreme Soviet reacted promptly by adopting a declaration of independence and a separate constitution for the peninsula, on 14 May. Since that time Crimean separatism has ebbed and flowed several times, with a high water mark in 1994 when the Russian nationalist Yurii Meshkov was elected president of the Crimean Republic. What seems to be a lasting solution was finally reached in December 1998 when a compromise formula for a Crimean constitution was adopted by the legislators in both Kiev and Simferopol, the capital of Crimea. While the politics of Crimean autonomy have passed through several serious crises, according to one knowledgeable observer, 'in the first seven years of Ukrainian independence, Crimean political autonomy played a significant role in maintaining political stability and preventing ethnoregional conflict.'[26]

In neighbouring Moldova, the Turkish-speaking Gagauz as well as the Russian and Ukrainian minorities reacted sharply against the strong ethnocentric tendencies in Moldovan nation-building under the Popular Front regime in 1989–91. In August 1990, the Gagauz-dominated areas in Southern Moldova were proclaimed a sovereign republic outside Moldova but inside the Soviet Union. Two weeks later the Slavic-dominated, Soviet-loyalist region on the left (eastern) bank of the Dniester river followed suit. Military conflict around Gagauzia was prevented by the intervention of Soviet military units, while the Dniester conflict escalated into full civil war, claiming approximately one thousand lives in 1991 and 1992.[27]

A solution to the Gagauz conflict was found in December 1994 when a special law established Gagauz Yeri as the homeland for the Gagauz, complete with its own constitution and legislative assembly. While this arrangement has been hailed by some as one of the most liberal minority regimes in Europe, other observers point out that the meagre financial resources at the disposal of the local Gagauz authorities give them very few actual possibilities to promote their own culture and language.[28]

The Dniester conflict still awaits final resolution. A bilateral agreement between the Moldovan and Russian presidents in July 1992 provided for a 'special status' for the Dniester region within a single Moldovan state. Both parties to the conflict, as well as the OSCE Mission to Moldova that has been trying to negotiate between them, agree that any future solution for Dniestria must be based on such a 'special status'. In 1995 the parties went one step further and agreed that the region shall be granted 'a legal status as a state' (*gosudarstvenno-pravovoi status*), but that is also as far as the agreement goes. During the seemingly endless negotiations the Moldovan side has made several important concessions but balked at any arrangement that to them looks like cementing and sanctioning the *de facto* independence that Dniestria enjoys today. To the Dniester leaders the special status as state means that Moldova must be transformed into a confederation in which each constituent part is free to conduct its own foreign policy and join different international organizations than the other party.[29] There is a strong suspicion among outside observers that the Dniester leaders are not really interested in achieving any final solution at all. As long as the parties continue to negotiate, the region can hold on to its *de facto* independence.[30]

Group 4

Finally, some regionally-based cultural groups in the former Soviet Union which did not enjoy TA in the Soviet period have presented demands in the 1990s for such autonomy that have not been met. In this category we find Rusyns (Ruthenians) in the Transcarpathian oblast of Ukraine; Russians in the north-eastern part of Estonia—the Ida-Viru county with the towns of Narva and Sillamäe; ethnic Poles in the Wilenszczyzna district outside Vilnius in Lithuania; and Russophone Europeans in some oblasts in Northern Kazakhstan, *in casu* Pavlodar, and Eastern Kazakhstan.

A referendum in Transcarpathia in December 1991 gave overwhelming support for TA in this oblast.[31] Initially some Ukrainian politicians signalled willingness to accept this demand, but at present Ukrainian authorities are holding out no offer of TA or any other kind of autonomy for the Transcarpathians. In fact, the Ukrainian state does not even recognize the Rusyns as a separate ethnic group, insisting that they are Ukrainians, plain and simple.[32]

In July 1993 the townships of Narva and Sillamäe arranged a local referendum on 'national-territorial autonomy'. Support for this proposal was over 95 per cent in both cities—with a turnout of 54 per cent and 60 per cent, respectively.[33] Estonian authorities, however, do not accept any kind of territorial autonomy for the Russian-speaking region, and the referendum was declared illegal by the Estonian state court. Considering the fact that some 70 per cent of Narva's population (in 1998), due to their lack of proficiency in the Estonian state language, do not qualify for Estonian citizenship and cannot participate fully in political life, Ida-Viru continues to enjoy less real local government than other Estonian counties.

In May 1991 local community leaders in the Polish-dominated Wilenszczyzna district outside Vilnius unilaterally proclaimed the establishment of a 'national-territorial Polish region', replete with its own flag, national anthem, and national bank. In August the same year Lithuanian authorities cracked down on this initiative on the grounds that Polish leaders in the area had supported the failed Communist coup in Moscow. In what many Poles in Lithuania see as an attempt to deny them any kind of self-rule whatsoever, Lithuanian authorities have designed—but not yet implemented—a redrawing of municipal borders in such a way that the Wilenszczyzna district will be split up and added to neighbouring municipalities.[34]

In Northern Kazakhstan, groups that push for TA are branded as separatist, and outlawed. This has particularly hit a number of Cossack units. In all regions in Kazakhstan, including the north, ethnic Kazakhs are replacing Russians and other russophones in leading administrative positions.[35] Kazakhs apparently regard the threat of separatism as real. On 19 November 1999, twenty-two men were arrested in East Kazakhstan Oblast, reportedly for having planned to organize an armed rebellion in the towns of Pavlodar, Oskamen, and Leninogorsk with the aim of establishing an 'Independent Republic of Russian Altai'.[36]

TA as a Minority Rights Regime in Post-Soviet States: Pros and Cons

This brief outline of the history of TA in the post-Soviet states indicates that the worst one can do is to take TA away from a group that enjoyed this kind of minority protection in the Soviet period. The chances that this will lead to civil war are great. It seems less problematic to deny TA to groups that cannot point to any historical precedence for such an arrangement in their area. True, the case of Dniestria, which was offered special status only after war had broken out, might indicate that denying TA to strong groups that did not enjoy it previously may indeed be fraught with violent consequences.

Violence, however, has been avoided in all cases discussed under Group 4 above, although usually at the expense of clear infringements of minority rights.

The granting of TA to a new group has yielded good results so far in two cases—Gagauzia and Crimea—but not as yet in the third case, Dniestria. It may be argued that differences in timing can account for this difference in outcomes. To hold out a promise of autonomy after a violent conflict through which mutual animosity and suspicion have been greatly enhanced is not quite the same as to do so before any blood has been shed. To the extent that state authorities in the post-Soviet states fear secessionist tendencies in parts of their territory, they might consider TA as a pre-emptive move.

However, national authorities in the new states will usually insist that as a strategy of pre-emption TA is unlikely to lead to the desired goal, rather to the contrary: groups that are granted TA will tend to use this as a jumping ground to achieve full independence. The Dniester case will be taken as proof of this, together with the Armenian-dominated Nagorno-Karabakh region in Azerbaijan, Chechnya in Russia, and Kosovo in Yugoslavia. Both Nagorno-Karabakh and Chechnya enjoyed autonomous status in the Soviet period, as an autonomous oblast and autonomous republic, respectively. The struggle for control over these regions has unleashed two of the worst wars in the post-Soviet space, with 20,000 deaths in the one case and 100,000 in the other.[37] In both of these cases, then, it seems that the separatists will be content with nothing short of complete secession.

In terms of principle, secession and TA are qualitatively different solutions, but in terms of practical politics they often shade into one another. S. W. R. de A. Samarasinghe has remarked that 'a separatist movement with modest aims that do not extend beyond devolution of power within the existing state can easily devolve into a full-blown secessionist movement.'[38] But, as Allen Buchanan has pointed out, the reverse may also be the case: a demand for a right to secede may merely be a strategic bluff to extract gains while remaining within the political union.[39] In retrospect we can see that this apparently was the case with the vast majority of independence declarations passed in the autonomous republics of the Russian Federation in the early 1990s—except Chechnya—and possibly also with the independence declaration passed by the Dniester republic in 1991.

Ironically, the clearest evidence in support of the suggestion that territorial autonomy within a state may be exploited as a springboard to achieve full independence, is provided by the Soviet successor states themselves. During perestroika the leaders in the union republics made maximum use of the territorial autonomy granted them in the Soviet constitution, and managed to engineer the dissolution of the Soviet state.[40] The political authorities in the successor states seem to be saying: since *we* misused TA, we cannot give TA to you, the current minorities.[41]

But even if the minorities were to somehow provide credible commitments or guarantees that they will refrain from stepping up the demand for TA into a demand for full political independence, they may be suspected of misusing in another way the limited political authority granted to them. In their autonomous unit they may discriminate against second degree minorities and/or against members of the majority population living in the area. Even worse, they may try to expel them. What is the record of TA arrangements in the post-Soviet space in this respect?

Sad to say, it is not a particularly good one. Many of the same exclusionary ruling techniques employed by the new majorities in the successor states indeed seem to be duplicated by the minorities whenever they get the chance. A common socio-psychological mechanism seems to be 'winner takes all'. In electoral politics this means that whoever wins in a national poll will feel entitled to fill all the most prestigious and well-paid jobs in the state with their supporters and dismiss the incumbents if they do not belong to their group. In autonomy politics it means that whoever gets control over a certain area will assume a right to give preferential treatment to their own group, not only culturally, but also in terms of political and economic power. Sovietologists are prone to call this the '*kto-kogo*' syndrome, after Vladimir Lenin's dictum that deep down 'who gets whom' is what politics is all about. A Western term to describe the same phenomenon is that politics is a zero-sum game.

In the ethnically defined subjects of the Federation in Russia the titular national group often manages to dominate local politics far out of proportion to their share of the total population. For instance, in the 1995 elections to the State Council of the Republic of Tatarstan, 73 per cent of the seats went to Tatars and 25 per cent to Russians, although both groups are about equal in size.[42] An even more remarkable case is Bashkortostan where the titular group, the Bashkirs, constitute a small numerical minority. Of the republic's population, some 22 per cent are Bashkirs, 29 per cent are Tatars, and 39 per cent are Russians—and yet, as of March 1995 Bashkirs accounted for 55 per cent of the republic's legislative assembly, with Russians having only 21 per cent, and Tatars, 15 per cent.[43] In this case, the titular group had managed to outmanoeuvre both the majority ethnic group in the larger state—the Russians—and a numerically strong second-degree minority, the Tatars.

In Crimea, the indigenous population of Crimean Tatars, returning from their war-enforced deportation to Central Asia, find themselves without political clout on the peninsula that is their ancestral home.[44] They also face enormous economic difficulties that they ascribe to systematic discrimination by the Slavic majority population. In the Dniester republic in Moldova many ethnic Moldovans complain that pro-Moldovan political parties are banned and they are not allowed to use their Moldovan language as they wish.[45] In Gagauzia the Gagauz are accused of discriminating against a second order minority, the Bulgarians.[46]

The situation in the Caucasian region is even worse. When Chechen nationalists took over in Chechnya in 1991 many Russians—not without reason—feared for their safety and left in droves. The introduction of Sharia as Chechen state law also clearly discriminated against the non-Muslim population of the republic. From Nagorno-Karabakh in Azerbaijan and from Abkhazia in Georgia, tens of thousands of Azeris and Georgians have fled since the Armenians and Abkhazians, respectively, took control. Similarly, in Abkhazia the Russian population fell from 28 per cent in 1926 to 17 per cent in 1979.[47]

Conclusion

Political leaders in the Soviet successor states often resent the advice issuing from Western political scientists and human rights experts on how they ought to accommodate their cultural minorities. Such advice often betrays condescending, paternalizing attitudes, they assert, and is also based on Western experiences and preconditions that do not obtain in their countries. Territorial arrangements for cultural minorities may perhaps work in stable, Western societies, it is argued, but not in newly established post-Soviet states where political authority is still shaky. Give the minorities an inch and they will take a mile.

These objections should not be brushed aside easily. Secession is not ruled out by international law but is legitimate only when it is based on mutual agreement between the parties. In no Soviet successor state, however, are the national authorities willing to countenance a truncation of state territory and they are entitled by international law to try to prevent it as long as they do not infringe on international law in another way, for instance, by using indiscriminate force against the civilian population such as Russia has done in Chechnya. But that argument does not lead to the conclusion that TA must be ruled out entirely. On the contrary, the new nationalizing states in the FSU may have a greater, not smaller, need to employ TA than do more consolidated democracies. What the post-Soviet states lack even more than strong political authority is mutual trust among the various groups in society. In any effort of confidence-building the stronger party has a greater responsibility than the weaker. In a national or nationalizing state the political groups representing the majority population must be assumed to be stronger than political groups representing the minorities.

In my view, cultural groups ought to enjoy cultural rights, that is, the protection, preservation, and development of their culture, including traditional language, religions, and way of life. This must apply to both majorities and minorities and these rights ought ideally to be enjoyed throughout the territory of the state. At the same time it is far from clear that cultural groups ought to enjoy any special economic or material rights, either nationally or locally. These are arguments that favour non-territorial (personal) autonomy over territorial autonomy as a minority protection regime.

Territorial autonomy is certainly no panacea for minority protection and leaves many problems unsolved. However, some arguments may be adduced that favour TA over other kinds of minority rights regimes. While the minorities ideally ought to enjoy cultural rights throughout the territory of the state, in practical terms these rights will often be far more easy to implement in a limited area designated as their homeland than elsewhere. While a regime restricting their cultural rights to one autonomous region may not be the optimal solution for the minority, it is certainly better than nothing. But the most important argument in favour of TA over other kinds of minority protection, as I see it, is that it gives the minorities some solid guarantees against encroachments from the majority population that no other minority protection regime may provide. Even while it does not make them 'masters in their own house'—as the titular nation in the state is regarded—it makes them at least 'masters in their own flat' within somebody else's house. This flat they may decorate as they see fit. There is a real danger that a TA arrangement may retard the consolidation of the perception that the entire house is the common home of all the tenants. But even a slow process towards the consolidation of civic nationhood must be preferable to all processes leading away from this goal, such as civil wars.

Finally, it should be pointed out that territorial and non-territorial schemes for minority protection are of course not mutually exclusive but may be employed simultaneously. Various combinations have been tried in a number of democratic countries with good results. A case in point is Finland, where the Swedish-speakers enjoy territorial autonomy in the Åland archipelago, as well as linguistic rights throughout the country. This arrangement has contributed to the Swedish-speakers' continued high degree of identification with the Finnish state and to a high degree of mutual trust between the two linguistic groups. In this and similar cases, then, the two kinds of minority protection complement and reinforce each other.

NOTES

1. In order not to be misunderstood I will emphasize that I do not regard ethnic groups as fixed, readily quantifiable entities. Groups do not exist 'objectively', but only by dint of the subjective allegiance of their members. Individuals who are born into a minority group may opt out of it, for instance by assimilation into the majority culture. My percentage estimates of minority populations in the former Soviet republics are based on 1989 Soviet census data. In this census the ethnicity of the Soviet citizens was registered according to their own self-description, not according to the official nationality recorded in their passports.
2. Pål Kolstø, 'Nation-Building In The Former USSR', *Journal Of Democracy*, 7/1, 1996, 118–32; Pål Kolstø, *Political Construction Sites: Nation-building in Russia and the post-Soviet States* (Boulder, CO: Westview Press, 2000).
3. Will Kymlicka, 'Introduction', in Will Kymlicka (ed.) *The Rights of Minority Cultures* (Oxford: Oxford University Press, 1996) 10. To be sure, exceptions do exist, such as bilingual Belgium, quadrilingual Switzerland, and so on.
4. A few states of the world have chosen either a minority language (Indonesia) or the language of the former colonial power as the official language, precisely in order not to favour one major group over the others.
5. The 1990 Belarussian language law proclaimed Belarussian as the sole official language in the former Belarussian Soviet Socialist Republic, but in a referendum in May 1995, Russian was introduced as a second state language alongside Belarussian.
6. Juan J. Linz and Alfred Stepan, *Problems of Democratic Transition and Consolidation. Southern Europe, South America, and post-Communist Europe* (Baltimore and London: Johns Hopkins University Press, 1996), 401ff.
7. Timothy D. Sisk, *Power Sharing and International Mediation in Ethnic Conflicts* (Washington DC: United States Institute of Peace, 1997) 49–53; John McGarry

and Brendan O'Leary, *The Politics of Ethnic Conflict Regulation* (London: Rout-ledge, 1997) 11–16; Graham Smith (ed.) *Federalism. The Multiethnic Challenge* (London: Longman, 1995); John Coakley (ed.) *The Territorial Management of Ethnic Conflict* (London: Frank Cass, 1993).

8. *The Document of the Copenhagen Meeting of the Conference of the Human Rights Dimension of the CSCE* (Copenhagen, 1990) 41.

9. Jan Wright, 'The OSCE and the protection of minority rights', *Human Rights Quarterly*, 18, 1996, 197.

10. Hélène Carrère d'Encausse, *The Great Challenge: Nationalities and the Bolshevik State, 1917–1930* (London: Holmes and Meier, 1992).

11. Some observers believe that this was more typical of the Asian than the European union republics. See Rasma Karklins, *Ethnic Relations in the USSR: The Perspective From Below* (Boston: Unwin Hyman, 1989) 77–100.

12. The number varied from census to census, reflecting changing political winds in Moscow as well as the effect of assimilatory processes on the ground. See Francine Hirsch, 'The Soviet Union as a Work-In-Progress', *Slavic Review*, 56/2, 1997, 251–78.

13. If they did have their own distinct settlements in the inter-war period, they no longer did after being forcibly deported to Central Asia during World War II.

14. Some Ukrainian-language schools existed in the Northern Caucasus and Moldova under Stalin, but the last of these were scrapped under Khrushchev.

15. Paul Kolstoe (Pål Kolstø) *Russians in the Former Soviet Republics* (London: Christopher Hurst and Bloomington: Indiana University Press, 1995); and Pål Kolstø, 'Territorialising Diasporas: The Case of Russians in the Former Soviet Republics', *Millennium—Journal of International Studies*, 28/3, 1999, 607–31.

16. Yuri Slezkine, 'The USSR as a Communal Apartment, or How a Socialist State Promoted Ethnic Particularism', *Slavic Review*, 53/2, 414–52; Ronald Grigor Suny, *The Revenge of the Past: Nationalism, Revolution, and the Collapse of the Soviet Union* (Stanford, CA: Stanford University Press, 1993). Many Soviet nationality experts will disagree wildly with this assessment. See e.g. Robert Conquest (ed.) *The Last Empire. Nationality and the Soviet Future* (Stanford, CA: Hoover Institution Press); Bohdan Nahaylo and Victor Swoboda, *Soviet Disunion: A History of the Nationalities Problem in the USSR* (London: Hamish Hamilton, 1990).

17. While the Slovaks received a separate territorial unit as a result of this arrange-ment, a number of other groups did not—the Hungarians in southern Slovakia, the Ruthenians (Ukrainians) in Eastern Slovakia, or the Moravians in the Eastern Czech lands.

18. Walker Connor, *The National Question in Marxist-Leninist Theory and Strategy* (Princeton, NJ: Princeton University Press, 1984).

19. *Asimmetrichnaya federatsiya: Vzglyad iz tsentra, respublik i oblastey* [Asym-metrical federation as seen from the centre, the republics and from the oblasts], (Moscow: Izdatel'stvo instituta sotsiologii RAN, 1998).

20. Kolstø, *Political Construction Sites*.

21. Helge Blakkisrud, *Den russiske føderasjonen i støpeskjeen* [The Russian federation in the melting pot], (Oslo: Spartakus, 1997); Graham Smith, 'Russia, Multiculturalism and Federal Justice', *Europe-Asia Studies*, 50/8, December 1998.

22. Barnett R. Rubin, 'Russian hegemony and state breakdown in the periphery:

causes and consequences of the civil war in Tajikistan', in Barnett R. Rubin and Jack Snyder (eds.) *Post-Soviet Political Order. Conflict and State Building* (London and New York, NY: Routledge, 1998).

23. Stephen Jones, 'Georgian: The trauma of statehood', in Ian Bremmer and Ray Taras (eds.) *New States, New Politics. Building The Post-Soviet Nations* (Cambridge: Cambridge University Press, 1997) 512.

24. The Georgians and Abkhazians have a long history of hostility, stretching back at least to the early decades of this century when the Abkhazians supported the Russian Bolsheviks against the Georgian Mensheviks. It would therefore be wrong to see the Georgians' abolishment of Abkhazian autonomy in 1992 as the only *causa belli*.

25. I omit from this survey any discussion of the autonomous republic of Nakhichevan in Azerbaijan. The population of Nakhichevan is compactly Azeri, that is, the same ethnic group as in Azerbaijan proper. This autonomous unit was not established as a minority rights regime, but for foreign policy reasons— to accommodate Kemalist Turkey in the 1920s. The other TA arrangement in Azerbaijan, the Armenian-populated Nagorno-Karabakh autonomous oblast, is also in many ways a special case. It has indeed unleashed an ethnically-motivated war with tens of thousands of casualties, but this is not a civil war. It is a war fought between two internationally recognized independent states, Armenia and Azerbaijan.

26. Gwendolyn Sasse, 'State-Building in Divided Societies: Crimean Regional Autonomy as a Means of Conflict-Prevention', paper presented at the fourth annual convention of the Association for the Study of Nationalities, New York, 15–17 April 1999, 27.

27. Pål Kolstø and Andrei Edemsky with Natalya Kalashnikova, 'The Dniestr Conflict: Between Irrendentism and Separatism', *Europe-Asia Studies*, 45/6, 1993, 973–1000.

28. For an upbeat assessment see Vladimir Socor, 'Gagauz Autonomy in Moldova: A Precedent for Eastern Europe?', *RFE/RL Research Report* 3/33, 26 August 1994, 20–8. For other viewpoints, see Charles King, 'Gagauz Yeri and the Dilemmas of Self-Determination', *Transition*, 1/19, 20 October 1995; Paula Thompson, 'The Gagauz in Moldova and their Road to Autonomy', in Magda Opalski (ed.) *Managing Diversity in Plural Societies. Minorities, Migration and Nation-building in Post-Communist Europe* (Nepean, Ontario: Forum Eastern Europe, 1998) 128–47.

29. Pål Kolstø and Andrei Malgin, 'The Transnistrian Republic—A Case of Politicized Regionalism', *Nationalities Papers*, 26/1, 1998, 103–27. In a conversation with this author in May 1995 the Foreign Minister of the self-proclaimed Dniester-Moldovan republic, Valery Litskai, suggested that Dniestria's relationship with Chisinau could also be modelled on Åland's relationship with Finland or on Liechtenstein's relationship with Switzerland.

30. See, for example, Charles King, *The Moldovans. Romania, Russia and the Politics of Culture* (Stanford, CA: Hoover Institution Press, 2000) 178–208.

31. Roman Solchanyk, 'Centrifugal Movements in Ukraine on the Eve of the Independence Referendum', *Report on the USSR*, 3/29, November 1991, 8–13.

32. Author's interview with officials of the Ukrainian Ministry of Migration and National Minorities, in September 1995.

33. Neil J. Melvin, *Russians Beyond Russia. The Politics of National Identity* (London: Royal Institute of International Affairs, 1995) 49.

34. Jørn Holm-Hansen, *Polish Policies in the European Borderlands. Ethnic institutionalisation and transborder co-operation with Belarus and Lithuania* (Oslo: NIBR, 1999) 149–55.
35. Ian Bremmer, 'Nazarbaev and the north—state-building and ethnic relations in Kazakhstan', *Ethnic and Racial Studies*, 17/4, 1994, 619–35; Pål Kolstø, 'Anticipating Demographic Superiority: Kazakh Thinking On Integration And Nation Building', *Europe-Asia Studies*, 50/1, 1998, 51–69.
36. *RFE/RL Newsline*, 22 and 23 November 1999.
37. The commonly accepted figure for death casualties in the 1994–6 Chechnyan war is 90,000. Since hostilities were resumed in 1999, at least 10,000 more people have died. It should be noted, however, that one Russian authority on the Chechen war, Valery Tishkov, has revised down drastically the casualty figures for the 1994–6 war to 35,000. See Valery Tishkov, 'Ethnic conflicts in the former USSR: the use and misuse of typologies and data', *Journal of Peace Research*, 36/5, 571–91, on 578.
38. S. W. R. de A. Samarasinghe, 'Introduction', in R. Premdas, S. W. R. de A. Samarasinghe, and A. Anderson (eds.) *Secessionist Movements in Comparative Perspective* (London: Pinter, 1990) 2.
39. Allen Buchanan, *Secession. The Morality of Political Divorce from Fort Sumter to Lithuania and Quebec* (Boulder, CO: Westview, 1991) 2.
40. In a referendum organized by Mikhail Gorbachev in March 1991, 70% of those who participated voted in favour of retaining a single Soviet state.
41. It is only fair to point out that the author of these lines is a Norwegian, that is, a member of a nation which achieved political independence under circumstances not too different from the Soviet republics, by pressuring the Swedes to accept a dissolution of the Swedish-Norwegian Union in 1905.
42. Valery Tishkov, *Ethnicity, Nationalism And Conflict In And After The Soviet Union. The Mind Aflame* (London: Sage, 1997) 256–7.
43. Il'dar Gabdrafikov, *Respublika Bashkortostan. Model' etnologicheskogo monitoringa* [The Republic of Bashkortostan. A Model for Ethnological Monitoring], (Moscow: Institut etnologii i antropologii RAN, 1998) 35.
44. In 1994 the Tatars were granted a special quota in the Crimean Supreme Soviet in excess of their share of the total population (14 seats). See Andrew Wilson, 'Politics in and around Crimea: A difficult homecoming', in Edward A. Allworth (ed.) *The Tatars of the Crimea. Return to the Homeland* (Durham, NC: Duke University Press, 1998) 299–302. The quota system, however, was abolished in 1998.
45. Cultural politics in the Dniester republic is complicated. The Moldovans are divided; some of the most fervent Russianizers in the republic are themselves ethnic Moldovans. The Dniester republic has three official languages—Russian, Moldovan, and Ukrainian—but Russian is used far more often than the other two.
46. Claus Neukirch, 'National Minorities in the Republic of Moldova—Some Lessons Learned, Some Not?', *South East Europe Review for Labour and Social Affairs*, 2/3, 1999.
47. While such *de facto* expulsions are absolutely inexcusable, they must be seen against the background of the demographic engineering pursued by the Azeris and Georgians over the last decades. When Nagorno-Karabakh was a constituent part of Soviet Azerbaijan the share of the Armenian population in this

autonomous oblast dropped considerably, from 91 per cent in 1939 to 80 per cent in 1970. Svante E. Cornell, *The Nagorno-Karabakh Conflict*, Working paper 46, Department of East European Studies, University of Uppsala, 1999, 11; J. Paul Goode, 'The Georgian-Abkhaz Conflict: A Triadic-Relational Analysis', unpublished manuscript, August 1999.

Nation-Building and Beyond

JÁNOS KIS

1. Introduction

In his article on ethnic relations and Western (liberal) political theory, Will Kymlicka proposes to take the nation-building state as given and to focus on variations in the ways ethnocultural diversity is handled in the course of the process of nation-building. '[T]he issue is not, he says, *whether* states engage in nation-building but rather what *kind* of nation-building.' I disagree.

To be sure, the political organization of any modern society requires a population that is literate, is capable of communicating with public officials, shares a sense of common identity, and recognizes the institutions claiming authority over it as its own. Call the population endowed with these characteristics a *political community*. In so far as the characteristics of a political community are not naturally given but need to be created before, in the course of, or after the emergence of the political organization, any attempt at establishing authoritative political institutions is preceded, accompanied, or followed by a process of transforming the subject population into a political community. Nation-building is such a process. But it is only a special case in building political communities, one which corresponds to the rise of the political organization usually called the *nation-state*.[1]

In the course of the last three centuries, the nation-state succeeded in displacing all the premodern systems of political authority. Unlike these, it is territorially based. Although premodern systems generally claimed control over an area, too, that claim was based on the fact that the area in question was the homeland of the people bound by ties of loyalty to a political ruler.

Unlike most premodern systems, the nation-state is characterized by centralized organization. That is, it has a body—a central government—vested with supreme authority such that any other body within the relevant territory is subordinated to it while it is not subordinated to any other body within the same territory.[2]

Unlike most premodern systems, the nation-state has direct access to all its subjects—those living on its territory—that is, at least some of their rights and obligations are defined at the level of the central government, and the enforcement is not delegated to intermediary bodies.[3]

Territoriality, centralization, and direct access are generally treated as jointly defining the state in its full-blown, modern sense.[4] The nation-state displays two further important characteristics. First, it claims exclusive authority over its territory, that is, the jurisdictions of two nation-states are not supposed to overlap—whenever two or more states claim control over the same domain, this fact is a symptom of an international dispute rather than of a mutually recognized, permanent *status quo*. Second, nation-states are supposed to be sovereign in their domestic affairs; they are not subjected to the rule either of distant colonial centres or of occupying forces, nor are they subordinated to any supranational body with government authority and enforcement mechanisms.

In this rejoinder, I will call those states that command unrestricted sovereignty over mutually exclusive jurisdictions, nation-states. My claim is that nation-building as we know it presupposes an international regime of nation-states.[5]

The nation-state as a form of political organization and the nation as a community of the state's subjects are linked by their name, but their connection is not a conceptual one. A state can have the characteristics of exclusive jurisdiction and unrestricted sovereignty without being the state of a nation. Absolute monarchies are illuminating examples. There is, though, a strong empirical connection between the two phenomena. The rise of the nation-state regime exerted, indeed, tremendous pressure on subject populations to consolidate themselves into nations.

The view that the state belongs to a ruling family or a ruling aristocracy to which all the other subjects owe their personal loyalty is extremely difficult to maintain in a territorially-based state with direct links between the centre and any anonymous individual. In order for the authority of such a state to be—and to be perceived as being—legitimate, the state must belong to all its subjects. Furthermore, the subjects, in their turn, must be tied to each other by horizontal bonds of loyalty. A modern state is in need of the shared belief that its subjects recognize each other as members of a political community and the state as their own political organization. Where the state is a nation-state, the political community shaped by it is a nation. Because the modern state system emerged as a system of nation-states, nation-building had virtually no competitors as a pattern of building modern political communities.

Nation-building starts from a situation where the subject population is divided by multiple and criss-crossing group identities. Individual subjects speak different languages and dialects, they profess different religions, and their ordinary lives are informed by different cultural practices, rules, and beliefs. The same individual might speak a regional dialect of language A, belong to a religious community mostly composed of speakers of dialects of language B, and indulge in practices characteristic of a region inhabited mainly by speakers of a dialect of language C. None of his or her identities dominates, by necessity, the others, nor is he or she necessarily tied by any of these to all those permanently living on the territory of the state. Nation-building has as its task, first, to consolidate some of these ties at the level of the whole state—for example, by substituting a literary language for regional dialects, and making it the official language of the state and used in all the public schools—and, second, to make them predominant, at least for political aims, over all other ties of loyalty. Unlike pre-political ethnic groups—which are shading into each other, share overlapping and fluid homelands, and allow for multiple identities—nations claim to divide the human population into 'insiders' and 'outsiders', so that participation in those reference groups is a matter of 'yes' or 'no', and aspire to be sovereign over an exclusive fatherland with sharp and fixed boundaries.

The historically predominant pattern of nation-building consisted of uniting one of the loosely connected regional, dialectal, and sub-cultural groups into a single national community. Members of those ethnocultural groups left out of the emerging nation were then confronted with the alternatives of assimilating into the nation, resigning to a marginal social position within the state, emigrating, or mobilizing as a group with the aim of seceding and establishing their own state.

This pattern of nation-building, which is generally called nationalist and which leads to the establishment of *one-nation states*, is the target of Kymlicka's criticism. There are fairly obvious reasons to abhor nationalism. It is dangerous for internal stability as well as for international peace. It is likely to generate situations of conflict where a high premium is put on terrorism on behalf of the minority and on preventive genocide and ethnic cleansing on behalf of the majority. Yet, even in the absence of such monstrous consequences, the nationalist path to nation-building would still be unacceptable because a one-nation state tends to be inherently *unjust*. Whenever the state has, within its jurisdiction, more than one ethnocultural community, the one-nation model fails to meet the standards of what Kymlicka calls 'ethnocultural justice'. It unfairly disadvantages ethnocultural minorities by depriving them—but not the national majority—of public status and of the politically allocated resources necessary for their culture to be preserved and to flourish. This is Kymlicka's central objection to nation-building as we know it.

In his discussion of the *kind* of nation-building in which states engage, Kymlicka leaves us with versions of one single alternative to the building of a one-nation state, an alternative which amounts to erecting a '*multination state*'. Unlike one-nation states, a multination state gives public recognition to minority groups as equal partners in the national community, and provides these groups with the rights and resources necessary for them to prosper.[6]

This rejoinder will not question the soundness of preferring, under conditions of ethnic diversity, the multination state to the one-nation state. I agree that the former is much closer to meeting the standards of ethnocultural justice than the latter. But I do not share the belief that alternatives to nation-building can be safely neglected.

The division of the world into nation-states is not the only conceivable modern state system. Institutions vested with political authority and powers of enforcement, more inclusive than the territorial states, can and do emerge. Some of these may have territorial jurisdiction—for example the European Court of Human Rights or its Latin American counterpart—others may lack it—such as the World Trade Organization. Some may have direct access to individual subjects—again, international courts are an example—others—bodies which supervise arms reduction—may lack it. Some may be specialized on a very narrow range of functions—a suprastate environmental protection agency is such a case—while others have a wide and potentially expanding range of functions—think of the European Union. And, jointly, these institutions do not submit to a central government. Although many organizations with a global reach—such as the United Nations—do exist, indeed, the majority of the other suprastate organizations are not subordinated to any authority with a global reach. Rather, they are drawing criss-crossing lines of authority. They are eminently political institutions because those under their control have an obligation to comply with their directives and because very often they are in possession of some enforcement mechanisms, but, with some exceptions, they fail to meet the conditions which are characteristic of states. The more the number of such suprastate institutions increases, and the wider their powers to interfere with internal matters become, the less is it justified to consider restrictions of state sovereignty as something trivial. The global regime of nation-states may be heading towards its end.[7]

This trend started towards the end of World War II, and has gone on at an accelerating speed since the 1970s. We have good reasons to believe that it will continue in the future. This is because the processes that give rise to a demand for co-ordination across state borders and, thus, for restriction of state sovereignty, are highly unlikely to be reversed. The rise of transnational corporations exposes the regulatory and taxation capabilities of nation-states to a severe test. The globalization of the financial markets reduces the ability of domestic governments to pursue social policies on their own. The increase in labour migration makes the clear-cut division between citizens and non-citizens, an important feature of the traditional concept of citizenry, more and more obsolete. Modern technologies, such as informatics, defy localized control. Cumulative external—such as environmental—effects on the well-being of one state continue as the result of economic activities in another state. Weapons of mass destruction become easily accessible to any government, even to non-governmental terrorist groups. Famines and epidemics caused by man have assumed unprecedented dimensions. The widening gap between rich and poor societies is more and more difficult either to justify or to tolerate without endangering international stability.

The fact of these pressures as well as the tendency of nation-states to adapt to their challenges by surrendering to suprastate organizations one chunk after another of their sovereignty, seem to be beyond controversy.[8] Less obvious is the possibility that, parallel to the erosion of the principle of state sovereignty, the principle of exclusive jurisdiction may start eroding as well. This rejoinder will try to show that there are chances for this second trend to take off and, that should the processes of restricting state sovereignty combine with those of establishing overlapping jurisdictions, the bases of nation-building as we know it might be undermined.

Section Two will attempt to establish the claim that if ethnocultural justice requires, as Kymlicka shows it does, that the one-nation state sometimes gives way to the multination state, then ethnocultural justice also requires that exclusive jurisdiction sometimes gives way to overlapping jurisdictions. The remaining part of this section will deal with the objection that such a development would be either unfeasible or unattractive.

Section Three will address a different kind of objection, that of practical irrelevance. Designing alternatives to the nation-state regime might be an interesting but fruitless exercise, so the objection runs, because we are very far from the situation where the nature of building political communities would be significantly affected by the changes in the global institutional environment. In support of my suggestion that this view is mistaken, I will describe an empirical story, that of the recent evolution in Hungarian nationalism. I hope to be able to show that the perception of the strategic options for the Hungarian nation is undergoing significant changes, which are, in their turn, induced by Hungary's getting into the orbit of the European Union. A brief note on the perspectives of this evolution will be offered in Section Four.

All this is not to deny that the multination state is an option by far superior to its one-nation rival in terms of justice and that it is not inferior to the one-nation state in terms of stability. My aim is rather to suggest that a third option is taking shape, that of gradually overcoming the nation-state altogether. If this is so, then there are good reasons to encourage the integration of post-Communist Eastern and East Central Europe into the web of suprastate organizations, and to encourage the involvement of these organizations with the task of handling ethnocultural diversity in this region.

2. *Self-Government Across Borders*

In what follows I will assume with Kymlicka that, in countries with ethnically mixed populations, minority self-government is among the requirements of ethnocultural justice. As it stands, this is a statement with vague contours. It leaves open the question of how robust a minority self-government is required by ethnocultural justice. One of the main issues that demand further elaboration concerns the *vertical reach* of self-government. Public administration has a complex hierarchical structure, and minority self-government might exist at various levels of this hierarchy. The question of vertical reach asks how far self-government must reach upwards in order that the autonomy requirement of ethnocultural justice be met.

Imagine a country with a municipal organization of three levels: local communities, counties, and regions. Suppose the country's population is divided into an ethnic majority and an ethnic minority. Call the minority homeland the geographic area where the minority represents more than, say, 50 per cent of the inhabitants. And let it be the case that the homeland in question extends over the territory of two counties. The story I would like to consider is this. The minority asks for self-government in a petition to the national legislature. The number of signatories is so large that the initiative can safely be taken as expressing the will of the minority community. The issue is put on the legislature's agenda.

No political actor denies that the minority has a right to self-government in its homeland. There is no agreement, however, as to the vertical reach to which the self-government authority has a right. Majority parties are unwilling to accept self-government on a level higher than that of the two separate counties. Minority representatives call for a redesigning of the state's regional division in such a way that the two counties are united in one self-governing region.

Do considerations of ethnocultural justice support the minority claim? Do they require that the state give way to the minority desire to erect its own government over the homeland it inhabits?[9] I can see three weighty reasons which support a positive answer.

First, higher-level decisions constrain the choices open to lower-level decision-makers. For example, many local communities might find themselves unable to establish a new school without external financial support. If the region is a level of effective municipal government where decisions about allocation of public funds—between competing aims and competing localities—are being made, then the minority has an obvious interest in getting control over that level. And even if the region were to be absent from the municipal organization of the state in question, the minority would still have an obvious interest in getting the counties of its homeland combined into a single higher-level administrative unit so that it has the means to govern that area as a whole.

Of course, the majority's interests conflict with the interest of the minority on this. But there is a weighty reason to give priority to the minority interest. In a country whose population is divided into a standing majority and a standing minority, the burdens and benefits of the political organization are distributed unevenly in the first place. To belong to the majority means to enjoy an initial advantage in access to public officials, to careers, and other resources allocated through political channels. To belong to the minority means to suffer cumulative disadvantages in all these respects. Justice requires, however, that the burdens and benefits of having a common state be allocated equally among the citizenry. Therefore, those who are structurally disadvantaged by the system need to be compensated for their disadvantages. The public institutions need to be designed in such a way as to countervail, in so far as this is possible, the initial bias against them. Securing municipal self-government over the minority homeland as a whole is one of the most important countervailing mechanisms. And so it is plausible to claim that ethnocultural justice requires providing the minority homeland with an autonomous municipal organization.[10]

Second, one of the channels through which social groups organize themselves is offered by the very institutions of public administration. Access to these institutions secures tremendous competitive advantages of self-organization over those groups to which such access is denied. The general strategy of liberal polities in treating this problem amounts to separating the public and the private, to making sure that no distinctive group can parasitize on government institutions for the aims of self-organization. A paradigm for such separation is presented by the liberal treatment of the relationships between state and church. However, ethnic divisions are to a large degree immune to the application of the separation strategy. The government can refuse to adopt any belief in religious matters—including atheism—as part of its official doctrine. It cannot refuse to adopt at least one language to serve as the medium of official communication. Nor can it avoid designating official holidays, identifying the founding fathers of the state, marking the great events of the state's history, and so on. As of necessity, some ethnic group will have access to public institutions, even if these are being strictly separated from all private organizations. In the dimension of ethnic diversity, therefore, the choice is not between making the state blind to the differences or allowing the largest ethnic group to prevail, but one between distributing access to public institutions as equally as possible, or allowing privileged access to some ethnic groups. The pure separation strategy amounts to allowing privileged access to the majority. Securing self-government at the level of the minority homeland is one way of equalizing access to the public channels of self-organization.

A third consideration is this. Beyond providing social groups with organizational and material resources, access to public institutions is a means for them to gain symbolic recognition as constitutive members of the political community. A group is not perceived as a constitutive part of the political community if it is denied that status in the public domain which other groups do enjoy as a matter of course. Such a deprivation is not remedied by the fact that the group's individual members have full citizenship and are free of personal discrimination. If it is true that the way an individual is perceived by his peers depends on the way his ethnic group is perceived by them—so that an individual whose group does not enjoy a status equal to that of others cannot expect to be treated with the respect due to an equal—then the right of the individual to be treated with equal concern and respect demands that the publicly recognized status of

all the ethnic groups within the state be equal. And so the requirement of equal public recognition demands that ethnic minorities are
not denied access to the highest levels of public administration that
can be subjected to its self-government without unjustly disadvan-
taging some other group.[11]

I conclude that ethnocultural justice demands that the minority
desire to establish self-government over its homeland be satisfied,
unless some overriding reason tips the balance in the other direction.
What could serve as such a reason? Rather than engaging in a general
discussion of this question, I will consider here one particular candidate for this role. Suppose the two counties into which the homeland
of our ethnic group is administratively partitioned lie on the territories of two different states. Suppose the ethnic group so divided enjoys
full recognition in both states, and is self-governing in each of the two
counties. However, a very large part of its members express their
desire, in a petition submitted to the two state legislatures, to unite
into a single autonomous political unit. Does the fact that the two
counties are separated by a state border rather than a mere administrative boundary make a difference for the moral standing of this
demand? Does it give rise to a reason against satisfying the minority
demand, and weighty enough to override it? The answer to this question will be decisive for the assessment of the claim I formulated at
the end of the first section. A positive answer would imply that the
extension of the right to minority self-government within the borders
of a nation-state to the right to minority self-government over an area
which cuts across state borders is mistaken. A negative answer would
support that extension.

There is a tendency to believe that the distinction between administrative boundaries and state borders is of decisive significance. In the
intrastate case, meeting the minority demand does not involve more
than redistributing government powers within the same state jurisdiction. The interstate case involves redesigning state jurisdictions
themselves. There are two standard ways to do this: either one of the
subgroups secedes from its state in order to join the other, or both
secede from their respective states in order to form their own independent state.

Secession, however, raises special problems, which the creation of
autonomous units within one and the same state does not. It deprives
the mother state of territory and natural resources. It confronts many
individuals with a coercive choice between accepting an involuntary
change of their citizenship or emigrating. These are serious concerns
in themselves, and they can give rise to further difficulties. Secession-

ist movements are likely to be resisted by means of force, to provoke oppression, genocide, and ethnic cleansing, to unleash internal wars or even wars between states. For all these reasons, unless it occurs by mutual agreement of all the concerned parties, secession cannot be claimed as a minority right on the grounds that the minority has a right to self-government over its homeland which, in this case, cannot be secured unless secession is allowed. The mere fact that the distribution of state jurisdictions unfavourably affects an ethnic group does not establish a case for the secession of the group. In order for such a case to be made, the minority must suffer systematic discrimination and persecution, including gross violations of individual human rights. Secession is a remedy of last resort for this kind of injustice.[12]

Thus, there is a significant moral difference between the claim to an autonomous region within the bounds of a state and the claim to seceding from that state. But this finding is not decisive for our question, unless it is the case that the standard ways to unite an ethnic group divided by state frontiers, that is, the ways which include secession, are the only conceivable avenues towards minority self-government over its homeland if that homeland cuts across state boundaries. I want to maintain that they are not. There is a further possibility, that of uniting the minority homeland under the joint authority of the two or more states. We know at least one attempt in contemporary Europe to resolve conflict in this manner, that of creating an autonomous government in Northern Ireland under the joint supervision of the United Kingdom and the Republic of Ireland.

One could quickly answer that even if it proves to be successful, the Northern Irish model is unlikely to be applied in other places of the world. The grounds seem to be obvious. Such a solution makes the policy options of a state which joins the agreement too closely dependent on the conduct of another state and, moreover, it involves the risk that giving up exclusive authority over a domain will ultimately lead to losing authority over that domain altogether.

This answer is all too quick, though. It relies on the tacit assumption that the world remains a home of nation-states, except that there will be some experimenting with ethnic self-government under joint authority of two or more states. So long as the nation-state regime remains intact, the chances for a political arrangement of overlapping state jurisdictions to be more than a transition from one regime of exclusive jurisdictions to another one are very slim indeed. But my argument is predicated on the assumption that the global state system is undergoing mutually reinforcing changes of restricting state sovereignty. Think of the European Union where national governments are more and more constrained from above by supranational bodies of the EU and from below by regions crossing state borders and gaining autonomy and direct access to the EU's central institutions. States enmeshed in a thick web of suprastate organizations have at hand an arsenal of practices, rules, and procedures that help to handle conflicts of overlapping authority, an arsenal that is not available to nation-states. Moreover, a long evolutionary experience of co-operation within such a web is likely to change the mutual expectations of the participants. The expectation that unilateral co-operative moves will *not* be reciprocated is a very strong motivating factor of nation-state action towards each other. This expectation might give way to more positive ones in a framework of suprastate institutions with powers of enforcement. Important sources of destabilizing behaviour might be fading away.

But if the stability of overlapping state jurisdictions relies on the growth of suprastate institutions, then there is a different kind of objection for us to face. From Immanuel Kant to John Rawls, liberal philosophers tend to agree that an 'amalgamation of states . . . would end in one universal monarchy', and that such a 'universal monarchy' would tend to be despotic on the one hand, and would risk falling prey to anarchy on the other.[13] I am not sure whether this gloomy prediction does indeed hold for a hypothetical world government. If, however, it is the nature of a centralized global state to involve the twin dangers of despotism and anarchy, then the objection does not apply to the evolution of the world upon which my argument relies. As already noted in the first section, the emerging suprastate institutions do not tend to unite under one single central authority. Rather than giving rise to an almighty Global Leviathan, their proliferation gives rise to a pattern of criss-crossing lines of authority, to something like suprastate checks and balances. Unacceptably slow and cumbersome decision-making at the suprastate level seems to be more of a danger than universal despotism spilling over into universal anarchy.

In sum, we must not assume that the format of an autonomous ethnic homeland simultaneously belonging to the jurisdictions of two or more states would either be inherently unstable or rely, for its stability, on a despotic suprastate organization. The joint jurisdiction solution is on the list of feasible and attractive options.

It is plausible to claim that delegating parts of state sovereignty to suprastate agencies and allowing for overlapping state jurisdictions enlarges the strategic options available for handling the problem of ethnocultural diversity in a just manner. But do these trends also affect the shaping of political communities? Do they point beyond what is generally called nation-building?

Because we are at the very beginning of the process of which I am talking, one can hardly make reliable, detailed predictions. But there are at least two important innovations that we can safely assume will play a role in shaping the political communities of the future. The first is this. Whether or not a nation-state is ready to allow the *individual citizen* to divide his or her loyalties between his or her particular ethnic group and the nation, in no case does it leave room for the *ethnic groups* inhabiting its territory to divide their collective loyalties. Not even a multination state can accommodate an ethnic group that splits its political loyalties between it and another state *on the same level*.[14] An arrangement wherein an ethnic homeland is united under the joint authority of two or more states allows for divided loyalties not only in the case of the individual but in the case of the ethnic group as well.

The other innovation is that ethnic groups inhabiting a state, which is enmeshed in a network of suprastate organizations, may find advantage in institutionalized access to such organizations whether or not they share the characteristics of territorial states. This is important because an organization without territorial jurisdiction cannot possibly host a political community. While some suprastate institutions are creating a higher-level framework for possible political identification—think of the incipient European citizenship—others offer purely instrumental levers for political action to social, including ethnocultural, groups. This might be a cause for worry from the point of view of the future of democracy, but it is a source of hope from the point of view of de-dramatizing inter-ethnic relationships.

Let me summarize this section's argument. I read Kymlicka as taking the world of sovereign states with exclusive jurisdiction as a given, and as assuming that ethnocultural justice can be achieved within such states. I argue, in part by appealing to Kymlicka's own arguments for minority rights, that if justice requires that ethnocultural groups located within the borders of one state have access to self-government over their homeland, then it also requires that ethnocultural groups located across state borders be able to develop some forms of common governance over their homeland. In a world of nation-states, the only way to develop such forms of common governance is through secession and irredentism, which is not morally justified except as a last resort. However, if we move beyond the assumptions of the nation-state, then we can envisage a form of common governance that involves joint authority. Such a model might not be stable if it were the only exception to the otherwise undisputed principles of state sovereignty and exclusive jurisdiction. There are wider processes, though, challenging the assumptions of the nation-state, and such a model of joint authority can take its place amidst the developing web of overlapping jurisdictions and shared sovereignty. These processes do not point in the direction of a World Government, so traditional worries about the rise of a Global Leviathan oscillating between despotism and anarchy—whether or not they are justified with regard to a hypothetical World Government—do not apply to it. Finally, we have some reasons to assume that the political communities informed by a post-nation-state political organization will lose at least some of the unattractive features of nations as we know them.

As developed above, my argument has direct application to the case where two or more kin groups, all of them in a minority position in their respective states, seek to associate with each other across state boundaries. We can imagine the Basques in Spain and in France entertaining such an aim. There are further cases that are different from the two-minorities case in important respects. An ethnic group might be distributed in such a way that one part of it is in a minority position in one country while the other makes up the majority in another. Such is the case of the Hungarians after the Versailles and Paris peace treaties. In order to fit these cases, the argument needs further elaboration. That is not part of this rejoinder, though. In order to challenge the claim I am attributing to Kymlicka, the more abstract reasoning made above must suffice.

3. The Hungarian Case

Even if defensible in principle, is the idea of overcoming the nation-state regime relevant for the contemporary world? Can it contribute to the process of devising viable strategies for handling ethnocultural diversity—here and now? The collapse of the Soviet world system left the successor states with an enormous amount of ethnic and national conflicts—can the thesis of this rejoinder be of any help in attacking them?

This question requires a drastic change in the level of discussion. The second section has presented an abstract normative argument. In this Section, we must turn to empirical description. I will try to show, using the example of recent developments in Hungarian nationalism, that the change in the international environment has already had an impact on the perception of political alternatives.

Let me begin by stating the 'national question' as Hungarians see it. The contemporary history of the 'Hungarian case' started when World War I was concluded by the Versailles peace treaty. Hungary found itself cut off, as a result of that treaty, from two-thirds of its historic territory and one-third of the ethnic Hungarian population. Dismemberment of the traditional state of Hungary came as a shock for the ruling classes, and they reacted by adopting an uncritical stance of irredentism, supported by a myth of Hungarian supremacy and special mission in the Carpathian basin. The central issue for Hungarian nationalists became how to undo the terms of the peace.

Official irredentism set the target of restoring the Kingdom of St Steven as it stood until the war, with a reckless disregard for the ethno-demographic realities in the areas detached from Hungary, and without giving serious thought to the strategic isolation of the country. Under the tutelage of France, the inheritor states were united into a so-called *Petite Entente* to contain Hungarian revisionist claims. In order to break out of the country's isolation, its rulers tried, first, to seek alliance with Great Britain, a power supposed to be interested in containing the influence of France in Eastern Europe. When this attempt failed, they turned to fascist Italy for support. Finally, in the second half of the 1930s, they ended up as satellites to Nazi Germany. In Hitler, they found a leader ready and able to return to Hungary large segments of its detached territories. Paradoxically, the two consecutive 'Vienna decisions' did what President Wilson promised to do: they brought state jurisdictions very close to the distribution of ethnic populations.

That outcome proved to be fatal, though. First, it sealed the isolation of the non-nationalist—Liberal, Social Democratic, and Communist—left which was very weak anyway. Second, the enormous popularity of the Vienna decisions defeated the only serious attempt to propose a more accommodating nationalist policy, the one made by the movement of populist intellectuals in the 1930s. The populists suggested that, confronted by a 'pan-Slavic danger' from the East and by a 'pan-Germanic danger' from the West, Hungary should give up its irredentist aims and join hands with the small peasant nations in the Danube area for their mutual defence. After the first Vienna decision, the idea of a Danube alliance vanished, of course.

Finally, and most tragically, the hope of gaining further territorial concessions and the fear of losing those already won propelled

Hungary into the war with Yugoslavia and with the Soviet Union. War participation led to the greatest national catastrophe Hungary suffered in its modern history: the deportation and extermination of about four-fifths of the Hungarian Jewish population, mob rule by the Hungarian Nazis at the turn of 1944–5, war destruction, an imposed peace treaty undoing all the territorial gains, and Soviet occupation for the next 45 years.

In the first decades of Soviet rule, the consequences of the two wars could not be discussed in public. As the single greatest beneficiary of the new international arrangements, the Soviet Union did not allow its satellites either officially to challenge the post-war *status quo* or even to tolerate unofficial criticism of it. Losers and winners alike were reduced to silence about the treatment of their ethnic brethren by neighbouring states. Until about the end of the 1960s, the mere fact of the existence of ethnic Hungarians beyond the borders of Hungary was largely ignored within the country.

The rebirth of Hungarian nationalism was marked by a rediscovery, in the course of the 1970s, of the Hungarian minority cultures and by attempts to reintegrate these into the general culture of the Hungarian nation. Literary magazines began to publish Hungarian authors from Transylvania, Slovakia, and the Voivodina, and in increasing numbers, young people visited the regions where minority Hungarians lived. A self-image of the Hungarian nation as cutting across the frontiers of the Hungarian state was slowly taking shape.

A leading role in this process of rediscovery and reintegration has been played by the new generation of populist intellectuals. New populism, like the old one, was driven by a concern for the mere survival of the Hungarian nation. A significant shift occurred, however, in the focus of this concern. In the midst of the turmoil of the inter-war period, the old populists perceived the main danger as the threat to the existence of what remained of the state of Hungary. These fears overshadowed the concern for the fate of the Hungarian minorities abroad. In the decades of Cold War stability, Hungarian statehood— even if not independence—seemed fairly secure. Thus, the anxiety for the Hungarians outside of Hungary, for their capacity to resist oppression and forced assimilation, became the main preoccupation of the new populists. To these worries, small-state nationalism and the virtual alliance of the Danube people could not possibly offer an answer. As soon as the movement of rediscovery reached the point where it raised political questions,[15] the new populism had to depart from the old one. It could either move backwards, in the direction of the suprematism and irredentism of the pre-war ruling classes, an ideology the old populists rejected with scorn and contempt, or else it could move forwards, in the direction of adopting the modern discourse of minority rights. Both possibilities have been experimented with in the 1980s. The playwright István Csurka, who was to emerge in the 1990s as the leader of an extreme right-wing party, voiced the first option.[16] The second option has been tried by the leading figure of the new populist generation, Sándor Csoóri. In a preface to the autobiography of Miklós Duray, a Hungarian minority rights activist in Slovakia, Csoóri identified Communist totalitarianism as the main culprit for the plight of minority Hungarians. It was the absence of multi-party democracy, of private property, and of church autonomy, Csoóri maintained, that deprived the minority of any institutional defence. Political, social, and economic pluralism emerged from this diagnosis as the bulwark which protects minorities against oppression, forced assimilation, and forced segregation.[17]

Actually, Csoóri's thinking represented an amalgam of these ideas and of traditional, anti-modernist rhetoric so dear to many of the old populists. Even so, his adoption of the talk of democracy and rights was to become a milestone in the evolution of Hungarian nationalism, one which deserves appreciation. A learning process had been started.[18]

As the rediscovery of the minority issue reached the political level in the early 1980s, nationalist intellectuals had to face the question of where to look for international support. The Soviet Union could not be expected to be a partner, so the populists had to turn towards the West.

This happened in the years following the conclusion of the Helsinki Accords. Some of the Western parties to that agreement, particularly the United States, were ready to make use of the changing international framework to pressure the Soviet Union and its dependencies to comply better with international human rights standards. To the degree that their perception of the complex game with the Soviet rulers permitted, they were responsive to complaints of East Europeans, provided those complaints were expressed in terms of rights-claims rather than nationalist grievances. This is why the politics of human rights of the region's democratic opposition could be successful in the international arena. And this is why Hungarian nationalists themselves had to engage in a process of learning the rights-discourse.[19]

When it came to the collapse of the Communist regime and to the transition to democracy, the political landscape of the country was significantly different from that between the two wars. First, non-nationalist parties held a solid share of the parliamentary mandates— somewhat more than 40 per cent in 1990, more than 70 per cent in 1994, and about 40 per cent in 1998. Second, non-nationalist and mainstream nationalist parties alike agreed on the priority of getting Hungary admitted to NATO and the European Union. József Antall, Chairman of the Hungarian Democratic Forum—a party issued from the populist movement which won the first free elections—proved to be as firm on this issue as any other political leader of the country. And, thus, the learning process continued.

At the beginning, Antall seems to have entertained some hopes that a firm Euro-Atlantic commitment might not conflict with attempts to exploit the post-Communist instability in the region to regain lost territories. In July 1991, he told the Italian president that the southern borders of Hungary were not established with Serbia by the two peace treaties but, in Versailles, with the Serbo-Croatian-Slovenian State and, in Paris, with Yugoslavia. Therefore, Antall concluded, in the case of a dissolution of the Yugoslav federal state, the status of Voivodina was open for renegotiation.[20] In the same year, his government facilitated secret arms shipments to Croatia, shortly before it seceded from the Yugoslav federation and the outbreak of war.

There is some indirect evidence that Antall might have been encouraged in this move by the then German Chancellor Helmuth Kohl. If so, then we have a plausible explanation for the absence of any follow-up to this adventure. After the outbreak of the war, Germany quickly abandoned its separate game in the Balkans, and Hungary's new leaders had to learn that the EU will not be a partner in challenging the *status quo*. It was made clear that no former Communist country can hope for admission to the EU until it makes credible efforts to resolve its historic conflicts with its neighbours.

At the same time, Europe offered a set of international standards, including provisions on minority rights, in terms of which conflict resolution could be sought. The Council of Europe was particularly active in this respect.[21] Thus, the Antall government was being pushed in the direction of exploiting the European legal and political framework in its search for an accommodation with the neighbouring countries. Minority rights, especially language rights and the right to minority schooling, as well as cultural and territorial autonomy became the key words in the government's vocabulary. A new strategy began to take shape.

In 1992, the Antall government struck a basic treaty with Ukraine, in which Hungary recognized the frontiers between the two countries as inviolable. True, in the parliamentary debate, Antall declared that he considered the Hungarian-Ukrainian treaty an exception, not to be followed by any parallel agreements with Romania and

Slovakia. The fact was, however, that the treaty set a precedent which the next government, elected in 1994, could follow.

The Socialist-Liberal government made a similar treaty with Slovakia in 1995 and with Romania in 1996. Both treaties improved upon the original model by including, along with a no-territorial-revendications clause, a long list of minority rights and privileges. They also contained, as an Annex, Recommendation 1201 of the Parliamentary Commission of the Council of Europe on minority rights—with a note, in the case of the treaty with Romania, to the effect that the parties read Recommendation 1201 as not entailing provisions of collective rights.

The right-wing opposition attacked both treaties in harsh terms. But it was cautious enough not to reject the very structure of the deal. What they objected to was mainly the list of rights and privileges pinned down by the two treaties, which they judged to be insufficient. Particularly, they blamed the government for not insisting on the inclusion of the principle of an ethnically-based territorial autonomy and for accepting, in the case of the treaty with Romania, that a note be added denying that Recommendation 1201 provided for collective rights as distinct from rights held by individuals severally. Although the rhetoric used in the debate was that of traditional nationalism—an analogy was drawn, by no less a political figure than the country's next Prime Minister, with the 1849 capitulation of the Hungarian army to the Russians—[22] the merit of the conflict was not in the clash between two opposite conceptions of the minority issue, but in two different strategic views of implementing the same conception.[23]

At the time I am writing this, Hungary faces a similar conflict between the Orbán government and its opposition, this time on the Yugoslav crisis. Orbán's strategy is to push for a linkage between the post-war Kosovo settlement and a settlement on Voivodina, the latter imagined as combining restoration of territorial autonomy for the province with special rights for the local ethnic—mainly Hungarian—minorities.[24]

His liberal critics agree that autonomy and minority rights are the key for the solution of the minority problem in Voivodina. However, liberals attack the strategy of linkage for two reasons. First, waging war for the Kosovo Albanians and interfering with the sovereignty of the Yugoslav state in dealing with the status of Kosovo was justified, they argue, by extreme violations of international humanitarian law. No comparable emergency situation has been created in Voivodina. Second, by pushing for a linkage, Hungary creates an image of itself as having participated in the war not for its declared aims but for promoting quite different interests. In so doing, liberals claim, it sends a dangerous message not only to nationalists in Serbia but also to possible democratic allies there and in other neighbouring countries.[25]

This debate reveals a deeper disagreement between the nationalist and non-nationalist understandings of the policy of minority rights. For non-nationalists, the commitment for such a policy is a matter of principle, a consequence of their more general commitment for freedom, equality, and individual dignity. Nationalists, on the other hand, adopt the rights-discourse as a matter of tactical accommodation to a *status quo*, not as a framework for principled settlement. That this is so is confirmed by further evidence. First, the mainstream nationalist conception fails to meet the universalization test. The presence of anti-Semitism in the ranks of the nationalist mainstream and its indifference towards the plight of the Romas are symptoms of a lack of willingness to apply the same principles of minority protection to domestic politics.[26] Second, the nationalist right treats individual human rights with neglect and contempt, and this attitude suggests that, very likely, the right-wing case for minority autonomy, rather than basing the claim of collective rights on individual interests, takes the former as basic and as capable of overruling the latter, should the two conflict.

Is there a chance for the tactical accommodation to give way to principled agreement, or has the evolution of Hungarian nationalism already reached the outer limits of its evolution? The answer to that question depends on the future of the relationships of Hungary to the European Union. Hungary is in the group of post-Communist countries that are candidates for admission to the EU in the first round. Should the admission process halt, a reversal in the evolution of Hungarian nationalism is possible. But if that process comes to completion in the foreseeable future, the movement towards a principled affirmation of the rights language is likely to continue.

Suppose this forecast is not grossly inaccurate—does it support the thesis of this rejoinder? Not really, or so it might look at first sight. After all, what the pressure of the EU environment has so far brought about does not amount to more than coming nearer to the concept of the multination state—and even then, as tactical accommodation rather than principled agreement.

But this is not the end of the story. The account given in the third section deliberately ignored such pro-nationalist authors whose voice is not echoed by the official right. In these circles, the idea that the 'Hungarian question' might find a solution in the framework of the

EU has been raised already. At least one of the authors I have in mind blames official Hungarian nationalism for being blind to the fact that, within the EU, large blocks of state sovereignty are delegated in part upward, and in part downward. Rather than trying to strengthen its central state powers, he claims, Hungary ought to proceed to region- alize its internal administrative structures as quickly as possible so as to facilitate the development of regions across state borders in the future. He maintains that the downgrading of the sovereign state and the upgrading of the regions below it, with a capacity for crosscut- ting state boundaries, might bring the problem of the Hungarians close to a solution.[27]

Suppose Hungary and its neighbours become members of the EU—which, in its turn, succeeds in overcoming the present tensions of integration. In this case, ideas such as the one cited in the above paragraph will find support in the strategic options inherent in the suprastate institutional framework of the Union. This might help these ideas to penetrate the mainstream nationalist right. Should this happen, the Hungarians will be on their way out of the era of nation- building, with their preferred ways of uniting politically based more and more on institutional structures that are different from and cross- cutting/restricting those of the nation-state.

This prediction relies on very optimistic assumptions, but my aim is not to make empirical forecasts about what is likely to happen. I am simply trying to show that something like this can possibly happen. And if there is some possibility for mainstream nationalism to evolve in the direction of overcoming the nation-state framework, then non-nationalists have good reason to take this alternative very seriously, both as a theoretical possibility and as a political option. That is the central claim I have tried to support in this article.

NOTES

1. On the rise of the nation-state and its defining features, see C. Tilly, 'On the History of European State-Making', in C. Tilly (ed.) *The Formation of Nation-States in Western Europe* (Princeton, NJ: The University Press, 1975).
2. The separation of powers is not an exception to this: so long as the division of competencies is functional in nature and, in cases of conflicts between directives issued by two separate powers there is a procedure to establish which power's directive takes priority, one can still speak of one central government made up of the supreme bodies of all the separate powers jointly.
3. Again, direct access is not abolished by a federal system. To be sure, a federal system delegates many of the powers over individual subjects to member states,

provinces, etc.—but the claim made above is not that the central government should have direct access to individual subjects in all politically relevant issues. I only claim that there are some individual rights and obligations that are defined at the level of and enforced by the central government.

4. See C. W. Morris, *An Essay on the Modern State* (Cambridge: Cambridge University Press, 1998), especially ch. 2. If the more general term of political organization is understood as entailing an institutional distribution of access to the legitimate use of violence, then that component of the state's definition, stressed by Marx and Max Weber, is implied by the above characteristics. A centralized political organization having direct access to those inhabiting its domain claims a monopoly in deciding who can legitimately use violence against whom and in what circumstances. But this aspect of the modern state will not play a role in the argument that follows.

5. This is the international order that emerged from the 1648 Westphalian settlement. For the significance of that settlement in shaping the European order, see A. Watson, *The Evolution of International Society* (London and New York, NY: Routledge, 1992), ch. 17. The characteristics of this order are accurately described yet unjustifiably taken as axiomatic for international relations by the so-called realist school. See H. J. Morgenthau, *Politics Among Nations* (New York, NY: Knopf, 1949).

6. In what follows, I will neglect the distinction Kymlicka makes between 'multi-nation states' and 'polyethnic states'. 'National minorities', in Kymlicka's usage, are those ethnic groups that have been permanently settled on the territory of the state for many generations. 'Ethnic minorities', on the other hand, are recent immigrants with a distinct ethnocultural identity. Disregard for this distinction is justified by two considerations. First, the 'polyethnic' phenomenon is absent from Hungary and its immediate neighborhood on which the interests of my rejoinder are focused—unless we treat the Roma minority as falling under this heading. Second, the 'polyethnic state' is exactly like the 'multiethnic state' in that it is predicated on the nation-state regime. Thus, I will take the liberty of calling both kinds of minorities 'ethnic' or 'ethnocultural'.

7. For this tendency, see J. Habermas, 'Die postnationale Konstellation und die Zukunft der Demokratie', in J. Habermas (ed.) *Die postnazionale Konstellation* (Frankfurt/Main: Suhrkamp, 1998), especially 107–9.

8. For a balanced assessment of these trends, commonly discussed under the label 'globalisation', see E. Hobsbawm, 'The Nation and Globalization', *Constellations*, 5, 1998, 1–9.

9. To be sure, self-government over the minority homeland is only one of the instruments for securing autonomy for a minority. Minorities with no homeland in which they could be the local majority can still enjoy functional self-government powers over special issues such as minority schooling, running of minority cultural centres, etc. Minorities having such a homeland, but also having subgroups dispersed among the majority, can enjoy, besides territorial self-government in their homeland, functional self-government outside of it. They also can obtain special procedural privileges such as veto rights in the national legislatures over issues that particularly concern them. But the richness of the instruments of minority protection does not play a role in my argument.

10. The argument in the above two paragraphs draws on ideas from W. Kymlicka, *Liberalism, Community, and Culture* (Oxford: Clarendon, 1989), 187 ff.

11. The above arguments draw on familiar ideas from W. Kymlicka, *Multicultural Citizenship* (Oxford: Clarendon, 1995), 26 ff., 75 ff., 108 ff.

12. The reasoning contained in this paragraph relies on A. Buchanan, *Secession: The Morality of Political Divorce from Fort Sumter to Lithuania and Quebec* (Boulder, CO: Westview, 1991); and on his 'Theories of Secession', *Philosophy and Public Affairs*, 26, 1997, 31–61.

13. See I. Kant, *Zum ewigen Frieden* [Perpetual Peace], in his *Werke*, vol. 9 (Darmstadt: Wissenschafliche Buchgesellschaft, 1993), 225. For Rawls endorsing Kant on this point, see his 'The Law of Peoples', in J. Rawls, *Collected Papers* (Cambridge, MA, and London: Harvard University Press, 1999), 539.

14. Simultaneous loyalty to a state and a federal or confederal government standing over it is possible, of course.

15. The transition from rediscovery and reintegration, a largely *cultural* process, to the public discussion of minority grievances, with which the populist movement regained its *political* dimension, was marked by a two-part article by Gyula Illyés, a leading poet from the first generation of populists. See 'Válasz Herdernek és Adynak' [A Reply to Herder and Ady], *Magyar Nemzet*, December 25, 1977 and January 1, 1978.

16. See I. Csurka, 'Levél az Írószövetség elnökéhez' [Letter to the President of the Writers' Union] and his 'Új magyar önépítés' [New Self-Building of the Hungarians], in *Minden, ami van* (All There Is), (Budapest: Püski 1998) Vol. 1, a collection of political writings and talks.

17. See S. Csoóri, 'Elszó' [Introduction], in M. Duray, *Kutyaszorító* (New York, NY: Püski, 1983).

18. Other figures, less central to the new populist movement, went much further than Csoóri in this direction. Outstanding among them was the literary historian and Polonist Csaba Gy. Kiss who tried to adopt a conceptual apparatus making possible the separation of the nation as an ethnocultural entity and the nation as a political unit. Kiss's central idea was that, in multi-ethnic contexts, equality could be secured by divorcing citizenship from nationality. See his 'Párbeszéd Európáért' [Dialogue for Europe], *Hitel*, 3, 1990, 38–40.

19. This learning process did not go unrelated to a dialogue between them and the democratic opposition in Hungary. In the 1980s, the democratic opposition made repeated attempts to raise the minority issue and to propose policies to tackle it within the framework of a non-nationalist concept.

20. On Antall's claim, see the statement made by his cabinet chief to the Hungarian News Agency, 'A békeszerződések a Vajdaság területét nem tekintik automatikusan Szerbia részének' [The Peace Accords Do Not Treat the Voivodina Automatically As Part Of Serbia], *Magyar Hírlap*, July 9, 1991.

21. See, e.g., the Recommendations 1134 (1990), 1177 (1992), 1201 (1993) and 1203 (1993) of the Parliamentary Assembly of the Council of Europe, issued at the time when the Antall government was in office, and their follow-ups in Recommendations 1255 (1995) and 1285 (1996).

22. See V. Orbán, 'Alapszerződés: Temesvár vagy Világos' [Basic Treaty: Timisoara or Siria], *Magyar Nemzet*, September 14, 1996. Timisoara is the city in Northern Romania where the parties came together to sign the basic treaty. Világos or Siria is the place where the Hungarian revolutionary army surrendered its arms in 1849.

23. For a somewhat biased but informative overview of the Parliamentary debate,

see G. Jeszenszky, 'The Debate On the Hungarian-Rumanian Basic Treaty', *Hungary's Political Yearbook 1997*.

24. The Kosovo war gave an opportunity to the Hungarian extreme-right openly to formulate revisionist demands towards Yugoslavia. Although the Prime Minister hesitated to condemn this move, in the end he was brought to distance himself from it in an interview to the *Frankfurter Allgemeine Zeitung*, August 25, 1999. His own proposals have always been formulated in terms of minority rights rather than in those of territorial revision.

25. See T. Bauer, 'Kétséges egység' [Dubious Unity], *Népszabadság*, May 22, 1999.

26. For anti-Semitic velleities in the Orbán government, see A. Sajó, 'A Kövér László kérdés' [The Kövér Question] *Népszava*, August 27, 1999. As to the disregard for Roma interests, it is helpful to consult the redesigning, in 1999, of the system of family allowances in such a way that conspicuously disadvantages the Romas as a group. See I. Riba, 'Padra fogva' [Forced to Study], *HVG*, September 9, 1999.

27. See G. Molnár, 'A történelmi Magyarország kísértése' [The Spectre of Historical Hungary], *Világosság*, 39, 1998, 73–7.

Ethnocultural Justice in East European States and the Case of the Czech Roma

Pavel Barša

Will Kymlicka's central question of the applicability of the concepts of Western liberal theory of ethnic relations to the current political predicaments in Eastern Europe may be fruitful not only from the perspective of developments in the region. Western political theory itself may gain, if only from a heightened consciousness of its own limitations and blind spots. Recall that it was precisely the myth of ethnocultural neutrality of the liberal-democratic state that made Western political thought look so helpless and futile when faced with the outbursts of nationalism in Eastern and Central European countries after the collapse of Communism.

Taken by surprise by this development, Western observers interpreted nationalism as yet another competitor of liberal democracy, that is, as an *Ersatzideologie* to Communism. This may be correct so far as exclusivist, collectivist, and authoritarian features of East European nationalism, in general, are concerned. But it is wrong when we consider that liberal democracy and nationalism are two responses to two different questions which not only have not been in conflict but historically have even complemented one another. While democracy is an institutional expression of the tenet of self-rule of the people, nationalism addresses the problem of who 'the people' are by identifying cultural borders with political borders.

Before 'the people' decide on the nature of their political regime, they must have already been associated into one collective body, recognizing themselves as 'one people'. Establishing the political community—that is, the state—is prior to and distinct from instituting a political regime. The legitimacy of the state and that of the regime are thus two separate levels of political legitimacy.[1] The first level concerns the state's boundaries and its internal structure according to the political standing of ethnocultural groups and the distribution of political power among them. It is on this level that questions arise of which ethnocultural groups should belong to a given state and which should have special status within the state. The problems of minority rights and ethnofederalism—in Kymlicka's words, of 'ethnocultural justice'—fall obviously on this level of legitimacy.

The break-up of the Soviet Union, Czechoslovakia, and Yugoslavia provided spectacular illustrations of the urge of post-Communist societies to transform themselves on both levels of political legitimacy. They were faced with two problems at once—the demarcation of an appropriate political unit, including the internal distribution of power among ethnocultural groups, and the establishment of liberal democracy. The success of nationalists stemmed from their ability to translate the issues of democratization into the language of national self-determination and thus to reduce the question of the legitimacy of a political regime to that of the legitimacy of the political unit or its structure. Liberals tried to do the same but in the opposite direction. By considering the sense of communal and national identity as ideas used only by demagogues and anti-democratic power-seekers, and irrelevant to democratic political life, the liberals reduced the problems of the politics of identity to those of the political regime and the values it embodies. This is the equivalent of saying that people hold together as one political body only by subscribing to liberty and equality, if they are democrats, or to hierarchy and community, if they are authoritarians. Liberals lost on many of the intellectual and political battlefields of the post-Communist world precisely because they did not acknowledge that there is an ethnocultural dimension of political modernity that is not reducible to the question of universal political values.

This strategy of denial leads nowhere: standard liberal norms and institutions simply do not address the issues of clashes of ethnic and national identities. Kymlicka's 'good news' is that the western world has already developed some conceptual and practical tools, however imperfect, to tackle these issues: liberal theory has realized that it cannot address the current political predicaments unless it enlarges its scope to encompass the relations between identity groups. Kymlicka's own reconstruction of liberal justice—through its extension to inter-ethnic and inter-nation relations—represents one attempt to address this issue. Although he developed his concept in response to Western problems, in doing so he targeted precisely those drawbacks of standard liberal theory that hindered its application to post-Communist politics. The experiences of the last decade in this part of the world have overwhelmingly confirmed his position: if liberal theory does not want to doom the multinational and multicultural states of Central and Eastern Europe to interminable civil strife and mimetic irredentism, it must acknowledge that alongside economic *interests* and moral and political *ideas*, the cultural *identities* of citizens are legitimate political concerns.

The three following comments should be understood in the context of my general endorsement of the propositions put forward in Kymlicka's paper. *First*, I want to show that a desired reconstruction of liberalism cannot be completed unless we also critically assess liberal nationalism alongside the liberal neutralism criticized by Kymlicka. *Second*, in contrast to Kymlicka, I will defend the distinction between immigrant and European countries as empirically—though not normatively—important. *Third*, I will apply Kymlicka's approach of ethnocultural diversity to Czech Roma to show that his concepts and their practical implications can be helpful even for the descriptive and normative assessment of groups that do not fit neatly into either of the two basic categories he proposes.

Neutralism and Nationalism: Two Sides of One Liberal Coin

With respect to the legitimacy of the state—or, more generally, of a unit of political organization—the mainstream of liberal political theory has wavered between two contradictory positions: neutralism and nationalism. Kymlicka criticizes the former by dismissing the assumption that adherence to the principles of liberal democracy provides the glue for national cohesion. Accordingly, he rejects the idea of a 'civic nation' defined only by membership in an already existing state embodying those principles.

Kymlicka sides with liberal nationalism, which acknowledges the cultural specificity of any feasible liberal-democratic state. He perceives this stance as superior to its culturally blind brother. I think, on the contrary, that their respective drawbacks are quite symmetrical. As with neutralism, liberal nationalism has no idea of how to deal with the problem of ethnic and cultural plurality within a state except through assimilation. The difference is that whereas neutralists can hide behind a façade of alleged cultural impartiality, liberal nationalists confess their partiality for forward nations upon which is conferred the moral right to absorb groups that lag behind in their historical progress. According to J. S. Mill, it is to the advantage of 'an inferior and more backward portion of the human race to merge and be absorbed in another' which is superior and advanced. He gave as examples Bretons and Basques in relation to the French, and Welsh and Scots in relation to 'the British nation'—obviously a euphemism for the English nation.[2]

Furthermore, Mill contended that a culturally homogenized, state-constituent people—that is, a nation—is the prerequisite of liberal democracy, since '[f]ree institutions are next to impossible in a country made up of different nationalities. Among a people without fellow-feeling, especially if they read and speak different languages, the united public opinion necessary to the working of representative government cannot exist.'[3] According to the tradition, represented by Mill, the liberal order of plurality of interests and ideas is to be erected on the unifying ground of a common identity. It comes as no surprise that this kind of theory cannot be of any more help than neutralism in situations where the common identity of a people is problematic.[4]

Whereas liberal neutralists virtually dismiss the very question of the legitimacy of a given political community or of the political standing of an identity group within it, liberal nationalists demand the coincidence of cultural and political borders. At the end of the day, however, both positions amount to the same: the starting point of liberal politics is supposed to be a homogenized nation-state taken by its citizens for granted as the proper unit of their political organization. The only difference is that one camp acknowledges the culturally distinct character of this political nation while the other denies it. In the context of Central and Eastern Europe, both approaches have to be rejected. Neither liberal neutralism nor liberal nationalism is able to deal with the diversity of identity groups within one state, especially when they are seeking some kind of political consideration, recognition, or, in the extreme, autonomy or secession.

Once we have dismissed both the neutralist delusion of the possibility of a culturally impartial liberal state and the liberal nationalist delusion of the possibility of a perfect coincidence of ethnocultural and political borders, we have to consider the justifiability of imposing the particular societal culture of a national majority upon minorities. In other words, if we accept the necessity of the existence of a national culture, albeit thin, as a prerequisite for the stable functioning of liberal society and, at the same time, take as inevitable the internal cultural plurality of those societies, then we have to explore the question of the moral admissibility of various forms of nation-building. Just as the core of social justice lies in the definition of the conditions for the legitimacy of social inequality—for example, Rawls's difference principle—the core of ethnocultural justice lies in the definition of the conditions for the legitimacy of majority nation-building.

Kymlicka's concept of two basic kinds of ethnocultural diversity is useful precisely as a conceptual tool for solving the problem of the normative differentiation of various minorities' demands *vis-à-vis* the majorities that control and impose a dominant societal culture. I think he is right in claiming that in principle these concepts can be applied to the ethnocultural diversity of Eastern and Central Europe and I will try to show this by using them to analyse the problem of the Czech Roma. Before dealing with this subject, however, I raise some objections to Kymlicka's dismissal of the relevance of differentiating between the national identities of Old and New World countries.

European and Immigrant Nations

In contrast to Kymlicka, I think that in comparing the various ways of dealing with ethnocultural diversity in different societies we have to keep in mind the basic difference between the immigrant countries that arose from European colonization and the European countries themselves. While the identities of the former were defined through projects for the future, the identities of the latter flowed from their relationship to the past. The identity of an American is based on his or her free will to abandon Europe and begin a new life in America, whereas the identity of a European stems from the relationship to his or her forefathers who have lived on the same land for centuries. The first stance is voluntaristic, the second deterministic. This is so even in the case of that nation which, since Ernest Renan, boasted that it was continually emerging from an 'everyday plebiscite': even in republican France the history textbooks used to begin with the expression *nos ancêtres les Gaulois*.

Politically speaking, a national of an immigrant country is not defined by ancestry but by participation in a common project of a people with various ancestries. That is why in principle those nations are more receptive towards ethnocultural diversity. Everybody, except for descendants of native people, is by definition from somewhere else and carries the traces of his or her origins, be it skin colour, religion, customs, or language. In contrast, the Europeans tend to believe in the continuity of one culturally distinct people living on the same territory and having rights to that territory. So immigrants are usually taken as something exceptional and foreign, possibly threatening the identity of the country.

This dichotomy is obviously ideal-typical and reflects not reality but an ideological self-consciousness of two kinds of nations. This holds both for European countries, whose identities have been of course the result of many migratory processes, and for the immigrant ones, which for most of their histories conducted exclusionary and racist immigration policies and were segregationist—not to mention their genocide of native peoples. Moreover, on either side of the dichotomy there are various degrees of orientation to the future or to the past, to voluntarism or determinism, and to inclusive openness towards ethnocultural 'otherness' or exclusive confinement to one's own particular identity.

On top of that, in the context of an immigrant country, an openness to the future and a readiness to include participants from various ethnic backgrounds may be in effect assimilationist, whereas a greater clinging to the past may entail more tolerance towards the maintenance of cultural diversity. To illustrate, it could be claimed that the main difference between the USA and Canada is that Americans are more future-oriented by virtue of their break with the United Kingdom.[5] Migration to Canada could occur without any strong changes to a migrant's identity, since he or she still remained within the borders of an ethnically plural Empire. This may be one of the reasons why, once 'Britishness' came under siege both from within—the quiet revolution in Quebec—and from without—the unsustainability of the British imperial idea as a result of decolonization—Canada chose as part of its new identity a cultural pluralism, rather than a melting pot. Bilingualism and multiculturalism as answers to the challenges of the 1960s can therefore be construed as a democratization of the hierarchical cultural plurality of the vanishing Empire.

As to the built-in xenophobia of European countries, there are big differences. These stem from the countries' historical encounters with non-Europeans, or lack of such contacts—this is the difference between countries with and without overseas colonies—and from their use of either a more ethnic or a more civic definition of a nation. Most countries of Central and Eastern Europe, including Germany, score badly on both points and so are predisposed by their history to be very xenophobic. For instance, the Austro-Hungarian Empire, of which many Central European countries used to be part, did not have overseas colonies. Also, nationalism in this region, in general, over-stressed the ethnic component of nationhood at the expense of the civic one, largely because these countries emerged and developed out of opposition to an imperial political structure—or against political fragmentation in the case of Germany—with the purpose of establishing an alternative kind of political organization, that is, a nation-state. Hence, it is not by coincidence that the ethnic concept of a nation is also called 'Eastern'. With the absence of a legitimate political framework as the starting point, the basis of such a future state could lie only in a pre-political identity group: an ethnic community was thus a prior and constitutive condition with respect to political community.

It is quite understandable, then, that the states established after the collapse of the three big empires of Central and Eastern Europe at the end of World War I were defined and constituted as the states of their majority ethnic nations.[6] This concept was adopted by Communist ethnofederalism—in the USSR each republic had its own 'titular nationality'—and its grip still holds today. Majority nations in Central and Eastern Europe have the tendency to conceive of the state in which they are dominant as 'their' state, that is, linked with their ethnically conceived history and symbols, filled out with their particular contents. If many of them are not even able to accept as equal citizens those members of another nation who have resided on the territory of their state for centuries, it should come as no surprise that they do not see their countries as points of immigration for other ethnic groups.

Normatively, I think that European countries do not have ways open to them of dealing with ethnocultural differences other than multinational federalism and multicultural integration as defined by Kymlicka. Empirically, however, it is clear that given the different historical backgrounds it is a tougher job to promote these policies in Europe than in the New World and, within Europe itself, tougher in the East than in the West. The implementation of these policies entails substantial changes in the identities of European nations.

Kymlicka's minimization of the difference between New and Old World does not seem to me very convincing. For instance, his reference to the successful integration of immigrants in France does not take into account that the French 'success' concerned mainly immigrants from Latin and Roman Catholic countries. This 'success' did not extend to the big non-European and non-Christian waves of immigration in the 1960s and 1970s. Moreover, the French republican integration was distinctively assimilationist; it did not leave any room for public development of group differences within the *nation, une et indivisible.* Indeed, it was the opposite of the multicultural integration Kymlicka himself advocates and, hence, can serve as a counter-example of his thesis.[7]

The British reception of non-European immigrants, on the other hand, was not based, prior to the Commonwealth Immigration Control Act of 1962, on a liberal tolerance of differences. On the contrary, it was the result of previous colonization, that is, based on the fact that the immigrants were already British subjects. More recently, the British have developed more culturally pluralist approaches, but only because of the tradition of a hierarchical pluralism of an Empire which boasted of its inclusiveness of many peoples, all ruled, nevertheless, by the dominant English. Because of this distinctively pre-modern yet surviving idea of a multinational Empire, Great Britain has been rather an exception among modern European nation-states and, hence, cannot serve as a paradigm.

As to Kymlicka's stress on the difference between Australia and Canada on the one hand, and the USA on the other, I think that it does not override their common traits as immigrant countries. The above-mentioned absence of any strong rupture from the past in Australia and Canada and their position as 'colonial outposts' does not erase the real and symbolic importance of immigration. The fact that migration occurred for a long time within the British Empire, and was racially or even ethnically restricted, does not make those countries any less immigrant. This characteristic proved crucial for the ability of Canada and Australia to carry out the shift to more universalistic and pluralistic policies. Once the political and cultural revolution of the 1960s gained momentum, nothing more was needed than to extend the range of people who were allowed to immigrate as future citizens and make room for pluralism and recognition of group identities.

If the aim of Kymlicka is to distinguish two kinds of national integration or nation-building—one qualified and self-limiting, respecting the entitlement of members of minorities to recognition of their group identities, the other absolutist and limitless, with no respect for cultural 'otherness'—then it corresponds to the contrast between immigrant and non-immigrant countries and, on a more specific level, between the European West and East. Looking at Kymlicka's distinction between liberal and illiberal politics of nation-building, I risk making a conjecture that at least five out of those nine differences—from 4 to 9—could also be taken as definitional for the ideal-typical difference between New and Old World countries and within the latter between Eastern and Western ones. These differences are:

4. greater inclusiveness, if assimilationist, 5. a thinner concept of national identity, 6. debunking the sacred idea of nation and allowing more space for other identities, 7. pluralistic openness to intercultural exchanges within one societal culture, and 8. the tendency to allow multiple or hyphenated identities, dual nationality, or even dual citizenship.

In contrast to Kymlicka, I think that recognition of the substantial differences between the New and Old Worlds does not prevent us from applying to both worlds his conceptual scheme of distinguishing between two basic types of ethnocultural diversity, where one consists of the political co-existence of different nations or national minorities in one state, and the other where immigrant groups maintain some cultural differences while integrating into a dominant national culture. Thanks to the difference in national self-definitions between the New and Old Worlds, however, the implementation in Europe of policies implied by this conceptual framework consists not simply of a *quantitative extension* of inclusiveness to other ethnocultural groups and non-European races but rather of a *qualitative transformation* of the European type of national identity towards that kind of open identity already latent in the concept and reality of the immigrant countries. As suggested above, moreover, this shift will be much more demanding for its Eastern than for its Western part where this transformation has already been taking place for some time.[8]

Czechs and Roma: Which Kind of Ethnocultural Diversity?

Let us move finally to the question of how useful Kymlicka's framework could be for analysing the situation of Roma living in the Czech lands. Like other regions in Central Europe, the Czech lands used to be an ethnoculturally diverse country—Slavs, Jews, and Germans had lived there for centuries. World War II changed this demographic situation drastically: the majority of Jews were exterminated and in the wake of the war most of the Germans were expelled. The small minority of Roma—around 6,000 before the war—were almost exterminated too. Since the end of the war there has been some migration of Slovaks to the Czech lands and several massive waves of Roma from Slovakia. In contrast to the Slovaks who tended to assimilate, the Roma, coming from poor agrarian villages to an industrialized urban setting, with their traditional family structure and non-European pedigree, have tended to stick together and be recognized as a conspicuously 'visible minority'. There are estimated to be at least 120,000 Roma currently living in the Czech Republic, one of the few significant minorities.

The Communists tried to force them to assimilate. In 1958, a law was passed forbidding them to travel—at that point, however, this ban concerned only some 15 per cent of the Roma as the rest had already settled—and they were dispersed among the rest of society. The Communists did not recognize Roma as a 'nationality', which meant that they did not allow them to develop their own cultural and social life. After 1989, the Roma were recognized as a minority with entitlement to some support for the development of their culture, associations, and media. They have lost, however, the caring hand of a paternalistic state, which had previously provided them with apartments and jobs. The Roma found themselves in a situation of triple exclusion. *Socio-economic exclusion* is illustrated by a 75 per cent rate of unemployment, low standards of housing and health, subordinate social status, and a disproportionately high involvement in crime. Their *cultural exclusion* is evidenced by the high number of Roma children transferred from elementary schools to the so-called 'special' schools for mentally retarded children, the insignificant percentage of Roma with high school or university degrees, and the absence of recognition of their culture, be it in the Czech school curricula or Czech public culture. Their *political exclusion* is shown by their almost complete absence in the political, administrative, and law-enforcement bodies of the state. If we reject this triple exclusion as morally and politically unacceptable, the Czechs and Roma have to explore ways of changing the terms of their coexistence. But what kind of group *vis-à-vis* Czech society are the Roma, if we assess them by Kymlicka's criteria?

Kymlicka himself sets the Roma in Central and Eastern Europe aside as a special case for which the Western experience does not provide a useful model. His main reason is the absence of a Roma homeland, drawing a possible parallel between them and African-Americans. In my view this comparison is fitting only in two ways: both groups have lost any real connection to their original 'homelands'—India and Africa, respectively—making a return unrealistic; and both are territorially dispersed, making autonomy within the state in which they live also unrealistic. There are, however, two big differences between them: first, Blacks in the USA stem from various ethnic groups and have formed a unified identity only because of the systematic repression and elimination of those original tribal differences. In contrast, a significant number of Roma living in Central Europe, despite the progressive withering away of their traditional way of life, still use various dialects of their language and maintain the sense of common ethnic descent; in other words, they are not a 'race' constructed by the contingent fact of white slavery, but an ethnic group. Second, Blacks were ferried to the USA in chains, while Roma came to central Europe voluntarily and, for most of the period of their presence, laws were passed and decrees issued to exclude and banish them—the assimilationist project of Maria Teresa and Josef II at the end of the eighteenth century was an exception to the rule. Thus, while the former were forced to come and stay, in the case of the latter, attempts were made, albeit unsuccessfully, to make them go away. Obviously, this point has important negative bearings on the possibility of using an analogy with Blacks to justify a policy of affirmative action for the Roma. The widespread endorsement of affirmative action for the Blacks in the late 1960s and 1970s was a reflection of the felt need of just compensation for the serious historical grievance inflicted by Whites in the enslavement and transatlantic transfer of Blacks.

The position of Roma within an industrialized society like the Czech lands seems more similar to that of indigenous peoples in Northern America or Australia. Like many members of these tribes, most Roma have lost their original way of life linked to the agrarian economy and now survive on the margins of modern society, carrying out the least qualified jobs and often completely dependent on the caring hand of the welfare state. If we add to this sociological likeness the historical fact that the Roma as an ethnically distinct group came to Central Europe at the beginning of the fifteenth century, we could draw the conclusion that Roma—similar to indigenous people in Kymlicka's typology—should be classified as a national minority with the right to self-government. In any case, it appears that Roma should be given a much stronger standing than that of an ethnic minority recently arrived into an already established modern nation-state. The Roma might be likened to the Hungarian minorities in Transylvania or Slovakia, which perfectly fit Kymlicka's definition of a national minority. I will suggest, however, four main reasons why Roma do not fit into this category and why the parallel with immigrant ethnic groups is more fruitful, at least in terms of formulating an appropriate policy of integration. First, thanks to their itinerant way of life, unlike all other minorities who lived for centuries in Central Europe with the exception of Jews, Roma did not work the land and did not congregate geographically. As already mentioned, they do not have a territorial basis in Central Europe that could substitute as a new 'homeland' for the mythical India. The absence of strong claims to land does not allow them to raise demands for territorial autonomy as is the case with indigenous people or European national minorities.

Second, unlike most other national minorities in Central Europe, the Roma are not Europeans. The types of difficulties affecting their coexistence with Central European ethnic groups have many similarities to the relationship of aboriginal peoples to their colonizers, and to non-European groups that came to the industrialized countries of Europe and North America from not yet industrialized parts of the world.

Third, the parallel with recent non-European immigrants to the developed countries can be further strengthened by the fact that, in spite of the presence of Roma in Central Europe for centuries, those Roma now living in the Czech lands came after World War II to this already industrialized country from the primarily agrarian Slovakia. Their population in the Czech lands is now at least twenty times more than before the war. So *de facto* they are recent immigrants to this country.[9]

Fourth, not only do Roma not have a territorial base from which they could claim the rights of self-government, but their language and literary culture in its present state could not serve as the medium for development of a societal culture that would fit the needs of a modern post-industrial society. In other words, they lack the cultural resources necessary to develop their own distinct society, if such a society should participate in the achievements of modernity.

In sum, on the one hand, the similarity of Roma to recent non-European immigrants is contradicted by their centuries-long presence in Europe while, on the other hand, their similarity to national minorities is undermined by the lack of a territorial base and of those cultural resources indispensable for a modern way of life. Kymlicka proposes for immigrants the policy of multiculturalism, conceived as a way of integrating them into a mainstream societal culture, and for national minorities the policy of ethnofederalism as a way to mutually accommodate distinct societies. If *descriptively* Roma do not fit into either of those ideal-typical categories, *practically* the policies for managing their problematic relationship with the Czech majority should draw on the parallel with immigrant ethnic groups. The aforementioned four points evidence that the basic prerequisites for Roma self-government and their development of a societal culture are missing. Therefore, the most realistic way of overcoming their triple exclusion is a policy of integrating them, in a multicultural context, into Czech societal culture.

Just as Canadians are able to include immigrant groups into their Canadian political identity and to add diverse cultural identities as new parts of an extended common heritage, while still maintaining the same French or English societal culture and language, the Czechs should make a space within their own political identity for Roma. Here, however, we encounter the basic difference between immigrant and East European countries. For Canadians the endorsement of multiculturalism was a handy solution once the 'Britishness' of Canada was not tenable any more—not to mention the balancing role which it has played with respect to the nationalism of the French-Canadians. This amounted to the continuation of the cultural pluralism of Empire without its imperial roof, that is, without the idea of a hierarchy of cultures. For Czechs, the endorsement of multiculturalism would amount to a substantial transformation of the concept of their society and state.

Creating a space for Roma within the framework of the Czech political identity would imply differentiating the Czech identity into its civic—if culturally specific—and ethnic parts, which have to date been conflated in the idea of an ethnic state. In other words, the consciousness of being a member of the Czech state with a Czech societal culture should be differentiated from the sense of membership in an ethnic group of Czechs. Only after this has happened could a Czech Roma recognize himself or herself as a member of the Czech political nation and, at the same time, remain loyal to his or her own ethnic group. In order to make such a change happen, Czechs are required to transcend the framework of their national identity as it was constructed during the nineteenth century and stabilized in the twentieth century. Still, according to a reconstructed concept of liberal justice—that is, one enlarged by an ethnocultural dimension—Czechs cannot claim to be forming a liberal society unless they are able to set out on this route.

The minimum condition for the development of this dual identity is to expand the curricula at elementary and secondary schools so that Roma history and culture would constitute a part of the history and culture of the Czech lands as the common homeland of both ethnic Czechs and Roma. There should also be preparatory classes for Roma children to help them bridge the gap between their background and the requirements of Czech schools—many such classes have in fact been established since 1993. In the case of schools with a higher percentage of Roma pupils, optional courses of Roma language, history, and culture would be desirable. Public support for the foundation and development of Roma cultural institutions—museums, folklore ensembles, theatres, magazines, and publishing houses—should be a matter of course—to some extent, this has been carried out since 1989. Alterations of national symbols and national holidays should also be considered: for instance, the Czech state emblem consists of four squares—in one is a Moravian eagle, in another a Silesian eagle, and in the remaining two a Czech lion. Why could not one of the Czech lions be replaced by the Roma wheel?

Because economic and social advancement and integration is directly proportional to, and dependent on, the level of education and qualifications, supporting the ethnic identity of the Roma has to be complemented and limited by their assimilation into Czech societal culture through the educational system. Reinstatement of the original Roma way of life, either nomadic or settled, is after many decades of interruption a utopian idea. In an urbanized and post-industrial society it is not only unfeasible, but undesirable, because it would simply confirm the role of pariahs that most Roma play in Czech society today.

As the cultural and economic situation of the Roma is reaching the point of exclusion, so also is their political position, as they hardly participate in the democratic process. The usual channels of political influence are at the mercy of the Czech majority, which monopolizes all political power. Given this political alienation and the resulting mistrust in the government and its law-enforcement apparatus, the situation could lead to ethnic conflict in the absence of group-differentiated political measures and procedures. The spontaneous call for the establishment of a Roma home guard in reaction to escalating xenophobic skinhead violence and similar radicalization on the Czech side can be seen as an ill omen. In the present situation the only realistic policy is the systematic consideration of Roma by the authorities and within political procedures. Roma advisors should be appointed in city and county councils, and measures should be taken to increase the number of Roma employed in public administration and the police—official initiatives in that direction have been developed since 1997. Finally, we should search for ways to include Roma in the process of political representation, either by special representation on party lists or by guaranteeing Roma some places directly in the parliament or Senate and in city councils where warranted by their proportion of the local population.[10]

NOTES

1. John Herz notes the difference between 'the legitimacy of the unit as such and that of its internal system', J. H. Herz, 'The Territorial State Revisited: Reflections on the Future of the Nation-State', in J. Rosenau (ed.) *International Politics and Foreign Policy* (New York, NY: The Free Press, 1969) 83.

2. J. S. Mill, *Considerations on Representative Government* (Oxford: Basil Blackwell, 1946 (1861)) 294–5. Kymlicka lists J. S. Mill among those great liberals who did not pay any sustained attention to the justification of nation-building processes. Mill's opinions on this matter may lack systematization, but he in no case avoided the issue. On the contrary, he was aware of its crucial importance.

3. Ibid., 292.

4. The same position as Mill's has been taken and reformulated more than one hundred years later by political scientists D. A. Rustow and R. Dahl. Rustow sets national unity as the main background condition for a successful transition to democracy and explicitly excludes from his theory of transitions to democracy situations of collapsing Empires beset by secessionist movements. He goes even further by requiring that national unity be unthinkingly and silently taken for granted by the people: 'Any vocal consensus about national unity, in fact, should make us wary.' D. A. Rustow, 'Transitions to Democracy: Toward a Dynamic Model', *Comparative Politics* (April 1970) 351. R. Dahl states that 'the problems of the proper scope and domain of democratic units'—that is, of the legitimacy of the state—lie outside democratic theory and democratic practice: 'If the unit itself is not [considered] proper or rightful—if its scope or domain is not justifiable—then it cannot be made rightful simply by democratic procedures.' R. Dahl, *Democracy and Its Critics* (New Haven, CT, and London: Yale University Press, 1989) 207.

5. Nathan Glazer, 'The Emergence of an American Ethnic Pattern', in Ronald Takaki (ed.) *From Different Shores. Perspectives on Race and Ethnicity in America* (New York, NY, Oxford: Oxford University Press, 1994) 19.

6. Multi-ethnic states such as Czechoslovakia and Yugoslavia were built upon an idea of Slavic nations as members of a larger but nevertheless ethnically-based 'family of nations' or as 'brother nations'.

7. For a brief review of the main European approaches towards post-war immigration see Umberto Melotti, 'International Migration in Europe: Social Projects and Political Cultures', in Tariq Modood and Pnina Werbner (eds.) *The Politics of Multiculturalism in the New Europe. Racism, Identity and Community* (London, New York, NY: Zed Books, 1997) 72–92.

8. For East European countries, the prototype for such a redefinition could be represented by the change of citizenship law promoted in Germany by the Greens. By allowing dual citizenship for German Turks, this law would strike a deadly blow to the ethnic definition of the German nation-state.

9. Of course *de jure* they are not, because they migrated within one state—Czechoslovakia.

10. Virtually all measures I have mentioned coincide with the idea of multiculturalism as defined by Kymlicka. One difference concerns special political representation for discriminated groups. Kymlicka sees this as a third form of dealing

with ethnocultural diversity, distinct from ethnofederalism for national minorities and multiculturalism for immigrants. See his 'Three Forms of Group-Differentiated Citizenship in Canada', in Seyla Benhabib (ed.) *Democracy and Difference. Contesting the Boundaries of the Political* (Princeton, NJ: Princeton University Press, 1996) 153–70.

2.11

Definitions and Discourse: Applying Kymlicka's Models to Estonia and Latvia

VELLO PETTAI

Will Kymlicka's application of Western political theory to the ethnopolitical conflicts of Central and Eastern Europe represents a provocative venture in normative conceptual thinking as well as an equally grounded analysis of empirical reality. His blend is obviously not trouble-free in a number of cases. However, such links must always be made. In my commentary, I will follow his example by tackling both theory and fact. I will begin with the theoretical dimension and raise a number of points in relation to the basic concept of 'ethnocultural justice' and Kymlicka's five models of ethnopolitical conflict. I find that while 'ethnopolitical justice' has indeed become the focal point of debate in all five of these contexts, a critical causal puzzle piece remains missing if we do not complement these *definitions* with the *discourses* ethnocultural groups use to wage their ethnopolitical struggles. In the second part of my essay examining the empirical reality of Estonia and Latvia, this is precisely the conclusion I suggest be drawn.

'With Liberty and [Ethnocultural] Justice for All . . .'

During the last quarter of the twentieth century, the Western world appears to have begun shifting away from a central political paradigm, which has hitherto governed the development of social communities for over three centuries. This paradigm concerns the interrelationship between ethnocultural societal groups and the predominant form of modern political power, the centralized state. Since the seventeenth century advent of the modern state as an integrated coercive, administrative, and ideological structure, we have seen the ways in which this unprecedented power has also begun to mould and synthesize disparate ethnocultural groups as part of what scholars for a long time quite benignly called 'nation-building'. It is this period and practice that now seems to be over.

In the historical drive to progressively homogenize ethnocultural systems, the state always held the long end of the stick. For it was the state which in any given society usually determined the essential proportion of existing symbols, languages, values, lifestyles, architecture, religion, and a host of other social-communicative elements, which individual people could use to build community and identity.[1] Since the state was the one that had the power to enact many of these elements by law, the state thus had a predominant role to play in shaping and determining society's sense of community and identity. Naturally, in each state's case there were people for whom the selected ethnocultural system was the one to which they themselves belonged— hence the cases where pure nation-states developed. Still, the state itself always played a central role in this process as the locus of ultimate coercive, administrative, and ideological power.

One of the central points of Will Kymlicka's chapter is that while the state itself has not disappeared as the reigning form of political organization in the world today, it is clear that ethnocultural groups for their part no longer bow submissively to the dictates of the state in terms of determining the communicative system of society. An essential crack has developed in the centuries-old franchise of the state to set the terms for social communication in society. These terms are now a matter of *negotiation* between the state and society, an issue for open-ended debate between the state and all ethnocultural groups affected.

This picture of three centuries of historical development, as I have just presented it, is admittedly most basic. Along the way since the 1600s there have in fact been many different stages, and most of these have actually signified a democratization of the original state-dominated nation-building practice. In his essay, Kymlicka addresses the penultimate stage of this evolution, namely, the 'liberal state' and its efforts to achieve ethnocultural 'neutrality' in its dealings with the ethnocultural groups under its jurisdiction. In contrast to the unapologetic nation-building—and hence nation-destroying— state of the nineteenth century, such as France, the liberal state has attempted to remain at least neutral or as unobtrusive as possible when setting the terms for social communication in society. The consequence of this more liberal attitude was that the state stepped away from an aggressive stance regarding its ability to mould social communication, and instead it moved toward a benign approach, in which it continued to play the dominant role, but in which it also understood its responsibility not to do undue harm to existing ethnocultural groups by forcibly imposing upon them entirely alien communicative elements or systems.[2]

Yet Kymlicka in his article makes the fundamental point that with the dawn of the twenty-first century even this liberal model of state-society relations is changing and that the state is now being opened up to a full-scale *negotiation* of social-communicative system management. As he says, it is no longer a question of ethnocultural neutrality on the part of the state, but of ethnocultural justice. This means that in a majority of Western states all meaningful ethnocultural groups are now *parties* to determining how the state will use its coercive, administrative, and ideological power to mould the society's system of social communication. Such groups are no longer merely the objects of state power.

Critiques

There are two main points to be made about this thesis. The first is that Kymlicka is right to go beyond this thesis and distinguish five essential *contexts* in which this paradigm shift from state-dominated nation-building is taking place. He makes the point that although in each of these five cases the historical circumstances are entirely different, the same dynamic concerning the *democratization* of state-society ethnocultural relations is taking place. Be it national minorities, racial/caste distinctions, immigrant groups, metics, or isolationist religious sects, the political-philosophical pressures are everywhere at work to give all ethnocultural groups their rights to preserve their own social-communicative systems in a much more conscious fashion than either the nation-homogenizing or even liberal-neutral state ever allowed. Thus, we are moving into a new era.

Still, in my view it is vital to notice that these same models actually reflect a much broader concept, which might best be called 'ethno-political situations' in the world. These 'situations' represent different patterns of how the modern state as a form of political organization spread across the societies of the world and of how it came to be imposed on ethnocultural groups in different ways and in different sequences. In some cases, such as national minorities, a consolidating state power simply conquered neighbouring ethnocultural groups and began the ethnocultural standardization process very rapidly. In other cases, political power was imposed from across great distances by colonial states. Although here the establishment of a common social-communicative system was more complicated, it was still attempted—and later continued by the post-colonial states themselves. Furthermore, both of these cases involved instances of state power *expanding* itself to outlying populations. Yet, with the expansion of human travel during the nineteenth and twentieth centuries, we have also seen the opposite process, whereby great numbers of individual people have moved *themselves* under a different political power and have thereby of their own accord been subjected to the social-communicative system fostered by that new state. Stated most simply, of Kymlicka's five models one could say that 'national minorities' and 'African-Americans' concern the first type of state *assumption* of new ethnocultural groups, while the remaining three—'immigrants', 'isolationist ethnoreligious groups' and 'metics' —concern the second trend of individual *transplantation* and submission to state ethnocultural power.

With this added distinction between Kymlicka's five models, we have in fact a powerful typology of five contemporary ethnopolitical situations and their salient dynamics. Each type captures not only a different historical pattern of state-society ethnopolitical interaction, but also the kinds of different claims and starting points the ethnocultural groups in question are likely to use and/or have available to them for negotiating their overall ethnopolitical position in the polity. Thus, not only do 'national minorities,' for example, differ from 'immigrants' or 'metics' in the historical ways through which they have come to face a state's ethnopolitical power, but they also clearly have different degrees of (a) political resources and (b) legitimacy which they can bring to that existential struggle.

The first of these two variables—resources—is in many ways an objective category. For example, it is well known sociologically that national minorities tend to have a greater potential for collective mobilization in defence of their ethnocultural interests than immigrant or metic groups. However, in relation to the second variable— legitimacy—an important degree of difference also exists. Namely, national minorities have generally been viewed as more entitled to 'ethnocultural justice' than immigrant or metic groups, even though in many Western countries this distinction, too, has begun to erode.

The second point to be made about Kymlicka's five-model framework is that although these categories are all very trenchant and conceptually objective, they fall short of alerting us to the fact that in any given ethnopolitical context these classifications are in reality always *an object of contestation themselves*. The consequence of this fact is that in many cases the group which succeeds in defining the ethnopolitical conflict first, is in the end also the group that most determines the ethnopolitical balance of power. Although we as scholars may attempt to assess certain ethnopolitical situations along Kymlicka's five different models, we are unlikely to be able to explain the *actual* ethnopolitical balance of power if we do not also study how the given ethnocultural groups themselves first sought to define the conflict. For, in general, ethnic groups will attempt to strategically cast their ethnopolitical situation by using terms that will give them as many resources and as much legitimacy as possible *vis-à-vis* other groups in the conflict. Thus, for example, situations, which to the outside observer might appear to involve racial or caste groups, might in fact play out on the ground as a metic-based conflict, since in the very beginning of the conflict one group was able to ascribe to another the category of 'metic', thus depriving the latter of certain resource and/or legitimacy claims. Likewise, one might encounter a situation where a *de facto* immigrant group has in fact perpetually been tainted as a metic group, and in the process been subjected to greater ethnocultural injustice than might otherwise have been the case. In these and many other instances, we must maintain a critical eye to the discursive struggles which groups undertake to define ethnopolitical situations, and see how these bear on the final ethnopolitical outcome. My empirical discussion of Estonia and Latvia will illustrate this theoretical assertion.

Definitions and Discourses in Estonia and Latvia

As Kymlicka correctly remarks in his opening chapter, the ethnopolitical situation in Estonia and Latvia represents perhaps one of the most striking sets of contrasting perceptions or discourses in the former Soviet Union. On the one hand, the minority Russian-speaking communities in both countries aspire to define themselves as national minorities. This is because although most of them came to these two Baltic states during Soviet rule and as part of a centrally planned russification policy, they were never themselves wholly conscious of this pawn-like role in a broader process, and instead came to view themselves as a legitimate group in society, which in turn entitled them to certain ethnocultural rights and power-sharing prerogatives regardless of the regime. In the Latvian case, this Russian feeling of belonging to a corporate minority community was buttressed by the historical fact that already before the Soviet occupation in 1940 there was a sizeable Russian population in the republic, especially in Riga and the eastern province of Latgale.[3] In this sense, the entire Russian-speaking population—both pre- and post-Soviet—could put this legacy to use as a claim to legitimacy as well as a source of self-worth. In Estonia, meanwhile, the Russian-speaking population had much weaker historical roots, since it was almost entirely the product of Soviet russification policy.[4] Nevertheless, that policy had also the effect of concentrating the Russians in key districts of Tallinn as well as in three main cities of the north-east—Narva, Sillamäe, and Kohtla-Järve. Thus, in this case the minority was located in compact enclaves and this meant that it could also mobilize relatively easily due to geographic concentration.

Indeed, to most outside observers the perception of the Russians as a 'national minority' is an objective one. From this, in turn, flows a number of conclusions following Kymlicka's model: for example, we should see in the two countries a move toward a 'multinational' model, where both the titular Estonian/Latvian as well as the minority Russian communities would, in Kymlicka's words,

> recognize that each constituent nation has an equally valid claim to the language rights and self-government powers necessary to maintain itself as a distinct societal culture. And this multinational character is typically manifested in some form of territorial autonomy for the national minority, and which may be explicitly affirmed in the country's laws and constitution. (p. 29 above)

The question then becomes, why is this *de facto* not so?

The reality of the ethnopolitical situation in Estonia and Latvia has been that most of the members of the two Russian-speaking communities have in fact been excluded from the overall political community as a result of exclusionary citizenship laws adopted by both states soon after the Soviet *coup* in August 1991. The reason for this was precisely the way in which the ethnopolitical situation had in the meantime been taken over by an *alternative definition* or *discourse* that portrayed Russian-speakers not as national minorities, nor even as immigrants, but essentially as metics and thus not even entitled to real inclusion within the polity.

The pathway to this kind of outcome began in the late 1980s when the winds of Mikhail Gorbachev's perestroika first reached Estonia and Latvia. On the one hand, the situation started off positively as most Estonians and Latvians were in fact fairly realistic and benevolent toward the Russian-speakers living in their societies. The main political movements to emerge during this period—the Estonian and Latvian Popular Fronts—were on the whole sober in their recognition of the Russian-speakers as a more-or-less permanent part of their societies and as such entitled to a substantive degree of participation in the political, as well as ethnopolitical, development of the two republics. On the other hand, these movements were not the only ones seeking to frame the new ethnopolitical situation. Just one year later, in 1989, a powerful, alternative discourse began to gain strength in Estonia and Latvia that was put forward by a new type of movement called the Citizens Committees. These leaders—who had generally originated from the old dissident circles of the 1970s and early 1980s—advocated a different discourse for the situation, which centred on the claim that in 1940 the Soviet Union had in reality illegally occupied and annexed Estonia and Latvia and that as a result the two states, along with Lithuania, were now entitled to the restoration of their sovereignty, much like Kuwait had been restored after occupation by Iraq or East Timor by Indonesia.

This argument was a very powerful one from the standpoint of breaking away from Moscow. However, state independence was only one of its implications. In addition, the Citizens Committees claimed that given this condition of illegal occupation all those who had moved to these territories during Soviet rule were also guilty of illegal colonization and that as a result they could not now be accepted into the new polity on some kind of automatic basis. On the contrary, as individuals who had 'illegally' settled on occupied territory, they could at best hope for lenient naturalization terms or other concessions. Barring such magnanimous gestures on the part of Estonia or Latvia, however, these immigrants would simply have to accept their fate.[5]

In the factual course of events, this alternative legalistic discourse eventually won out. During 1989 and 1990 the Citizens Committees grew rapidly in strength, and although for a period in early 1991 their influence waned, they staged an impressive comeback after the failed Soviet *coup* in August and the Baltic states' leap to freedom. For in the weeks and months following that unexpected event the Citizens

Committees pushed hard for an institutionalization of their legalistic political principles, most importantly via a definition of citizenship, which limited these rights to those who had held them before 1940, together with their descendants. Conversely, all those who had come to Estonia and Latvia during the Soviet occupation—together with their descendants—were excluded from automatic citizenship rights and were allowed instead only a chance at future naturalization based on certain residency and language requirements. Thus, in one fell swoop the idea of the Russian-speaking community as a national minority was definitively ruled out, largely through discursive definition. Instead, there were now only metics, 'long-term residents who are nonetheless excluded from the polis.' The Russian-speaking minorities in Estonia and Latvia did not formally qualify as 'metics' in the same sense that Kymlicka, for example, refers to 'guestworkers' in Germany. As noted above, the Russians did not migrate to these republics knowingly as 'colonists', 'migrants', or 'guestworkers'. Nevertheless, I use the term in this essay to draw attention to the Estonian and Latvian governments' attitude toward these populations once the legalistic doctrine was adopted. From that perspective, these persons were indeed seen as essentially illegitimate residents. In addition, it is true that a certain degree of inclusion was possible for these individuals if they were persistent enough to go through certain naturalization procedures made available to them.[6] But in reality these barriers were themselves quite high and in any case the state that was on offer to such 'legalized metics' was now respectively an Estonian or Latvian nation-state, and not in any way a multinational partnership, which would have been the case had the Russians been defined as a national minority.[7]

In sum, the Estonian and Latvian cases show how a great deal of ethnopolitical outcomes are in fact often determined by the effective reframing of otherwise objective situations by ethnopolitical entrepreneurs, and that rigorous conceptual schemes are only half the recipe for explaining real ethnopolitical dynamics. One can always argue that just as a certain degree of framing can lead to one particular outcome, so too can a different type of framing lead to another. For normative political theorists this is precisely their point of departure in criticizing ethnopolitical entrepreneurs for framing divisive ethnopolitical situations. If all discourses are relative, they argue, then it is the task of responsible élites and theorists to construct positive counter-discourses. However, often this is not so easy. On the contrary, it is more likely that over time ethnopolitical élites will simply moderate their own discourses or new élites will emerge to reframe the debate toward a new evolutionary stage. At the beginning of the year 2000, this was precisely the crossroads at which Estonia and Latvia stood.

Conclusion

During 1997–8 both the Estonian and Latvian governments embarked on a new direction in their ethnopolitical policies after it became clear that six years of large-scale exclusion was only deepening ethnic separation in society. Instead, the two governments began to work out comprehensive schemes for 'integrating' Russian-speakers and other minorities into Estonian and Latvian society. This shift in discourse involved two essential steps. On the one hand, both governments finally admitted that the large number of non-citizens in the two states—330,000 in Estonia and some 650,000 in Latvia—had to be reduced through the active promotion of available naturalization procedures. In so doing, the two states admitted that metic status for such a large share of the Russian-speaking population was undesirable and that all individuals should be encouraged to become full members of the community. As Kymlicka, too, notes, Estonia and Latvia thus began to move toward an 'immigrant' definition of the ethnopolitical situation.[8]

Still, even in this liberalized setting, 'ethnocultural justice' for the Russian minorities continued to focus mainly on their integration into an *Estonian-* and *Latvian-dominated* societal culture, not a broader, multicultural societal, or ethnopolitical structure. Thus, for example, there remained a general reluctance in both countries to go the next step and begin reassessing existing social institutions to see how their rules, structures, and symbols actually accommodate immigrants or how minority political participation could be actively encouraged. Such steps were perhaps premature, given the mere decade that had passed since independence. Too many Estonian and Latvian memories of Soviet russification remained, while the Russian communities themselves were slow to really mobilize their strength and press for meaningful change.[9] However, these questions would eventually be on the agenda, for over time the notion of ethnocultural justice will almost surely expand and it will also no longer be so easy to categorize Soviet-era immigrants as metics.[10] Thus, even exclusionary ethnopolitical discourses were being challenged by inclusive notions of ethnocultural justice. Still, the two phenomena remain closely linked, and any explanation of a country's shift from one ethnopolitical regime to another must, in my view, take into account both dimensions.

NOTES

The author would like to thank Will Kymlicka and Andrew Valls for helpful comments on earlier drafts of this essay.

1. In this essay I use the term 'social communication', as originally defined by Karl Deutsch, to mean that system of symbols, values, lifestyles, languages, and other practices by which individuals communicate information to each other about what can be expected of themselves and how to act in relation to them. It is not far from Kymlicka's basic term 'ethnocultural'. However, it focuses more on the functionalistic processes of ethnicity. That is to say, ethnic identity in my view is most extensively derived from the communicative congruence or efficiency that a person feels when interacting with other individuals, and not from simply vague emotions. In this sense, states obviously have a major influence on ethnic identity to the extent that they build or impose an efficient social-communicative system for their people.
2. In this respect, the liberal state is said to have adopted a stance toward ethnocultural systems similar to that which it had assumed already in relation to religion. Just as religious groups were allowed at one point in the eighteenth century the freedom to practice their different faiths, so too would ethnocultural groups now be permitted essential existential rights.
3. For example, before 1940 Latvia was only 78 per cent ethnic Latvian.
4. It is estimated that in 1945, Estonia was over 95 per cent Estonian.
5. Kymlicka makes the argument in Part 1 of this volume that because most countries recognized the borders of the USSR, international law implicitly condoned the influx of Russians to all parts of the Soviet Union. In the Baltic case, however, Baltic politicians cited the West's concomitant policy of non-recognition of the Soviet occupation, as a result of which they argued that international law was on their side.
6. In Estonia, moreover, permanent residents can vote in local elections.
7. Indeed, some authors have gone so far as to declare Estonia and Latvia 'ethnic democracies' or 'ethnic control regimes', instead of bona fide democracies. See Vello Pettai 'Emerging Ethnic Demoracy in Estonia and Latvia', in Magda Opalski (ed.) *Managing Diversity in Plural Societies. Minorities, Migration and Nation-Building in Post-Communist Europe* (Nepean, Ontario: Forum Eastern Europe, 1998) 15–32; Graham Smith, 'The Ethnic Democracy Thesis and the Citizenship Question in Estonia and Latvia', *Nationalities Papers*, 24/2 (June 1996) 199–216.
8. p. 78 above.
9. In Estonia, for example, Russian political parties became hopelessly split during the March 1999 parliamentary elections, such that only four of their members were actually elected to the 101-seat assembly. This was in comparison to the non-Estonian community's estimated 15 per cent share of the citizenry, and over 30 per cent share of the general population.

10. For example, in 1996 Estonia ratified the Council of Europe's Framework Convention for the Protection of National Minorities, in the context of which it was obliged in 1999 to begin preparing a state report as to how it was implementing the Convention's provisions. Although upon ratifying the Convention, Estonia had declared that it defined national minorities as only citizens of Estonia—thus excluding once again the non-citizen Soviet-era immigrant population—there remained a question as to whether Estonia was fulfilling the Convention even in regard to these people. See 'Vähemusrahvuste Ümarlaua töögrupi analüüs Vähemusrahvuste kaitse raamkonventsiooni täitmise kohta Eestis', Presidential Roundtable on National Minorities, 22 January 1999.

Universal Thought, Eastern Facts: Scrutinizing National Minority Rights in Romania

Gabriel Andreescu

It is to a certain extent surprising for me—a researcher who is geographically removed from the Western academic world—to discover that a scholar like Will Kymlicka is sceptical about the application of the instruments of his own discipline to Eastern Europe. According to Kymlicka, the limitations are apparent in Western political theory and in the challenges posed by Eastern Europe. When Kymlicka states that, 'Western political theory may have relatively little to offer to people in [Eastern European countries] struggling with the sorts of ethnic conflict discussed in this book', he implicitly separates Western reality from the state of affairs in Eastern Europe, and Western thought from the concepts by which Eastern European peoples are supposed to manage their ethnocultural diversity. Does such a separation match the facts?

The generic West that Kymlicka has in mind is itself extremely diverse in the way it deals with ethnocultural diversity. Kymlicka himself notes that there is an important difference between Canadian and Austrian or German policies towards the communities of immigrants that have entered these countries during the last decades. There is an equally significant difference between the manner in which France and the Scandinavian countries deal with the nature and meaning of a 'national minority'. But is this not also true of Hungary, Romania, and the Federal Republic of Yugoslavia? Do Croatia and the Baltic countries face the same issues? Is the gap separating the Czech Republic from Portugal wider than that dividing the former from its neighbour Slovakia? I think not. I doubt even more that we can speak of distinct Western and Eastern European concepts and doctrines for the management of ethnocultural diversity. I will look at the examples offered by Will Kymlicka from a different perspective. My underlying premises are:

1. There are universal ethical values, just as there are universal human rights, and the former are the fundamental reference point for solving the problems of minority issues.
2. The main questions facing today's Western and, to a greater extent, Eastern European societies do not arise from different histories but, mainly, from the necessity to face modernity.
3. The focus on modernity is even more crucial when we deal not with the internal dynamics of these societies, but with their interconnectedness in a global society.[1]
4. A society is first and foremost a functional system, the task of which is to identify and solve the problems of its members.

These four premises are in themselves controversial. I agree, though, with Richard Falk, who states that 'virtually any cultural heritage is rich enough that it can, under some circumstances, make inspirational contributions to the struggle for human rights, democracy and social justice.'[2] I would simply add that this is equally true in the struggle for minority rights.

Romania's Multicultural Diversity

Romania's 1992 census recorded sixteen national minorities whose populations ranged from 1,620,199 Hungarians to just 2,023 Armenians. The total population of Romania was 22,760,449.[3]

Ethnic diversity in Romania is enormously complex. Fourteen small minorities are integrated into the majority population and are thus beyond the tensions that 'nationality' can invoke. With the exception of the German and the Jewish traditions, their contribution to the country's multicultural make-up is peripheral.

The Roma minority raises serious social problems. Their level of education and standard of living are considerably below the average. Discrimination against the Roma is acute: Roma have the lowest 'sympathy index' among the rest of the population.

The Romanian Hungarians are a political challenge typical to many other countries. Transylvania, the region where the greatest part of the Hungarian minority is situated, was for a long time an autonomous principality, which subsequently became a part of the

Hungarian Kingdom within the Austro-Hungarian Empire. In 1918, Transylvania became a part of Great Romania. Today, Hungary is Romania's neighbour at the Transylvanian border. Although the Hungarians are living in a compact community in the centre of the country—the Harghita and Covasna counties—rather than near the border, the possibility of Transylvania becoming a Hungarian province is a constant theme in the Romanian collective imagination. The situation where a powerful community has become a minority after the borders were redrawn, and which furthermore inhabits a region neighbouring its ethnic 'mother-state', is not uncommon. Italy, Slovakia, and Finland, to name just a few European countries, provide similar examples.

The Exercise of Majority Rule and the Struggle for Political Legitimacy

The manner in which Eastern European countries have treated the problem of national and religious minorities after 1989 was aptly captured by Adam Michnik's well-known phrase: 'Nationalism is the continuation of communism'. Before the fall of Communist regimes, nationalities legislation and the status of ethnic minorities in these countries presented a patchwork of diversity. One can hardly compare Poland, where the Germans were not allowed to use their national language, to Romania, where Hungarians enjoyed higher education in their own language. Similarly, it is impossible to draw parallels at that time between the complex association of ethnoreligious groups in the former Yugoslavia and Hungarian policies.

In all of these countries the end of Communism brought the beginning of a desperate battle by the old élites for political survival. Nationalism was the only ideology left intact. Nevertheless, as Michnik himself noticed, the nationalist doctrines confronting democracy did not have the same content, amplitude, and consequences throughout Central and Eastern Europe.[4] Nationalism led to civil war and bloody secession in the former Yugoslavia. It triggered the peaceful dismembering of Czechoslovakia. It marginalized Romania in the process of European integration. It posed problems in the definition of statehood and citizenship in the Baltic countries and influenced political life in Bulgaria. But it affected Poland only a little and barely touched Hungary. In this sense, although Michnik's phrase remains generally true, it is relevant to only some of the countries in the region. Romania is one of them.

Nationalism as a form of political legitimization belongs to a wider concept defined by Jon Elster as 'majority rule'.[5] In a 1993 paper dealing with the possible conflict between majority rule and individual rights in post-communist Eastern Europe, he remarked: 'To exaggerate somewhat, there has been a shift from the despotism of the Party to the despotism of majority, both inimical to the protection of minority rights.'[6] Elster was referring to a number of developments: the attempt of the parliamentary majority to remain a majority by manipulating electoral mechanisms; the state appealing to the passion of *amour-propre*; confiscatory measures against property owners; and majorities acting under sudden impulses and momentary passions— 'the turbulence and follies of democracy'. While this is part of the story, in Romania there was more to it. The mentality discerned in the abuse of national minorities by majority rule—as part of the struggle for political legitimacy—fed upon the national-Communist legacy. And national-Communism in turn had amply benefited from the Romanian cultural traditions of the end of the nineteenth and first half of the twentieth centuries, when nationalist discourse was pervasive. A demagogically impregnated political imagination, which was easy for the actors vying for political power and influence to manipulate, was quickly restored.

The Victory of Nationalism in Romania: 1992–6

Romania adopted a new Constitution in December 1991. Some of its articles, and especially those referring to the nature of the Romanian state, were the subject of serious parliamentary debate. Two articles in particular—Article 1 (1) and Article 4 (1)—expressed a clear nationalistic approach.[7] But this approach does not actually support the assimilation of ethnic minorities, as demonstrated by several constitutional provisions.[8] These suggest not only that the Romanian Constitution does recognize national minorities, but also that it accepts special measures to strengthen and affirm their identities. Nevertheless, this is only one side of the coin. The other is that the nationalist ideology managed to affect negatively some formal provisions of

Romanian law before 1990, in addition to some fundamental rights and freedoms.

Meanwhile, the nationalist and extremist forces had consolidated their positions. The October 1992 elections brought four parties to power. The winner, the Party of Social-Democracy in Romania (PDSR), formed a coalition with the Party for National Unity in Romania (PUNR), the Great Romania Party (PRM) and the former Communists (PSM). At least two of these groups can be labelled hyper-nationalist, in John Mearsheimer's definition of the word.[9] These developments have been the subject of several papers and studies by Western scholars concerned with the region's stability.[10]

The birth of extremist parties is inseparable from the insanely aggressive mass-media campaign that started in 1990. Racist, xeno-phobic, chauvinistic, and anti-European propaganda was used on a large scale. The scapegoats were predominantly the country's main minorities—the Hungarians and the Roma. The new members of the governmental coalition managed to pass a new Education Law in 1995 that substantially reduced the linguistic rights of the national minorities.

The hyper-nationalism associated with the country's governance suggests that during the 1992–6 period Romania confronted an 'ethnocratic' problem. Important institutions of the Romanian state, such as the Supreme Council of National Defence and the Romanian Intelligence Service, displayed nationalistic tendencies in their activities. It is apparent that these organizations were constantly under pressure from political actors of the extremist-nationalist orientation.

The situation became particularly serious in relations with the Hungarian minority. After 1989 the Hungarian minority had its own form of political representation, positively sanctioned by the whole community: the Democratic Union of Hungarians in Romania—DAHR, known by the Hungarian acronym UDMR. The DAHR's draft laws and programmes were built on the notions of internal self-determination and a system of autonomy.[11] The Hungarian com-munity's efforts to get their draft laws adopted failed. Moreover, not only did the Parliament refuse to consider the proposals for self-government and autonomy. Instead it adopted a new law, the previously mentioned Education Law, that was obviously targeted against the Hungarians in so far as it eliminated the previous provision for taking exams in the mother tongue and restricted the range of Hungarian university training. It thereby dissolved one of the most important assets for defining the Hungarian identity.

The Romanian-Hungarian Reconciliation

The worsening of inter-ethnic relations in Romania was reversed after the 1996 elections. The DAHR was invited to join the winning coalition of the Democratic Convention and the Democratic Party. Romanian authorities enhanced the standards for the special protection of national minorities. Concomitantly, Romanian extremist groups—be they cultural or political—were pushed to the periphery of public life. In May and June 1997, the government adopted new legal norms in the most sensitive area—use of the mother tongue in administration and education.[12] At the same time, Romania signed new international documents that have positively affected the status of national minorities.[13]

As a result of those developments, the Hungarian minority implicitly agreed to give up its own solution for self-protection—the system of internal self-determination and autonomy—which does not accord with the Romanian constitutional framework. The pragmatic wing of the DAHR realized that some objectives are, at least for the time being, unrealizable. A constitutional change involves securing at least two-thirds of the parliamentary votes and compliance with an intricate procedure. Under the current circumstances this is impossible to achieve and, given the fragility of democracy in Romania, it would probably also be wrong. Fortunately, the political leaders who accepted the compromise understood the limits of negotiations.

The political class that accepted new standards for minority protection in Romania's post-1996 political life did so, sometimes against their personal beliefs, in order to comply with the new political environment. NATO and the EU regarded the resolution of minority problems as a compulsory criterion for integration. The will to integrate overcame the reluctance of the political class to turn Romania into a multicultural society.[14] Moreover, the situation of the Hungarian minority in Romania is also an issue for regional stability. The Hungarian state took upon itself in its Constitution the task of taking care of the Hungarians outside its borders. All Hungarian governments after 1990 placed the support of Hungarian nationals in Romania and Slovakia on their agendas. Max van der Stoel, the OSCE High Commissioner for National Minorities repeatedly toured Budapest and Bucharest to discuss the issue of the Hungarian minority. It is significant that he was less interested in the status of the Roma, in spite of the numerous and serious incidents against their community.[15] From the international perspective, it seems that the question of national minorities in Romania is primarily a question of the status of the Hungarian community.

Do We Need a New Political Theory to Deal with Diversity in Romania?

The lengthy description of the evolution of the struggle for minority rights in Romania—as well as the struggle against minority rights—was meant to show that the resolution of minority issues depends in large part on the internal and international contexts. Empirically speaking, the arguments that were invoked in forging inter-ethnic relations in post-1989 Romania belong to a common pool of ideas and practices. Nationalist clichés, principles of international law, democratic catchwords, and European or North American examples have been woven into an eclectic discourse on nationalities policy. But this did not simply result in a couple of words on paper. It led to practical, if not always effective, political actions and legal norms.

Probably the most relevant example of this is the political struggle around the Hungarian minority's demand to establish a state university in their mother tongue. The proposal was firmly rejected by the nationalist forces that dominated political life before 1996. But then, after the 1996 election, the principle behind the notion of a Hungarian university was accepted by the new governing coalition in 1997. The nationalist opposition, however, saw this as an Achilles' heel of the majority coalition and launched a campaign opposed to the proposed legislation. As a result, laws to promote the use of the Hungarian minority's mother tongue in administration and education, which had been adopted by the government in the first half of 1997, have been stuck in Parliament.

The issue has not disappeared. In fact, the main theme of political life between the summers of 1997 and 1999 has been the right of the Hungarian minority to have a Hungarian state university. Everybody has been involved in the debate. The manner in which political leaders, including those governing the country, the Ministry of National Education, and a significant part of the media have responded to the claims of the Hungarian minority is in a way reminiscent of the pre-1996 nationalistic policy. This endangers the reconciliation process between the Hungarian minority and the majority that was initiated recently and risks a return to inter-ethnic tension. What were the main arguments?

Some regard the idea of a Hungarian state university as a rejection of cohabitation. Part of the leadership of Romanian universities, university professors' associations, and the Ministry of National Education have described the Hungarians' demand as a 'federalization of education', an 'enclavization of education', or a 'development of education on ethnic bases'. One of the most significant documents of this kind, entitled *The Ethnic Segregation of Higher Education in Romania is Untimely*, was published in August 1998 by the State Secretariat for Higher Education. A typical passage reads: 'The State Secretariat for Higher Education has been constantly facing urgent requests for ethnic segregation that take various institutional forms which range from the establishment of self-managed departments on ethnic criteria to the establishment of state universities in the Hungarian language.'[16]

The response of minority rights activists and of the representatives of the Hungarian minority is relevant to the issues raised in Will Kymlicka's paper. Associations for the protection of national minorities legitimized the Hungarian community's requests by making reference to international law. They invoked Romania's obligation to act in conformity with Article 27 of the *International Covenant on Civil and Political Rights*, adopted by the UN in 1966 and ratified by Romania in 1974. An interpretation of the *Covenant* by the Geneva Committee for Human Rights, as well as reference to the status of Hungarians in Romania as the most numerous minority in Europe—apart from the CIS countries—were used as supportive arguments.

The Hungarian minority's arguments concentrated on its tradition as a Transylvanian community and on the way that other states treat their minorities. Its favourite examples were Finland, where there are several bilingual universities with instruction in Swedish for the approximately 285,000 Swedes who make up 5.8 per cent of Finland's population; the system of higher education in South Tirol, Italy, for the 303,000 German speakers—0.5 per cent of the population; Switzerland, with its 1.3 million French speakers and 500,000 Italians speakers—18 per cent and 7 per cent of the population, respectively; as well as Great Britain and Canada—the University of Ottawa.

Is there an original argument in this whole debate? I do not think so. Defending national identity in a European country like Romania drew upon international documents, tradition, the spirit and the letter of the law, the values of liberal policies, the meaning of international contexts and of the national interest. These references have been constant ingredients in the struggle for inter-ethnic peace. Western thought and Western ideas have been consistently summoned to aid both the minority representatives and minority rights activists, and they have found their way into legislation. This should be enough to refute Will Kymlicka's main thesis.

Principles of Cultural Autonomy: Special Measure versus Autonomy

Generally speaking, Romanian public opinion has been rather sceptical about the principles of cultural autonomy, and even more so about the territorial autonomy that is legitimized in the writings of authors such as Hurst Hannum, Patrick Thornberry, or Will Kymlicka. This is not to say that a tradition of autonomy has been altogether absent. On the contrary, Transylvania, the province with the most diverse ethnic composition, has been accustomed to radical forms of autonomy. An autonomous region in the centre of the country existed in the 1950s.

Opposition to the concept of cultural autonomy through 'special measures' was dramatized by the dispute over the proposal for a Hungarian-language state university. The notion of two entirely separate types of protection gained credit: autonomy and special measures. However, special measures do actually warrant, at least implicitly, a certain form of cultural autonomy for minorities. The right to civil and political association, the right to one's own institutions, the right to use one's mother tongue privately or publicly, and the right to education in one's own language are practical tools for minorities to develop their cultural life freely. This is the very substance of cultural autonomy.

Principles of Justice

How is one to interpret the Romanian disputes over nationalities policy in terms of an academic analysis of the principles of justice in a multicultural society? Richard Rorty has an interesting position on this question. For Rorty, human rights—and minority rights by extension—need passion and courage rather than reason and theory. The quest for secure philosophical foundations of human rights, he argues, is doomed to fail and is practically useless.[17] Maybe this is too radical, as well as unfair to the merits of theorists. But I believe that the most important resource for the knowledge of ethics in political life is the battle for concrete rights. This is not to say, of course, that it is all a matter of pure attitude. The struggle for justice needs concepts because it needs nuances and effectiveness. Nevertheless, the process of conceptualization cannot be isolated from the scientific solidarity of the academic community throughout the world. The solutions themselves have worldwide applicability, even if applying them from one case to another is not determined *in nuce* by the general theory.

In applying general principles to the Romanian case one obviously needs to take into account the specific context—the state of transition. I have referred to the struggle for political legitimacy. It is no wonder that the ethnic issue was defused in Poland, Hungary, and the Czech Republic, countries where the political élites were radically changed and where institutional and economic reform was successful.

Another aspect of transition is the existence of a 'waiting list'. One cannot move forward by jumping over particular stages. The issue of immigrants is significant in this sense. By concentrating on the Hungarian problem and having to face the dramatic challenges posed by the Roma community, there was little room left for the rights of newcomers on the political agenda.

There is another characteristic of transition that I find crucial—the relation between rights and their costs. Different sorts of rights—purely individual rights, individual rights exercised in a community, collective rights exercised individually, and purely collective rights[18]—can support and enforce one another. It is therefore natural to expand and develop the system of rights, irrespective of country, while taking into consideration the historical, numerical, and cultural specificities. The challenge for scholars is to make, theoretically and practically, individual rights and group rights compatible with one another in order to avoid contradiction. However, such an endeavour has several constraints. One of them is the actual costs of rights. Looking at rights in terms of costs may suggest a real distinction between the fate of minority rights in the West and in Eastern Europe.

My conjecture is that there are three important levels of costs: the costs of civil and political rights; the costs of special measures; and the costs of social and economic rights. The first is generally affordable and a matter of political will. Because social and economic rights carry substantial costs, they are considered by many a *desideratum*.

Between these two extremes there are the costs of special measures—the basic instrument of minority rights.

How can one evaluate the costs of different sorts of rights? A decision on civil and political rights depends on the Parliament or another authority with the same competence. In principle, the implementation of this decision does not impose significant costs. Granted, the institutions of a democratic society do need money. But maintaining the institutions of a democratic order is not more expensive than maintaining the institutions of oppression. In other words, civil and political rights do not require extra costs.

An indicator of the cost of minority rights would be the price paid for special measures in particular fields. Consider the case of education. What is the cost of a bilingual university, in comparison to a unilingual one? The supplementary cost of bilingualism at the University of Ottawa is about 10 per cent of the provincial subsidy received by the university.[19] There are cases where special measures incur higher costs. Such is the case of education for the Roma minority, which becomes a dilemma in times of economic scarcity.

In general, though, it is clear that the costs of minority rights are not very high. Many societies can afford to pay them. I believe that in most countries minority rights are a matter of political will rather than cost. Real limits exist only under circumstances of severe scarcity. This is to a certain extent true in Romania. Although there is no real financial obstacle in solving the Hungarian demand for a Hungarian-language state university, there are limits in promoting an affirmative action programme for the Roma.

Conclusion

At the end of the continuum of the political evolution of Central and Eastern European countries there are democratic and, one hopes, prosperous societies. These societies understand their socio-political structure in functional terms. The region embodies no particular 'essence' that suggests treatment of its minority problems in a way that differs from the conceptions and standards prevalent in the West. The problems pertaining to costs and political will, typical of transition periods, will be overcome sooner or later. What follows will be a process of *internal accommodation*, marked by debates that will probably be similar to those now current in Western societies.

NOTES

1. I have in mind a global society that has gone beyond the interaction of traditional political actors, that is, states. Gordon Christenson's 'world civil society' is a symptom of this new development. See Gordon Christenson, 'World Civil Society and the International Rule of Law', *Human Rights Quarterly*, 19/4, November 1997.

2. Richard Falk, 'Cultural Foundations for the International Protection of Human Rights', in Abdullahi Ahmed An-Na'im, ed., *Human Rights in Cross-Cultural Perspectives* (University of Pennsylvania Press, 1995) 54.

3. The 1992 census indicated 1,620,199 Hungarians; 409,723 Roma (Gypsies); 119,436 Germans; 66,833 Ukrainians; 36,688 Russian-Lippovans; 29,533 Turks; 29,080 Serbs; 24,649 Tatars; 20,672 Slovaks; 9,953 Bulgarians; 9,107 Jews; 5,800 Czechs; 4,247 Poles; 4,180 Croatians; 3,897 Greeks; and 2,023 Armenians. Other persons declared that they belonged to the Carashovans (2,775) and the Changos (2,165). The census figure for the Roma does not reflect the actual size of this minority. Roma organizations offer different figures, most of them somewhere between 1 and 2 million. Also, see E. Pons, *Les Tsiganes en Roumanie: des citoyens à part entière?* (L'Hartmann, 1995). Pons refers to some 2.5 million Roma. A useful synthesis of the Romanian minorities is to be found in Renate Weber, 'The Protection of National Minorities in Romania: A Matter of Political Will and Wisdom', in Jerzy Krantz, ed., (in co-operation with Herbert Kupper) *Law and Practice of Central European Countries in the Field of National Minorities Protection after 1989* (Warsaw: Center for International Relations, 1998) 199–269.

4. George Carpat-Foche, 'De la communism la nationalism' *22 magazine*, 3, January 24–31, 1992.

5. Jon Elster, 'Majority Rule and Individual Rights', in Stephen Shute and Susan Hurley, eds., *On Human Rights: The Oxford Amnesty Letters 1993* (Basic Books, 1993) 175–217.

6. Ibid., 176.

7. Article 1 (1) defined the state as follows: 'Romania is a sovereign, independent, unitary and indivisible national state.' Article 4 (1) says: 'The state foundation is laid on the unity of the Romanian people.'

8. For example, Article 6 (1) states that: 'The State recognises and guarantees the right of persons belonging to national minorities to the preservation, development and expression of their ethnic, cultural, linguistic and religious identity'. Article 15 (1) says that: 'All citizens enjoy the rights and freedoms granted to them by the Constitution and other laws and have the duties laid down thereby'. And Article 59 (2) states that: 'Organizations of citizens belonging to national minorities, which fail to obtain the number of votes for representation in Parliament, have the right to one Deputy seat each, under the terms of the electoral law.'

9. John Mearsheimer, 'Back to the Future: Instability in Europe After the Cold War', in *International Security*, 15/1, Summer 1990, 5–56.

10. For example, 'Projet de Rapport Spécial—Roumanie: une transition inachevée' (Commission des Affaires Civiles, Assemblée de l'Atlantique du Nord, May 1992, AJ 75, CC (92) 5); Stephan Iwan Griffiths, *Nationalism and Ethnic*

Conflict: Threats to European Security (SIPRI Research Report, OUP, 1993) especially 23; Dominique Rosenberg, *Les minorités nationales et le défi de la sécurité en Europe*, Travaux de Recherche no. 21 (Institut de Nations Unies, New York, 1993) especially 17; Michael E. Brown, 'Causes and Implications of Ethnic Conflict', in Michael E. Brown, ed., *Ethnic Conflict and International Security* (Princeton University Press, 1993) especially 3; Lothar Ruehl, 'European Security and NATO's Eastward Expansion', in *Aussenpolitik*, 45/2, 1994, especially 119; and Hans-Joachim Hoppe, 'The Situation in Central and Southeast European Countries', in *Aussenpolitik*, 45/2, 1994, especially 143.

11. See Gabriel Andreescu and Renate Weber, *The Evolution of the DAHR Conception on the Rights of the Hungarian Minority* (Bucharest: Center for Human Rights, 1995).

12. See Renate Weber, 'Romania si drepturile omului: standarde interne, standarde internationale (I)', *Revista romana de drepturile omului* 13, 1996, 27–38.

13. Two examples are the *Charter of Minority and Regional Languages* and the *Charter of Local Autonomies*. Other important international documents became part of internal law after the ratification of the treaties with Hungary (1996) and Ukraine (1997). See Gabriel Andreescu, 'Recommendation 1201 and a Security Network in Central and Eastern Europe', *International Studies*, 3, 1997, 49–63.

14. See Gabriel Andreescu, 'The Central European Divide', *War Report*, June/July 1997, 27–8.

15. A 1995 Helsinki Watch report counted some 35 such incidents between 1990 and 1995.

16. *APADOR-CH Report* (Bucharest 1998).

17. Richard Rorty, 'Human Rights, Rationality and Sentimentality', in Shute and Hurley, *On Human Rights*, 112–30.

18. I have elaborated this concept, which seeks to complete the general system of minority rights, in Gabriel Andreescu, 'Drepturi colective exercitate individual', *Revista Romana de Drepturile Omului*, 13, 1996, 38–50.

19. Jean-Michel Beillard, 'Bilingualism at the University of Ottawa', paper delivered at the round-table meeting in Snagov, Romania, 6–8 February, 1998.

Perspectives on a Liberal-Pluralist Approach to Ethnic Minorities in Ukraine

VOLODYMYR FESENKO

An Overview of the Ethnocultural Situation in Ukraine

Ukraine is a multi-ethnic society comprised of more than 120 ethnic groups. Ethnic Ukrainians constitute 37 million, or 72 per cent of the population. Russians, the largest group after the Ukrainians, number 11.3 million (22 per cent). The remaining ethnic groups each number fewer than 500,000 people, eight with populations of 100,000 to 500,000. About 90 ethnic groups have fewer than 1,000 people.[1] Six of the largest ethnic minorities are geographically concentrated near Ukraine's borders, in areas contiguous with their respective kin-states.

Of the five types of ethnocultural groups discussed by Kymlicka, four can be found in Ukraine: national minorities, immigrant ethnic groups, metics, and Roma, who number about 48,000. The specific ethnocultural problem of the Rusyns should also be noted. The Rusyns are an ethnocultural group living in the Ukrainian Transcarpathians and in Slovakia. Unlike Slovakia, Ukraine does not recognize the Rusyns as a distinct national group, considering them instead to be one of the regional subcultures of the Ukrainian nation.

The division of Ukrainian society along linguistic, ethnocultural, and regional lines is deepened by serious religious differences. More than half of the religious communities and believers in Ukraine are orthodox. Ukrainian orthodoxy, however, is divided into three churches that are firmly in opposition to one another: the Ukrainian Orthodox Church of the Moscow Patriarchate (UOC-MP),[2] the

Ukrainian Orthodox Church of the Kyivan Patriarchate (UOC-KP)[3] and the Ukrainian Autocephalous Orthodox Church (UAOC).[4] The Ukrainian Greek Catholic Church (UGCC) also figures in the religious antagonisms. Greek Catholics (the Uniates) account for 10 per cent of all believers in Ukraine. The UOC-MP is oriented to the Russian-speaking population of Ukraine in the eastern and southern regions, while the UGCC's influence is mainly in the western part.[5]

Although most of Ukraine's ethnocultural groups are small in size, many of them yearn for the preservation and development of their ethnic identity and cultural uniqueness. To this end, institutions have played an important role. In early 1995, there were 237 ethnocultural, non-governmental organizations, including 16 that operate through-out Ukraine.[6] At the beginning of 2000, these numbers had risen to 275 and 35, respectively. Representatives of 31 ethnic groups have established national cultural societies of their own.

The Special Case of Russians in Ukraine

Russians are concentrated mainly in the east and south of Ukraine, the Crimea, and nine other regions, constituting 20–67 per cent of the local population in each region. Judging solely by the demographic size and territorial concentration of Russians in some regions of Ukraine, one might deduce that the relationship between Russians and Ukrainians constitutes the basic ethnic problem of the young Ukrainian state. Some politicians in Russia, and sometimes even in Ukraine, think along these lines. In fact, however, it is a much more complicated matter.

The vast majority of Ukrainian-Russians were born in Ukraine, socialized in the bilingual and bicultural medium of the large cities and, to some extent, have adopted Ukrainian cultural values. Approximately one quarter of the Russian population (4.3 million people) came to Ukraine at a mature age and have not had enough time to imbibe the 'Ukrainian spirit'.[7] The dual culture of most Russian-Ukrainians is also characteristic of a significant segment of ethnic Ukrainians, especially those living in large cities in eastern and southern Ukraine.

According to sociological research conducted in 1994 and 1995 by the Sociological Institute of the National Science Academy and the Centre for Democratic Initiatives, the population of Ukraine as a whole can be divided into three linguistic groups of roughly equal size: families using only Ukrainian as the language of communication;

families using only Russian; and families using both Ukrainian and Russian, depending on the circumstances. Table 2.13.1 provides the regional breakdown for these three groups.

The approximately equal size of these three dominant ethno-linguistic groups creates, on the one hand, a situation of ethnic equilibrium; on the other hand, it makes it impossible to speak about the Russian-speaking—meaning linguistically Russian not culturally Russian—population as Ukraine's ethnic minority. That bilingual people constitute a third of the population of the country represents a specific feature of Ukrainian society, highlighting the ethnic complexity and instability of ethnic identification amongst the Ukrainian population. We can also assume that the high percentage of bilingual people inhibits the development of aggressive nationalistic manifestations, both Russian and Ukrainian.

The proximity and centuries-old cross-fertilization of the Russian and Ukrainian cultures and languages have created a special ethno-cultural situation in Ukraine. 78 per cent of the population of Ukraine speaks fluent Russian and 77 per cent speaks fluent Ukrainian.[8] Perhaps this explains why language has not become a serious source of conflict despite the gradual exclusion of the Russian language from official use.

For most of its history the territory that now makes up Ukraine developed as parts of different state formations. The inevitable result is profound socio-cultural differences between the western region, and the eastern and southern part, sometimes referred to as 'right-

TABLE 2.13.1 *Language of communication in families: regional variations, May 1994, (%)*

	Only Ukrainian	Only Russian	Ukrainian and Russian (depending on circumstances)
Kyiv	16	39	46
Western Ukraine	79	5	16
Central Ukraine	60	8	32
Eastern Ukraine	13	53	35
Southern Ukraine	22	47	31
Crimea	4	86	11
All Ukraine	37	33	30

Source: Politychnyi potret Ukrayiny. *Biuleten' doslidno-navchal'noho centru 'Demokratychni initsiativy'*, 14 (1995) 66.

bank' and 'left-bank' Ukraine. The significant linguistic variations between the western region and the eastern and southern part are clearly shown in Table 2.13.1. This regional ethnocultural cleavage is a dominant feature of the country's political life.

The peculiar ethnocultural and ethnopolitical identification of the Russian-speaking population of Ukraine is determined not only by its marginal, 'boundary' socio-cultural status, nor by its only partial conformity to the ethnocultural standard of either ethnic Ukrainians or ethnic Russians. It must also be appreciated that the Russian-speaking population in Ukraine—as well as in the other former non-Russian republics of the USSR—represents the remnant of Soviet society. Many Russian-speaking people to this day identify themselves as 'Soviet people'. They are nostalgic for the single united state, the USSR, and support the idea of the recreation if not of the USSR, then at least of a union of the Slavic nations of Russia, Ukraine, and Belarus. The Russian-speakers' desire for some form of reunification represents another profound cleavage within the Ukrainian nation.

How Liberal is Nation-Building in Ukraine?

The key problem of Ukrainian ethnic policy is balancing Ukrainian majority nation-building with respect for ethnic minority rights. This explains a paradoxical but, at the same time, logical mixture of liberal and illiberal elements in the nation-building process.[9] The more illiberal elements are rooted in a peculiar post-colonial 'Russian syndrome', which drives Ukrainians to distance themselves from Russia and strengthen the legitimacy of the independent Ukrainian state. At the same time, though, the policy of nation-building in Ukraine is moderate and open to compromise. It reflects the current balance of forces within the political élite of the country as well as among the country's different regions and main ethnocultural groups.

Given its ethnocultural make-up, Ukraine offers ample scope for the application of a liberal-pluralist approach to minorities policy. But do the legislative basis of official Ukrainian policy towards ethnic minorities and the liberalization of majority nation-building in Ukraine meet liberal-pluralist standards? The Ukrainian legal framework governing inter-ethnic relations does have a significantly liberal character. But this liberalism has defined limits, which stop short of such ideas as the right of national minorities to territorial autonomy.

Ukraine belongs to the relatively small number of post-Communist states that have managed to avoid serious ethnic conflict. Nevertheless, the uniqueness of Ukraine's ethnocultural and ethnopolitical configuration poses a variety of problems. Overcoming these depends on the process of nation-building in Ukraine. Seven key elements of this process are examined.

Alternatives for the Territorial-State Arrangement of Ukraine

The choice of territorial-state organization for Ukraine has been the subject of the most animated political discussion since the moment of independence. The specific nature of the ethnocultural structure of Ukrainian society, as well as the existence of significant ethnocultural and socio-economic differences between various regions of Ukraine, would seem to provide a compelling argument in favour of some sort of federation. Those political forces speaking for the Russian-speaking population of Ukraine supported the idea. National democratic parties and movements were, however, against federation, upholding instead the unitary-state model. In their opinion a federal arrangement would stimulate the separatist aspirations of the regions, thus consolidating existing cleavages within Ukrainian society. The potential instability of federations is confirmed by historic experience, most recently in the examples of the USSR, Yugoslavia, and Czechoslovakia.

Disputes over Crimean autonomy did nothing but increase negative perceptions of federalism. For example, when the draft Law on National Minorities was being considered by the Ukrainian legislature, it contained a clause on the establishment of autonomous administrative units for minority groups.[10] The clause was voted down. The reasons for dismissing the idea of territorial autonomy for minorities were the same as for rejecting federalism. Supporters of a unitary Ukrainian state suspected that the idea of federation was a strategy by the opponents of Ukrainian independence to seek to re-establish the USSR or at least reunite Ukraine with Russia. Some Ukrainian politicians were so concerned that they proposed the introduction of a constitutional prohibition of any manifestations of federalism.

In the end, Ukraine decided in favour of a unitary form of territorial-state organization, and enshrined it in the Constitution.[11] However, this choice can in no way be considered final and irrevocable. Even the opponents of the idea of federation understand the objective predisposition of Ukraine to a federal form of state organization. As a compromise, Leonid Kravchuk, the first democratically

elected President of Ukraine, proposed a unitary but decentralized
state model. While supporting a unitary state, Viacheslav Chornovil,
the leader of Narodnyi Rukh (People's Movement), the pre-eminent
national democratic party, accepted the possibility of a federation in
the future, but only after the independent Ukrainian state had
strengthened its position and overcome centrifugal trends.

Russian Language Status

The 1989 Law on Languages regulates relations among language
groups in the state. Adopted even prior to the announcement of
Ukrainian independence, it represents the cornerstone of Ukrainian
majority nation-building. The Law for the first time entrenched the
official status of the Ukrainian language and formulated a programme
ensuring its priority development and eventual application in all
spheres of public life in Ukraine. At the same time, the Law allows
any language to be used at a regional level providing it is acceptable
to the whole population of that region. Although no language is
specifically mentioned, it is well understood that Russian is the language in question.

   As often happens when decisions are the result of compromise, the
Law satisfied neither the supporters of Ukrainian majority nation-
building nor most of the Russian-speaking population. The former
believed that the Law on Languages was insufficient in that it did not
provide an adequate enforcement mechanism. The latter viewed the
Law as an instrument for the imposition of the Ukrainian language
and culture on Russian-speakers. Among Russian-speaking politicians the idea of granting official status to the Russian language was
very popular. In the end, the Constitution of Ukraine confirmed
Ukrainian as the sole official language, making provisions for its comprehensive development and use in all spheres of social life throughout the entire territory of Ukraine.[12] The Russian language was placed
on a par with the languages of national minorities, though it was given
specific mention: 'In Ukraine the free development, use and protection of Russian, and other languages of national minorities of Ukraine,
is guaranteed'.[13]

   Those opposed to granting Russian official language status used the
following arguments:

1. It would not right historic injustices. Official status must be
   granted solely to the Ukrainian language in part to overcome the
   legacy of Russian linguistic and cultural domination.

2. The slogan of official bilingualism is simply a way to preserve the Russian language monopoly, and mask an unwillingness to study the Ukrainian language.
3. Granting official status to the Russian language would strengthen existing cleavages within the Ukrainian nation.
4. The Ukrainian language is the most important instrument, the organic principle, of nation-building in Ukraine. The rebirth of Ukraine is impossible without the revival of its language.
5. Official status for the Russian language would lead to techno-logical and cultural dependence on Russia and would amount to continuing Russian imperialistic control over Ukraine.

The paradox of Ukrainian language policy, as implemented, is that in spite of the language legislation, Russian is widely used in the public life of Ukraine. Approximately half of Ukrainian schoolgirls and boys are taught in the Russian language, and most of the print media is in Russian.

On the other hand, the provisions of the Law on Languages that allow official status for Russian in places of territorial concentration of Russians, or Russian-speakers, have not always been implemented. Recent developments in Kharkiv illustrate this. In 1996, the City Council decided, in keeping with the Law on Languages, to grant official status to the Russian language, as it is spoken by a large major-ity of the city's population. However, the Regional Public Prosecutor overturned the decision, citing the Constitution provision that only the Ukrainian language can have official status. What seems to have emerged in practice is a situation of informal 'peaceful coexistence' between official monolingualism and spontaneous bilingualism, that is, the simultaneous usage of both Russian and Ukrainian in the public sphere.

The Status of the Crimea and Crimean Tatars

The most painful ethnopolitical problem facing Ukraine is the status of the Crimea. This is complicated by its close connection to the acute foreign policy issues of Russian territorial claims and the status of the Black Sea fleet. The Crimea is the only region where ethnic Russians make up the majority of the population—about two-thirds—and where separatists are politically organized and constitute a real threat to the territorial integrity of the region.

At the time of Ukrainian independence, the Crimea enjoyed the status of autonomous region, the only such case in Ukraine. The peninsula's inhabitants confirmed this autonomous status in a referendum and Kyiv was forced to accept the decision. In the subsequent constitutional debates, opinions over Crimea were divided. In official circles, the reasons that underlay opposition to the idea of federation also applied to the notion of autonomous status for Crimea. A number of right-wing deputies of the Ukrainian legislature proposed terminating Crimean autonomy, while deputies of left-wing parties suggested that the Crimea be granted full-fledged autonomy. In the end, the autonomous status of the Crimea, albeit with restricted powers, was confirmed by the Ukrainian Constitution.

The current status of ethnocultural and political rights for the Crimean Tatars is rather contradictory. On the one hand, the rights of the Crimean Tatars in the spheres of education and culture are ensured to a much greater extent than the rights of the ethnic Ukrainians residing in the Crimea. For example, as of 2001 there were ten Crimean Tatar schools operating in the Crimea and just two Ukrainian ones, though there are twice as many ethnic Ukrainians as Tatars residing there.[14] Furthermore, the Crimean Tatars are the only ethnic group in Ukraine that has managed to create a well-developed and efficient structure of economic, political, and educational institutions. On the other hand, the problem of acquiring Ukrainian citizenship by newly arrived Crimean Tatars has become more complicated and, as a result of a change in the electoral system, the number of Crimean Tatar representatives in the Crimean legislature has dropped significantly.

The current situation reflects the dual policy Kyiv has adopted toward the Crimean Tatars. In the first half of the 1990s, for example, when strong separatist tendencies emerged in the Crimea, Kyiv used the Crimean Tatars as a counterbalance and an ally in the struggle against chauvinistic manifestations by Crimea's Russian community. Furthermore, Kyiv had to be sensitive to the international community's focus on the Crimean Tatars' problems. By claiming the status of 'deported nation' and 'indigenous people', the Crimean Tatars attracted the attention of the international community and won support for their efforts to return to their historic native land. As soon as the wave of separatism began to wane, however, Kyiv's interest in the Crimean Tatars dropped sharply.

The Problem of Citizenship

The 1991 Law on Citizenship of Ukraine ensures equality before the law of all permanent resident citizens, regardless of their ethnic, cultural, linguistic, or religious identity. The Law was passed in its so-called 'zero option' form, that is, it granted Ukrainian citizenship to all who resided on Ukrainian territory at the time the law was passed. At present, decisions regarding the acquisition of Ukrainian citizenship tend to be based either on ethnic affiliation, as an expression of national solidarity, or on humanitarian grounds for those fleeing persecution in their home countries. Citizenship may also be granted for historical reasons, such as compensation for previous injustice. This would apply, for example, to formerly deported peoples.

The most acute disputes have been generated by the problem of dual citizenship. In the first half of the 1990s, the idea of dual citizenship was widely popular with ethnic Russians, especially those residing in the Crimea. During Ukrainian-Russian negotiations over the status of the peninsula, the Russian side insisted on putting the principle into practice. However, Kyiv objected to the principle allegedly on the grounds that if dual citizenship were introduced it would lead to a number of thorny legal conflicts over citizens' rights and responsibilities in both countries. In reality, Kyiv feared that dual citizenship would be an instrument through which Russia could intrude into the political life of Ukraine, and possibly provide a legal basis for the unification of Crimea and Russia. As a result, single citizenship was entrenched in the Constitution of Ukraine.[15]

The Problem of 'Ethnic' vs. 'Civic' Nationalism

Heated discussion about the meaning of 'Ukrainian nationality' has arisen in several contexts. The most animated debate was over the reference to nationality in the Ukrainian passport. What does one write in the 'nationality' column of the passport? Phrases such as 'the Ukrainian nation' and 'the nation of Ukraine' are ambiguous: do they refer to the ethnic or political nation? The phrase 'Ukrainian nation' is generally understood to refer to 'ethnic nation', that is, a nation made up of ethnic Ukrainians as opposed to national minorities. In other contexts, however, the terms 'nation' and 'nationality' have a political (civic) connotation, that is, they refer to Ukraine as a political entity embracing ethnically diverse groups. The terminology used in Ukrainian law and policies, which is often the result of compromise, tends to perpetuate rather than resolve the conceptual ambiguity over these terms.

The failure to clearly define the terms 'nation' and 'nationality' reflects the underlying uncertainty about the appropriate process of nation-building for Ukraine. The alternatives are clearly delineated:

either nation-building through integration and unification of Ukrainian society on the basis of the Ukrainian language and Ukrainian culture, or the formation of a civic, multi-ethnic, multicultural, and multi-religious society in which Ukrainian ethnicity plays a fundamental, but not hegemonic, role.

Ensuring the Rights and Conditions to Maintain and Develop the Ethnocultural Identity of National Minorities

Ukraine is developing a legal framework for protecting minority rights through domestic legislation and by signing and ratifying international conventions. On 1 November 1991, the Verkhovna Rada (parliament) adopted the Declaration on the Rights of Nationalities, which says that the Ukrainian state guarantees all peoples, national groups, and citizens residing on its territory equal political, economic, social, and cultural rights. In territories where ethnic groups are concentrated, they can use their native language along with the state language. According to the Law on National Minorities in Ukraine, adopted by parliament in June 1992, a person belonging to an ethnic minority, while being a citizen of Ukraine, can express his or her national self-awareness and affinity with members of any particular ethnic group. The state guarantees to all ethnic minorities the right to national and cultural autonomy, which includes:

(1) the use of, and education in, their native language and the study of the native language in state educational institutions or through national-cultural societies; and

(2) the development of national cultural traditions, use of national symbols, celebration of national holidays, religious practice, pursuit of cultural endeavours—literature, art, mass media—creation of national cultural and educational establishments, and any other activity that does not contradict the existing legislation.

Ukraine is actively involved in preparing and adopting international accords on the protection of national minorities. In 1992, it ratified the Bishkek Agreement of the CIS countries on issues related to the restoration of rights of deported persons, and ethnic minorities and peoples; in 1994, Ukraine signed the Moscow Convention of the CIS Countries on ensuring the rights of persons belonging to national minorities. In September 1995, Ukraine was the first CIS country to accede to the Council of Europe's European Framework Convention for the Protection of National Minorities.

Illegal Migrant Problem

The issue of immigrants, either legal or illegal, is relevant to an understanding of the country's ethnocultural diversity. Excluding ethnic Ukrainians who have returned to their historic homeland upon its gaining independence, the largest immigrant groups in Ukraine are the descendants of the people deported from the region during Stalin's regime. This includes Crimean Tatars, Germans, Greeks, Armenians, and Bulgarians. Originally, it was expected that the total number of such immigrants and their descendants would reach about 500,000 by the year 2000. However, their numbers have turned out to be significantly less and consist mainly of Crimean Tatars, whose population has increased more than five times between 1989 and 1997.[16] At present, Crimean Tatars number approximately 260,000.

The specific problem of illegal immigrants, or 'metics' to use Kymlicka's terminology, is being exacerbated by the continued growth in their numbers from year to year. In 1997, 16,500 'illegals' were detained at the border,[17] a figure comparable to the population of many ethnocultural groups residing in Ukraine. For the majority of illegal migrants, Ukraine is just a transfer point, a stopover on their way from the East to the West. Those who are detained usually remain inside Ukraine for only a short time. Ukrainian law states that illegal migrants are to be deported from the country. In practice, however, administrative bodies have money neither for deportation nor for settlement—even temporary—of these people on the territory of Ukraine.

Nevertheless, the number of illegal immigrants who have chosen to settle in Ukraine for a longer period of time is growing. They are mostly citizens of Asia and Africa, usually former students who studied in Ukraine. Although no exact information exists on the number of such illegal immigrants, one can judge the scale of the phenomenon by the following example. During the first nine months of 1998 in Kharkiv alone—the second largest city in Ukraine with 1.6 million people—5,000 foreign citizens were prosecuted for violation of the law on the legal status of a foreigner, and more than 200 illegal immigrants were detected, of whom 47 were deported.[18]

Illegal migrants are becoming an increasingly significant source of crime and conflict. Under these conditions it is difficult to expect a favourable attitude towards the idea of granting Ukrainian citizenship to foreigners who happen to find themselves on Ukrainian territory.

Now, as the borders of the European Union are approaching Ukraine, one can predict an aggravation of the problem of illegal migrants. Solving this is possible only within the broader European context, with the participation of all concerned parties.

Implications for the Future

Although the new Ukrainian Constitution of 28 June 1996 addressed many controversial issues such as the form of the territorial-state arrangement, Russian language status, and Crimean autonomy, this does not mean that the ethnic problem will no longer obscure the Ukrainian political horizon. There will be continued debate on the subject. In this debate, there is no doubt that the liberal-pluralist approach to solving minority issues is relevant to the dilemmas faced by contemporary Ukraine. However, in the current political environment this approach is unlikely to prevail in Ukraine, at least in the short term.

The political landscape in Ukraine is much more complicated and contradictory than the straightforward dichotomy of Communist (illiberal) versus democratic (liberal) forces. For example, many Ukrainian national democrats oppose the pluralist model of ethno-cultural development, while some leftists support a federal system. In the final analysis, though, it remains that Ukrainian policy-makers, who are former members of the Soviet-era *nomenklatura*, take a centrist stand on issues dealing with minorities policy. And while many of the (former Communist) bureaucrats have adopted pro-Western attitudes, this reflects more a desire for prosperity than an embrace of liberal-pluralist beliefs. This means that, to a large extent, residual illiberal elements in the post-Communist, post-Soviet transition period determine policies toward ethnic minorities. Thus, 'ukrainization' policy is not so dissimilar from the Soviet-era policy of russification.

In the current political environment, a much greater effort is required to propagate the liberal-pluralist perspective. Attitudes favouring Ukrainian majority nation-building, and its logical outcome of 'ukrainization', dominate the ideological discourse. Many authors, politicians, and scientists decisively reject the idea of a more pluralist approach to minority issues, citing its negative impact on the transition process in Ukraine.[19] Their arguments are, first, that ethnocultural diversity undermines the integrating national idea by fostering antagonistic group interests that result in the growing fragmentation of society. Second, diversity promotes irredentist tendencies among those ethnic groups that have neighbouring kin-states—for example, several political movements in Crimea seek reunification with Russia and similar tendencies can be observed in some sections of the Romanian community in Bukovina. Third, the significant increase of organized crime activity during the transition period is attributed in part to national minority groups—for example, there is a disproportionately high percentage of non-Ukrainians involved in organized crime groups. Fourth, Russian cultural nationalism is on the rise. Many Russian-speakers remain culturally oriented toward their 'great motherland' despite the collapse of the Soviet Empire and subsequent social crisis in Russia.

The prevailing view in Ukraine has therefore been that under conditions of transition, ethnic diversity constitutes a source of problems and conflicts rather than of social dynamism. Multi-ethnicity is recognized as a political reality but it is rejected as a principle for the organization and development of Ukrainian society. Likewise, federalism is regarded as a mechanism for preserving ethnic diversity but is superseded by a rather broadly accepted formula for solving ethnic problems that aims to avoid conflicts, develop a national idea—but not on a narrow ethnic basis—and integrate society around it. This prevailing view incorporates the negative stereotypes of the multi-ethnic, pluralistic model of development, and reflects the anxiety of Ukrainians during a period of social crisis. Overcoming these stereotypes will not happen quickly or easily, but it is possible.

First, the fortunes of the liberal-pluralist approach can be enhanced by linking them with Ukraine's gradual advancement into European institutional structures. Kyiv is prepared to make serious domestic policy concessions in instances where the integration of Ukraine into European structures is at stake. The best example is the introduction in Ukraine of a moratorium on capital punishment following pressure from the Council of Europe, despite the fact that a considerable part of the political élite and the majority of the population—according to the data of sociological surveys—support the death penalty.

Second, there are multi-ethnic regions in Ukraine, such as the Crimea and Transcarpathia, where principles of ethnocultural justice simply cannot be ignored. The internal ethnocultural diversity and need to incorporate the interests of different ethnic groups make anything but a multi-ethnic, pluralistic model of development unthinkable. These regions could become 'experimental fields' to perfect policies that would ensure ethnocultural justice and the development of multi-ethnicity. Such experimentation would provide an opportunity to anticipate potential legal and political pitfalls and to prepare the ground for the further liberalization of ethnic policies in other regions of the country.

To adopt a broader liberal concept of ethnocultural justice, the country's political élite must be assured that it is an appropriate and secure model of development for Ukraine. In this respect, one of the thorniest issues relates to immigrants, including illegal ones, acquiring the right to become citizens. This only stimulates the stream of migrants to the developed countries. With an expected toughening of immigration legislation in Western European countries, the countries of Central and Eastern Europe that do not become members of the European Union may become a 'hotbed', if not 'dumping ground', for illegal immigrants. Will they accept this role? If so, would the new millennium not begin with another mass migration of peoples?

The liberal concept of ethnocultural justice poses a worthy theoretical challenge to the ideology of illiberal nation-building. 'Integration through ethnocultural diversity' is a good motto and an important practical task for the twenty-first century. But how universal and effective is this formula for solving all ethnopolitical problems?

NOTES

1. Based on data from the 1989 USSR census.
2. The UOC-MP is the successor to the Russian Orthodox Church in Ukraine.
3. The UOC-KP was created in 1992 to counterbalance the UOC-MP. The leader and the founder of the UOC-KP is Filaret, ex-metropolitan of the Communist-era Russian Orthodox Church in Kyiv. The UOC-KP, which has pretensions to be the only national church in Ukraine, supported right-wing political parties during the 1998 parliamentary elections in Ukraine.
4. The UAOC was created in 1921 and declared its independence from Moscow. The Communist government liquidated the autocephalous churches in Ukraine in the 1930s. The UAOC, revived in 1990, is supported by the pro-Ukrainian urban intelligentsia. Two-thirds of UAOC adherents are located in Galicia (western Ukraine). The UOC-KP has tried, unsuccessfully, to join with the UAOC.
5. The religious structure of Ukrainian society is striking in its diversity. Members of approximately seventy religious denominations, schools, and doctrines reside in Ukraine. Together with the four main churches, the Roman Catholic, Evangelical Christian Baptist, Christians of Evangelical Belief, Seventh Day Adventist, the Watch Tower Society, Muslim, Reformatory, and Judaic religions represent 97% of religious adherents. See, M. Rybachuk, ' "Svoi" i "chuzhie" u

khrami: religiynyi faktor mizhetnichnyh vidnosyn', *Viche*, 2 (1996) 138. The 1990s witnessed the appearance of unconventional cults, spiritual trends, and movements. Many of them are socially insular, avoiding participation in politics or civil society. Their activities are unusual in the Ukrainian context, and sometimes lead to conflict with mainstream society.

6. Ukrainian Ministry for Nationality Affairs, Migration and Religion, *Information Bulletin*, 1 (1995) 31–2.
7. F. D. Zastavnyi, *Skhidna ukrayins'ka diaspora* (L'viv, 1992) 21.
8. Based on data from the 1989 USSR census.
9. The eclectic combination of liberal principles (laws) and non-liberal social practices—or, vice versa, bad legal arrangements and spontaneous self-regulatory social mechanisms—is an essential feature of the post-Communist, post-Soviet society. This situation may appear perplexing for western theorists, but it is the real picture. It can be solved by gradually improving legal arrangements and liberalizing social practices and the political and civic culture.
10. In the 1920s, Soviet authorities established a large number of minority autonomous regions at all administrative levels. In 1931, a few years before they were eventually abolished, there were twenty-five autonomous districts—eight Russian, seven German, three Jewish, three Bulgarian, three Greek, and one Polish—and a few hundred autonomous rural communities in Ukraine. Is this not a good example of a minority policy based on the principle of ethno-cultural justice? Today, the episode is a closed chapter in Soviet nationality policy.
11. *The Constitution of Ukraine*, Article 1.
12. Ibid., Article 10.
13. Ibid., Article 10.
14. The following reasons explain the extremely minimal number of Ukrainian-language schools in the Crimea: in comparison to Crimean Tatars, ethnic Ukrainians in Crimea are not as persistent in protecting their cultural rights; the Crimean government, influenced by the international community, pays more attention to the cultural and educational problems of Crimean Tatars than of ethnic Ukrainians; and about 50% of ethnic Ukrainians in Crimea are Russian-speakers.
15. *The Constitution of Ukraine*, Article 4.
16. *Den'*, 7 February 1998.
17. *Uriadovyi kur'er*, 27 August 1998.
18. *Sloboda*, 13 October 1998.
19. This attitude is most thoroughly treated in the article of S. Grabovs'kyi, 'Polietichnist' u perehidnykh suspil'stvakh: perevagy I nebezpeky', *Suchasnist'*, 10 (1997) 81–4.

Can Will Kymlicka Be Exported to Russia?

MAGDA OPALSKI

Chances for the successful import of liberal political theory into Russia can be assessed, at least in part, by looking at the state of the theoretical debate on liberalism. Before 1989, attempts to adopt liberal policies in Eastern Europe were few and isolated.[1] In Russia, the 1990s have witnessed the emergence of what some Russian liberals call a 'conceptual liberalism', that is, a liberal interpretation of the country's problems after Communism.[2] This paper examines how this stream of liberalism approaches the question of ethnocultural diversity in Russia. What modes of accommodation of diversity and specific policy prescriptions does it propose? What are the prospects for liberal pluralism in Russia and, more specifically, for the adoption of Will Kymlicka's concepts of minority rights and ethnocultural justice?

In exploring these questions, I adopt a definition of Russian liberals proposed by a Russian liberalism expert, Susanna Matveeva. It emphasizes the modernization of Russia through its integration into the world economy and based on a vision of global liberal civilization. Oriented toward the future, this liberal view is in opposition both to Russia's imperial past and values, and to 'restorationist' forces in post-Communist society. In addition to their commitment to a market economy and private property, which is not linked to any specific form of capitalism or stage of socio-economic development, Russian liberals adopt human rights of individual citizens, the rule of law and the 'civic' concept of nationhood as the highest principles of nation-building. 'Nation', in their view, includes all communities within state borders whose members are officially recognized, and who recognize themselves, as equal citizens accepting some responsibility for the fate of their state.[3]

Nation-Building, Traditional Russian Ideas of 'Nation', and Western Terminology

After the collapse of the Soviet Union, all of the newly independent successor states embarked on the road of nation-building. This process defines who 'we the people' actually are and fosters that people's national identity, that is, their sense of belonging to a distinct community. The central problem of post-Soviet nation-building, whether in Russia or the other successor states, is the reconciliation 'between the dominant nationality and ethnic minorities of their civic identities, based on inclusive citizenship, and their exclusive ethnic identities, based on shared culture, religion, language, and common ancestry'.[4]

For Russia, these processes have been complicated by the fact that Russia had traditionally been the centre of an empire, which raises questions of the 'just borders' of the new state. In addition, Russians have always been the *Staatsvolk*—the dominating people of a multinational state—which has a profound impact on the national identity of ethnic Russians. These historical circumstances weigh heavily on the so-called '*russkii vopros*' (Russian question), that is, 'the question of the position of ethnic Russians in relation to the other groups in a multinational state'.[5]

In analysing the process of Russian nation-building and the nature of the Russian nation, contemporary Russian intellectuals refer both to Russia's current political situation and traditional concepts of 'nationhood' and 'nationalism'. Many look for inspiration in traditional, and largely obsolete, pre-revolutionary, émigré and Soviet sources. The most influential authors include the Slavophile thinkers of the 1840s, the late nineteenth century Pan-Slavist, Nikolai Danielevsky, historian Vasilii Klyuchevsky, and early twentieth century philosophers Nikolai Berdyaev, Georgy Fedotov, Ivan Ilin, and Vladimir Soloviev. The so-called 'Eurasianists', members of the émigré intellectual movement of the inter-war period, are also widely read.[6] Soviet concepts of nation and nationalism, themselves strongly influenced by the pre-revolutionary thinkers mentioned above, remain influential. For example, Stalin's 1913 definition of nation remains, with very minor modifications, a cornerstone of present-day

Russia's nationalities policy.[7] The theory of ethnos, including the socio-biological views of Lev N. Gumilev, had a strong impact on Soviet understandings of what makes a nation and how nations relate to each other. Finally, contemporary Western theories of nationalism and inter-ethnic relations, particularly models developed by Ernest Gellner, Donald Horowitz, Arend Lijphard, Eric Hobsbowm, and Benedict Anderson have had a discernible influence on a small group of advocates of a 'civic' definition of Russian nationhood. Their influence, however, is limited in comparison to that of the traditional approaches.

Three views, common in the current debate over the 'Russian question', reflect the impact of the traditional sources. The first is that the multinational Russian empire, which historically preceded the formation of Russian ethnic awareness, played a crucial role in defining Russians as a nation. The second idea is that the process of intermingling within the Russian and Soviet empires created a new type of community, different from European nations. The third view is that Russian national identity was historically shaped, and should continue to be shaped, in terms of opposition to the broadly defined 'West' and rejection of Western political theory.

These traditionalist views raise specific questions in the contemporary environment. Russians today—much like pre-revolutionary thinkers—are divided on whether the entanglement of national and imperial identities is a handicap or blessing for Russia. They also disagree on what the distinct Russian community implies for the present and future of their state: should Russians recreate the empire in some form, or should they see its collapse as an opportunity to engage in the long-overdue process of building a Russian nation-state?

Recently, several typologies have been offered that conceptualize post-Communist Russian nationhood.[8] Most of them, in one way or another, place competing concepts of Russian nationhood on a scale bounded by two extremes: an ethnocultural understanding, identified by the term *Russkii*, and a state-territorial meaning, referred to as *Rossiiskii*. In common parlance, however, *Russkii* and *Rossiiskii* are used interchangeably in reference to the Russian state. The confusion generated by these terms and their relation to 'nation' and 'state', as well as the conflicting, vested political interests that are associated with them, run deep, as revealed in heated debates about whether new Russian passports should identify the nationality of their carriers.

The statist (*Rossiiskii*) identity is not synonymous with the Western concept of 'civil nation', understood as an ideal type, even though this is frequently implied, not least in English language sources and

English translations from Russian. Nevertheless, the statist identity implied by *Rossiiskii* comes closest to the Western model of democracy, civil society, and voluntary membership in a nation, all of which are central components of 'civic nationalism'. Thus, the statist notion inherent in the term *Rossiiskii* could conceivably serve as a springboard for the development of the concept of civil nation in Russian society, as some students of Russian nationalism suggest.

Both 'civil society' and 'civil nation' are new concepts in the Russian political vocabulary; they had no place in the political discourse of either pre-revolutionary or Soviet Russia. Neither did the distinction between 'civic' and 'ethnic' nationalism take root in political or even academic discourse. Even today, when they appear in newer publications, these terms have all of the characteristics of 'imported intellectual novelties'.[9] The Russian language has no separate term for 'ethnonationalism' because any form of nationalism is assumed to be 'ethnic'. In the words of Valery Tishkov, a leading academic and, in 1992, head of the State Committee on Nationalities, nationalism in the 1990s continued to mean 'all forms of political propaganda and activism on behalf of, and benefiting, a given ethnic group referred to as a "nation".'[10]

Characteristics of Three Approaches to the 'Russian Question'

Current approaches to the 'Russian question' can be roughly divided into three categories: neo-imperial, ethnonationalist, and liberal.

The neo-imperial view of the Russian nation is typically seen in terms of hegemonic nationalism. It defines Russians as an imperial people who have created a unique civilization, a new type of human community, or as a people whose defining characteristic is a historical mission to create a large, supranational state. Rooted in Pan-Slavist and Eurasianist thought, this approach made a vital contribution in shaping the concept of 'Soviet people', the new entity that had emerged from the Soviet melting pot. The mission of the ethnic Russians is to build a 'Eurasian home' for themselves and countless non-Russian nations residing on the territory of Russia. Historically, such 'homes' eventually became—as in the cases of tsarist Russia and the USSR—a playground for Russian language and culture. Vera Tolz observes that even those Eurasianists who went so far as to claim that all the peoples of Eurasia had merged into one anthropological entity within the USSR, 'never defined the community of peoples of the Russian empire in terms of common citizenship and political loyalties, but only in terms of cultural and religious assimilation, or harmonious coexistence.'[11]

Liberal critics of the neo-imperialist approach are concerned not so much by its potential for further territorial conquests but, rather, the continuous dependence of neo-imperialists on an imperial system of government and imperial values, which remains pervasive in Russia and which, they feel, is incompatible with modernization.[12]

The ethnonationalist approach, also referred to as ethnocratic or ethnocultural, encompasses a large cluster of concepts whose common denominator is a shared culture based on common ancestry. Accordingly, it understands the Russian nation as a linguistic and cultural community. Proponents of this view currently see ethnic Russians as stateless people: the dissolution of the USSR left them with no ethnically defined state to call their own, and in urgent need to conceive a nation-state with borders coinciding with Russian cultural territory. There are several territorial options for a Russian (*Russkii*) national state. It could coincide with the territory of the present Russian Federation, where the ethnic Russian majority is comparable to that of the ethnic French in France; be a part of that territory; or be a larger territory, by incorporating the Russian-inhabited areas in neighbouring republics.[13]

Some forms of the ethnonationalist view focus primarily on language as the main characteristic of national identity. This implies the inclusion of all Russian-speakers, regardless of their ethnicity, into a community based on language. The underlying vision of Russian society, however, goes far beyond language and assumes, as do all variations of the ethnonationalist perspective, a massive cultural assimilation of non-Russians.

Another popular variation of the ethnocultural approach, inspired by Klyuchevsky and more recently associated with the name of Solzhenitsyn, is often linked to hegemonic nationalism. It sees Russians as a nation of eastern Slavs, sharing with Belarussians and Ukrainians a common culture, language, religion, and descent from Kievan Rus. This idea was opposed by early Ukrainian nationalists who claimed that Russians' historical roots went back to the Moscow principality, while Ukrainians descended from Kievan Rus. In pre-revolutionary and Soviet times, the idea of reuniting the three separated Slavic brothers fostered policies aimed at undermining the sense of distinct identity in Belarus and Ukraine. In territorial terms, this meant a state comprising all three eastern Slavic republics and, potentially, territories outside their borders populated primarily by eastern

Slavs. Interestingly, some designs for an eastern Slavic/Russian state, notably one articulated by Solzhenitsyn, consider the *exclusion* of some non-Russian territories that are currently part of the Russian Federation.[14]

The neo-imperial and ethnonationalist approaches are sometimes tainted by racist views, wherein a nation is perceived as a phenomenon of nature rather than in strictly social terms. Like a great living organism, a nation emerges from the process of evolution, goes through a life cycle, interacts with its physical environment, possesses an individual character, mentality, and needs, and has a biologically defined potential for conflict. At its most extreme, this approach advocates endogamy.[15]

The third 'liberal' approach is implied in Matveeva's definition of Russian liberalism. This vision sees Russia as a 'bourgeois'-type nation aspiring to reach the level of development of advanced industrial and post-industrial societies. It opposes isolationism, that is, accepts the view that Russia can draw on the experiences of other societies in contributing to the formation of a liberal global civilization. Russian societal culture, the culture of an overwhelming majority of citizens, constitutes the basis of the nation-building process. Provinces and regions can keep their distinctive traits, including linguistic distinctiveness, so long as cultural preservation does not entail special 'privileges' and is compatible with Russia's 'national interest'. Minorities are entitled to state support in their quest to redress past injustices and establish equal chances in society—to the extent to which the latter is compatible with the 'national interest' and the principle of the equality of citizens. Liberal prescriptions on how to balance these potentially contradictory principles have ranged from various types of autonomous regimes to national self-determination. However, given the escalation of the ethnonationalist challenge in the former USSR, most liberals have moved toward more 'statist' positions, emphasizing the need for the compatibility of minority and majority rights and intensifying their criticism of minority nationalism.

Today, the liberals give priority to human rights over ethnocultural affiliation. Under ideal circumstances, the state should stay away from ethnic identity issues, which are more appropriately viewed as the private business of its citizens. Although in the imperfect conditions of post-Communist Russia ethnicity had to be accommodated, this was hardly the highest priority of the state. The most urgent task was to fight those forces opposing Western-style modernization. Because of their propensity to underestimate the role of ethnicity in a modern state, liberal reformers were late in joining the debate on the management of ethnocultural diversity in Russia.

Russian liberals advocate a 'civic' nation that incorporates a non-ethnic, state-centred concept of Russian identity. It refers to a Russian nation whose members, regardless of their ethnic, racial, or cultural backgrounds, are united by their citizenship in the Russian Federation, and by their loyalty to the constitution and newly emerging political institutions. This fundamentally novel approach, for Russians, is referred to as *sograzhdanstvo* (co-citizenship) or *grazhdanskaya natsiya* (a citizenship-based nation). Critics dub it 'national nihilism', alluding to the 'thinness' of societal culture this concept implies, especially in comparison with the 'thickness' of the Soviet understanding of nation. Some opponents interpret the concept of 'civic' nation as a frontal, post-modernist, or idealist assault on the legacy of historical materialism, and as a radical rejection of rationality and objectivity.[16] They say that the 'civic' concept's emphasis on identity, subjectivity, and the irrationality of national ties precludes any objective study of nation-related phenomena, let alone a rational ethnic policy.[17]

The Debate over Federalism

Liberals differ significantly in their understanding of federalism, a key issue in the debate over the direction of nation-building and state-building in Russia. This ambiguity is reflected in the absence of a common liberal position on federalism and its role in managing the country's ethnocultural diversity. The views expressed by Russian liberals range from the perception of federalism as the most suitable tool for integration in large multicultural states[18]—sometimes described as the only formula capable of preventing the country's disintegration[19]—to rejection of federalism. While most liberal sceptics criticize the type of federalism that exists today, and particularly its 'asymmetrical' quality, others reject the federalist principle itself, opting instead for the 'French' or other non-federal state models.

Vladimir Pastukhov is among a handful of liberals to theorize on a federalist model for Russia. He posits that 'genuine federalism'—not to be confused with pseudo-federalism of a Soviet or post-Soviet variety—is a 'product of individualisation and rationalisation of modern social life', reflecting 'the quest for self-government' by individuals who desire to leave traditional society for a modern, rational one. The freedom-seeking individual is the creator, real political subject, and main actor of federalism. His or her sovereignty can only be realized through 'splitting' state sovereignty. In this sense, federalism is an organic element of the state-building process. It can be conceptualized as a three-way power-sharing contract, involving the federation, the subject of the federation, and the individual. According to this view, federalism is particularly required when, as in Russia, there is no tradition of local self-government, and the population is unwilling or unable to self-organize. Large, ethnoculturally diverse states with a huge government apparatus, such as Russia, also need federalism to counterbalance the growth of bureaucracies at the expense of individual freedoms.

Federalism greatly increases the potential for states to establish a democratic order: it can be the fourth pillar in the division of powers in those states where the traditional division into legislative, executive, and judicial branches does not adequately protect the individual freedoms of citizens. In this sense, a federal state represents the most advanced form of democracy. Conversely, a unitarian state would spell disaster for the democratization process in Russia where, as Pastukhov posits, transformation into a modern nation can only be achieved through genuine federalism.[20]

Given the current legislative basis for federal relations, including the 1993 constitution, 'genuine' federalism cannot be realized in Russia. Russia's current '*dogovornyi* (bargaining) federalism', based on a complex mix of legislative acts—the constitution, a federal treaty, and a collection of bilateral treaties with the republics—stands no chance of success. Federalism is a strictly constitutional arrangement rather than the outcome of a bargaining (*dogovornyi*) process between the subjects and the centre of a federation, or among its subjects.

In addition to constitutionality, Pastukhov argues, genuine federalism must meet at least three more conditions. First, unlike in today's Russia, all its subjects should be equal in their relations with the centre. Second, republican authorities should not be appointed by the centre, but democratically elected. Third, the executive branch should be reformed so that the centre and the subjects of the federation develop separate, non-overlapping bureaucracies, security forces, and tax systems.[21]

There is no indication that Pastukhov's model of federalism is conceived as an instrument of accommodating ethnocultural diversity, an omission not uncommon among liberal authors who, like Pastukhov, place individual rights and freedoms at the centre of their pro-federal argument. It also reflects the fact that in contemporary Russian discussions, the management-of-diversity function of federalism is not well-theorized. The relationship between federalism and diversity is examined chiefly in the context of: (1) the pros and cons of 'ethnic' federalism, that is, the principle that bases a federal system on ethnically defined subjects; (2) the 'asymmetric' nature of federal arrangements, meaning legal inequalities among constituent units, primarily between those that are ethnically and territorially defined; and (3) territorial vs. non-territorial forms of minority autonomy and the related question of minority rights. Liberals can be found on all sides of these and related issues, even if a minority opposes federalism *in abstracto*. This broad distribution of liberal voices seems to echo the widespread view that federalism, in the words of a Russian official responsible for nationalities policy, is 'both a means of salvation and a destructive force'.[22]

One of the main targets of the liberal criticism is the ethnic foundation of Russian federalism. Some liberals even equate 'federalization' with the proliferation of an aggressive, illiberal form of nation-building in the Russian 'periphery'.[23] According to this view, ethnic republics play a 'destructive' role by providing a breeding ground for ethnonationalism, which most liberals identify as their arch enemy and primary cause of political instability and ethnic unrest in Russia.[24] At the most extreme, it is claimed that 'nation-building based on whatever ethnicity—Tatar Kalmyk, Bashkir, Ossetian, Russian or otherwise—contradicts the basic principles of democracy, undermines efforts to build civil society and establish the rule of law in Russia, violates fundamental human rights, divides societies into frist and second class citizens, fosters inter-ethnic conflict and threatens to destroy the unity of Russia as it destroyed that of the USSR.'[25]

The evil inherent in ethnic federalism has many faces. Some liberals blame the 'territorial principle', that is, the idea that nations are organically tied to a territory on which they exercise their right to self-determination. Not accidentally, conflicts classified as 'ethnoterritorial' occupy a central place in social and political research, both of which have a strong focus on conflict studies.[26] Other critics stress the propensity for ethnic federalism to create and institutionalize inequalities among ethnic groups. Most agree that the ethno-republics should not be granted the status of states.

Liberal critics note that contemporary Russian federalism inherited from its Soviet predecessor a complex stratification of ethnic groups, with some favoured more than others; in fact, it further expanded and consolidated those ethnic hierarchies. As a result, nominally equal nations of the Russian Federation differ widely in terms of their political, legal, and economic standing, depending on whether they are titular or non-titular, repressed or non-repressed under Stalinism, aboriginal or non-aboriginal; whether their status is that of minority, nation, nationality, or ethnic group; and whether they reside in or outside of their territorial autonomies. These differences in status, which were merely symbolic before the collapse of Communism, were translated into the language of power politics in the 1990s.

In multicultural societies, according to this view, a combination of territoriality and strong political stratification along ethnic lines tends to be explosive. In this respect Russia is hardly an exception. In addition to generating ethnic strife, separatism, and inequality, ethnically based federalism fosters authoritarianism in its constituent parts, turning national republics into centralized, oppressive 'ethnocracies' that engage in ruthless economic competition and isolate their citizens from the beneficial influences of universal culture.[27] In these circumstances, the prime objective of any reform of the federation is to curb the ability of titular nations to mobilize along ethnic lines.

There is no demographic argument for the preservation of ethnic federalism, the liberals claim. They never tire of repeating that the number of direct beneficiaries of the system is, in fact, limited. The largest non-Russian nation, the Tatars, make up only 3.8 per cent of the population of the Russian Federation, followed by Ukrainians (2.3 per cent) and the Chuvash (1.2 per cent). Although nominally ethnic autonomies—twenty-one republics, ten okrugs and one oblast—make up 53 per cent of Russia's territory, the respective ethnic groups make up only 18 per cent of the combined population. Titular nations form majorities in eleven of the thirty-two autonomous districts, with only one being a significant majority. In contrast, twenty-one autonomous districts have Russian majorities, three of which feature large Russian majorities.[28] An overwhelming majority of non-Russians live outside ethnic autonomous districts, let alone autonomous districts in which they are the titular nation.[29]

Liberals who share this view urge that ethnic federalism in Russia should be gradually abandoned, and replaced by less ethnic or, ideally, non-ethnic forms of federalism. The solutions they propose regarding the future architecture of the state frequently involve the German, American, and French models. Widely distributed on the scale between centralization and decentralization, their proposals range from a de-ethnicized federation—with ethnically neutral republics but robust, non-territorial cultural 'autonomies' at the local level—to the *gubernizatsiya* of Russia. The latter scenario sees the country divided into territorial-administrative and ethnically neutral *gubernii* (provinces), similar in name and function to those operating in pre-revolutionary Russia.[30] Here, the liberals come close to the unitary vision of the state, a perspective shared by an assortment of nonliberals, including monarchists, great power nationalists, and the political gadfly Vladimir Zhirinovsky.[31]

This quest for de-ethnicization of the federation and, by implication, for curtailment of the right to self-determination, is not exactly a new current in Russian political thought. In the early Soviet period, it was articulated by some Bolshevik activists who considered ethnic republics to be a temporary arrangement because, they argued, the ethnic principle had nothing to do with socialism.[32] In the 1960s, calls were heard again for a quick transformation from federation to unitary state, based on the premise that the process of the voluntary merger of nations was close to completion, thereby eliminating the need for ethnic federalism.[33] The last and most powerful wave of criticism of the ethnic principle took shape in the late 1980s and gained momentum in the first half of the 1990s. One of its leading advocates was Valery Tishkov.[34]

Questioning both the legitimacy and political advisability of preserving the ethnic character of the republics, Tishkov promoted a nonterritorial form of cultural autonomy for those ethnic minorities who either do not posses their own administrative homeland or live outside the ethnorepublics claimed by their titular co-nationals. A departure from the idea that minorities can be best accommodated in their own ethnic states, the new liberal concept seems to have enjoyed some popularity in official circles in the early 1990s.[35] It was eventually embodied in a federal law on national and cultural autonomy in April 1996[36].

Inspired by the ideas of nineteenth-century Austrian Social Democrats Karl Renner and Otto Bauer, and Stalin's autonomization drive of the 1920s, this form of autonomy would be based on voluntary ethnic associations along cultural, socio-economic, and political lines. Because the republican and ethnic borders rarely overlap—for example, only a quarter of Russian Tatars live in Tatarstan—such cross-cutting networks and alliances would promote integration across administrative boundaries, dilute the existing ethnoterritorial divisions and, most importantly, reduce the fervour of ethnonationalist mobilization in the republics.[37] Cultural autonomy at the local level with no territorial base would be more easily compatible with a broader civic Russian (*Rossiiskii*) identity. In a political environment of cautious decentralization and strong local government, which most liberals favour, cultural autonomy could become the main tool for accommodating Russia's ethnocultural diversity. Tishkov stresses the important role of official bilingualism or multilingualism in the republics, even if 'on the functional, non-official level, bilingualism in Russia will keep its "unequal"—that is, Russian-dominated—character.'[38]

Predictably, this approach is criticized from many ideological quarters, ranging from liberals who remain loyal to the traditional concept of national self-determination to neo-Marxists. The critics object to the juxtaposition of territorial autonomy and cultural non-territorial forms of autonomy, which they deem artificial and unnecessary. The two, they argue, have a vital role to play in the Russian mosaic and should complement each other. If the ethnorepublics are 'neutralized', cultural autonomy will not sufficiently accommodate diversity, and could never meet the needs of non-Russians.[39] Still more radical critics see cultural autonomy as an attempt to water down the status of ethnorepublics as states in order to promote unitarianism and russification.[40]

Using the language of ethnocultural justice, similar to the intentions of Soviet federalism that were meant to compensate for tsarist policies, the critics of the liberal approach point out that until 1991, federalism and other forms of minority autonomy existed mostly on paper. The acute crisis of inter-ethnic relations that followed the collapse of the USSR was not caused by a federal system unleashing the monster of ethnonationalism. On the contrary, the source of Russia's predicament was the totalitarian nature of the Soviet state that precluded the implementation of any genuine federalist arrangements. Both Russian and Soviet empires destroyed states and state-like structures built by peoples they subjugated, a fact that fully justifies offering them national-territorial autonomy: the national sovereignty of non-Russians is an act of historical justice. The proponents of de-ethnicization, their critics also argue, forget that national republics accommodate not just loose collections of individual citizens, but ancient ethnic groups living in their historic homelands. These groups are distinct social organisms for whom, at their present level of historical development, state-building is the most natural form of self-expression.[41]

Russian critics of territorial autonomy show little patience for arguments based on the concept of ethnocultural justice. Their responses to suggestions for rehabilitation, upgrades of political and administrative status, and other attempts to redress the injustices of the past, are profoundly ambivalent. They present extensive evidence to show how such compensatory measures aggravate inter-ethnic tensions by reinforcing and deepening the ethnic cleavages established under Communism.[42] More importantly, such proposed actions are misguided, and even counter-productive, because they are rooted in the idea of collective rights, which many liberals oppose. They blame past excesses of collectivism for the establishment of a political culture that gives 'low priority to individual lives and human rights', a major reason for Russia's current predicament.[43] Some liberals warn that even measures intended for minority protection, if based on collective rights, can backfire by deepening and politicizing intergroup divisions. As such, they harm the very minorities they are seeking to protect.[44]

Tishkov's definition of a national republic as 'a state of an ethnos for that ethnos alone', and his tendency to blur the distinction between republican nationalism and ethnonationalism, are indicative of the distaste of some liberals for minority nationalism.[45] Critics argue that the concept of nation in some of the national republics may be far less exclusive than these liberals believe, and that the illiberal impulses of minority nationalists are defensive in nature, and largely due to past abuses by the centre. Sovereignization is just a stage of a process, a *maladie de croissance*.[46] Moreover, they discern a growing consensus among the republics that they are states for all citizens, not exclusive domains for the titular nations. This is reflected in the constitution of the Russian Federation—which identifies the 'multi-ethnic Russian nation' as the only source of power—and in the constitutions of many other ethnically defined republics, including Sakha, Bashkortostan, Tatarstan, Khakassya, and Buryatya. The advocates of de-ethnicization, say their opponents, unfairly dismiss the potential of the republics for civic nationalism.[47]

The defenders of the ethnic principle warn against attempts to radically divorce the process of nation-building from the ethnic principle. Russia's best choice at its present stage of transition, some say, is to tolerate the uneasy coexistence of ethnic identities with a Russian civic (*Rossiiskii*) identity. For example, the Deputy Chairman of the Federation Council, Ramazan Abdulatipov, opposes the concept of civic nation not so much as a matter of principle, but in terms of its feasibility and advisability under present socio-political conditions. Rushing the process would mean repeating the mistakes of the Bolsheviks as they pushed for the merger of nations. The nations of Russia, Abdulatipov posits, are unprepared for this. They value collective ethnic rights over individual human rights. In Russia, the latter have not acquired, and will probably never acquire, the status they enjoy in the West. Moreover, their victory in the West has been achieved through 'the eradication of entire tribes and nations, which were sacrificed on the altar of "humanism".'[48]

Defenders of ethnic federalism also point to the inconsistencies in the critique of minority nationalism. Why is the ethnic principle acceptable at a lower level of the federal structure, but unacceptable at a higher echelon? Why do liberals assume that cultural autonomy will prevent minority mobilization? Why do they reject the idea of 'Soviet people', the closest approximation of the concept of civic nation?[49] Paradoxically, arguments in defence of ethnic federalism strike a chord with some more old-fashioned Russian liberals who still believe that 'the essence of liberal policy is to guarantee the rights of nations to self-determination'.[50]

Reshaping Russia's Nationalities Policy

In addition to promoting non-territorial cultural autonomy, calls for the limitation of the ethnic principle entail appeals for changes in Russia's nationalities policy. Among those current practices most criticized by the proponents of greater 'de-ethnicization' is that of delegating the management of inter-ethnic relations to the republican governments. This practice, it is argued, leaves minorities within the republics, the so-called double minorities, at the mercy of titular nations and their illiberal nation-building. Therefore, nationalities policy in the Russian Federation should be recentralized and executed from Moscow, bypassing local authorities.[51] Underlying this and many similar policy recommendations is the assumption that majority nationalism is quantitatively different from, and preferable to, minority nationalism.

The proponents of greater ethnocultural neutrality of the state also recommend an aggressive promotion of ethnically neutral, inclusive national symbols.[52] In the early and mid-1990s, they frequently called for an end to Russian domination of the federal system, and its replacement by a legally enshrined, pluralistic system of proportional representation. The discussion of cultural autonomy spawned the idea of establishing a new body, the Assembly of the Nations of Russia, which would provide adequate federal representation to ethnic groups. Representation in that body would be non-territorial and free of republican domination, and would downplay the role of the republics as states. In this way, the Assembly would provide, for example, adequate representation to all ethnic Tatars of the Russian Federation, not just the minority that happens to reside in, and be recognized as, citizens of Tatarstan.[53] Laws should be based on individual rights only. Tishkov has repeatedly suggested basing Russia's nationalities policies on the 1992 UN Declaration of the Rights of Individuals Belonging to National Ethnic, Religious and Linguistic Minorities.[54] Any differentiation along ethnic lines—for example ethnically based political parties—should be banned from public life. Political coalitions that cut across ethnic lines should be fostered by central authorities.[55]

It should be noted that liberals are not the only users of the rhetoric of individual rights and freedoms when discussing ethnicity. Ironically, this rhetoric is also used by some Russian nationalists in the defence of majority rule. Their rejection of group rights and promotion of individual rights is bound up with reclaiming their own national homeland of Russia from the Soviet regime which was perceived as promoting territorial rights of minorities.[56]

Obstacles to the Creation of a Civic Nation

Tishkov identifies three major obstacles in Russia to the adoption of the idea of civic nation. Other liberal intellectuals generally echo his views.

The first is the persisting weakness of civil society in Russia. Accordingly, Russians should be considered a proto-nation, rather than a mature nation in the Western liberal sense of the term[57]—some liberals suggest that the immaturity of the Russian nation may be a blessing in disguise if it makes Russians less prone to create ethnocracies.[58] Because of its weak civic culture, Russia lacks 'societies structured by other interests and ideologies than ethnicity', which, in turn, accounts for its 'vulnerability to ethnonationalist ideology and practice.'[59]

The second obstacle is opposition from an important segment of non-Russian political leaders and intelligentsia who see minority nationalism as a democratizing, constructive, anti-totalitarian and pro-Western impulse. Acutely aware of the negative connotation of nationalism, minority nationalists seek to rehabilitate its tarnished image. They do this by promoting a distinction between minority nationalism, which they describe as 'liberal' or 'democratic', and the aggressive hegemonic nationalism of the Big Brother.[60] Seeing the proposed de-ethnicization of Russian federalism as a potential threat to their minority rights, and as russification in disguise, republican élites oppose the civic definition of nationhood. For the same reason, they have been 'in unison' in condemning attempts to abolish the declaration of nationality in Russian internal passports.[61] This opposition is usually rooted in the Soviet understanding of nation as a primordial, socio-biological phenomenon. Paradoxically, minority leaders share this stance with their main opponents—Russian nationalists.

Proponents of civic nationalism and the ethnocultural neutrality of the state tend to portray 'ethnic entrepreneurs', as they often refer to non-Russian élites, in the same way they portray minority nationalism: as inherently illiberal. Republican leaders, say the liberals, foster prejudice, discourage integration, campaign against mixed marriages, and cynically manipulate human rights. Having little respect for the latter, minority élites are driven by narrow ethnonationalist ambitions and personal careerism. By defending the national autonomous districts, they merely seek to preserve their power-base in the Russian Federation. Although some liberals portray majority and minority nationalism even-handedly, that is, in equally unflattering terms, majority nationalism generally comes across in their discourse as more civil and benign, and certainly more responsive to state control.

The third barrier is a political culture based on the 'objective' primordial understanding of ethnicity. 'Primordialism', which has been on the decline in the West for some time, continues to dominate post-Soviet social and political sciences, and is deeply ingrained in the political culture. Because of its importance, it is worth discussing this approach more fully.

According to primordialism, ethnicity is apparent in objective entities such as territory, language, recognizable membership, and a distinct collective 'mentality'. At the most extreme, it is thought of in socio-biological categories of natural selection and kinship ties. This understanding of ethnicity is reflected in Stalin's 1913 definition of nation, according to which a nation represents a higher, more advanced form of ethnicity.[62] An influential pseudo-science was developed around the concept of ethnicity, defining and classifying such terms as 'ethnos', 'super-ethnos', and 'meta-ethnos'. Such notions provided the conceptual framework for Soviet and post-Soviet ethnonationalism. Having permeated the political and judicial systems, and state institutions at both the central and local levels, its position was unchallenged under Communism.

The theory of ethnos, rejected as unscientific by liberals, was developed by generations of Russian academics. It acquired its mature shape and influence thanks to the efforts of Lev Gumilev, as well as Yulian Bromley and his many followers.[63] According to this theory, ethnoses are socio-biological phenomena created in the course of evolution. As living organisms, they become integrated, to the extent of achieving total internal homogeneity. As 'carriers of biological energy', ethnoses are subjected to the 'laws of nature', which differ from strictly social laws. The lifecycle of an ethnos is typical of a living organism—birth, maturity, ageing, and death—and possesses count-less anthropomorphic features, including an ability to express will, sense emotions—it appears that the fear of extinction is endemic among post-Soviet ethnoses—and develop distinct psyches, com-patible or incompatible with those of other ethnoses. According to Gumilev, the coexistence of diverse cultures and peoples on the terri-tory of Russia was possible only because of the natural compatibility between Russian, Siberian, and 'Grand Steppe' ethnoses.[64]

Gumilev distinguished three types of relations among ethnoses. The first, 'symbiosis', amounted to a peaceful coexistence of self-contained ethnoses occupying specific ecological niches and preserv-ing their cultural distinctiveness. The second, 'xenia', was a parasitic relationship in which a smaller ethnos lived on the 'body' of a larger ethnos. As long as the guest-ethnos inflicted no harm on the host-ethnos, inter-ethnic peace could be preserved. 'Xenia', however, easily slipped into 'chimera', the third pattern of inter-ethnic relations, which made bloody conflicts unavoidable, and typically resulted in the annihilation of one of the sides. 'Chimera' also occurred when a territory was shared by ethnoses belonging to mutually incompatible super-ethnoses that possessed different levels of 'bioenergy'. The Jews, for example, were perceived as a permanent source of chimera. Although they were seen as one of the seven super-ethnoses inhabit-ing Russia, they never occupied their own territorial niche. In this theory, the enormous energy of the Jews was additionally heightened by their urban lifestyle and alienation from nature.[65]

Ethnoses grew deep territorial roots. But only one ethnos, the indigenous one, could lay claim to a specific territory. To establish the socio-cultural development of ancient ethnoses, which invariably began with the discussion of archaeological artefacts, anthropologists and ethnographers spent decades tracing the evolution of ethnoses from Neolithic times and mapping their material culture.

With the emergence of ethnic politics in the crumbling USSR, ethnographic primordialism took on an added dimension. It held potential for the construction of new identities as well as for the purposes of political discourse. The latter days of perestroika and the early post-Communist period witnessed a proliferation of ethno-graphic and historical publications tracing the origins of ethnic groups, especially of titular nations. The term ethnos became a central theme in intellectual and political debates of that time. Today, the historical records are being reworked and reinvented on a massive scale by ethnic élites seeking to elevate the status of their groups in the political hierarchy of ethnoses. Even the Cossacks, a military caste, embarked on a massive campaign to prove that they, too, were an ancient ethnos, or super-ethnos, in an effort to claim a higher political status.[66] Non-Russian élites fiercely reject the liberal notion that many of these identities are relatively modern, construed and reconstrued by arbitrary political decisions, and sometimes elevated to the status of autonomy.[67]

The intellectual mess left by Soviet nationalities policy and its theoretical underpinnings requires a massive clean-up effort. Rethinking the concepts of nation and ethnicity and their relationship to the state, Tishkov writes, is a precondition for the political modernization of Russia.[68] So far, however, the liberals have suffered more setbacks than victories in their promotion of civic nationalism.

Among their brief victories were President Yeltsin's support of the concept of *grazhdanskaya natsiya*, and a short tenure of liberals, such as Galina Starovoitova and Valery Tishkov, as chief presidential advisers on nationalities policy. Their impact on the Concept of State National Policy of the Russian Federation, a document signed by the President in 1996, is discernible.[69] In the end, though, the liberals could not prevent the subsequent shift of presidential support from the concept of civic nation to more nationalist positions.[70] Analysing early symptoms of the new trend, sociologist Vladimir Solovei accurately predicted the continuous 'ethnicization'—that is, 'nationalization' in the *russkii* sense of the term—of Russian politics. He linked it, among other factors, to the short- and long-term impact of the Chechen war.

Conclusions

Russian liberals are still at an early stage in their efforts to articulate a vision of post-Soviet Russia, and have only begun to translate it into policy prescriptions. Uniting them conceptually are the priority given to individual rights and freedoms, an aversion to a societal culture rooted in collectivist and primordial values, the yearning for an ethnically neutral state based on the civic loyalties of citizens, and a universal culture mediated by the Russian language. On the other hand, Russian liberals lack a common position on a number of crucial issues that preclude the formulation of even a consensual liberal nationalities policy. They differ widely on the price they are willing to pay for controlling minority nationalism. This is reflected, for example, in the absence of a common liberal stand on federalism in Russia and, despite a formal commitment to decentralization, flirtation with a centralized, and even unitary, vision of Russia. A superficial examination of current discussions of federalism suggests little or no correlation between stances on federalism and the ideological credentials of Russian liberals. If this is true of intellectuals matching the narrow definition of 'liberals' adopted in this paper, the same is likely to apply to a much broader stratum of those who are commonly described in Russia as 'liberal'.

By identifying minority nationalism as a major source of political instability in the country, the liberals seek primarily to neutralize, contain, dilute, or in other ways minimize the impact of mobilized ethnicity. The problems they confront resemble those of the previous generation of Western liberals who built their vision of modern society on the assumption of the ethnocultural neutrality of the state. Russian liberals may have a much keener sense than their Western colleagues of the ethnic challenges that lie ahead in Russia, but for a variety of reasons—including the newly won freedom to think of society in individualistic terms—they are unlikely contributors to, and consumers of, a liberal theory of minority rights as conceptualized by Will Kymlicka.

But if the liberals, a minority with limited—and decreasing—political influence, are unlikely to act as transmitters of liberal pluralism into Russia, this is not to say that Kymlicka's ideas could gain more support from the dominant political culture. Slow to liberate itself from the legacy of the Soviet system, this culture continues to rely heavily on the language of institutionalized ethnicity, ethnic federalism, and ethnic group rights. Underlying this culture is the assumption that, as Aleksandr Ossipov puts it, society is a collection of 'collective individuals possessing ethnic rights and ascribing ethnic sense to social relations'. Built on the assumptions of ascribed status, collectivism, and primordialism, Russia's current political culture provides no fertile soil for the adoption of Kymlicka's model of liberal pluralism.

NOTES

1. Jerzy Szacki, 'Avtonomiya lichnosti i grazhdanskoe obshchestvo', *Polis*, 5, 1997, 71.

2. Susanna Matveeva, 'Sovremennyi kontseptualnyi liberalism v Rossii', *Obshchestvennye nauki i sovremennost'*, 2, 1993.

3. Susanna Matveeva, 'Vozmozhnost' natsii gosudarstva v Rossii: popytka liberalnoy interpretatsii', *Polis*, 1, 1996, 154; see also 'Natsional'nye problemy Rossii: sovremennye diskussii', *Obshchestvennye nauki i sovremennost'*, 1, 1997, 52–62.

4. Vera Tolz, 'Forging the Nation: National Identity and Nation Building in Post-Communist Russia', *Europe-Asia Studies*, 50/6, 1998, 993.

5. Sven Gunnar Simonsen, 'Raising the "Russian Question": Ethnicity and Statehood, "Russtie" and "Rossia"', *Nationalism and Ethnic Politics*, 2, Spring 1996, 91.

6. Andrei Zdravomyslov, *Mezhnatsionalnye konflikty v post sovietskom prostranstvie* (Moscow 1997) 204–5; Tolz, 'Forging the Nation', 944–5.

7. Valery Tishkov, 'O natsii i natsionalisme', *Svobodnaya mysl'*, 3, 1996.

8. See, for example Simonsen, 'Raising the "Russian Question"'; Valery Tishkov, *Ethnicity, Nationalism and Conflict in and After the Soviet Union. The Mind Aflame* (London and New Delhi: Thousand Oaks, 1996) 228–45; Tatyana Solovei, 'Russkoye i sovetskoye v sovremennom samosozdanii Russkikh', *Identichnost' i konflikt v postsovetskikh gosudarstvakh*, (Moscow 1997) 346–57; and Tolz, 'Forging the Nation'. I have used some of Tolz's suggestions in my own typology outlined below.

9. Tolz, 'Forging the Nation', 993–1022.

10. Tishkov, *Ethnicity, Nationalism*, 1996, 230.

11. Tolz, 'Forging the Nation', 997.

12. Matveeva, 'Vozmozhnost', 154–62; Anatoly Vishnievsky, 'Edina i nedelimaya', *Polis*, 2, 1994, 26–38.

13. Viktor Kozlov, *Etnos. Natsia. Natsionalism* (Moscow, 1999) 340; Simonsen, 'Raising the "Russian Question"'.

14. Aleksandr Solzhenitsyn, *Kak nam obustroit Rossiu* (Leningrad, 1990) reprinted in *Literaturnaya Gazeta*, September 18, 1990.

15. Yulian Bromley, 'Etnos i endogamiya', *Sovietskaya etnografiya*, 6, 1969.

16. Kozlov, *Etnos*, 19–22.

17. See, for example, Sergei Cheshko, 'Chelovek i etnichnost', *Etnograficheskoye obozrenie*, 6, 1993 and his critics, Eduard Tadevosian, 'Rossiiskii federalism i natsioal'no-gosudarstvennyi nigilism', *Gosudarstvo i Pravo*, 10, 1996; Kozlov, *Etnos*; and Viktor Kozlov, 'Problematika etnichnosti', *Etnograficheskoye obozrenie*, 4, 1995.

18. Tishkov, *Ethnicity, Nationalism*, 276; and Valery Tishkov, *Ocherki teorii i politiki etnichnosti v Rossii* (Moscow, 1997) 161.

19. Vladimir Pastukhov, 'Novyi federalism dla Rossii. Institutsionalizatsiya svobody', *Polis*, 3, 1994, 98.

20. Ibid., 95–105.

21. Ibid., 101–4.

22. Interview with Vadim Pechenev, First Deputy Minister for Nationalities Policy, *Nezavisimaya Gazeta*, April 28, 1999.

23. Aleksander Ossipov, 'Krasnodarskii Krai: Migration, Nationalism and Regionalist Rhetoric', in M. Opalski (ed.), *Managing Diversity in Plural Societies: Minorities, Migration and Nation-Building in Post-Communist Europe* (Ottawa, 1998) 273–4.

24. Tishkov, 'O natsii i natsionalisme'; Tishkov, *Ethnicity, Nationalism*, 273–4. Cf. 'Rossiikii sotsium 1994', *Sotsiologicheskie issledovania*, 2, 1995.

25. V. M. Delaev, *Paradigma federalism v kontekste reform Rossiiskoy gosudarstvi-ennosti* (Moscow 1999), 123.
26. E. Stepanov, 'Otchestvennaya konfliktologiya: k voprosu o stanovlenii i razvitii', *Sotsiologicheskoe issledovanie*, 1998, 50–6; Vladimir Streletskyi, 'Etnoterritorial'nye konflikty: sushchnost', genezis, tipy', *Identichnost' i konflikt v postsovietskikh gosudarstvakh* (Moscow, 1997) 225–49.
27. Tishkov, 'O natsii i natsionalisme'; Tadevosian, 'Rossiiskii federalism', 1–14; and Boris Fedorov, *Shto i kak my budem delat* (Moscow, 1994).
28. Cameron Ross, 'Federalism i demokratsiya v Rossii', *Polis*, 4, 1999, 21.
29. Valery Tishkov, 'Strategiya i mekhanismy natsional'noy politiki Rossiiskoy Federatsii', *Etnograficheskoye obozrenie*, 5, 1993, 12–34.
30. Fedorov, *Shto i kak*.
31. Interview with Vladimir Zhirinovsky, *Izvestiya*, April 23, 1994. Zhirinovsky urged Russians to 'forget about the federation as one forgets a bad dream'.
32. Eduard Tadevosian, *Sovietskaya natsiona'lnaya gosudarstvennost'* (Moscow, 1972) and his 'Edinstvo internatsionalnogo i natsionalnogo v gosudarstvennosti narodov SSSR', *Kommunist*, 18, 1973, 66–76.
33. Tadevosian, *Sovetskaya natsional'naya*; Grey Hodnett, 'The Debate Over Soviet Federalism', *Soviet Studies*, 28/4, 1967.
34. Valery Tishkov's article, 'Narody i gosudarstvo', *Kommunist*, 1, 1989, opened public debate on the issue.
35. Roundtable on 'Interethnic Contradictions in Russia. The Strategy of Political Parties and Social Movements', *Russian Politics and Law*, September–October, 1994, 6–31.
36. For a detailed discussion of the law and the concept of cultural autonomy, see Mikhail Goboglo, *Mozhet li dvuglovyi orel letat's odnom krylom?* (Moscow, 2000).
37. V. A. Pechenev, 'O natsional'noy i regionalnoy politike v Federativnoy Rossii', *Etnopolis*, 1, 1994, 84.
38. Tishkov, 'Strategiya i mekhanismy'.
39. Tadevosian, 'Rossiiskii federalism'; and 'Etnonatsia: mif ili sotsial'naya realnost'?' *Sotsiologicheskie issledovania*, 6, 1998, 61–8.
40. Mikhail Nikolaev, (President of the Republic of Sakha), 'V bratskoy sem'e—no bez ottsa narodov', *Rossiisakaya gazeta*, 9 August 1996.
41. Tadevosian, 'Rosiskyi federalism', 2nd 'Ethnonatsia'.
42. For a discussion of federalism as the institutionalization of complex ethnic hierarchies, see for instance Galina Soldatova, *Psikhologiya mezhetnicheskikh naprazhennosti* (Moscow, 1998). Soldatova presents Russia's rehabilitation of nations deported by Stalin as a source of ethnic unrest in the Caucasus.
43. Tishkov, *Ethnicity and Nationalism*.
44. Ossipov, 'Krasnodarskii Krai', 260–73.
45. Valery Tishkov, 'Sotsialnoye i natsional'noye v istoriko-antropologicheskoy per-spektive', *Kommunist*, 1, 1990; 'Narody i gosudarstvo', *Kommunist*, 2, 1992; Vestnik RAN (Rossiiskoy Akademii Nauk) 8, 1993.
46. Interview with Nikolai Ryzhov, the head of the Narodovlaste faction in the State Duma, *Etnograficheskoe obozrenie*, 3, 1999, 126.
47. Ildus Ilishev, 'Russian Federalism: Political, Legal and Ethnolinguistic Aspects', *Nationalities Papers*, 26/4, 1998; Tadevosian, 'Etnonatsia', 67–8.
48. Ramazan Abdulatipov, 'Poslanie Prezidentu Rossiiskoy Federatsii B. N. Yeltsinu. O federativnoy i natsional'noy politike rossiiskogo gosudarstva', *Nezavisimaya gazeta*, March 14, 1995, 3.

49. Ibid.; and Kozlov (1995).
50. Roundtable on 'Interethnic Contradictions', 22.
51. Tishkov, *Ethnicity, Nationalism*, 64; 'Kontseptsia gosudarstvennoy natsional'noy politiki Rossiiskoy Federatsii utverzhdena spetsialnym ukazom prezidenta ot 15 yunia', *Nezavisimaya Gazeta*, June 21, 1996. Goboglo, Mozhet.
52. Ibid.
53. Vladimir Kalamanov, 'Rossii nuzhna Assambleya narodov', *Rossiiskaya Federatsia*, 7, 1997; Sergei Alekseev, Vladimir Kalamanov, and Andrei Chernenko, *Ideologicheskie orientiry Rossii*, Vol. 2 (Moscow, 1998) 30–6.
54. Valery Tishkov, 'Rossiia kak natsional'noye gosudarstvo', *Nezavisimaya gazeta*, 26 January 1994.
55. Ibid.
56. Graham Smith, 'Russia, Multiculturalism and Federal Justice', *Europe-Asia Studies*, 50/8, 1998, 1398–9.
57. T. Alekseeva, B. Kapustin, and I. Pantin, 'Kakovy ideologicheskie uslovia obshchestvennovo soglasia v Rossii?', *Polis*, 7, 1999, 19, 41; Solovei, 'Russkoye i sovetskoye'; Matveeva, 'Vozmozhnost', 162. See also Eduard Bagramov, 'Natsiya kak sograzhdanstvo?', *Nezavisimaya gazeta*, 15 March 1994, 5.
58. Matveeva, 'Vozmozhnost'.
59. Tishkov, *Ethnicity, Nationalism*, 274.
60. See the papers and comments by Faozia Bayramova, Davit Berdzenishvili, Vyacheslav Chernivil, Refat Chubarov, Paruir Hairikyan, Mart Nutt, and Ali Kerimov at the conference, 'The Rise of Nationalism in the Former Soviet Union', Kyiv, Ukraine, November 29–December 1, 1996, *Uncaptive Minds*, 9/3–4, 1997.
61. For an extensive discussion on the so-called 'fifth point' see Sven Gunnar Simonsen, 'Inheriting the Soviet Toolbox: Russia's Dilemma Over Ascriptive Nationality', *Europe-Asia Studies*, 51/6, 1999, 1069–87.
62. Joseph Stalin, 'Natsional'nyi vopros', in *Voprosy Leninisma* (Moscow, 1945) 45–52.
63. Sergei Shirokogorov is best known for his classification of ethnoses. Yulian Bromley's typology of ethnoses and 'ethno-social processes' identified the 'socialist nation' as the highest evolutionary form. Lev Gumilev offered a socio-biological interpretation of the theory.
64. On the 'negative' and 'positive' 'mutual compatibility' of ethnoses see Igor Shishkin, 'Simbiosis, xenia i khimera: Lev Gumilev o etnosakh Rossii', *Zavtra*, 4, 1995, 60.
65. Ibid.
66. In the authoritative encyclopedia *Narody Rossii*, edited by Valery Tishkov (Moscow, 1994) 169–74, the Cossacks are presented as an ethnos. On the Cossack struggle for the status of a nation, see Magda Opalski, 'The Cossack Revival: Rebuilding an Old Identity in a New Russia', in M. Opalski (ed.), *Managing Diversity in Plural Societies: Minorities, Migration and Nation-Building in Post-Communist Europe* (Ottawa, 1998) 75–101.
67. Tishkov, *Ethnicity, Nationalism*.
68. Ibid.
69. Tishkov, *Ocherki teorii*, 138–73.
70. Valery Solovei, ' "Natsionalizatsia" rezhima budet prodolzhatsia', *Nezavisimaya gazeta*, 7 March 1996.

Nation-Building, Culture, and Problems of Ethnocultural Identity in Central Asia: The Case of Uzbekistan

ALEKSANDR DJUMAEV

Will Kymlicka has prompted an interesting exchange of ideas on some crucial concepts of Western political theory. He expresses the hope that the countries of Eastern and Central Europe (ECE), learning from the mistakes made by Western democracies, will avoid repeating them in their management of ethnocultural relations. Kymlicka is aware of the diversity and uniqueness of the problems facing the countries of the former Communist bloc, as well as the differences among ECE countries and Russia. His paper, in fact, is addressed to the specialists of those countries, that is, countries with a Christian heritage.

This raises a question of the extent to which the Western European experience is applicable to the former Soviet, and now newly independent, countries of Central Asia that have a Muslim culture. Political scientists and a segment of the intelligentsia in Central Asia, including Uzbek intellectuals, have long been wrestling with this question. The latter's scepticism about the applicability of the Western model is based on an understanding of the level of conservatism within the traditional society, which is currently growing and consolidating after being shaken in Soviet times.

The question is not, however, only about the traditional conservative structures and mentality associated, at least to a certain extent, with Islam or its origin. More importantly, every newly independent Central Asian state has its own 'Islamic factor' that is capable of directly influencing the nation-building process. Central Asian politicians are forced to take into account this factor, albeit in a different way in each country. It is manifested in a special way in Uzbekistan and Tajikistan where, as the events of recent years have shown, it can assume a form of political opposition, including the claim to create its own state structures.

In present-day Central Asia, state- and nation-building are strongly linked to cultural and ethnic processes. In every newly independent country in the region, these factors are in a state of heightened dynamics, contradiction, and instability. This makes analysis more difficult, and general conclusions and forecasts more complicated. Forecasts are, nevertheless, being made. Many of them predict that inter-ethnic and other types of conflicts will intensify in several regions of Central Asia, especially in the Fergana Valley.[1]

Many researchers consider that such conflicts could be triggered not only by the further deterioration in economic, social, political, and ecological conditions—all of which have a direct impact on the coexistence of, and relations among, nations and neighbouring countries—but also by the historical miscalculations of Soviet nationalities policy. Thus, since the latter half of the 1980s, there has been an open and lively discussion, initiated primarily by Tajik authors, on the sensitive topics of historical injustices associated with the redrawing of national borders in Soviet Central Asia, of the infringement of human rights, and even of the genocide of an entire nation. The books by R. Masov[2] gave new impetus to this discussion, generating a wave of new publications.[3] When it reaches a critical mass, this discussion threatens to expand from a local (Tajik-Uzbek) debate into a regional one involving other ethnic groups and nations.[4]

In this situation, the principles developed in Western democracies can not only be 'potentially applicable to ECE countries' but, in many cases, to Central Asian countries as well. Even if they provide no satisfactory answers to the specific problems of the region, they should nevertheless be studied carefully. Their adoption would depend on successfully overcoming at least three contrasting visions apparent in Central Asian society:

(1) the above-mentioned scepticism of the élites regarding the applicability of the Western model, based on the assumption that the traditional society, particularly in Uzbekistan, will resist radical social change;
(2) the view that Central Asia's own experience in harmonizing and managing inter-ethnic relations—developed in antiquity, in the Middle Ages, and at the beginning of the twentieth century—can provide a viable 'alternative to the West'; and

(3) the idealization of inter-ethnic relations in Western Europe, whereby their laws and democratic norms, if transplanted to Central Asia, would automatically bring about harmony, lasting peace, and stability in inter-ethnic relations.

Kymlicka's picture of ethnic relations in Western democracies, however, shatters the pleasant myths and wishful thinking. He argues that ethnocultural conflicts constitute a permanent feature of modern Western democracies and that 'the achievement of democratization, prosperity, and tolerance has gone hand in hand with increased ethno-cultural mobilization'. He also states that 'democracy, economic prosperity, and personal tolerance are all great goods, of course—valuable in and of themselves. But they are not by themselves, or even when taken together, an answer to the issues of ethnocultural diversity. The accommodation of ethnocultural diversity will remain a powerful source of conflict—and may indeed increase in strength—even when all of these other goods are in place. This is the most important lesson which the West has had to learn.'

If, as Kymlicka states, Western theoreticians have long neglected research in ethnocultural relations and conflicts because they considered ethnicity to be a marginal phenomenon that would disappear as a result of modernization, or for other reasons, then what can be said of the countries of Central Asia? Here, accelerated modernization conducted, but not completed, in Soviet times, did not lead to the eradication of ethnicity. On the contrary, ethnic and national awareness was strengthened. During the perestroika period, people started to speak openly about inter-ethnic and ethnocultural problems in the Soviet Central Asian republics. It was primarily journalists, poets, and writers who fanned the flames of their 'wounded national identity'. Even party leaders openly tried to 'sort out' inter-ethnic and international relations. At a 1986 conference[5] organized by the Central Committee of the Communist Party of Uzbekistan and other organizations, certain ethnocultural problems and trends, such as the rewriting of history and the destruction of the cultural heritage of Central Asian nations, were raised. Today, they are public knowledge. Yet, it has only been in the last few years, in great part due to the initiatives and support of international organizations, that problems of inter-ethnic and international relations started to be studied seriously and discussed publicly at the national and regional levels in Central Asia.[6] These discussions, which included topics such as the cultural legacy of Soviet times and the place of contemporary Central Asian cultures in state- and nation-building, showed that after the dissolution of the

USSR and the collapse of Communist ideology, different and some-times contradictory understandings of the ethnocultural process began to take shape in Central Asia.

Kymlicka's assessment that 'the newly democratizing countries of ECE are following the model of the "nation-building" state' seems to be fully applicable to the Central Asia of today. Almost every one of the newly formed countries of Central Asia is multi-ethnic and multi-national. In the opinion of the President of the Uzbek Republic, Islam Karimov, the region 'is going through the irreversible process of cre-ating national states with a multi-national population.'[7]

At the same time, the policies of several Central Asian states, including Uzbekistan, are far from neutral towards ethnocultural diversity. The 'myth of ethnocultural neutrality', which Kymlicka dispels using the examples of Western liberal democracies and the 'newly democratizing countries of ECE', has never been apparent in Central Asia. The majority of leaders and institutions concerned with nation-building in the newly independent Central Asian states do not conceal their priorities and the single-mindedness of their eth-nocultural policies. There is an active effort to bring to 'completion' the process of nation-building of the titular nations, to consolidate their positions and promote national mobilization based on their own ethnocultural symbolism, to free them of the Soviet identity and mentality, to bring them into the fold of the world community, and to define their place within the system of international relations.

Independence has made it possible for Central Asian countries to make choices and manoeuvre, which are necessary in defining and conducting their own policies. Every country in the region has adopted its own nation-building programme. Uzbekistan has given priority to the development of its state institutions, creating an integral programme for building a national government with its own 'national ideology of independence', presented by President Karimov himself.

Nevertheless, independence did not prevent the emergence of new and complex problems in inter-ethnic and international relations. First, serious divergences arose among Central Asian states in their understanding of a series of issues, caused by different development priorities and the different paths chosen to achieve them. The differences include attitudes toward the Soviet past and its cultural heritage, an important component of which is Russian culture and the Russian language. Second, the post-independence period laid bare the contradiction between the process of modern nation-building and tra-ditional Central Asian management of multi-ethnicity, ethnocultural diversity, and multiculturalism. Third, ethnocultural differences within Central Asian society grew deeper. In Uzbekistan, this is especially true of urban civilization, to which both Tajiks and Uzbeks lay claim. Each of these problems is examined in greater detail.

Relationship to Soviet Cultural Heritage: Language and Culture

Russian and National Languages

The problem of Soviet cultural heritage is only briefly touched upon by Kymlicka, and then only in terms of the status of Russians and the Russian language in the successor states, using the Baltic States as an example. He puts the Baltic republics into a group of cases 'for which there are no obvious analogues in Western experience, and for whom the West provides no useful models or principles'.

Yet, to examine the impact of Soviet heritage, it is necessary to take into consideration the particularities of the regions and republics that were once part of the USSR, even if there were shared traits. The situation in the Baltic republics—where the Russian language is primarily an indicator of national affiliation—is essentially different from the one that has developed in the states of post-Soviet Central Asia. Here, Russian is not only the language of the Russian diaspora—which has shrunk in the last few years—and a means of international communication in everyday life. It is also a channel for the transmission of universal modern culture, a function it acquired over the last 130 years in the Russian colonial and Soviet periods. Analogies can be made with the historic role Arab, Persian, French, and English languages have played in the development of different civilizations. The approach to language as an ethnic identifier, frequently the first and primary indicator of ethnicity—as in 'one nation, one language, one territory . . .'—is currently widespread among a part of the Uzbek intelligentsia. This is apparently one of the spontaneous (subconscious) manifestations, albeit temporary, of a mind-set reflecting deeply rooted neo-Bolshevik thinking.

Recent practice, however, shows that this tendency has not become prevalent. Its influence on the nation-building process in Uzbekistan is felt gradually and within established channels. The coexistence of two languages and cultures must be balanced anew. The Russian language is used to communicate the newest achievements in culture, technology, and the humanities, in response to the contemporary boom of intellectual and publishing activity in Russia. It is especially noticeable in Uzbekistan, given the acute shortage of published materials and the concentration of intellectual endeavours on the popularization of its own history. The attitude to the Russian language and culture, particularly in Uzbekistan, depends on the situation in Russia: the stabilization of political life and the consolidation of state power and institutions in Russia strengthen the position of the Russian culture and language in Uzbekistan, and vice versa.

In the newly independent countries of Central Asia, the national language plays a crucial role, especially in culture and the arts, in the acquisition of ethnocultural and national identities, in the building of national unity, and in achieving cultural, and even political, independence. Of all the Central Asian countries, this is most evident in Uzbekistan. To a certain degree, a parallel can be drawn with Hebrew in Israel, which is now a factor of national integration. At the same time, a recent study[8] concludes that 'the promotion of Uzbek to the rank of a state language did not restrict the many language groups of the Uzbek population. The Republic has created positive conditions for the functioning and development of other languages spoken by peoples in Uzbekistan.'[9] Unfortunately, this does not apply to the Tajik language, a situation that requires rethinking as a historical and cultural phenomenon in Uzbekistan.

In looking at the coexistence of Uzbekistan's two main languages, Uzbek and Russian, the picture is complicated and riddled with contradictions. First of all, one must note that, in different fields, such as business, culture, and politics, Uzbek, as a state language, has different meanings, status, and ranges of applicability. It is only natural that, in post-Soviet Uzbekistan, Uzbek considerably strengthened its position in the national culture and has become a tool in the struggle for national cultural revival. The return of the Uzbek language to its long-lost position in society has laid the groundwork for 'cleansing' the Uzbek national culture and 'separating' it from the general Russian and Soviet cultures. Secondly, its revival has considerably weakened Russian cultural influence and, at the practical day-to-day level, has limited the participation of Russian-speakers in Uzbek national culture, practically excluding them from their former fields of activity. This has seriously curtailed the opportunities for Russian-speakers to pursue their professional careers. In almost all Uzbek cultural organizations, all meetings, scientific councils, and other public activities are conducted in Uzbek. Uzbek is also the only language in which official documents are produced. To a certain extent, one can speak of the partial delegitimization of Russian-speakers in several areas of Uzbek culture and science—especially the social sciences and history—as public attitudes are highly ambivalent towards everything that is created, said and written in the Russian language. If need be, speaking Uzbek can always be used as 'an ace up one's sleeve', that is, Uzbeks can always be masters of a situation by speaking their own language.

This situation is strongly reminiscent, in reverse, of one that existed in the 1970s and 1980s, during the so-called years of *zastoi* (stagnation), when Russian represented one of the main elements of Central Asian culture and determined one's status in cultural affairs.[10] The current position of the Uzbek language can be seen as 'tit-for-tat', or a manifestation of 'the pendulum principle', that is, a reaction to the long-dominant status of Russian. The 'defenders' of the Uzbek language during perestroika and the first years of independence were frequently those members of the Uzbek intelligentsia who had built their careers in the Russian language and had contributed nothing to the development of the Uzbek language during Soviet times.

The reinstatement of the Uzbek language as the primary language of the national culture changed the general direction and the paradigms of cultural and scientific thinking, the choice of methodological approaches and research methods. Yet, on the whole, the legislated status of the Uzbek and Russian languages does not entirely coincide with reality and Russian continues to maintain its position of importance.

From the standpoint of maintaining ethnic peace and stability in Central Asia, the most effective approach to Russian culture and language would be a policy oriented to a redefinition of their place in the new nation-building process. Because Russian culture and language are a common heritage of the Central Asian people, they have a place in the region's future. They can play this role in each country of the region, especially in Uzbekistan with its ethnocultural differences. No one is confident that the Russian-speaking population in Uzbekistan will learn the Uzbek language. Most probably, Uzbekistan and other Central Asian countries will remain bilingual and most Uzbeks will know Russian as well.

Russian and Soviet Cultures

Towards the end of the 1980s, culture consisted of three 'layers' in each of the Central Asian nations: traditional national culture, Russian/European culture, and modern national culture. The modern culture in the nations of Central Asia was nurtured by the single-minded cultural policy of the Communist Party of the Soviet Union and the Soviet government and, on the whole, falls within the concept of 'Soviet culture'. However, the latter should not be equated, as is commonly done, with 'Russian culture'.[11] One needs to talk about the new type of Europeanized culture, one that was based on the synthesis of Russian/European traditions and the native cultures of Central Asia. In my opinion, and with some obvious reservations, this modern Central Asian culture is compatible with the concepts of 'territorially concentrated culture' or 'societal cultures', as proposed by Kymlicka. The recognition of this culture as 'national' occurred in varying degrees in all countries of Central Asia. The 'fifth point' factor—the reference to 'nationality' in Soviet passports—played a role in this process.

Cultural policies conducted during the Soviet years produced some positive results leading to the formation of several generations of cultural, scientific, and artistic élites capable of creating highly professional spiritual and artistic treasures. In spite of the domination of the Russian language in Soviet times and of the policy of 'russification', as a rule the cultural interests of the titular nation were given priority. This was particularly so in Uzbekistan where the 'fifth point' factor, that is, identifying oneself as Uzbek in the Soviet passport, was possibly even more important than membership in the CPSU. It was a very important factor, frequently implemented unofficially and informally as a means of resisting the policies of internationalism in employment and other areas. This preferential policy is now fully implemented in Uzbekistan and the middle management of the public service apparatus is dedicated to its enforcement.

After the disintegration of the USSR and the fragmentation of a single cultural entity, cultural cleavages occurred in each of the former Soviet republics in Central Asia. Throughout the region, Soviet culture was subjected to a review and re-evaluation, and some of its elements were rejected. The newly independent states are developing their own forms of 'nationalization' and rethinking ethnocultural issues from state- and nation-building perspectives. Each of the Central Asian states is putting its individual stamp on this process. Kyrgyzstan, known as 'a little island of democracy' in Central Asia, paradoxically retained not only Soviet culture but also many basic political attributes and symbols of Soviet power—such as monuments, including those to Lenin, and street names. Uzbekistan has adopted a different approach, conducting an accelerated dismantling of the Soviet political system and the destruction of a significant part of the Russian and Soviet cultural legacies—for example reducing the number of hours of teaching in Russian, a change of names and symbols, the removal of monuments to figures of Russian and Soviet culture, and a thorough cleansing of libraries. In the arts, to quote the Tashkent art critic, Boris Chukhovich, 'a new ideological banner was unfurled—art that is national in form and content' and, 'in spite of the declared freedom from Soviet stereotypes, artistic life and even figurative thinking are becoming much more monotonous than they were ten years ago.'[12]

As noted above, the attitude to the Soviet past and to its cultural legacy is one of the more notable points of divergence in the policies of the newly independent Central Asian states. The political leaders of Kyrgyzstan and Kazakhstan, for example, have an appreciation for the Soviet period and its cultural legacy. When appraising the legacy of the Soviet period, the president of Kyrgyzstan, Askar Akaev, stated:

In the years of Soviet power, the national statehood of the Kyrgyz people benefited enormously even though, to a considerable extent, this was a facade. I am not talking about the fact that the Kyrgyz people were saved from genocide, but that a cultural structure was built which cannot but elicit admiration, regardless of its cost. A relatively civilised system of governing was established, and a civic, political and legal consciousness has taken root in Kyrgyz society. (*Slovo Kyrgyzstana*, 11 October 1994).

This position was incorporated into Akaev's electoral platform, which stated that, 'we should be more careful with, and more attentive to, the precious and positive heritage of the past, including the seventy years of Soviet power.'[13]

The national intelligentsia in Central Asian countries is divided into two camps—those who opt for a moderate re-evaluation and retention of some positive aspects of the Russian cultural presence in the region, and those who opt for the re-establishment of 'pure' national traditions. This dichotomy is apparent when comparing Kazakhstan and Uzbekistan.

Among the Kazakh intelligentsia, traditionally inclined to a philosophical interpretation of their history and culture, there is an active search for new paradigms to explain their culture and national mentality. They do not view the problem of the Kazakh and Russian languages, even within the context of global cultural challenges, as their leading problem. Instead, they feel an 'insistent need to comprehend the condition of Kazakh culture which, after the fall of the Soviet Union, seems to be suspended in a vacuum.'[14] The bilingual Kazakh poet and thinker Auezkhan Kodar has written:

It is not a secret that modern Kazakh culture is artificial, having been created in high-level Kremlin offices and it, therefore, harbours the traces of dual dependence—first, from the colonial policies of Imperial Russia and, second, from the exhausting intellectual pressure of Soviet ideocracy. It is not surprising that dependence on Russian standards is an inherited malaise of our intelligentsia. It is natural that there should be two trends in a sovereign Kazakhstan: different forms of russophobia among the Kazakh intelligentsia, and the conciliatory tactics of Russian-speaking intellectuals who are operating under the 'one house' banner. Now, when passions have cooled after five years of post-colonial existence, it is time to ask whether it is possible to identify common cultural elements in a multi-ethnic country, and which is the criterion of differentiation—ethnicity or intellectual provincialism? (Kodar, 'Mesto predisloviya', 3).

In a newspaper interview with the evocative caption of, 'Right after the Russian Cannons came Pushkin', the Kazakh poet, Meirkhan Akdauletov, discussed the complex search for and difficult process of building a historic ethnocultural identity which, he believes, inevitably leads to its opposite.

When independence was 'declared' I, too, welcomed everyone's wish to know his or her ancestors to the seventh generation. But now, all of this is becoming somewhat sinister. The identification of one's ancestral line is a very particular kind of genealogical chronology, which is called *shezhire* in Kazakh. But we ourselves barely noticed how this led us to a concept of society based on blood ties, which then developed into a *zhuz* ideology. Initially, this was meant to be a search for one's roots. On the other hand, I would probably be seriously bending the truth if I did not say that there was nothing natural in this. Having freed themselves from the 'socialist whores', Kazakhs needed a direction. They started searching and found it, not at their doorstep, but two centuries away. This was the old archetype but no one was bothered by this. On the contrary, this 'archaization' evoked a favourable response. (Dzhabinek Suleev, 'Vsled za ruskimi pushkami prikhodil Pushkin', interview with Meirkhan Akdauletov in *451° Fahrenheit*, 18/6, Summer 1999).[15]

For Akdauletov, it seems inevitable that Kazakhstan will maintain ties with the Russian culture, in spite of the political games of Russian and other nationalists who are exploiting the topic of discrimination against Russians and Russian-speakers in Kazakhstan.

Recently, Mr Bunakov... again announced to the entire country that there is discrimination against Russians and Russian-speakers. Never mind; that's politics. That is maybe even Russian politics. After all, everyone is looking out for himself in this harsh world. It would seem that I have many more reasons to take offence against the Russians. After all, in 1986, they broke two of my ribs, not Bunakov's. But I did not hold this against the entire Russian people. I consider that stupid and highly irrational. No matter how dramatic this sounds, without Russian culture, which opened other worlds to us, things could be even worse for us. As a Tatar wise man once said, 'After the Russian cannons came Pushkin.' Fate brought us together. Yes, we were colonised. We were nomads. That is our fate. (Suleev, 'Vsled za ruskimi')

A diametrically opposed approach toward Russian and Soviet history and cultural heritage is developing in Uzbekistan in spite of the fact that, among Central Asian countries, Uzbekistan inherited the most from Soviet culture and the Soviet cultural model. The implementation of a consistent Soviet cultural policy in the republic created a completely new cultural strata and new artistic types and genres. Nevertheless, in the official ideology of Uzbekistan, the Russian and Soviet periods are, on the whole, appraised very negatively. Lately, they are not even being differentiated, and are being lumped together as one 'colonial period' in Uzbekistan's history.[16] It seems that there are several factors influencing this position. The two primary ones are the distancing from Russia politically, a guiding principle in the policies of Uzbekistan in the last few years, and the desire on the part of the previous Communist Party *nomenklatura*, as well as parts of the national intelligentsia, to 'wash away the damned past', to denigrate and criticize it in order to preserve their status and privileges, which they had acquired in Soviet times.

Such an approach, which has become the basic trend in the official historiography and ideology of Uzbekistan, is to a certain extent discernible in other newly independent states of Central Asia. Yet, in Uzbekistan, the negative attitude toward the Soviet and Russian past, as expressed in most publications, is practically canonized and enjoys a monopoly in the official stance of the establishment. Contrary to what occurs in neighbouring states, the press is not allowed to articulate an opposite point of view. This is evident in the very negative commentaries, which sometimes border on the absurd. There are many examples where the word 'Soviet' was struck from scientific and other publications and replaced with other expressions, and where illustrations in the press that showed Soviet symbols were retouched. Most frequently, it is suggested that this entire period in the history of Uzbekistan should be forgotten or eradicated from people's memory.[17] It is presented as being an exclusively colonial period when Uzbek people fought for their independence.

The official press cannot reflect the entire range of opinions prevalent among the opponents and supporters of the national version of

Uzbek history. The new version of Uzbek history, however, was expressed most succinctly in a watershed article by the historian Hamid Ziyaev entitled, 'Our road to freedom was not easy', published in Russian in two editions of the newspaper *Narodnoe Slovo*.[18] It characterizes the Soviet period in Central Asian history as a 'new stage in the enslavement of the people' in which policies have reached their peak' and the state system was 'a new type of society run by slave drivers'.

Judging by a sample of responses from intellectuals who were questioned about Ziyaev's article, as well as similar publications, the Russian-speaking intelligentsia reacted very negatively. The proliferation of such views put them in a state of depression, and caused many to withdraw from social life, and even to emigrate from the republic.

On the whole, the political and ideological climate that developed in Uzbekistan led to the 'eradication' of an entire historical period, from the beginning of Russian colonization to 1991; it was deemed to be illegal and historically illegitimate. The 'eradication' of Russian and Soviet legacies happened in conjunction with the search for national cultural paradigms. Hundreds of articles, published in such magazines and newspapers as *Mulokot, Guliston, Tafakkur, Shark Yulduzi, Uzbekiston adabieti va sanati, Khurriat* and many others, are dedicated to the foundations and treasures of the national culture. These publications predominantly refer to the great past, the work and deeds of great scientists and philosophers, military and national leaders, Sufi leaders, saints (*avlie*), law-makers, and the keepers of sacred stories about the prophet Muhammad (*khadis*).

The return to Islamic religious values is frequently proposed as an option in the development of culture and art, and the search for a national identity. 'We are a Muslim people', writes one of the authors. 'For many centuries, our culture, our art, our concepts were based on an Islamic foundation'.[19] Great importance is also attributed to the study of the *jadids* (wise men) and the reinstatement of their legacy. They have become the symbol of the movement for national independence, and are frequently seen as an alternative to Western and Russian cultural values and models of development. Yet, it is apparent—and this is noted by some researchers in Uzbekistan—that the intellectual legacy of the *jadids* also contains ideas that are capable of adversely influencing the formation of a multi-ethnic and multi-cultural society in Uzbekistan and other Central Asian states.

At the same time, a trend has started to integrate world, especially European, cultural values into Uzbek society—for example, translations from English and other languages. Most recently, there has been state support for strengthening the general secular Soviet cultural development in the country. No doubt, the events of 16 February 1999—when a series of terrorist explosions shook Tashkent, followed by a struggle with religious extremism—provided a strong impetus for this.

An intense re-evaluation and criticism of Russian, European, and Soviet forms of art also took place at the beginning of the 1990s.[20] These art forms were considered to have no relevance or to be foreign to national artistic traditions and mentality. National poets and writers expressed ideas about how unnecessary opera, musical theatre, symphonies, and other types of modern art are to the Uzbek people. One of the more prominent figures is Muhammad Salikh, who had espoused nationalistic positions from the mid-1970s through the 1980s.[21] Nationalistic views on culture were also being formulated by some former members of the Communist Party *nomenklatura*, who until recently actively worked on promoting Soviet culture in Uzbekistan.

These views were not, however, supported by the leaders of the country and, as a consequence, remained localized and failed to become a general trend. A series of decisions taken by Islam Karimov, aimed at developing Uzbek traditional art, was instrumental in easing tensions. In addition, sponsored support for both traditional and modern art by various diplomatic missions, international organizations, foreign foundations and companies also helped to mute the more radical views toward Russian, European, and Soviet art.

The future existence of the formerly modern Soviet, and now modern national, culture, as well as the survival of the Russian language, will depend on several factors, including:

(1) the political orientation of newly independent Central Asian states;
(2) the maintenance of ties with Russian and European culture, inasmuch as modern national culture is organically linked to it; and
(3) the degree of openness and interaction with world culture.

Although the sphere of operation of the Russian culture and language has been substantially reduced, it is unlikely that their influence will disappear entirely in the near future.

Nation-Building and Ethnocultural Diversity

The policy of active nation-building implemented in the new Central Asian republics could not but affect the status of national and ethnic minorities, and non-titular nations. As Kymlicka notes, a natural reaction of national and ethnic minorities to majority nation-building is to mobilize minority communities and create their own nation-states. To date, this has not occurred, with the possible exception of Kazakhstan, where a cohesive, strong Russian Cossack diaspora has become active—but this is a particular case that does not fall within the parameters of this article.

In reality, the response of national minorities to the mobilization of titular nations was mass emigration to their 'historical homelands' for various reasons, including economic ones. After the near-total exodus of Jews—both European and 'Bukharan' Jews—and the emigration of Germans, Greeks, and the first wave of Russians and Russian-speakers, this process has slowed somewhat. But the potential is there for it to increase again.[22]

Although the multi-ethnic and multinational traditions in Central Asian states have been maintained, the out-migration is changing the broad ethnonational picture of Uzbek society. Titular nationalities in each of the states are increasing their share of the total population, largely due to the decrease in the Russian and Russian-speaking populations and, to a lesser extent, due to repatriation from other countries. The dynamics of change in the structure of the ethnic and national compositions can easily be traced by comparing demographic data for the last few years.[23]

In Uzbekistan, several cultural factors have been identified by members of the Russian and Russian-speaking artistic and scientific intelligentsia as reasons for emigrating—it is possible that these factors, which relate to nation-building policies, are characteristic of the entire region. They include the general psychological condition of minorities, in particular, insecurity about the future; a rapid change in the cultural and ethnocultural environments; increased promulgation of national Uzbek values and ideals; the re-establishment of medieval and mythical heroes, and of the originators of absolute moral codes, as symbols and idols of nationhood; reduced opportunities for satisfying the cultural needs and expression of non-titular nations; the political reorientation towards the USA and NATO, and away from Russia; restrictions on culture and information; and, most importantly, a feeling of inferiority and a sense of illegitimacy as a citizen.

The feeling of inferiority and illegitimacy arises from many sources, two of which are the overt and covert ethnocentric nation-building process, and the absence of strong ties to the native culture of Central Asia, or of the feeling that this is their (second) homeland. For example, even though Russians represented 32.2 per cent of the total population of Kazakhstan (1997 data),[24] Kazakh political scientists admit that the country's president, Nursultan Nazarbaev, is conducting ethnocentric policies to strengthen clan and family ties.[25] As a result, Russians and Russian-speakers play no political role whatsoever in the building of the new state because they lack 'legitimacy'.[26] They feel besieged by the 'titular nation'. This situation exists, to a greater or lesser extent, in each of the Central Asian states. It seems that it is least evident in Kyrgyzstan and most evident in Uzbekistan. In the latter, it is only now that attempts are being made to explain the proverbial 'passivity' of the Russians.[27] From the perspective of the newly independent states, however, the feeling of 'illegitimacy' by Russian-speakers and other ethnocultural groups is a psychological and mental, rather than legal, condition.

The reasons for the lack of strong ties to Central Asian culture among Russians and Russian-speakers range from the decline in the Russian intelligentsia's knowledge of local traditions, languages, and customs,[28] to the generally more negative view of Russians. In this latter context, Russian and Soviet cultures and their Russian and Russian-speaking carriers are seen as inherently alien to Central Asia; their presence bore tragic results for the cultures of the people of the region, especially the Tajiks.[29] It is thought that the changes for the worse were exacerbated in the 1970s and 1980s. In Uzbekistan, the first major break in ethnocultural relations occurred as early as the second half of the 1960s, after the Tashkent earthquake. Thousands of workers were sent to Tashkent from Russia, Ukraine and other republics to rebuild the city. For the majority, the traditions, customs, and culture of the Uzbeks, and the fairly harmonious interethnic relations that existed in the city, were completely alien and incomprehensible to them.

Ethnocultural differences between Russians, Russian-speakers, and the native people of Central Asia, and their different, incompatible lifestyles, surfaced sporadically over decades. Meirkhan Akdauletov, citing the words of the famous Kazakh poet and writer Olzhas Suleimenov, reminds us that, 'unfortunately, as Olzhas said in his time, Kazakhs and Russians, living in one land, lived within different parameters, almost in different worlds. He said and wrote it at the dawn of sovereignty. But it continues and remains true to this day.'[30]

According to the Kyrgyz researcher, G. A. Bakieva, the way out of this painful problem for the Central Asian region lies in 'changing previous stereotypes and developing new arrangements for those for whom Central Asia is not a historical homeland. This primarily refers to Russian-speakers who, even today, are still oriented towards Russia in every way. There are, probably, objective reasons for this. Yet, in the minds of the Russian-speaking population, old stereotypes of the republics of Central Asia still prevail, which do not let them come to terms with the new situation in the region. Therefore, it is essential that those who consider Central Asia—Kazakhstan, Kyrgyzstan, Tajikistan, Turkmenistan and Uzbekistan—as their home be ready to "adopt the political culture of their new homeland without rejecting the cultural forms that exist in their countries of origin"'.[31]

In Uzbekistan, some academics view the adjustment of Russians and Russian-speakers to the way of thinking, way of life and behaviour of the modern Uzbek nation—known as '*uzbekchilik*', meaning 'uzbekization'—as the way to solve the current problem. They assume that *uzbekchilik* is possible for all people in Uzbekistan and is, therefore, a tool for bringing all ethnic groups together.[32]

The social base of the *uzbekchilik* movement consists primarily of small and medium-scale merchants, the 'New Uzbeks' who came from deep within traditional communities (*makhala*). For Europeanized Uzbeks, as well as for Russian and Russian-speaking intelligentsia, the *makhala*-based culture has both positive and negative connotations. The *uzbekchilik* movement has absorbed the cultural and social conservatism of the *makhala*, including the observance of certain traditional norms of behaviour and lifestyle. These norms are an extension of the traditional single-mindedness and social coherence that are foreign to a Europeanized way of life. This is why, in this Europeanized milieu, *uzbekchilik* usually becomes the object of ironic comments and jokes. Sometimes one comes across highly negative attitudes toward *uzbekchilik*. This is epitomized in the expression 'doing business the Uzbek way', which refers to such traits as close-mindedness, giving priority to family and clan interests, corruption, bribery, and other unsavoury commercial practices.

Another important factor, Uzbekistan's drifting away from Russia, has many causes. The most significant is the ever-present danger of Russian intervention under the pretext of defending the curtailed rights and interests of the Russian minority in Uzbekistan. The subject of the 'oppression' of Russians is raised every once in a while by Russian journalists, politicians, and nationalists. This problem is described extensively by Kymlicka in Part 1.

Putting more distance between the Central Asian states and Russia also weakens the political and cultural influence of Russia. It is appreciated, though, that the destruction of Soviet ideals and symbols could also increase the nostalgia for the Soviet past. For this reason, the debunked ideals have been replaced in each of the new states with specific, new ones around which, according to the thinking of national ideologues, the nation should rally and mobilize. In Uzbekistan, it is Amir Timur, the great conqueror and founder of the Timurid Empire of the fourteenth and fifteenth centuries; in Tajikistan, the Iranian dynasty of the Samanids—ninth and tenth centuries; in Kyrgyzstan, the national epic hero Manas; in Kazakhstan, to a certain extent, the ancient Turkic god Tengri; in Turkmenistan, President Turkmenbashi himself; in Russia, Peter the Great; and in Mongolia, Ghengis Khan.[33] Nurturing these idols in film, prose, poetry, fine art, theatre, and in the sciences creates a national alternative for the official art of each of the Central Asian states. 'The Seven Commandments of Manas' and Timur's 'Code', as well as other canonized texts, have been called upon to resolve moral and ethical problems, and to create a secular, nationally-based code of ethics that would parallel religious ideals.

In Uzbekistan, the distancing from an unpredictable Russia is made more difficult by the considerable Russian diaspora. Practically every Russian and Russian-speaker has relatives either in Russia or in other countries of the Commonwealth of Independent States.[34] After the dissolution of the USSR, the weakening of contacts with the historic homeland was first due to the disruption of transportation and communications. In the circumstances of the first years after independence, a new attitude towards the problem of national and ethnic minorities was developed in Uzbekistan, in parallel with the idea of national renaissance. This was the question of dual citizenship. It was addressed by President Karimov in the following way:

Politicians in certain states are raising the question of the right of their co-nationals to dual citizenship. Our answer to this is clear and simple. If one considers the situation in Uzbekistan, it would be necessary to give dual citizenship not only to one, but to many nations residing in the republic. Wouldn't such a situation constrict Uzbeks the most? What country should a person with dual citizenship love? Of which country should he be a patriot? And for which land, if circumstances should so dictate, should he give his life? We consider that the best situation is where all those who live in Uzbekistan are fully equal citizens, regardless of their origins, nationality or religion! We must live as one friendly family and fight together for a worthy future both in happy times and in times of tribulation! (Islam Karimov, 'Podnimaem vyshe potentsiali prestizh rodiny [We Will Raise the Potential and the Prestige of our Homeland]', speech given at the fourteenth session of the Supreme Soviet of the Uzbek Republic *Narodnoe Slovo*, (Tashkent) 248, 30 December 1993.)

In the last few years, the idea of a 'single friendly family' has started to take shape in Uzbekistan as a model of international and inter-ethnic relations. It is possible that, in many ways, it resembles the model of the former USSR. One of the main problems in its reali-zation is not only political and cultural distancing from Russia, but also distancing from Russians and Russian-speakers who live in Uzbekistan. The way to achieve this would be to unite them around a titular nation of Uzbeks—an 'older brother' of sorts—which would take the responsibility for the maintenance of international and inter-ethnic harmony in the government and in society. For this, it is essen-tial, on the one hand, to raise the status of the Uzbek nation as an ethnos with a great past and a great future, and bolster national con-sciousness and national pride. On the other hand, Russians, Russian-speakers, and all other resident nationalities should be mobilized in support of a strong and independent Uzbekistan and encouraged to participate on an equal footing with the titular nation in building a new democratic state with a great future. This approach promotes and reinforces the feeling among Russians and Russian-speakers in Uzbekistan that they are different from Russians in Russia. In this respect, some authors even talk about the formation in Uzbekistan, and in Central Asia in general, of a fundamentally different type of ethnocultural association of Russians and Russian-speakers.

To this end, cultural centres for national minorities were already being created in Uzbekistan in 1989 so that they might realize their cultural and other rights, and to give them equal opportunities in the development of their national consciousness. 'With the purpose of co-ordinating their activities, the Republican International Cul-tural Centre (RICC) was established to assist government agencies and public organisations which are engaged in cultural activities for ethnic minorities living in Uzbekistan.'[35] According to the RICC, Uzbekistan currently has more than thirty national cultural centres and associations including Armenian, Azerbaijani, Bashkir, Belorussian, Jewish, Kyrgyz, Korean, Russian, Tatar, and Ukrainian.[36] A new model of Uzbek culture to replace the model of Russian and Soviet culture can become a standard and rallying point for the entire range of ethnocultural expression in Uzbekistan.

It is evident that Uzbekistan's policy of balancing the development of the titular nation and various ethnocultural groups has led to a relatively stable intercommunal *modus vivendi*, and that 'consensus and pluralism is preserved in the polyethnic and multi-civilisation society of Uzbekistan.'[37] Yet, what are the chances of maintaining and strengthening this consensus? That is a question that is difficult to answer unequivocally because of the existing disagreements, which are practically never discussed publicly in Uzbekistan, between Uzbeks and Tajiks.

Uzbeks and Tajiks

The weight of mutual historical wrongs that has been accumulating between Uzbeks and Tajiks over a long time has, in the last few years, seriously spilled over into open polemics and discord. This schism is evident in practically all aspects of political and cultural activity. A strong, almost permanent, fuel for this discord is provided by the political and cultural history of the two nations, which has been interpreted in both countries in the last ten to fifteen years from a narrowly nationalistic point of view. The civil war, which exploded in Tajikistan and brought great material and intellectual loss to the country, has somewhat attenuated the nationalistic mood among certain Tajik politicians and members of the intelligentsia. Yet it did not, nor could it, eradicate the problem of Uzbek–Tajik relations.

The basic area of disagreement is that of culture, cultural heritage, and language policy. Two peoples who, for a long time, had close cultural relations, and even a cultural symbiosis, chose confrontation and warfare in the twentieth century, especially after Soviet authorities drew international borders in Central Asia. For the Tajiks, this demarcation of boundaries, which gave to Uzbekistan the two ancient centres of Tajik culture, Bukhara and Samarkand, constituted a great loss to national Tajik culture. This loss was significantly exacerbated as a result of assimilationist policies conducted by the leadership of Uzbekistan in Soviet times.

In fact, such policies, especially the language policy, were aimed at constraining and eradicating the Tajik language in bilingual (Tajik-Uzbek) cities of Uzbekistan. This, as well as the fight for mutual historical and cultural legacies, was common in Soviet times, perpetrated on many levels by the powers-that-be in Uzbekistan. The explanation for this policy should be sought, on the one hand, in the doctrine of 'Soviet nationalism' and, on the other, in the idea of Uzbek statehood.

It is no secret that in the young Uzbek nation, 'Uzbek national identity is a 20th century phenomenon and a direct product of Soviet policy on nationalities.'38 Yet, in spite of its youth, Uzbekistan has a great historical and cultural heritage and potential. For many historical and political reasons, primarily the existence in the last few centuries of Uzbek khanates, this heritage integrated the great cultural wealth created by various Central Asian peoples. The foundations of Uzbek culture were laid by the synthesis of two basic parts—Irano-Tajik and Turkic-Uzbek. Moreover, these correlate with two types of cultures—steppe and urban. Because of its diversity and conflict, this complicated synthesis holds huge potential for future development and, importantly, offers a permanent mechanism for integrating cultural values that were absorbed in the centuries-long process of interaction with other ethnocultural traditions.

After Uzbekistan declared independence, the Uzbek intelligentsia trebled its efforts in adopting and integrating cultural treasures that had been created on the territory of their country. This trend was supported by defining the temporal boundaries of Uzbek nationhood (2,700 years) and by including Ancient-Iranian ethnic foundations into the Uzbek ethnogenesis. An enormous job of translating texts from Persian to Uzbek and publishing literary, historical, and other sources dating from the Middle Ages was begun. Many Uzbek members of the intelligentsia who were educated in Soviet times have fully embraced the view that all religious treasures created on the territory of Uzbekistan belong exclusively to the Uzbeks. This trend fed directly into the new concept of the Uzbek national state, which is being built on a different set of historical assumptions than those existing at the time of the Uzbek khanates or even in the Soviet period.

In Tajikistan, hopes and illusions to reverse this situation still existed at the beginning of the 1990s, that is, after perestroika and before the civil war. At that time, a group of scholars from the Academy of Sciences of the Tajik Republic sent to Uzbek President Karimov, 'An Address to Academics and the Creative Intelligentsia of Brotherly Uzbekistan'.39 It expressed the hope of the Tajik intelligentsia that, 'in the period of revolutionary reconstruction and openness' attention will be given 'to the fair resolution of those problems which, in the years of the cult of the individual and *zastoi*, precluded to a certain extent our mutual understanding and mutual respect.' The address referred, in part, to the necessity of rejecting the ongoing policies of assimilation of the Tajik population, eliminating the idea of a common cultural heritage with Uzbeks, expanding opportunities for studying the Tajik language, adopting the Tajik language in Bukhara and Samarkand, and maintaining a 'fertile basis for the further development of Tajik culture' in the name of the 'traditional brotherhood and friendship' of the two peoples.

Observations made in the last few years show that efforts to address these specific issues and, in general, to solve the problem of Uzbek–Tajik relations have led, on the whole, toward the integration of Tajiks into the large independent Uzbek state. At the bottom of this lies the idea of kinship and even unity of the two peoples. This was made clear by President Karimov in one of his comments about the events in Tajikistan. 'More than any other country,' he said, 'we always helped the Tajik people, especially by supplying humanitarian aid and, as President of Uzbekistan, I am announcing that we will continue to help the suffering people of Tajikistan, who were always close to us both as a result of a shared historical past and in our religious traditions. I have spoken about this in the past and again state: *basically we are one people that speaks two languages, Tajik and Uzbek*'[40] (author's emphasis).

The idea of one people speaking two languages could serve as a basis for a true resolution of the problem, especially if the status of the Tajik language in Uzbekistan were changed. Expanding its use and possibly, in future, introducing it into school curricula could potentially resolve the basic problem of relations between Uzbeks and Tajiks. It would also address a whole range of other, no less important, problems, including access to the Persian-Tajik sources of the history and culture of Central Asia. This type of programme has direct historical analogues to the teachings of pre-revolutionary Central Asian wise men (*jadids*), including Bekhbudi, who proclaimed the necessity of studying several languages. Perhaps then the Tajik and Uzbek languages will be seen as two parts of a single Central Asian culture and not just as an indicator of national affiliation. This would help to resolve the problems between Uzbeks and Tajiks and support the rich historical past, whose renaissance has been spoken about so much in our times.

Conclusion

This article examined some of the problems that arose after the Central Asian republics acquired true independence. The conditions of the transition period open new avenues for solutions to existing problems. At the same time, though, the many differences that are emerging among Central Asian states, especially in the area of politics, are exacerbating the search for joint solutions to regional problems, including international and inter-ethnic relations. Should solutions not be found, the situation will remain unpredictable.

Political theorists, academics and politicians are constantly reminding us that multi-ethnic, multicivilizational, multicultural groups seem to be solidly entrenched in Central Asia. But will they be able to progress from rhetoric to real measures in the development of a multi-ethnocultural society and ethnocultural pluralism? This is a question for the entire post-Soviet territory, including Russia,[41] which is now broken into many 'small USSRs'. It seems that in building a new state, the leaders prefer to use old, well-tested methods, rather than following their stated approaches. For example, they fall back on ethnocultural homogeneity as a key element in building a new state and establishing cultural policies. And yet, the sad experience of world history has shown us that, 'the belief in the fact that the state-political community is only strong when it is based on ethnocultural homogeneity is one of the most tragic preconceived notions of the 20th century.'[42] It remains to be seen whether this preconceived notion can be abandoned and overcome in the twenty-first century.

NOTES

1. Much has already been written on the problem of the Fergana Valley, in Russian and other languages. One of the most recent studies was conducted by the Kyrgyz researcher, Anara Tabyshalieva. See 'The Challenge of Regional Co-operation in Central Asia. Preventing Ethnic Conflict in the Fergana Valley', *Peaceworks*, 28 (Washington, DC: United States Institute of Peace, June 1999).

2. R. Masov, *Istoriya topornogo razdeleniya [History of a Clumsy Partition]*, (Dushanbe, 1991) and *Tajiki: istoriya s grifom 'sovershenno sekretno' [Tajiks: A History Stamped 'Top-Secret']*, (Dushanbe, 1995).

3. In particular, see the monograph by Saidinisso Khakimova, 'Zalozhniki imperii [Hostages of the Empire]', 1998, 540.

4. The necessity for open discussion of the potentially explosive issue of inter-national borders was discussed at the conference, 'Problems and Prospects of Multilateral Cooperation in Central Asia', organized in August 1999 in Issyk-Kul by the Kyrgyz Institute of Regional Studies.

5. The conference, entitled 'The Improvement of National Relations in Light of Decisions Taken at the XXVII Congress of the CPSU', was held in Tashkent in April 1986.

6. One of the avenues for discussion was seminars held within the framework of the project called 'Central Asian Forum', organized by the Kyrgyz and Kazakh chapters of the Soros Foundation.

7. Islam A. Karimov, *Uzbekistan na poroge XXI veka. Ugrozy bezopasnosti,*

usloviya i garantii progresa [Uzbekistan on the Threshold of the Twenty-first Century. Threats to safety, conditions and guarantees of progress], (Tashkent, 1997) 69.

8. Sociological research for this study was conducted by the Department of Applied Sociology of the 'Ijtimoij Fikr' Public Opinion Centre of Uzbekistan.

9. Rano Ubaidullaeva, Yakov Umanskiy, Akmal Saidov *et al.*, 'Interethnic and Inter-confessional Relationships in Independent Uzbekistan', (Tashkent, 1999) 47. The material is based on the results of a sociological poll.

10. The high status awarded to the Russian language was the object of particular concern for the central and local party organs. Tremendous efforts in promoting the Russian language were made personally in Uzbekistan by Sharaf Rashidov, First Secretary of the Central Committee of the Communist Party of Uzbekistan. See, for instance, his article that defined the programme, 'Yazyk druzhby, edinstva i sotrudnichestva [Language of Friendship, Unity and Co-operation],' in Sharaf Rashidov, *Sobranie sochinenii [Collected Works]*, vol. 5 (Moscow, 1980) 250–321.

11. The 'tradition' of equating Russian and Soviet cultures was established, it seems, by Sovietologists during the Cold War and has been maintained to this day.

12. Boris Chukhovich, 'Kulturnyi mir molodykh khudozhnikov Uzbekistana, ikh sotsialnoye povedenie i tvorcheskyi vybor. Konets 80-kh i nachalo 90-kh godov [The Cultural World of Young Artists in Uzbekistan, their Social Behaviour and Creative Choices. End of the 80s and Beginning of the 90s', *Tsentral'naya Aziia [Central Asia]*, 15/3, 1998, 114.

13. *Slovo Kyrgyzstana*, 19–20 December 1995.

14. Auezkhan Kodar, 'Mesto predisloviya [In Lieu of a Foreword]', in *Kulturnye konteksty Kazakhstana: istoriya i sovremennost'. Materialy mezhdunarodnogo seminara posviashchenogo 100-letiyu M. O. Auezova [Cultural Contexts of Kazakhstan: History and Modern Times. Material from the international seminar dedicated to the 100th anniversary of M. O. Auezov]*, (Almaty, 1998) 3.

15. 'Vsled za ruskimi pushkami prikhodil Pushkin [After the Russian Cannons Came Pushkin]'. *451° Fahrenheit* is an independent socio/political weekly newspaper published in Irtysh. The Russian title of the article contains a play on *pushki*, the Russian word for cannon. *Zhuz* is the traditional division of Kazakh people into three groups, or *zhuz*—great, middle, and little.

16. The following quote is an example: 'This is the period of conquest by Russia of Central Asia and the establishment of Soviet power in Uzbekistan until the proclamation of state independence (from the second half of the nineteenth century to 1991).' Akmal Saidov, *The Legal System of Uzbekistan: History, Traditions and Renewal*, (Tashkent, 1998) 13.

17. One frequently finds articles and notes with distinctive titles such as, 'To Be Struck From Memory'. See, for example, *Pravda Vostoka [Truth of the East]*, 15 November 1997.

18. *Narodnoe Slovo*, 22 and 23 August 1997.

19. M. Iiuldoshev, 'Millatga Khos Iimon', *Guliston* (Tashkent) 6, 1996, 9.

20. See, for instance, Frunze Djuraev, 'Uzbekka opera kerakmi? [Do Uzbeks Need Opera?]', *Mulokot* (Tashkent) 5, 1991, 23–8.

21. The poet's work of this time can be found, in part, in Ruth Daibler, *Muhammad Salik i politicheskie preobrazovaniya v Uzbekistane v 1975–1995 godakh [Muhammad Salik and Political Reform in Uzbekistan in 1975–1995]*, (Bloomington, 1996) 16–27.

22. The process of re-immigration to Uzbekistan, which also occurs, is less important and does not equal emigration. Regarding re-immigration into Uzbekistan, see R. Ubaidullaeva, Ya. Umanskiy, M. Khodjimukhamedov, O. Atamirzaev, and A. Vakhidova, 'Re-immigration in Uzbekistan', *Public Opinion* (Tashkent) 2, 1998, 121–2.

23. See, for example, I. K. Faizullaev and Galina Saidova (eds.), *Independent Uzbekistan Today* (Tashkent, 1997) 62; M. M. Arenov, A. I. Babkin, S. V. Gmyrya, and K. K. Murzakhmetov, *Respublika Kazakhstana: informatsionnyi pasport [The Republic of Kazakhstan: Information Passport],* (Almaty, 1996) 4 and 5; and E. Yu. Sadovskaya, 'Vneshnaya migratsiya v respublike Kazakhstana v 1990-e godu: prichiny, posledstviya, prognoz [Internal Migration in the Kazakh Republic in 1990: reasons, consequences, prognosis]', in *Tsentral'naya Aziya i kul'tura mira [Central Asia and World Culture],* (Bishkek) 4/1, 1998, 56.

24. E. Yu. Sadovskaya, 'Vneshnaya migratsiya', 56.

25. Nurbulat Masanov, 'Politicheskaya i ekonomicheskaya elita Kazakhstana [The Political and Economic Elite of Kazakhstan]', in *Tsentral'naya Aziya i Kavkaz [Central Asia and the Caucasus],* 1, 1998, 82 ff. See also, Petr Svoik, 'Natsionalnyi vopros v Kazakhstane: vzgliad "ruskoyazychnogo" [The National Question in Kazakhstan: point of view of a "Russian speaker"]', in *Tsentral'naya Aziya [Central Asia],* 15/3, 1998, 28–38, as well as other articles in this issue. In a contrasting point of view, conjectures about the 'pro-Kazakh and anti-Russian policy that is apparently being conducted' are being written by 'advocates for the rights of the Russian-speaking population' and 'emissaries from Russia'. See Saken Amanzholov, 'Migratsiya, izmeneniya v etnokulture i rynok [Migration, Changes in the Ethnic Structure and the Market]', *Shakhar* (Almaty) 1993, 1, 33.

26. Masanov, 'Politicheskaya i ekonomicheskaya elita Kazakhstana'.

27. See, for instance, A'lo Khuzhaev, 'Uzbekistonda demokratiyaning Rivojlanishi va jamoatchilik fikri fenomeni [Development of Democracy in Uzbekistan and the Phenomenon of Public Opinion]', *Ujtimoii Fikr [Public Opinion],* (Tashkent) 1, 1998, 89.

28. This point of view is developed in part in newspaper articles and fiction of the Kazakh writer Morris Simashko. See, for instance, his novel, *Padenie Khanabad [The Fall of Khanabad]* in Volume 2 of his *Izbrannye v trekh tomakh [Collected Works],* (Alma Ata, 1992) 363–75. See also, 'Teni proshlogo—na stsena i v zhizni [Shades of the Past—on stage and in life]', (conversation between Yu. Egorov and Mark Weill) in *Literaturnaya Gazeta* (Literary Newspaper) 37, 10 November 1997.

29. Sh. Shukurov and R. Shukurov, 'O vole i kulture [On Will and Culture]', *Tsentral'naya Aziya i Kavkaz [Central Asia and the Caucasus],* 3/2, 1999, 196–205.

30. Suleev, 'Vsled za ruskimi'.

31. G. A. Bakieva, 'Sotsialnaya pamyat i tolerantnost' [Social Memory and Tolerance]', *Tsentral'naya Aziya i kultura mira [Central Asia and World Culture],* (Bishkek) 4/1, 1998, 40, with reference to Yu. Habermas, *Demokratsiya. Razum. Nravstvennost'. [Democracy. Reason. Morality.]* (Moscow, 1995), 243.

32. Akmal Saidov and Yakov Umansky, *The Factor of Polyethnicity in Uzbekistan—Challenges Regarding Security, Human Rights and the Potential for Development,* (Tashkent, 1998) 14.

33. On the resurrection of the cult of Ghengis Khan in Mongolia, see Morris Rossabi, 'Mongolia in the 1990s. From Commissars to Capitalists?' *Occasional Paper Series,* (The Project on Open Society in Central Eurasia) 2, August 1997, 5–6, 8.

34. 'Interethnic and Inter-confessional Relationships in Independent Uzbekistan', 28.
35. Ibid., 24.
36. Ibid., 26.
37. Saidov and Umansky, 'The Factor of Polyethnicity in Uzbekistan', 28.
38. Shahram Akbarzadeh, 'Nation-building in Uzbekistan', *Central Asian Survey*, 15/1, 1996, 24.
39. Dated at the beginning of 1990, this letter was only published for the first time seven years later in the Tajik newspaper *Chunbish*, 6, October 1997.
40. *Pravda Vostoka* (Truth of the East), 1 December 1998.
41. See, for instance, Vladimir Malakhov, 'Natsiya i kulturnyi pluralism. My poprezhnemu delaem vid zhiviom v odnorodnoy stranie [The Nation and Cultural Pluralism. We Are Again Acting as if We Were Living in a Homogeneous Country]', addendum to *Nezavisimaya Gazeta* [The Independent Newspaper], (Moscow) 7, June 1997, 2.
42. Ibid.

3

REPLY AND CONCLUSION

WILL KYMLICKA

REPLY AND CONCLUSION

Will Kymlicka

The commentaries raise many profound and complex issues, and I cannot address them all in this brief reply. Several of the commentators express general sympathy for the liberal pluralist approach I defended, and I'm encouraged by their support. For the purposes of this reply, however, I will focus on the main areas of disagreement. I'm grateful to the authors for the thoughtfulness and fair-mindedness of their criticisms, and for allowing me to have the last word.

I will look at four general worries about liberal pluralism that emerged repeatedly, in different forms, and which seem to me to underlie many of the more specific points regarding the application of liberal pluralism in particular countries. They are:

1. The role of élites in defining and manipulating minority claims. The worry here is that the sort of liberal pluralism I endorse would, in the ECE context, accord legitimacy to inauthentic claims, invented by self-appointed ethnic entrepreneurs, which do not reflect the real identities or interests of members of ethnocultural minorities.

2. The problem of intolerant minorities. The worry here is that liberal pluralism, in the ECE context, would simply change the scale or unit of oppression, rather than remove it. Minorities that were formerly oppressed by the central state would use their new-found rights and powers to establish oppressive regimes at the substate level.

3. The relative priority of democratic consolidation *vis-à-vis* minority rights. In order to avoid the first two sorts of concerns, it is clear that liberal pluralism will only work properly where there is genuine democratic accountability of leaders and firm protection of individual rights of both members and non-members. This raises the question whether we should defer minority rights until these liberal-democratic safeguards are well-established. The worry here is not just that minority rights would be potentially dangerous in

the absence of these safeguards, but also that the premature adoption of minority rights would make it more difficult to achieve democratic consolidation.[1]

4. The appropriateness of territorial autonomy. The concern here is that, even if liberal-democratic safeguards are in place, there may be features of the ECE that make Western-style models of federal or quasi-federal forms of territorial autonomy inappropriate.

I will address these points in turn. These are all important questions, and I cannot hope to resolve them fully here. However, I will try to show that many of the concerns about minority rights in ECE have also arisen in the West, and that there may be successful strategies for tackling them. I acknowledge that the barriers to the implementation of Western models are great in many ECE countries, and that the prospects that these models will be voluntarily adopted is quite slim in the foreseeable future. However, I will argue that these same barriers often make alternative strategies for accommodating diversity even less likely to succeed.

This suggests that the prospects for significant progress in ethnic relations are minimal in many ECE countries, at least in the absence of external pressure. And this in turn suggests that the evolution of minority rights in ECE may depend in large measure on the role of the international community. What role, if any, should international organizations—such as the EU, NATO, the Council of Europe, or the OSCE—play in encouraging or pressuring ECE countries to change their approach to minority issues? I address this in sections 5 and 6, and argue that while we must be modest in our expectations about the impact of external pressures, there is more that the international community can do to promote a healthier context for the discussion of minority rights claims. I then conclude with some more general reflections on the role of East–West—and Old World–New World—comparisons in the area of nationalism and minority rights (section 7).

1. The Role of Élites

One of the most common concerns raised in the commentaries is that ethnic élites in ECE are not representative of the members they claim to speak for. Élite constructions of 'group interest' are said to be 'more or less arbitrary' and do not reflect the real aspirations of group members. For example, Ossipov argues that most members of national minority groups in Russia accept and indeed prefer integration into the dominant Russian society—while maintaining their 'marginal' culture in 'private'—rather than seeking to form or maintain their own distinct societies with their own autonomous public institutions. It is only a handful of self-serving nationalist leaders who endorse minority nationalism. He worries that my approach would accord 'automatic' acceptance to their nationalist claims, regardless of the level of actual support for autonomy amongst members of minority groups.

This is a legitimate concern, of course, but how should we respond to it? The liberal pluralist response would be to insist on two safeguards. To ensure that self-proclaimed leaders of a group really do speak for the members of the group, we must establish forms of democratic accountability. For example, before we accord legitimacy to the claims of a political party advancing minority nationalist claims, we see whether they have been able to gain support in a free and fair election, where voters have a choice amongst many parties, and have access to information through a free press about government policies and about the platforms of these different parties, and can exercise a secret ballot to support the party which they find most attractive.[2] If nationalist parties cannot win in a free and fair election, we know they do not speak for the majority of group members. But if they do win such an election, then we can safely assume that they represent the desires of many citizens, and that their interpretation of the group's interests is not 'arbitrary', but rather is truly representative.

The experience of Western democracies shows that even when these mechanisms of democratic accountability are in place, nationalist parties can consistently gain clear victories in elections. In Catalonia, Scotland, Quebec, Flanders, and Puerto Rico, nationalist parties seeking greater autonomy consistently do well in free and fair elections, and there is every reason to believe that they reflect very widespread beliefs and interests of group members. Should we not expect that minority nationalist parties in ECE will also do well under conditions of democratic accountability?

It is possible that the ECE will be different from the West in this regard, but what is the evidence for thinking that national minorities in ECE will turn out to be less nationalist than national minorities in the West? This was the point of my concluding section, where I challenged the assumption that once ECE countries liberalize and democratize, ethnonationalist mobilization will decrease. As I said there, if the Western experience is an indication, it is possible that minority nationalist mobilization will actually be even stronger with liberalization and democratization. Perhaps truly accountable political leaders will be even more insistent in demands for language rights and political autonomy–although hopefully they would have a more liberal conception of how to exercise these national rights and powers: see section 2 below.

It may be difficult to establish such mechanisms of democratic accountability in some ECE countries. I discuss that question in section 3 below. Where accountability is absent, we shouldn't simply take the word of self-appointed ethnic entrepreneurs. We should look critically at whether they have genuine public support for their demands, and exercise our best judgement about what most members of a group would support if they had effective democratic rights. But we should do this in an even-handed manner. We should also look critically at the level of support for those self-proclaimed minority leaders who *reject* minority rights and argue instead for greater integration into the larger society. I can't see any reason for assuming that their pro-integration views are 'authentic' whereas the pro-nationalists are 'arbitrary'. The former can be just as self-serving as the latter, and just as out of touch with the views of the average member of the group.[3]

The strength of minority nationalist sentiment will vary from group to group, as it does in the West. But my guess is that, in many cases, members of national minorities, in free and fair elections, would provide substantial popular support to nationalist parties, just as they do in the West. To assume in advance that demands for autonomy or language rights do not reflect popular sentiments seems like wishful thinking.

The lack of democratic accountability is a serious issue, but it is important not to misdiagnose the problem. The accountability of political élites and the legitimacy of minority nationalist claims are two separate issues: you can have accountable élites supporting minority nationalism—as in the West—and unaccountable élites supporting integration—as in Russia. A liberal pluralist will want political leaders to be accountable, but will not try to pre-empt or prejudge what sorts of minority rights accountable leaders will demand.

Of course, even if minority nationalist parties can gain the support of most members of the group, there will still be some individuals who would prefer to integrate. And so we need a second procedural safeguard: namely, an individual right of exit from the minority group, which should be guaranteed by the constitution. This is a basic part of my liberal pluralist position, and is firmly guaranteed by Western constitutions.

I believe that when we have these two safeguards in place—effective mechanisms of democratic accountability, and individual rights of exit—then we have the means to assess the extent to which minority nationalist claims are truly representative. Under these conditions, group members are free to opt for integration both as individuals—via exit—and collectively—by voting for non-nationalist parties. If the nationalist parties nonetheless continue to win elections, then the interests promoted by nationalist parties are no more 'arbitrary' than any other political interests—be they class, or region, or environmentalist, or whatever. To say that minority nationalist construals of group interest are inherently illegitimate even when most group members have freely rejected the option of integration would be illiberal: this would be tantamount to saying not only that group members should be free to integrate—as guaranteed by the two safeguards—but that they should be forced to integrate: that is, they should not have the option of democratically choosing to resist integration and to maintain their own societal culture with their own self-govering institutions. And no liberal pluralist could accept that claim.

2. Intolerant Minorities

Several commentators raised the problem of intolerant minorities. If it is wrong for the state to coercively assimilate national minorities within the state, then it is equally wrong for minority nations to coercively assimilate smaller ethnocultural groups at the substate level. Yet in many ECE countries, we find that minorities who are free from oppression by the state exercise their freedom by oppressing internal minorities. This is part of what Dimitras and Papanikolatos call the paradox of minority rights.

This points out another of the many dilemmas and inconsistencies which plague public policies and public attitudes on this topic. In my paper, I mentioned how majority groups often exercise blatant double standards in evaluating minority rights claims. Majorities throughout the region deny rights to minority groups that they claim for themselves—and/or their kin-minorities in other countries.[4] But as the commentators note, we often find a comparable sort of hypocrisy amongst minority groups. They decry the injustice of being subject to nation-building pressure from the state, and of being excluded from a state which is said to 'belong' to the dominant group. Yet they impose precisely the same pressures on their own internal minorities, and claim that the substate region is 'theirs', and refuse to share public space with any other groups.[5] The prevalence of this sort of hypocrisy throughout the region is another manifestation of the weakness of any tradition of debating minority issues in terms of universal principles of justice and rights.

I tried to emphasize the need for a consistent approach to these questions in my paper. I argued that where federal or quasi-federal forms of minority autonomy have been adopted, nation-building policies will exist at both the state and substate levels, and we need to apply our liberal norms consistently at both levels. As I put it, 'national minorities should have the same tools of nation-building available to them, subject to the same liberal limitations' of respect for the rights of individuals and other ethnic groups. And as I noted, the point of these limitations is, *inter alia*, to reject any notion that a state or substate government belongs exclusively to one group.

So I agree with the commentators that the language of minority rights must not become a smokescreen behind which intolerant minorities oppress their own internal minorities. The goal of a liberal pluralist approach is to eliminate this sort of intolerance and injustice between ethnocultural groups, not simply to devolve tyranny from the state to substate levels.[6]

We may disagree, however, about how to deal with this danger. Some authors take the paradox of minority rights as a reason to reject self-government claims, at least until minorities have proven themselves to be liberal and tolerant of diversity.[7] Otherwise, recognizing self-government will simply shift the unit of oppression, rather than resolve the problem. Of course, if the central state is not tolerant, minorities may legitimately fear oppression. But some people think it will be easier to liberalize the majority culture and the central state apparatus than to liberalize the minority culture and the sub-state government. So even if the danger of intolerance arises at both levels, the two cases are not seen as symmetrical. The illiberalism of the majority is seen as easily remedied, whereas the illiberalism of the minority is seen as more deeply-rooted. Indeed, some people seem to think that it is intrinsically impossible to liberalize minority nationalisms.

This view is widely endorsed by both liberals and nationalists from the majority group in ECE. For example, as Opalski notes, this seems to be an implicit assumption of many Russian intellectuals.[8] This view often receives a receptive audience amongst many Western liberals, who also have typically assumed that minority nationalisms are inherently illiberal and 'ethnic'.[9]

I would argue, however, that the problem of oppression at the sub-state level can and should be handled in the same way as at the central level—namely, by developing judicially-enforceable constitutional safeguards for diversity and dissent. I see no reason to assume *a priori* that national minorities are less able or willing to abide by liberal constraints than the majority. The evidence from the West strongly suggests that national minorities have the same capacity to abide by constitutional norms and the rule of law as the majority. Minority nationalisms in the West are just as capable of being open and tolerant as majority nationalisms, and of respecting the rights of immigrants, refugees, and other ethnocultural groups. To be sure, minority nationalisms in the West vary in how well they score along the nine dimensions of liberal nation-building that I identified in my paper. Some score well on some criteria, and less well on others. This is equally true of majority nationalisms in the West. And the general trend throughout the West, for both majority and minority nationalisms, is towards a more open and liberal conception of nation-building.[10]

Perhaps the situation in ECE is different. Perhaps national minorities in ECE are less capable of liberalizing than majorities. But what is the evidence for such a claim? On what basis can we assume that the ethnic Hungarian minority in Slovakia is less capable of respecting constitutional limitations than the Slovak majority? On what basis can we assume that the Turks in Bulgaria are less capable of liberalization than the Bulgarian majority? No doubt there are some cases where the minority is less capable of liberalization than the majority, but I see no general rule here, and in some cases the opposite may be true. I don't mean to underestimate the difficulty of establishing meaningful constitutional limitations on governments in ECE, and I return to this in the next section. But there is nothing in logic, or in the Western experience, to suggest that this is inherently more difficult for substate governments than for central state governments.

In any event, it seems hypocritical to insist that minorities prove their liberal credentials before acquiring self-government rights when the majority doesn't face the same test.[11] This can just be an excuse to allow the majority to maintain indefinitely its oppressive rule over minorities. After all, it is extremely difficult for minorities who are being oppressed to prove their capacity for liberal governance. One needs a certain freedom of expression and political mobilization and self-governance to develop and prove this capacity. It is hypocritical for central states to suppress a minority's ability to exercise responsible government, and then point to the lack of responsible governance as a justification for its continued domination.[12]

In short, the problem of intolerant minorities is a real one. But the solution is to promote and support their liberalization, not to suppress their legitimate claims for autonomy. We should promote meaningful constitutional restrictions, enforced by an independent judiciary and international monitoring, on all forms of government, at the state or substate level. This is a crucial part of the success of liberal pluralism in the West, and it is surely the aim in the ECE as well. To be sure, substate governments will need assistance to liberalize in this way, as indeed will the central states. As Dimitras and Papanikolatos note, the international community must provide the means by which all governments in the region can live up to international standards of human and minority rights.

Some people think that multination federalism, even when circumscribed by liberal norms, involves a different kind of double standard, since it grants some kind of 'special status' to national minorities, rather than insisting on 'equal treatment'.[13] This too was a familiar refrain amongst many Western liberals in the past. But what does equal treatment mean in a multination state like Russia? Does it mean that everyone has an equal right to attend Russian-language schools? Or does it mean that everyone has an equal right to mother-tongue education? Some people claim that the former is 'equal treatment' and the latter is 'special status'. But I would argue just the opposite. To insist that all public institutions operate in Russian is to give the majority national groups a 'special status', whereas guarantees of mother-tongue education provide truly 'equal treatment'.

Some people might say that forcing everyone to learn Russian is not giving Russians any 'special status' because this is simply the result of democratic majority rule in which everyone has an equal right to vote. But this just pushes the question back a level: does equal treatment require giving everyone an equal vote in a centralized state, so that all decisions are made in a forum where ethnic Russians form a majority? Or does it require decentralizing decision-making so that important decisions are sometimes made in forums where national minorities form a local majority? Here again, some people think that the former is 'equal treatment' and the latter is 'special status'. But I would argue just the opposite. Requiring all major decisions to be made in forums where ethnic Russians form a majority is to give them a special status, and effectively disenfranchizes national minorities; whereas adopting multination federalism creates a genuine form of equal treatment, by giving national groups the same power to govern themselves and to live and work in their own language that the ethnic Russians have.

The whole language of 'equal treatment' and 'special status' is systematically ambiguous. Unless these terms are defined, they are rhetorical rather than analytical. Critics of minority rights describe whatever they dislike as a form of 'special status', but this just begs the question, since one can equally see minority rights as guaranteeing equal treatment. Indeed, the whole point of the liberal pluralist approach is precisely to say that 'special' minority rights achieve greater equality, by remedying disadvantages which national minorities face in unitary nation-states. Some people might deny that national minorities face disadvantages in multination states, or they might deny that the minority rights being claimed actually rectify the alleged disadvantage.[14] But to simply describe minority rights as 'special status' is not an argument against them. Critics need to explain how or why these forms of special status do not help achieve greater equality between the members of majority and minority groups.

In short, I agree with the claim that we should avoid double standards when evaluating majority and minority nationalism. But I would argue that multination federalism of the sort I described is an attempt to apply the same liberal standards to both majority and minority nationalism. Liberal pluralism says that both majority and minority nations are allowed to demand forms of self-government and to establish public institutions operating in their own language— where their members democratically express their wish to do so—but it also puts limits on the ways in which both majority and minority nations engage in this sort of nation-building: for example, they must give political rights to all permanent residents, they must allow a right of exit, they must respect the rights of other nations within their territory and be willing to share public space with them, and so on. So far as I can tell, this sort of liberal-pluralist view does not involve any double standards.

3. *Priority of State-Building and Democratic Consolidation*

So far, I have emphasized that liberal pluralism will only work successfully when liberal-democratic safeguards are in place. Norms of democratic accountability, tolerance, and human rights are not in conflict with norms of minority rights, but rather are integral to the successful practice of liberal pluralism and multination federalism in the West.[15] A liberal-pluralist approach would argue that the long-term goal in ECE should be the same: to endorse a robust set of minority rights with firm protections of democratic accountability and tolerance at both the state and substate levels.

Some commentators agree that this model of 'minority rights within liberal constraints' should indeed be the long-term goal for ECE, but disagree about how best to get there. I have implicitly suggested that we should promote minority rights and liberalization/ democratization simultaneously. Others, however, argue that we should give priority to the democratic consolidation of ECE states, and only then turn to issues of minority rights.

This is an important issue that I did not address in my paper. Drawing on the Western experience, I suggested that the idea of a 'liberal pluralism' is a coherent ideal, and a desirable long-term goal. But in the West, pluralization of the nation-state typically occurred after democracy was well established, whereas in ECE claims for pluralization of the state are occurring at the same time as the transition to democracy. This raises important complications that were not present, by and large, in the Western experience of implementing liberal pluralism. Even if the idea of liberal pluralism is a coherent and desirable one in the long-term, perhaps in the short-term we need to give priority to liberalization and democratization before addressing pluralization.

This is an urgent issue because some ECE states are structurally very weak. The problem is not simply the lack of effective liberal-democratic constitutional safeguards, but even the lack of any state capacity to implement policy and to enforce the law. As Doroszewska notes, the liberal-pluralist approach assumes that states are able to adopt and implement laws and policies, to uphold the rule of law, and to enforce rights. It assumes that states 'have the political will to solve problems resulting from their ethnocultural diversity; that there exists some sort of national 'majority' which defines the state's policy towards national 'minority'; and finally that the state has a vision of what this policy should or should not be, and makes the appropriate decisions to meet these objectives'. She argues that these assumptions are 'unwarranted' in many ECE countries, where quasi-criminal ruling élites are simply interested in privatizing public wealth, and not interested in social or minority issues (see pp 126–7 above).

Talking about minority rights is perhaps idle where there is no coherent framework of state power capable of adopting and implementing policies and upholding laws and rights. Discussing the merits of Western models of minority rights may seem pointless when some post-Soviet states aren't even able to collect taxes and investigate crimes.[16]

No doubt this varies from country to country. Not every ECE country is in the same condition of near-anarchy as Albania. But even in those countries that need desperately to increase their state capacity, what exactly follows from this for issues of minority rights? What is the relationship between adopting minority rights and improving the tax-collecting and law-enforcing capacity of the state? Would adopting minority rights help or hinder the effort to enhance state capacity?

Some people seem to think that the 'premature' adoption of minority rights would make it more difficult to achieve democratic state consolidation. On this view, granting language rights or territorial autonomy to minorities would detract from efforts to build state capacity, and so we need to defer the former until the latter is well-established.

That claim may be true, but it is not self-evident to me. How would denying autonomy to the Russians in Crimea make it easier for Ukraine to collect taxes? How does denying language rights to Hungarians in Slovakia make it easier for the Slovak government to investigate crimes, stop corruption, and enforce the rule of law? Why suppose that the only or best way to improve state capacity and the rule of law is to deny minorities their autonomy or language rights?

On the contrary, as Vàrady suggests, dealing with minority issues may in fact be a precondition to the modernization of the state. For one thing, as Schöpflin notes, the only way to build state capacity in modern societies is to do so consensually, and this requires the voluntary participation of citizens. Moreover, refusing to address minority issues can play into the hands of radicals and authoritarians amongst both the majority and minority. Since minorities will feel excluded from state-building, they will be visibly dissatisfied, which will reinforce majority fears that the minority is disloyal, and hence reinforce the power of intolerant majority nationalists, who say that democracy and liberalism must be subordinate to issues of national security. It will also reinforce the illiberal and authoritarian tendencies within the minority. Denied their legitimate rights by the majority, they exercise ever-tighter control over what little power they do possess (Reaume 1995: 121). Deferring minority rights in the name of promoting democratic consolidation is, therefore, likely to be counter-productive.

Here again, this may vary from country to country. But it seems to me that Russia and Ukraine would be much worse off today if they had not come to an accommodation with their national minorities, and that Serbia and Slovakia will be better off when they come to such an accommodation. We can also find indirect support for this in the

West. As I noted earlier, in many cases in the West, minority rights were only adopted after democratic consolidation had occurred. But there are a few exceptions, such as Spain. And virtually every commentator on the transition from dictatorship to democracy after the death of Franco agrees that the decision to federalize the country in order to accommodate Catalan and Basque nationalism aided in the consolidation of democracy. Why should the same not hold in the transition from dictatorship to democracy in ECE?

Minorities in ECE are often told that they should support 'democratic reformers' within the majority, and defer their minority rights claims until these democrats have successfully defeated the former Communists and democratized the state. Such a voluntary deferral of minority rights claims is supposed to help prove the loyalty and democratic credentials of the minority, and make the majority more sympathetic to their claims over the long-term.

No doubt this may be a sound strategy in some cases. However, much depends on the views of these 'reformers'. In Serbia, for example, the 'democratic opposition' in the 1990s was systematically hostile to minority claims.[17] There is no reason to believe that once in power, such reformers will miraculously convert to minority rights, rather than seeking to permanently entrench a highly centralized, majoritarian vision of democracy, and perhaps reduce even further the scope of minority autonomy and minority language rights. If anything, the fact that these countries are undergoing a transition is precisely a reason to tackle, rather than ignore, issues of minority rights. As Donald Horowitz notes, 'times of transition are often times of ethnic tension. When it looks as if the shape of the polity is being settled once and for all, apprehensions are likely to grow' (1985: 190). And as Pettai notes, this is what we see now in the Baltics. There is little doubt that over time, Russians in the Baltics will acquire greater rights and influence. But 'the shape of the polity' will already be fixed as a unitary, centralized nation-state, and Russians will have to find whatever bits of power and resources they can find within such a structure. There will be little chance of reopening questions about bilingualism or federalism that were 'deferred' in the name of democratic consolidation. These claims will not be deferred, but dead. This may or may not be an acceptable outcome for the Baltics, given their unique history, for the reasons I described in my paper. But I think it is a very dangerous idea to defer minority rights in countries like Romania or Macedonia if in the meantime notions of a highly centralized unitary nation-state are being permanently entrenched in the constitution—often by 'democratic reformers'.

More generally, it's simply wishful thinking to suppose that democratic reformers from majority groups in ECE are reliable allies for minorities. They are sometimes called—or call themselves—'liberals', but in many cases this simply means that they are anti-Communist and support a market economy. It doesn't mean that they are defenders of liberal-democratic values. As Schöpflin notes, these reformers have embraced certain democratic 'forms'—particularly majority rule—but not democratic 'values' of self-limitation, feedback, moderation, commitment, responsibility, and recognition of the value of independent and competing multiple rationalities.

So I see no basis for assuming as a general rule that minority rights should be deferred in the name of state consolidation. Moreover, as Fesenko's discussion of Ukraine shows, the weakness of legal arrangements has mixed consequences for minorities. On the one hand, minorities may actually benefit from the inability of the state to enforce its laws. For example, the fact that Ukraine is unable or unwilling to enforce its official language law probably helps the Russian-speakers, and the conflicts which might have arisen due to this law are being diffused by spontaneous self-regulatory social mechanisms—that is, legal requirements regarding the use of Ukrainian are replaced by informal bilingualism on the ground. More generally, minorities may benefit from the fact that states are weak or distracted by other issues and priorities—as noted in Doroszewska's commentary.

But the weakness of legal arrangements is a mixed blessing for minorities, since some self-regulatory mechanisms work in the opposite direction. For example, state policies, not just spontaneous self-regulation, are needed in cases where minorities require rectification of severe historic injustices—as with the Crimean Tatars. More generally in Ukraine there are liberal laws on national minorities that the state is unable to implement in practice due to the lack of resources or expertise—the same is true in Russia.[18]

This suggests a complex picture of the relationship between law and ethnocultural justice. In some cases, minorities benefit from the fact that a restrictive law is not implemented in practice; in other cases, minorities suffer from the inability of the state to implement a progressive law. The former suggests that a certain looseness in the application of laws can help ensure ethnic peace, the latter implies we need to strengthen the rule of law so that just laws can be better enforced.

A further complication, as Vàrady notes, is that even the best-designed and best-enforced legal rules often lack the sensitivity to

discern and prevent many of the common ways in which the majority can distort decision-making procedures in its favour. Laws can
only deal with certain formal or structural questions, leaving much
scope for the discretion of public officials. He argues that injustices
to minorities can only be contained by a 'group-sensitive' state that
is sincerely committed to informal codes or conventions of ethnic
fairness when making these discretionary decisions (Vàrady 1997:
43). In some countries, the presence of strong informal codes of
power-sharing can help mitigate the lack of formal minority rights
guarantees. But in other countries, the informal codes of decision-
making work to exclude minorities. To take one example, since independence Latvia has not had a single Russian member elected to
the National Radio and Television Council, despite the fact Russians
form 40 per cent of the audience of public radio and television in
Latvia.[19]

All of this suggests that it is unreasonable to ask minorities to
defer their minority rights claims in the name of state consolidation
unless they can be assured that: (a) the state will not use its enhanced
capacity to more rigorously enforce illiberal laws; (b) the state will
not use this period of transition to permanently or constitutionally
entrench centralized forms of majority rule that will be difficult to
renegotiate later on; and (c) the state will promote informal norms of
power-sharing, and a culture of tolerance, even if it cannot yet adopt
or implement more formal minority rights. So far as I can tell, few
ECE states show much willingness to abide by these constraints, and
so it is not surprising that few minorities are willing to defer their
claims.

None of this resolves the question of the lack of effective state
capacity. It remains true that adopting progressive minority rights
policies will have little tangible effect in many cases, since the state
cannot implement them. It may seem pointless, therefore, to adopt
progressive laws and constitutional provisions before they can be
implemented. But I would argue that even if these laws will only exist
on paper for the foreseeable future, they are important as indications
of a long-term approach and because institutions have enduring per-
formative effects. It is even possible, as in Russia, to adopt these policies simply as statements of aspirations rather than legally enforceable
duties. This may seem symbolic, but symbols are important. In any
event, this seems preferable to the alternative one often hears in ECE:
namely, telling minorities not to worry about illiberal laws or constitutional provisions on the grounds that the state cannot enforce them
anyway. This cavalier approach gives minorities a reason to fear and

resist the enhancing of state capacity, rather than a reason to co-operate as partners in building functioning democratic states.

4. Territorial Autonomy

The final issue raised by the commentators that I want to address concerns the desirability of adopting federal or quasi-federal forms of territorial autonomy (TA) as a mechanism for accommodating national minorities. Several commentators argue that while this mechanism may work in the West, it is not applicable to the ECE.

This scepticism of TA is widely shared, not only in ECE, but also amongst Western organizations dealing with minority rights in ECE. For example, Max Van der Stoel, the OSCE High Commissioner on National Minorities, has said that while minorities in ECE often seek TA, there are

good reasons for minorities to consider a pragmatic approach. Even though the [OSCE's] Copenhagen Document mentions territorial autonomy as an option, minorities should take into account the fact that such a demand will probably meet maximum resistance, whereas they might be able to achieve more if they concentrated on legislation that enabled them to have a greater say in fields of special interest for them, such as education and culture, or if they tried to concentrate on matters which, as well as having their support, also had the sympathy of many amongst the majority, such as an increase of the powers of local government   (van der Stoel 1999: 111–12).

He has also said, 'in my view, insufficient attention has been paid to the possibilities of non-territorial autonomy' (1999: 172). And indeed, as I discuss below, the OSCE has actively discouraged several minorities in ECE from demanding Western-style models of TA.

Several reasons are given for this reluctance to promote TA. One reason is the fact that the necessary liberal-democratic safeguards are not present in some ECE countries, so that minority leaders are not accountable, and human rights are not adequately protected. I have tried to address these points above. But others argue that even if and when these liberal safeguards are in place, TA would not be appropriate, for two major reasons: the dispersed and intermixed nature of ethnic settlement patterns in ECE; and the level of distrust between majority and minority groups.

I want to say a few words about each of these arguments. I should emphasize that my concern here is not to defend federalism or TA as such. TA is just one tool amongst many for promoting ethnocultural justice, and we should be open-minded about which of these tools work best in particular circumstances. What matters is that minorities are adequately protected from injustice at the hands of nation-building states, not that any particular mechanism be adopted for this purpose. However, I believe that TA has worked well in the West, and is worthy of serious consideration in ECE, and has not yet received a real hearing in the region. I also believe that the standard arguments given against TA in ECE reflect a misunderstanding of how TA works in the West and/or an underestimation of the sorts of injustices minorities can face in unitary systems. So my goal here is not to defend TA *per se*, but rather to clarify what is at stake when evaluating it or other possible tools for promoting ethnocultural justice.

The most common argument against TA is that national groups are intermixed in the ECE, and do not inhabit discrete, ethnically-pure homelands. No matter how the boundaries of a self-governing territory are drawn, there will be some people who live on that territory who do not belong to the national minority asserting rights of self-government—what I called 'internal minorities', such as ethnic Russians in Tatarstan. There will also be members of the national minority who live outside the self-governing territory—what we can call the minority's diaspora, such as ethnic Tatars who live outside Tatarstan, or ethnic Albanians who live outside Western Macedonia. In short, territorial autonomy is both under- and over-inclusive as a way of protecting national minorities. As a result, it is said, we should look for some other non-territorial mechanism.[20]

For example, Clause Offe says that territorial solutions 'won't do given the mixed and dispersed pattern of settlement of ethnic groups in Eastern Europe. . . . These peculiarities preclude the Spanish solution of granting the ethnic minorities inhabiting the Basque Lands, Galicia and Catalonia a statute of limited autonomy' (1993: 34).

I think this is a misleading argument. The intermixing of national groups exists in the West as well. In some cases, like Catalonia, there is only a small minority diaspora, but a very large internal minority—that is, there are only a few Catalans in Spain outside Catalonia, but ethnic Catalans formed a bare 52 per cent majority within Catalonia when autonomy was adopted. In other cases, like Puerto Rico, there is an enormous minority diaspora, but few internal minorities—around 50 per cent of Puerto Ricans have moved to the continental United States, but there are few minorities within Puerto Rico. And in yet other cases, like Quebec, there are both sizeable internal minorities and a sizeable minority diaspora—there are over a million non-francophones within Quebec, and over one million francophones outside Quebec. One could give many other examples. Consider the sizeable internal minorities in Flanders, the sizeable Swedish population in Finland living outside the autonomous area of the Åland Islands, or the native Indian population in North America, 50 per cent of whom live outside the self-governing reserves.

Indeed, internal minorities and minority diasporas can be found in virtually every Western example of territorial autonomy. The ECE is not so different in this respect. If TA were given to the Hungarian-populated areas of southern Slovakia, or the Albanian-populated areas of Western Macedonia, the size of the resulting internal minorities and minority diaspora—either as an absolute number or as a proportion of the population—is well within the range we find in Western examples of TA. Indeed, it would be less than in many Western examples. Offe's claim that the intermixing of peoples in ECE is radically different from that of the West is simply not true.

This raises an interesting question. If internal minorities and minority diasporas exist in the West, why do we see such a trend towards TA? Why hasn't the West adopted non-territorial models of minority rights instead of TA? I think there are three reasons, all of which may apply to ECE as well:

1. These options are not mutually exclusive. That is, the adoption of TA does not preclude adopting non-territorial forms of minority rights to protect the rights of internal minorities and minority diasporas. For example, francophones outside Quebec have certain non-territorial rights wherever they live in Canada—for example, to mother-tongue schools, to the use of French in federal courts, access to French-language TV.[21] But these are combined with special protections which arise through TA within Quebec—for example, that French is the language of public administration in Quebec; that Quebec has veto power over most constitutional changes. This is what we see throughout Western multination federations: a combination of territorial forms of minority autonomy with non-territorial principles of individual civil, political, and cultural rights. Commentators in ECE often assume that these are mutually exclusive options, but it doesn't work that way in the West, and I see no reason to assume it would be different in the East.

2. While TA primarily benefits minority members who live within the area of self-government, it also indirectly benefits the minority diaspora who live outside the territory. For example, it benefits French-Canadians living outside Quebec to have a French-

majority province with strong legislative powers to nurture French-language TV, radio, literature, institutions and so on. That francophones outside Quebec benefit from TA is evidenced by their strong support for Quebec's autonomy. Similarly, most Catalans living in Madrid support autonomy for Catalonia; most Puerto Ricans living in New York support autonomy for Puerto Rico, most ethnic Welsh living in England support autonomy for Wales; and so on. Perhaps it would be different in ECE, but I doubt it. My guess is that most ethnic Albanians in Skopje would support autonomy for Western Macedonia, and that most ethnic Tatars in Russia support autonomy for Tatarstan. States in ECE often invoke the interests of a minority diaspora as a reason for rejecting TA. But this is often hypocritical and paternalistic, particularly given that most of these states have made no effort to ask these minority diasporas whether they support TA.[22]

3. Why do members of the minority who live outside the self-governing homeland support TA? Perhaps because non-territorial forms of minority rights haven't protected national minorities from slow assimilation. For example, even with the most complete set of language rights, French-speakers were assimilating into English outside of Quebec. This is what sociolinguists call the 'territorial imperative' regarding languages in modern, industrialized societies. Language communities can only thrive and prosper if they have a robust set of institutions; and institutions can only survive if they both have concentrations of numbers and if they can offer avenues of advancement and opportunity; and these institutions can only offer avenues of advancement and opportunity if their language is the language of public life in the society. So even with the most generous set of language rights, French-Canadians in Vancouver lack the numbers to maintain the required institutions, and even if they had the numbers, these institutions cannot offer avenues of advancement since all economic and political opportunities in Vancouver are in English.

Members of minorities can see this plainly. They know that French will only survive in Canada if there is a place in Canada—that is, Quebec—where French is the dominant language of public life, and hence where French-language institutions offer avenues for advancement and opportunity. This is ensured by TA in Quebec, and by legislation that establishes the official status of French as the language of public life in Quebec, so that others who move to Quebec will have to learn French if they wish to advance and succeed.

In short, without TA, French will lose everywhere in Canada. With

TA, it will thrive in one place, and while this doesn't prevent long-term assimilation elsewhere, it can slow the process, since members of the minority outside Quebec benefit indirectly from the cultural production in Quebec. The same is true of linguistic minorities in Belgium, Spain, or Switzerland. In all of these cases, members of the minority diaspora outside the zone of TA believe that their linguistic community will suffer without TA, and that they benefit indirectly from the strength and security it provides.

Hence the trend in the West is in fact towards *greater* territorialization of minority rights regimes for national minorities. Consider Switzerland or Belgium or Canada. In all of these cases, there has been a shift in the balance between purely personal bilingualism—in which you take all of your language rights with you wherever you live in the country—and territorial bilingualism—in which each language group is self-governing in its territory, with fewer language rights outside.[23]

In short, the claim that non-territorial solutions are preferable to TA is subject to three major objections: (a) these aren't mutually exclusive options—it isn't an either/or choice; (b) without TA, national minorities will be subject to long-term assimilation no matter how strong their non-territorial protection; (c) TA is a benefit to, and is supported by, members who live outside the TA zone.

There is a very widespread belief—or hope—amongst many ECE intellectuals that non-territorial policies will be sufficient to accommodate ethnic diversity. This has become a veritable mantra amongst most commentators. However, the experience of the West provides little support for this belief. Perhaps the situation would be different in ECE, but I haven't seen any clear arguments or evidence to think so.

A second major objection to TA concerns the history and ongoing level of distrust between majority and minority. Several commentators have argued that trust is necessary for the successful functioning of federalism, and that the required level of trust is absent in ECE.[24] As Liebich puts it, the dissolution of the three Communist federations left

in their wake a strong suspicion amongst state elites (and perhaps the hope among minorities) that federalism is a step toward separatism. It is useless to argue that these federal states were fundamentally vitiated by their long experience of communism. Federalism has suffered a severe setback in Eastern Europe and all efforts to protect minorities must take account of this fact. We need to recognize legitimate fears about secession and give support to non-territorial forms of autonomy (Liebech 1995: 317).

As I noted in my paper, this preoccupation with issues of loyalty and state security is a defining feature of the public debate in ECE today, and any credible proposal must deal with this fact. Some commentators have argued that to be 'pragmatic', we must set aside any minority claims which will evoke or fan these majority fears. However, I think it is a mistake to filter every minority demand through the lens of the majority's fears about loyalty and security. I believe this is not only unjust, but indeed counter-productive from the point of view of peace and stability.

Throughout the region, states have tried to remove from the political agenda any minority claim which might lead to secession. They hope to do this, in part, by eliminating any talk of multination federalism or territorial autonomy. For example, the first sentence of the post-Communist Romanian constitution says 'Romania is a unitary and indivisible state'. Similarly, the Bulgarian constitution explicitly rules out the granting of territorial autonomy to any group for any reason—and indeed says that there are no minorities in Bulgaria, even though ethnic Turks are 10 per cent of the population.

The point of putting such statements in the constitution is to make the renouncing of claims to territorial autonomy the test-case for the loyalty of minorities. Anyone who even suggests federalism is, by definition, disloyal to the constitution, and hence can be ignored, denied a seat at the political table, and perhaps put under police surveillance as a security threat.

In this and other ways, the state says to its minorities 'we will talk to you about your interests and needs, but only if you first agree to renounce all claims to territorial autonomy, for ever'. There is a systematic effort throughout the region to delegitimize any mention of federalism, and to label anyone who even mentions it as radical, disloyal, and a traitor.[25]

But the loyalty test doesn't stop with renouncing claims to autonomy. After all, federalism isn't the only political mechanism that can be used as a basis for future secession or irredentism. For example, consociationalism—the solution proposed by Schöpflin—often involves recognizing a minority as one of the 'constituent nations' or 'state-founding peoples'. But if the minority is seen as having helped to found or constitute the state, then presumably it can decide to un-found the state, as it were. So countries in ECE firmly resist any notion of consociationalism which recognizes the equality of minorities as co-founders or co-possessors of the state.[26] Proposals to give a minority's language equal status as a co-official language—as exists in Belgium, Canada, or Switzerland—are rejected for the same reason.[27]

Similarly, any talk of 'collective rights' is often rejected as illegitimate and disloyal, since it can be seen as implying some notion of collective agency, and hence of self-government, and hence of potential secession. Some countries have even asserted that having universities in the minority's language is a threat to the existence of the state (Pritchard 2000). In short, minorities are required to renounce any claim that implies that the country is a *multination* state.

Put another way, the majority does not simply reject a particular means of sharing power with a minority—such as federalism—they reject the very principle of sharing power with a 'disloyal' minority—and a minority can only prove it is loyal by abandoning any claim to share power, and asking instead for only minor cultural rights.

This is the difficult situation confronting minorities today in many ECE countries. The state requires that minorities renounce forever any claim which might, however indirectly or remotely, at some indeterminate in the future, imply some claim to self-determination. This is required to get a seat at the political table. Any minority that won't renounce these claims is labeled as disloyal, radical, and a security threat. The first casualty of this attitude is minority demands for federalism or territorial autonomy, and so minorities turn instead to demands for consociationalism, veto rights, collective rights, official bilingualism, or universities in their language. But demands for any of these rights are interpreted as prima facie evidence, not of the desire to be accepted as a partner in the state, but of disloyalty to the state. As a result, virtually every major minority rights claim falls victim to the majority's fears and phobias.

If minorities are required to renounce all these claims as proof of their loyalty, in order to gain a seat at the political table, what then is left to negotiate? In effect, there are two sorts of claims which majorities are prepared to contemplate and negotiate: mother-tongue primary schools, and token forms of non-territorial political representation. These have been accepted by even the most virulently nationalist governments, such as Croatia under Tudjman or Slovakia under Meciar. They are accepted, I believe, largely because they are consistent with the goal of the long-term assimilation of minorities. Indeed, this was precisely the argument given to persuade countries to accept mother-tongue elementary education under the League of Nations minority protection scheme.[28] So long as all higher education is in the majority language, and so long as all legal and political institutions are centralized, then all avenues for economic advancement and political influence will require integrating into majority institutions. The minority group will be 'decapitated'—its educated élite will either assimilate or emigrate. Providing mother-tongue elementary schools provides the window-dressing of tolerance, but is not able, and is not intended, to reverse or slow down this process of minority decapitation. As Ina Druviete puts it, this sort of approach involves letting a minority group 'walk to their grave with their boots on' (Druviete 1997: 165).[29] Of course, countries cannot openly admit that this is their long-term goal, which helps to explain the oft-noted fact that these countries offer 'no coherent vision of the future' regarding their minorities. They reject federalism and territorial autonomy, but offer no alternative in its place (Mihalikova 1998).

If this is an accurate description of the situation today, then we can safely conclude that there is little chance for the internally-generated and democratically-mandated adoption of significant minority rights. Few ECE countries have gone beyond mother-tongue schools and token political representation, and where they have it is typically the result of external pressure and/or extra-parliamentary power-grabs by the minority. Where those two factors are absent, states have not adopted significant minority rights. That is the record we see since 1989,[30] and I suspect it will remain true for the foreseeable future.[31] (This also makes the Russian exception more interesting).[32]

On this issue, therefore, the East and West appear to be moving farther apart. In the West, it is considered legitimate that national minorities demand territorial autonomy, and indeed these demands are increasingly accepted. Most national minorities in the West have greater autonomy than before, and none have been stripped of their autonomy. The idea of territorial autonomy is accepted in principle, and adopted in practice. The old self-image of states as unified nation-states is being replaced with the new self-image of states as multination federations and/or as partnerships between two or more peoples.

By contrast, in ECE, many national minorities have less autonomy than they had 30 or 50 years ago, and it is considered illegitimate for minorities to even mention autonomy, or to make any other proposal which would involve redefining the state as a multination state. ECE countries cling to the old model of unitary nation-states, in which minorities ideally are politically weak, deprived of intellectual leadership, and subject to long-term assimilation.

These are generalizations, of course, and I've emphasized that there are exceptions in each case. In the West, France and Greece remain adamantly opposed to multination federalism, and in the East, Russia has adopted it. But these are anomalies.[33] As a rule, the prospects for the internally-generated adoption of significant minority rights in ECE are dim.

I believe that the hostility to federalism in ECE must be understood in this wider context. It is just one manifestation of an underlying condition that makes any reasonable accommodation of diversity impossible. I believe that the inability to accommodate minority nationalism in ECE is potentially detrimental not just to the minorities, but to democracy itself, and to the existence of a peaceful civil society. There is a clear correlation between democratization and minority nationalism. Those ECE countries without significant minority nationalisms have democratized successfully—Czech Republic, Hungary, Slovenia, Poland—those countries with powerful minority nationalisms are having a more difficult time—Slovakia, Ukraine, Romania, Serbia, Macedonia, and Georgia. The minority issue is not of course the only factor here, but I believe it is an important one.

In an interesting essay first published in 1946, Istvan Bibo provided a thoughtful analysis of this problem. He argues that the experience of nineteenth-century Hungary taught leaders that their minorities might use their democratic freedom to secede. Ever since, ECE states have feared the exercise of democratic freedoms by minorities. As a result, they have consistently tried to suppress, dilute or contain these democratic freedoms, sometimes by embracing fascism or other forms of authoritarianism—that is, by suppressing everyone's freedom—sometimes by disempowering minorities—that is, by suppressing the minority's freedom. But in either case, the result is a stunted and fearful form of democracy. As he puts it,

In a paralyzing state of fear which asserts that freedom's progress endangers the interests of the nation, one cannot take full advantage of the benefits offered by democracy. Being a democrat means, primarily, not to be afraid: not to be afraid of those who have different opinions, speak different languages, or belong to other races. The countries of Central and Eastern Europe were afraid because they were not fully developed mature democracies, and they could not become fully developed mature democracies because they were afraid (Bibo 1991: 42)

I believe that this remains true today. Most ECE states with minority nationalisms have the shell of liberal democracy, but remain afraid of the full and free exercise of democratic freedoms.

5. Minority Rights and European Integration

If this is right, the fate of minority rights in Eastern Europe will depend heavily on whether or how external pressure is applied to ECE countries. In particular, will Western organizations pressure

ECE countries to adopt more robust forms of minority rights? Western organizations clearly have the *ability* to impose enormous pressure.[34] The West has said that admission into NATO or the EU is conditional on meeting certain minority rights standards, but has not yet clarified what these standards are, and could in principle set them quite high. Many countries in ECE would probably accept these conditions, since they are desperate to get into Western organizations, which they believe will help ensure their security and prosperity. And they have little bargaining power with which to challenge these conditions. ECE countries need the EU and NATO much more than the EU and NATO need ECE countries. These Western organizations would survive and thrive perfectly well if some or all ECE countries stayed outside the fold. So at least for the foreseeable future, Western organizations can afford to set strong conditions for admission. For example, the Council of Europe has successfully insisted that ECE countries abolish the death penalty, despite very strong public opinion—including élite opinion—in favour of it in many countries. Similarly, it would be possible for Western organizations to set strong standards regarding minority rights, and to get ECE countries to agree to the monitoring and enforcement of them as a condition of 'rejoining Europe'. If the EU said that Macedonia can only join if it creates an Albanian-language university in Tetovo, as the Albanian minority wants, Macedonia would probably accept, however reluctantly. If the EU said that Romania can only join if it restores autonomy to Transylvania, Romania would probably accept. If NATO said that Estonia can join only if it grants immediate citizenship to all its Russian residents, Estonia would probably accept.[35]

And indeed the West has used its leverage to pressure various ECE countries to improve their treatment of minorities. But it has done so in a curious way that has evolved over time. The initial strategy involved what we can call a justice-based approach. This involves codifying a set of 'universal' standards that all countries within the EU, NATO, the Council of Europe, or the OSCE would have to meet. It seemed in 1990 that Western countries had agreed to establish such a code of minority rights. The outlines of such a universal code were sketched in the 1990 Copenhagen Declaration of the OSCE, and reaffirmed in its Geneva Declaration. These OSCE declarations were statements of political commitments, rather than legally binding treaties or international law, but it was assumed that a legally binding convention would soon follow, and indeed the Council of Europe began to draft such a convention. The premise of this justice-based approach is that minority rights are indeed matters of *rights*, and of fundamental justice, and hence are a necessary supplement to traditional human rights. These minority rights standards would be designed to protect minorities from the standard sorts of threats they face within modern nation-states.

There is no reason to assume that such a justice-based approach would or should insist on any particular form of federalism or TA. After all, TA is just one possible means for achieving justice in a multi-nation state, not an end in itself. The underlying principle is a more general one that the minority should have some meaningful form of self-government; or, put the other way around, that the minority should have some guarantee that it will not be outvoted or outbid on matters that are fundamental to the survival and flourishing of its culture and community. This can be achieved by various means, either by allowing the minority to govern its own institutions, or by ensuring that the minority can exercise a veto over the governance of common institutions. But in either case, it involves some explicit form of power-sharing, to reduce the vulnerability of the minority to the economic and political power of the majority. What we would expect, then, in a justice-based approach, is a general principle of power-sharing, either on a territorial or consociational basis.

We saw the outline of such an approach in the initial 1990 OSCE Copenhagen declaration. This endorsed TA as a good practice, but did not impose any obligation to grant TA in particular, recognizing that there were alternative ways of ensuring the fair accommodation of diversity, including more consociational arrangements. But the implication was that states were under an obligation to do something to ensure a fairer distribution of political power and public resources between majority and minority. The strongest endorsement of autonomy by any Western intergovernmental organization came in Recommendation 1201 of the Council of Europe Parliamentary Assembly, adopted in 1993, which contains a clause (article 11) stating that 'in the regions where they are a majority, the persons belonging to a national minority shall have the right to have at their disposal appropriate local or autonomous authorities or to have a special status, matching this specific historical and territorial situation and in accordance with the domestic legislation of the State'. This Recom-mendation was not legally binding, but still in the early 1990s it seemed that there was some movement in the direction of endorsing a universal principle that justice required some or other effective mechanism for sharing power between majority and minorities, specifically mentioning TA as one such mechanism.

Since then, however, there has been a marked movement away from the endorsement of TA. This is for two reasons. First, as the OSCE High Commissioner on National Minorities has noted, claims to TA are likely to meet 'maximal resistance' on the part of states in ECE, and so would require maximal pressure from Western states to achieve. This would make relations with ECE states much more conflictual and costly. Hence it is more 'pragmatic' to focus on more modest forms of minority rights (van der Stoel 1999: 111). Second, and equally important, there was strong opposition to the idea of entrenching a right to TA for minorities *in the West*, and also to the idea that there would be international monitoring of how Western states treated their minorities. As I noted earlier, France, Greece, and Turkey remain adamantly opposed to the very idea of self-government rights for national minorities, and indeed deny the very existence of national minorities.[36] And even those Western countries that accept the principle do not necessarily want *their* laws and policies regarding national minorities subject to international monitoring. This is true, for example, of Switzerland and the United States (Chandler 1999: 66–8; Ford 1999: 49). The treatment of national minorities in various Western countries remains a politically sensitive topic, and many countries may not want their majority-minority settlements, often the result of long and painful negotiation processes, reopened by international monitoring agencies. In short, while they were willing to insist that ECE states be monitored for their treatment of minorities, they do not want their own treatment of minorities examined.[37]

This sort of double standard was an explicit part of the earlier minority protection scheme under the League of Nations, and is widely viewed as one of the reasons for the failure of that system (Alexanderson 1997; Burgess 1999). In an attempt to avoid the appearance of a similar hypocrisy today, Western countries have moved along two different and somewhat contradictory tracks. On the one hand, they have maintained but weakened the commitment to a universal, justice-based, minority rights track; on the other hand, they have created a new contextual, security-based minority rights track. Both tracks raise interesting and important questions.

Let me start with the universal minority-rights track. Western organizations have maintained a commitment to the idea of developing such general standards, but have diluted both their content and enforcement. The legally-binding document which was eventually adopted by the Council of Europe in 1995—the Framework Convention for the Protection of National Minorities (FC)—is weaker than either the 1990 OSCE declaration or the 1993 Recommendation 1201 of the Parliamentary Assembly. Whereas these earlier documents recommended or even required some form of self-government for minorities, the FC makes no reference to this idea.[38] Similarly, the FC says nothing about issues of official language status, or mother-tongue universities, or consociationalism. Moreover, the West rejected any attempt to make the FC judicially enforceable. It was originally proposed that individuals would be able to take cases of violations of their FC minority rights to the European Court of Human Rights, just as individuals can take violations of their human rights under the European Charter of Human Rights. But this was dropped from the FC, and there is now no effective enforcement mechanism.[39]

Much the same applies to the universal minority rights norms articulated by the OSCE, such as its recent recommendations on linguistic, education and participation rights.[40] While these recommendations clarify some of the rights listed in the FC, they too do not broach issues of official language status, territorial autonomy, consociationalism or mother-tongue universities. Indeed, the OSCE, like the Council of Europe, has backed away from the idea that there is a right to autonomy or any other form of power-sharing, and mentions autonomy only as one possible option on a 'shopping list' of good practices which states are free to adopt or not as they see fit (Thornberry 1998: 112).[41] Even when autonomy is listed as one possible option, it is never linked to any right or principle of self-government (Zaagman 1999: 5, n13; Zaagman 1997: 250). And in any event, the OSCE's universal norms have no legal force. They are considered political documents, not international law, and there is no judicial overview of these norms, nor any obligation of states to report on their adherence to them.

In short, the sorts of universal norms which have been developed by Western organizations since 1995 are quite weak in both content and enforcement. Partly in order to appease those Western states that opposed substantive and/or enforceable minority rights, the obligations of all states were weakened.

It was clear, however, that this weak Framework Convention would not solve minority issues in ECE. The FC provides far less than most minorities—in either the East or West—feel entitled to. Almost all the cases of serious ethnic conflict in ECE involve issues that are left unaddressed by the FC, such as the desire of Albanians in Macedonia for official-language status, the desire of Russians in Crimea for territorial autonomy, or the desire of Hungarians in Romania for a mother-tongue university.

In order to help resolve these conflicts, the West needed some other basis to advise and pressure ECE countries to do more for their minorities than was required by the FC. To this end, the West created a second minority rights track, defined in terms of 'security'. On this second track, the OSCE was given the mandate to monitor the status of national minorities, not whenever universal minority rights were violated, but whenever ethnic conflict threatens international security. Even if an ECE country was meeting all of its obligations under the Framework Convention, the OSCE could still intervene in order to help defuse majority–minority tensions that threatened violence or regional stability.

The main instrument for pursuing this security-track is the office of the High Commissioner on National Minorities (HCNM) within the OSCE, created in 1992—the office so far has been held continuously by the Dutch diplomat Max van der Stoel. It is important to emphasize that the mandate of the HCNM is to promote international security, not to monitor or enforce international principles of minority rights. As he himself repeatedly emphasizes, he is the High Commissioner ON national minorities, not a High Commissioner FOR national minorities (van der Stoel 1999: 133). He is neither an advocate for the rights of national minorities, nor an ombudsman to investigate the violation of such rights. Rather his mandate is to provide early warning and advice regarding potential sources of instability.[42]

The fact that the OSCE/HCNM's mandate is security-focused has two important implications. First, it provides a rationale for the differential treatment of East and West. The HCNM's activities to date have focused exclusively on ECE countries—he has not initiated an investigation into, or offered recommendations regarding, any Western country's minority rights record. The justification for this is that even where Western states contain secessionist movements—as in Quebec and Scotland—or terrorist groups—as in Northern Ireland and the Basque Country—these conflicts are not 'security' issues in the relevant sense, since they are not a threat to international peace, however much they cause domestic anxiety (Chandler 1999).[43] So whereas the first track of universal minority rights applies identically to all countries, and imposes the same (weak) obligations on East and West, the second security track provides a rationale for differential treatment of East and West.

This is an important contrast from the League of Nations minority protection scheme, which involved a more explicit double standard. The inter-war League of Nations system was premised on the idea that 'although justice would require identical obligations from everyone, in practice some countries, enjoying a higher standard of civilization, "had already grown out of" the period of intolerance, and thus did not deserve to be under any limitations' (Burgess 1999: 52). Hence the League did not ask or expect Britain to sign international agreements regarding the Irish, or France regarding Algeria, or the US regarding the blacks. In the current two-track system, the differential treatment of East and West is more subtle. On the one hand, the first justice-based track does mandate respect for an identical set of rights under the FC on all countries, and imposes identical reporting requirements. On the other hand, the second security-track focuses exclusively on ECE, and generates levels of intervention and monitoring of ECE not found in the West. It is now security considerations, not differential legal obligations or levels of 'civilization', which are supposed to explain the differential treatment.

The security mandate has another important implication. The HCNM is allowed by his mandate to recommend forms of minority rights beyond those required by the FC, if in his opinion they would help to ensure stability. He can recommend that ECE states provide territorial autonomy, or official language status, or consociational veto rights, or mother-tongue universities, even though none of these are required under international law. While these recommendations are not legally binding, they are extremely important, since the EU has said repeatedly that ECE countries seeking accession to the EU are expected to follow the HCNM's advice. The EU and NATO have in effect delegated to the HCNM the task of judging whether ECE countries have 'done enough' in terms of minority rights.[44]

This new security-based track has become the dominant means by which Western states seek to pressure ECE states regarding minority issues. It is increasingly clear that admission to the EU and NATO requires not only ratifying the FC, but also accepting the recommendations of the HCNM, which often go beyond the requirements of the FC.

In principle, this new security-track creates the potential for Western states to pressure ECE states to adopt strong forms of minority rights—including perhaps multination federalism—in the name of security, without endorsing these rights as a matter of justice—and hence as an obligation of Western states. After all, as I discussed earlier, many commentators believe that accommodating minority nationalism through self-government arrangements has promoted stability in Western states, and would do so in ECE as well.[45]

In fact, however, the West has sent out mixed signals regarding TA in ECE. The HCNM is generally sceptical of TA, and has tended to assume that it is a threat to security in ECE. Van der Stoel has been 'very reluctant to propose territorial solutions for minority issues', on the grounds that 'states are mostly not willing to contemplate such arrangements, as is reflected in OSCE norms and OSCE state practice which give little support for claims to territorial autonomy'. It is only in 'exceptional cases' or 'atypical cases' like Crimea or Gaugazia that the OSCE has explored the possibilities of autonomy—that is, as a last resort, when the only alternative is civil war (Zaagman 1999: 16; Zaagman 1997: 253–4). Even where the OSCE has promoted autonomy, it has done so not as a 'right' or as a 'constitutive premise'—that is, not on the premise that the minority has any inherent right of self-government—but simply as a voluntary act of devolution by the central legislature. OSCE principles entail that each state is the sole possessor of sovereignty within its borders.[46]

Indeed, the OSCE is actually now *discouraging* demands for territorial autonomy on the part of some national minorities. Such demands are discouraged on the ground that, while they may promote a fairer distribution of power or resources within the country, they jeopardize international stability. As van der Stoel puts it, 'I would oppose the choice for territorial autonomy if such a formula would lead to potentially dangerous tensions. In fact, my mandate requires me to take this line' (van der Stoel 1999: 26). On this basis he has discouraged the Albanian minority in Macedonia from demanding autonomy, since this would inflame passions in an already-tense region. So too with the Hungarian minority in Slovakia (Mihalikova 1998: 162). As one commentator puts it, the OSCE operates on the premise that demands for autonomy 'would only result in a strong increase in tensions, instead of building them down. Such arrangements are only a real option when relations are already more or less relaxed and not a useful instrument for making them relaxed' (Zaagman 1997: 253).[47]

So, as part of its security approach, the OSCE is now telling some minorities to give up their aspirations to TA.[48] This is understandable given that 'demands for territorial autonomy are almost always rejected out of hand by the government concerned' (Zaagman 1997: 253). It makes a certain amount of sense for international organizations to tell minorities to be more 'realistic' in their demands. And the OSCE has had definite success in moderating some of the more repressive laws in some countries.[49] But I have reservations about this strategy. There probably was a need to combine a justice-based track, involving the codification of universal minority rights, with a security-based track, involving country-specific recommendations to defuse dangerous tensions. But the particular way these two tracks have been combined raises a number of questions.

First, it is still perceived as containing a double standard in the treatment of West and East. The claim that it is only in ECE countries that ethnic conflict has international security implications is dubious. Of course, much depends on what we mean by 'security'. In its traditional understanding, international security means the absence of war between states, and this indeed is the crux of the HCNM's mandate: his office is 'a security mechanism aiming at the prevention of armed conflict between [OSCE] states' (Packer 1996: 265).

If this is the concern, then it is very difficult to understand why the OSCE has intervened regarding the Hungarian minorities in Romania and Slovakia. No serious commentator has supposed that there was a potential for war between Hungary and its neighbours. And while there were initial fears about possible armed conflict between Russia and the Baltics, most commentators today stress that the likelihood of this happening has now vanished. Yet the HCNM continues to aggressively monitor and pressure Latvia and Estonia regarding their minority policies. The OSCE missions to these countries continue long after any credible threat of interstate war has disappeared. It is also difficult to understand why the HCNM has taken such an active interest in the plight of the Roma in ECE countries, which can hardly be seen as a cause of international war.

In order to explain this continuing intervention in ECE countries, the OSCE sometimes refers to a more diffuse notion of interstate 'tensions'. It is certainly true that the rights of the Hungarian minority remains a source of 'tension' between Hungary and its neighbours, or that the rights of Russians are a source of 'tension' between Russia and its Baltic neighbours. But this is hardly unique to the ECE. The rights of the Catholics in Northern Ireland are a source of tension between Ireland and Britain; the rights of the German-speakers in South Tyrol are a source of 'tension' between Austria and Italy; Finland has complained about the treatment of Finnish-speakers in Norway; Slovenia has complained about the treatment of Slovenian minorities in Austria and Italy; and the treatment of the Basques has been a source of tension between France and Spain. There is little chance of these tensions escalating into armed conflict, but that is true in many ECE countries as well.

In explaining its activities in ECE, the OSCE also sometimes appeals to a different and broader notion of security: what is called 'comprehensive security'. This includes not just the absence of war, but also economic development and the 'human dimension' of democracy, justice, and human rights. According to this 'comprehensive security' doctrine, true or full security will only be achieved when states develop an inclusive and democratic political culture free of xenophobia, racism, and discrimination. Interpreted in this expansive way, 'security' considerations can justify intervening in ECE countries even where the minority issues pose little or no threat of international war or even international tensions—for example, with the Roma. Interpreted in this expansive way, however, one could equally argue that OSCE intervention is needed to fight racism and discrimination against African-Americans in the US, or against Turks in Germany, or against the Roma in Spain.

The point is that the criteria of security seem to be applied differently in the ECE and the West. When applied to the West, 'security' is interpreted narrowly to mean the absence of war between states, and on this basis, Western states are exempted from OSCE scrutiny.[50] But in ECE, the notion of security is expanded in various directions to justify intervention in countries where there is little or no prospect of interstate war. More generally, we could say that when Western organizations were developing this new security track, they were very careful to craft it in such a way as to minimize the likelihood that the HCNM would intervene in the West, while providing maximal freedom to intervene in ECE. This reinforces the widespread perception that the West is imposing minority rights on ECE as a matter of power politics, rather than sincere conviction.[51]

Second, and relatedly, there appear to be inconsistencies and double standards in the way this security track operates *within* the ECE. The demands made by the OSCE vary enormously from country to country. Compare Estonia, Slovakia, and Serbia. In Estonia, the OSCE has been demanding citizenship for the Russian minority, but has done little to stop Estonia from closing down Russian-language schools and institutions. In Slovakia, the OSCE has been demanding mother-tongue schools for the Hungarian minority, but has not supported demands for TA or a Hungarian-language university, and has not protested the redrawing of internal boundaries to disempower the Hungarian minority.[52] In Serbia, the OSCE has been demanding not only Albanian schools, but also an Albanian-language university and the restoration of Kosovo's territorial autonomy.[53]

It is not clear to most East Europeans what logic or principles underlie these actions. The problem is not only that the demands seem to vary from country to country, but also seem to change over time for a particular country: the goal posts keep moving.[54] These varying and evolving recommendations may reflect a sensible assessment of what would best promote security—in one or more of the senses discussed above—in the particular circumstances of each country at a particular time. But at least in some cases, they seem instead to be driven by considerations quite unrelated to the actual conditions on the ground. For example, the claim that Slovakia's mistreatment of Hungarians during the Meciar administration could lead to war was widely disputed in ECE, and was seen as a pretext for the fact that most Western countries despised Meciar, and wanted to put the screws to him (Burgess 1999). Conversely, when the West needs a friend or ally, as with Russia or Turkey, it turns a blind eye to the mistreatment of minorities, even when these really do have serious implications for international security, as in Chechnya or Kurdistan.[55] As a result, Western concerns about minority rights are widely seen as arbitrary and disingenuous in ECE.[56]

Third, the security track approach provides a perverse incentive for both the state and the minority to escalate the conflict. It gives the state an incentive to invent or exaggerate rumours of kin-state manipulation of the minority, so as to reinforce their claim that the minority is disloyal and that extending minority rights would jeopardize the security of the state. It also gives the minority an incentive to threaten violence or simply to seize power, since this is the only way its grievances will reach the attention of the international community. Merely being treated unjustly is not enough to get Western attention or sympathy these days.[57]

For example, consider the OSCE's approach to TA. As we've seen, the OSCE has discouraged TA in several cases, including in Slovakia for the Hungarians, or Macedonia for the Albanians. But the OSCE has in fact supported autonomy in several other countries, including Ukraine (for Crimea), Moldova (for Gaugazia and TransDneister), Georgia (for Abkhazia and Ossetia), Azerbaijan (for Ngorno-Karabakh) and Serbia (for Kosovo). What explains this variation? The OSCE says that the latter cases are 'exceptional' or 'atypical' (Zaagman 1997: 253, n84), but so far as I can tell, the only way in which they are exceptional is that minorities seized power illegally and extraconstitutionally, without the consent of the state.[58] Where minorities have seized power in this way, the state can only revoke autonomy by sending in the army and starting a civil war. For obvious reasons, the OSCE discourages this military option, and recommends

380 Reply and Conclusion

instead that states should negotiate autonomy with the minority, and accept some form of federalism or consociationalism that provides after-the-fact legal recognition for the reality on the ground. Hence the HCNM recommended that it would be dangerous for Ukraine to try to abolish the autonomy that Russians in Crimea (illegally) established (van der Stoel 1999: 26).

By contrast, wherever a minority has pursued TA through peaceful and democratic means, within the rule of law, the OSCE has opposed it, on the grounds that it would increase tensions. According to van der Stoel, given the pervasive fears in ECE about minority disloyalty and secession, any talk about creating new TA arrangements is bound to increase tensions, particularly if the minority claiming TA borders on a kin-state. Hence his recommendation that Hungarians in Slovakia not push for TA, given Slovak fears about irredentism (van der Stoel 1999: 25).

In short, the security approach rewards intransigence on the part of both sides. If minorities seize power, the OSCE rewards it by putting pressure on the state to accept an 'exceptional' form of autonomy; if the majority refuses to even discuss autonomy proposals from a peaceful and law-abiding minority, the OSCE rewards it by putting pressure on minorities to be more 'pragmatic'. This is perverse from the point of view of justice, but it seems to be the inevitable logic of the security-based approach. From a security point of view, it may indeed be correct that granting TA to a law-abiding minority increases tensions; while supporting TA after it has been seized by a belligerent minority decreases tensions.

This might not be as perverse as it seems if there were any arguments for supposing that autonomy is morally more appropriate for Russians in Crimea or Abkhazians in Georgia than for Hungarians in Slovakia or Albanians in Macedonia. But the OSCE has provided no such reason—that is, no reason for thinking that the former minorities are more in need of, or more rightfully entitled to autonomy than the latter. The differential response in these cases seems to be entirely a matter of the power wielded by the minority, and hence its threat to state security, not the justice of its claims.

It is interesting to note that the OSCE often argues that its proposals are grounded in justice, as well as security. Hence federalism and/or consociationalism for Crimea, Abkhazia, Ngorno-Karabakh, Kosovo, Gaugazia, and Trans-Dneister are said to embody principles of fairness and equality for the various national groups. Of course, for strategic reasons, the OSCE has to say this, since these settlements are unlikely to be stable if the majority believes them to be an unjust capitulation to minority belligerence. So in these contexts, the OSCE emphasizes the fairness that is embodied in models of power-sharing, and defends them in terms of justice as well as security.

Conversely, when the HCNM rejects TA in Slovakia or Macedonia and encourages instead non-territorial solutions, he insists that this too is what justice requires. He argues that TA for Hungarians in Slovakia is not just dangerous from a stability point of view, but also unnecessary from the point of view of justice (van der Stoel 1999: 25–6). And here again, strategically, he has to argue this, since these non-territorial solutions are unlikely to be stable if the minority views them as an unjust capitulation to state power or hegemonic majority nationalism.

In this way, the OSCE tries to reduce the operational distance between the justice track and the security track, by dressing up security-based recommendations in the language of justice. The problem, of course, is that these justice-based rationales for security-based recommendations seem to contradict each other. If justice requires TA for Russians in Crimea, why not for Hungarians in Slovakia? Conversely, if non-territorial approaches can secure justice for Albanians in Macedonia, why are they insufficient to secure justice for the Armenians in Ngorno-Karabakh? No Western organization has provided any principle of justice that would explain these apparent inconsistencies.

It is one of the most striking features of the HNCM's activities that he is continually trying to find universal norms to justify security-driven recommendations. Wherever possible, he cites international law and norms to back up his recommendations, and where there are no existing norms, he attempts to develop them.[59] He emphasizes that security without justice is impossible, and that these issues cannot be resolved purely in terms of short-term balance of power (van der Stoel 1999: 118–22). This continuing attempt to inject considerations of justice into a security-defined mandate is admirable in many ways. The problem is that the sort of 'justice' one gets seems to depend on the sort of power one exercises. Where belligerent minorities have seized power, we are told about the justice-enhancing properties of federalism and consociationalism; where minorities are peaceful and law-abiding, we are told to forget about federalism and consociationalism, and to think instead about the justice-enhancing properties of non-territorial forms of cultural autonomy.

This would not necessarily be a problem if there were compelling arguments to show that non-territorial forms of cultural autonomy can in fact achieve justice for minorities. But the OSCE has not offered any credible alternative to TA. The OSCE talks in vague terms about 'non-territorial' alternatives, but without any clear indication what these are, or how they protect minorities from the threats they face within nation-building states. As Zaagman puts it, the OSCE assumes that the 'self-realization' of the minority does not 'require a territorial expression but could often be realized through legislation promoting the development of the identity of the minority in various fields—for instance, culture, education, local government, and so forth' (Zaagman 1997: 254). This almost ritual invoking of 'non-territorial autonomy' is rarely accompanied by any clear account of how this would actually work in practice, or of any examples where it has successfully worked in practice, or how it would avoid the limitations which have necessitated TA in the West discussed in section 4 above.

It would be one thing if the OSCE were recommending a strong form of consociationalism in place of federalism, with a guarantee of a coalition government and a minority veto over legislation. That indeed would be a credible alternative to territorial self-government, since it would equally ensure that the minority cannot be outvoted or outbid on key decisions affecting its culture and institutions. But this is not what the OSCE is recommending in most cases. It is merely pushing for a set of educational and cultural rights that are limited in scope and that have a weak legal status—that is, they can easily be revoked whenever a new government is elected. Many minorities have understandably viewed this as 'paternalism and tokenism' (Wheatley 1997: 70).[60]

Fifth, this approach may simply be deferring the problem until after ECE countries gain entry into the EU. There is a waiting game going on in ECE. The majority is waiting to get into the EU because it thinks that once accepted, it will no longer be subject to the humiliating and hypocritical monitoring of its minority policies, and will have the same freedom as France or Greece to declare itself a homogenous centralized unitary state.[61] Minorities, by contrast, are waiting to get into the EU because they expect that once included, they will start to get the same rights as the Catalans, Scots, Flemish, South Tyroleans, and other Western national minorities (Liebich 1998). Minorities in ECE can see that most Western democracies accord territorial autonomy, official bilingualism, minority-language universities, and/or consociational veto rights to their national minorities, and so they ask themselves why they shouldn't also get these rights once they are 'in Europe'—and this seems a perfectly legitimate question to me. In other words, the apparent success of the OSCE in getting states and minorities to 'agree' on certain reforms may be quite misleading.[62] The majority may view OSCE proposals as hypocritical and unjustified, but accepts them as a temporary measure until they get into Europe, at which point they expect to have the same freedom from monitoring that Western countries have demanded for themselves. And the minority may view these Western proposals as inadequate and far less than they are entitled to, but may agree to withdraw their more robust demands for minority rights until they get in the EU, at which point they expect to get the same rights as other national minorities in the West. The security approach, whatever its other merits, hasn't developed a consensus within ECE about the justice of minority rights policies. It is exerting pressure on the majority, perhaps on a temporary basis, without changing either the majority or minority's views of what they are rightfully entitled to. So the security track may just be deferring conflicts—and once both sides realize that they may be wrong about the consequences of EU accession, the temporary agreements may unravel.

Finally, this new security track may simply be reproducing the beliefs and assumptions that were the cause of the problem in the first place. That is, it does not challenge the idea that minorities in ECE are first and foremost a *security* issue. As I argued earlier, as long as states view minorities in the framework of loyalty/security, they are unlikely to understand or act upon notions of fairness or justice. OSCE intervention has undoubtedly helped to improve the status of particular minorities in particular countries, at least in the short-term. But the basis on which the OSCE demands these reforms is not that they are just or fair, but rather that they are needed to defuse international security threats—an argument which may simply confirm the state's view that minorities are above all else a security problem.[63] The state mistreats its minorities because it views them as a security problem; the OSCE comes along and says 'you need to change your minority policies because we have a security problem here'. This approach cures some of the symptoms, but has not tackled the underlying pathology.[64]

More specifically, the OSCE's decision to discourage autonomy claims may be legitimating and reinforcing the state's view that there is something inherently suspicious about minorities seeking territorial autonomy, and something unnatural about a binational or multination state. ECE states have cited Western reluctance to support TA as proof that their distrust of minorities was justified. They say: 'Look, even Western organizations agree that claims for TA are radical and dangerous. We were right to view minority claims as threats to security and loyalty'. ECE countries cite Western objections to TA as evidence that the normal democratic state is a 'nation-state' with a hegemonic majority and weak minorities. Rather than promoting the ideal of a multination federation as a normal and natural and just solution to divided societies, the OSCE is tacitly, and sometimes explicitly, endorsing the view that this is a 'radical' idea.

The result has been to entrench serious misconceptions about what are normal practices in the West. For example, the Latvian scholar Ina Druviete claims that 'more collective linguistic rights are granted to the Russian-speaking population in the Baltic States than are granted to minorities in any Western country' (Druviete 1997: 180). An association of ethnic Macedonians sent an open letter to the OSCE saying that 'the Republic of Macedonia is under constant pressure to expand the rights of the Albanian minority, even though not even one European or other country has done the same for its minorities as Macedonia has done for the Albanians who live there'.[65] Meciar claimed that Slovakia under his rule provided more rights to its Hungarian minority than any Western country, and indeed he demanded a report on minorities in EU countries and said 'if the results show that there is a higher level of minority rights in other countries we will be glad to adapt' (quoted in Chandler 1999: 71).[66] He said that accepting the claims of the Hungarian minority would make Slovakia 'a guinea pig for Europe' (quoted in Nelson 1998: 319).[67]

These are staggering misperceptions about the West. If such a report were written, it would show that wherever national minorities in Western democracies are as numerically or proportionally significant as the Albanian minority in Macedonia, or the Russian minority in Latvia, or the Hungarian minority in Romania or Slovakia, they have far greater minority rights, including territorial autonomy, equal or even dominant official status for the language within that territory, and higher education in their own language.[68] This is obvious when we consider the largest national minorities in the West, like the Quebecois, Puerto Ricans, Catalans, and Walloons, all of whom are over 2.5 million. But it is equally true of smaller national minorities, like the Swedes in Finland—285,000 or 6.8 per cent of population; German-speakers in South Tyrol—303,000 or 0.5 per cent of population; the Italian-speakers in Switzerland—500,000 or 7 per cent. All of these groups have territorial autonomy, official language rights, and universities in their own language. Yet they are smaller in number, and form a smaller percentage of the population, than the Hungarians in Romania—1.6 million or 7.1 per cent; the Hungarians in Slovakia—600,000 or 10.8 per cent; the Russian-speakers in Latvia—1 million or

34 per cent and Estonia—500,000 or 30 per cent; or the Albanians in Macedonia—600,000 or 33 per cent.[69] Were these minorities located in almost any Western democracy besides France or Greece, it would be considered perfectly natural and normal for them to demand, and indeed to have, substantial territorial autonomy, official language status and higher education in their own language.

So too I believe it should be seen as normal and natural for territorially-concentrated national minorities in ECE to want some kind of TA, official language status, and mother-tongue higher education. There may be good reasons in particular cases for rejecting or deferring some of these claims, but it should be acknowledged that there is nothing wrong or illegitimate in advancing them. So when ECE states claim that such demands are 'radical', untested, and not present in the norms and practices of Western democracies, the OSCE should directly challenge these misperceptions. Instead, the OSCE is tacitly reinforcing the view that such claims are abnormal and dangerous, and that a normal state is a unitary nation-state.[70]

I'm not saying that the OSCE should necessarily endorse minority claims for TA, let alone seek to impose them on ECE states, but rather that the OSCE should do more to emphasize that the advancing, debating, and negotiating of such claims is a normal and healthy part of democratic life in a multination state. My concern is not with federalism *per se*, which is just one tool amongst many for accommodating diversity, but rather with the larger intellectual framework within which such tools are debated and evaluated. Federalism may or may not be a good idea in particular ECE countries—there may be other or better models for some countries.[71] However, while the fair accommodation of diversity need not require federalism, it certainly requires that people can engage in a free and open debate about the merits of federalism or territorial autonomy. In that sense, I think it is a fair test of the progress of democracy in ECE whether states are willing to tolerate an open debate about federalism. As I've tried to show, the fact that most ECE states are unwilling to even consider federalism, and have attempted to stigmatize anyone who mentions it, is not a healthy sign for democracy. It is a manifestation of an underlying set of assumptions that minorities are disloyal, that ethnic relations are zero-sum, that the exercise of democratic freedoms by the minority is a threat to the nation, and that the status of minorities is above all an issue of national security. These interrelated assumptions have created an atmosphere that makes any reasonable accommodation of diversity—federal or otherwise—impossible. The paranoia about federalism suggests not only that the majority is addicted to a model of the state as unitary and centralized, but also that the majority sees the minority as a threat rather than a partner in building a multination state, and cannot see any way in which a strong and flourishing minority can help to build a strong and flourishing country.

My worry is that the current 'security' track approach of the OSCE and other Western intergovernmental organizations is unintentionally reinforcing, rather than challenging, these assumptions. By not challenging the majority's view that it is 'radical' to seek TA, they are tacitly legitimating the view that a normal state is a unitary nation-state, and that there is an inherent conflict between strengthening the state and strengthening minorities.[72] Even if Western states cannot or should not impose a more 'multination' conception of the state on such countries, they can at least do more to emphasize that such a conception is a normal and natural model for multiethnic democratic societies. They can encourage a freer debate about such alternative models, in the hope that, over time, the underlying framework for discussing minority issues will change from one of security/loyalty to one of justice.[73]

Put another way, rather than saying that Crimea and Gaugazia are 'exceptional' in exercising autonomy, I think that the OSCE should say that autonomy is normal for territorially-concentrated national minorities, and that if autonomy is inappropriate in other countries like Slovakia and Macedonia, it is because there is something exceptional about these countries. This may seem like a minor semantic question, but debates about minority rights in ECE are often couched in terms of what is a 'normal' state. We are unlikely to make long-term progress in desecuritizing issues of minority rights if we cannot change majority views about what a normal state is, and hence about what forms of minority rights threaten the state.

For all these reasons, I think the West needs to rethink the relationship between the justice-based track of universal minority rights and the security-based track of conflict prevention. I think that both tracks are needed, but the content of each, and the relationship between them, could be clarified.

What we currently have, in effect, is:

(a) a very weak justice-based track, which defines a minimal set of universal minority rights that are weakly enforced in both the East and West; and

(b) a very powerful but selective security-based track, which imposes minority rights of varying strength solely on ECE countries as a condition of EU and NATO accession. These rights range from mild forms of non-territorial cultural rights all the way up to confederation or associated statehood, based on controversial assessments of 'security'. These security-based recommendations are rarely seen as morally legitimate by either the majority or minority, since they are not grounded in principles of justice, and are widely seen as creating double standards in the treatment of East and West, and indeed in the treatment of different ECE states.

What we need, I think, is to strengthen the former track, and clarify the latter track. Ideally, the West would enlarge its original justice-based approach, strengthening both the content and enforcement of a universal code of minority rights that would be monitored and applied in an even-handed way to both Western and ECE countries.[74] Because the obligations imposed on Western countries by the justice track are currently so weak, OSCE interventions in ECE are widely perceived as arbitrary, hypocritical, and more a matter of power relations than of genuine concern for minorities. As a result, it has done little to change anyone's views about the actual legitimacy or desirability of minority rights. Western interventions in ECE would be more credible and convincing—and also more justifiable—if they were tied to a principled account of minority rights that was applied even-handedly to both the West and East. It's important to have this at least as a supplement to the current security track.

Perhaps, given the intransigence of France and Greece, and the 'maximal resistance' of ECE states, there is no feasible way to establish a universal and impartially-administered set of minority rights that will tackle the difficult issues raised by minority nationalisms. If so, the current security track approach may be the best we can hope for to at least prevent violent conflicts. But then we should recognize that Western interventions in ECE are likely to continue to be seen with deep resentment in many countries, and to have only limited long-term success in changing the underlying dynamics of majority–minority relations.

6. Federalism and Secession in the ECE

So far, I've argued that any effective long-term strategy for enhancing minority rights in ECE needs to shift the framework for discussing minority issues from one of loyalty/security to justice. Of course, this is a long-term process, and so we need to be modest in our expectations about the short-term prospects for major reform in the region.[75] It will be a slow process of overcoming this 'maximal resistance' to TA. Indeed, it is not even clear how to start this process of addressing majority fears about loyalty and secession. There are many issues to be dealt with here, including the role of historic memories, and the appropriate role of kin-states and bilateral treaties.[76] But let me focus on one specific aspect of this process—namely, the relationship between TA and secession.

Any proposal for TA in ECE must grapple with the widespread fears of secession. But how do we make majorities less fearful of TA? One strategy is to try to draw a watertight separation between TA and secession, and to persuade ECE states that adopting TA will not and indeed could not lead to secession. The idea here would be to encourage states to think about TA in an open-minded way, without challenging their view that secession is unthinkable and that secessionist mobilization is intolerable. The goal would be to persuade ECE states to put TA on the political agenda, while agreeing with these states that secession cannot be a legitimate topic of public debate or political mobilization.

This could be done in a variety of ways. In particular, the international community can provide strong assurances regarding secession. It can make solemn pledges guaranteeing the integrity of state borders in ECE, and can insist as part of its TA proposals that the minority agree to some 'loyalty clause' which affirms their acceptance of state borders. And it can insist that kin-states renounce all irredentist territorial claims on neighbouring states, and indeed pressure these states to sign bilateral treaties guaranteeing the borders. With these guarantees against secession in place, the international community can then encourage states to think in a more open-minded way about TA, and about the role it can play in promoting greater trust, co-operation, and stability in multination states.

Much of this has already been done in ECE, and yet it has had little success in persuading ECE states to consider TA in an open-minded way. These states obviously do not trust international guarantees regarding state borders, and understandably so. For one thing, the international community has a rather mixed record on this issue. In some cases—like Abkhazia, Chechnya and Trans-Dneister—it has indeed refused to recognize *de facto* secessions, and continues to support the principle of the integrity of state borders. But in other cases, notably in the former Soviet Union and Yugoslavia, it was very quick to recognize secessions. ECE states assume, perhaps rightly, that Western powers will sacrifice the principle of the integrity of state borders if they have some larger geopolitical reason for doing so.

More importantly, even if the international community does hold firm to this principle, it doesn't really solve the problem of what to do with a territory where the local majority has clearly and democratically affirmed a desire to secede. Imagine that a national minority achieves TA, and begins to conduct democratic elections for the new territorial government. At first, none of the political parties may be explicitly secessionist, partly in order to ensure international cooperation with the new TA regime. But certainly some parties will be pushing for greater autonomy. And over time, perhaps in response to some manifestation of majority intolerance, some people will begin to discuss the merits of secession. Perhaps they won't call it secession, but rather some form of 'confederation', or 'sovereignty-association', or 'associated statehood', in which the seceding territory maintains some nominal link with the larger state, while becoming *de facto* independent. And let's imagine that a party promoting some such form of (quasi)-secession is created, and after a few elections eventually becomes the governing party. As part of its platform, it holds a referendum on its proposals for confederation or sovereignty-association. Perhaps this referendum is defeated at first—as every such referendum has been defeated in the West—but there is always the chance that it will win, and then the territorial government declares (quasi)-independence.

Now what? What does the state do? Let's imagine the international community keeps its promise, and refuses to recognize the declaration of independence. Still the territory has proclaimed independence, and perhaps is beginning to implement this on the ground. Let's say it is refusing to pay taxes to the central government, adopts and enforces laws which violate the state's constitution, adopts its own currency, and refuses to have its citizens drafted into the state army. In principle, the state could send in the army to crush this secessionism—that is, civil war. But even assuming that the state army could win such a civil war—which was not true in several ECE states—the fact is that the international community is unlikely to accept this sort of response. The international community may not favour secession, but nor does it favour military suppression of democratically elected and non-violent secessionist governments. They will favour 'negotiation', the end result of which may be to accept *de facto* independence, even if the fiction of state unity is maintained.

Of course, the state could try to short-circuit this scenario by passing a law that secessionist parties cannot run for office. But how do we know which parties are secessionist, and who is to judge? Are parties supporting 'confederation' secessionist? Will we send the secret police to attend party rallies to find out what the party really wants? Or perhaps the state could pass a law forbidding the holding of a referendum on secession. But even if we could define such a law— would it forbid a referendum on confederation?—there is still the problem of enforcing it. Let's imagine that the territorial government says that it will hold the referendum anyway: will the state send in the army to break up the balloting stations?

The fact is that there is no obvious way for a free and democratic country to prevent a self-governing region from electing secessionist parties, and from holding referendums on secession. This, at any rate, appears to be the lesson from the Western multination federations, all of whom have grudgingly accepted the legitimacy of secessionist political mobilization. The state can only prevent this by undemocratic and illiberal means. And even if these means worked, they would undermine the whole point of the exercise. After all, the point of having TA was to give the minority some sense of secure self-government. The minority will not feel any security if the larger state decides which minority parties are free to run for office, and which questions can be put to a referendum.[77] If the minority needs the majority's permission for every proposed law, political party or referendum, it is not a meaningful form of self-government. Notice that even those members of the minority who are not in favour of secession are nonetheless typically in favour of the right of secessionist parties to run for office. That the state allows such parties to run is considered proof that it is genuinely committed to democracy and autonomy.

My point is not that federalism inevitably leads to secession. Just the opposite. I believe that democratic federalism reduces the likelihood of secession. But I think democratic federalism only works, or best works, to inhibit secession when secessionist political mobilization is allowed—indeed, federalism is only democratic if it allows this. Minorities will only find TA an acceptable form of self-government if they have the right to freely debate their future, including freely debating a range of options from assimilation to secession. If the state decides for them which options they can debate, and which parties they can vote for, the minority has neither freedom nor democracy, and this will just increase their desire for true independence.

On my view, then, in order to get the full benefits of federalism, we need to accept the legitimacy of secessionist parties, and that entails accepting the possibility, however slim, of a democratically-mandated secession. Federalism of this form reduces the chance of secession actually taking place, but it requires accepting as legitimate the presence of secessionists in the political debate. Attempts to promote federalism while prohibiting secessionist mobilization are likely to be undemocratic, illiberal, and in the end counterproductive.

In short, federalism is unlikely to work where the state views secession as unthinkable, and secessionist mobilization as intolerable. Defenders of TA in ECE have typically tried to promote TA without challenging this fear of secession. They want to put TA on the agenda, while keeping secession off the agenda. But I doubt this strategy will work. In the Western experience, accepting TA has gone hand in hand with accepting the legitimacy of secessionist mobilization, and accepting the possibility of a democratically-mandated referendum on secession. ECE states can see this perfectly well. They know that Western-style TA has not 'solved the problem of secession', and that international guarantees about state borders will not solve it either. They know that if Quebec, Scotland, Puerto Rico, or Catalonia votes one day for secession, there is little that the state, or the international community, can do to prevent it.

If we want to promote TA in ECE, therefore, we need to consider a second strategy. We need to challenge the assumption that eliminating secession from the political agenda should be the first goal of the state. We should try to show that secession is not necessarily a crime against humanity, and that the goal of a democratic political system shouldn't be to make it unthinkable. States and state borders are not sacred. The first goal of a state should be to promote democracy, human rights, justice, and the well-being of citizens, not to somehow insist that every citizen views herself as bound to the existing state 'in perpetuity'—a goal which can only be achieved through undemocratic and unjust means in a multination state.[78] A state can only fully enjoy the benefits of democracy and federalism if it is willing to live with the risk of secession.

This indeed is the conclusion which Istvan Bibo reached in his 1946 essay. I quoted earlier his claim that ECE states were unable to 'take full advantage of the benefits offered by democracy' because they feared the exercise of democratic freedoms by national minorities, and his view that being a democrat means 'not to be afraid of those who have different opinions, speak different languages, or belong to other races'. He went on to argue that 'Under these conditions, a clear-sighted, brave and democratic public opinion can pursue only one course of action: It can offer minorities the greatest opportunities within the existing framework and use its own initiatives to satisfy the boldest minority demands, accepting even the risk of secession' (Bibo 1991: 50).

Of course, as Bibo notes, this sort of 'brave and democratic' approach is only possible if we reduce the stakes of secession. I believe that the acceptance of secessionist mobilization in the West is tied to the fact that secession would not threaten the survival of the majority nation. Secession may involve the painful loss of territory, but it is not seen as a threat to the very survival of the majority nation or state. If Quebec, Scotland, Catalonia, or Puerto Rico were to secede, Canada, Britain, Spain, and the United States would still exist as viable and prosperous democracies. In ECE, by contrast, it is widely believed that 'the secession of foreign-speaking or minority territories forebodes national death'. According to Bibo, accepting the risk of secession was not possible in ECE because of a 'political consciousness burdened by fear of survival' (Bibo 1991: 50, 55).[79]

Similarly, the increased acceptance of secessionist mobilization in the West is also tied to the fact that secession would not necessarily dramatically affect the rights or interests of people in the seceding territory. If Quebec, Scotland, Puerto Rico, or Catalonia were to secede, there would be few changes in the legal rights of people within those regions, or the distribution of power between groups, or in the language of public institutions. Whether these groups have self-government within a larger state, or exist as separate states, they will in either case promote their national language and culture within the constraints of a liberal-democratic constitution which ensures respect for the rights of internal minorities. The seceding group does not gain much by going from a multination federation to an independent state, and internal minorities do not lose much.

In ECE, by contrast, secession is often viewed almost as a matter of life and death. Since politics in unitary nation-states is typically seen as a zero-sum, winner-take-all battle, it is of the utmost importance whether you are a majority or a minority in the state. If you are the majority, it is your language and culture which monopolizes public space and which is a precondition for access to jobs and professional advancement, and every important political decision is made in a forum where you form a majority. If you are the minority, you are faced with political disempowerment—that is, no important decisions are made in a forum where you are the majority—cultural marginalization, and long-term assimilation. It is no wonder, therefore, that secession is viewed with such dread by ECE states.

If ECE states are ever to accept the risk of secession and hence accept the risk of a democratic TA, we need to reduce these stakes of secession. We need to find a way of assuring states that the loss of a minority territory does not 'forebode national death', and of assuring potential internal minorities that secession does not mean that they will lose their rights or jobs or identities.

I believe that such a change in attitudes towards secession is needed, in the long-term, if we are ever to have the genuine accommodation of ethnocultural diversity in ECE states. To summarize a complicated argument, I think that the fair accommodation of diversity requires that states be willing to consider claims for TA or other forms of power-sharing; and that states will only consider these claims in an open-minded way if they are willing to accept the legitimacy of secessionist mobilization; and they will only accept the legitimacy of democratic secessionist mobilization if they no longer see secession as tantamount to national death.

This, at any rate, is the lesson I draw from the Western experience. I believe that federalism has worked well in the West to ensure ethnocultural justice, and to reduce the likelihood of secession. But it has been able to achieve this in part because citizens accept the legitimacy of secessionist mobilization. And they accept this legitimacy because the stakes of secession have been dramatically reduced, both for the majority group in the rump state and for internal minorities.

I think there is much the international community can do to reduce the stakes of secession, and thereby increase the willingness of states to adopt forms of democratic TA. But it involves a rather different approach than that currently taken by the international community. At present, the focus is on trying to provide guarantees against secession, not on reducing the stakes of secession. In my view, the goal shouldn't be to provide iron-clad guarantees of existing state borders—which cannot be done in a free and democratic society—but rather on providing firm guarantees that the rights of internal minorities will be protected in the event that state borders change, and that the majority group will survive as a nation even if it loses some minority territory.

This sort of change in attitude can only be a very long-term process. And many people think it is completely unrealistic. However, I see no plausible alternative.

7. Conclusion

The commentators have raised several important difficulties regarding the implementation of a liberal pluralist approach in ECE. I have tried to give a qualified defence of this approach, in part by showing that many of these difficulties have arisen in the West as well, and have been tackled more or less successfully. Of course, it is possible that the strategies adopted in the West would not work in ECE, and I have tried to identify some questions in this regard for which we do not yet have good evidence: for example, about the likely strength of nationalist mobilization under conditions of democratic accountability; about the relative ability of central and substate governments to liberalize; about the impact of minority rights on the process of democratic transition; about the relationship between security and justice. These are all issues on which we need further debate and investigation.

I hope that this discussion has helped clarify the strengths and limits of the liberal pluralist approach. But some people might think that this entire discussion rests on a mistaken premise—namely, that all liberal-democratic states should converge on a single set of principles for accommodating various forms of diversity. This is said to ignore the fundamental differences between various kinds of liberal states— in particular, the difference between New World and Old World democracies.[80]

I have given my reasons in Part I for thinking that this is not a useful distinction for our purposes. I argued there that while there are of course differences between New World and Old World countries, these are often less significant than the differences between types of groups *within* both Old World and New World countries. National minorities in the New World are completely unlike immigrant groups in the New World, in terms of their needs and aspirations, although they are very much like national minorities in the Old World. Indigenous peoples in the Old World—for example, Lapps in Sweden—have little in common with immigrants in the Old World, although they have much in common with the indigenous peoples of North America or Australasia.

However, let's accept for the sake of argument that the distinction between New World and Old World democracies is a useful one for the purposes of normative theories of liberal pluralism. How would this change our notions about the legitimacy of minority rights claims? According to Walzer, Old World countries, including ECE countries, are likely to adopt 'thicker' forms of nation-building than

New World democracies. He argues that this is legitimate if in return these states give greater corporatist rights to minorities, and not just to national minorities but also to immigrant groups. If the state promotes a thick majority identity that makes it difficult for minorities to integrate, it must allow these minorities—immigrant and national— the rights and powers needed to promote their own thick identity. He argues that this package of thick nation-building and thick minority rights is not only more likely in the Old World, but is also morally legitimate. We should not expect or require that ECE countries follow the New World model of thin nation-building and immigrant multiculturalism.

I have two reservations about this argument. First, I think it is a mistake to suppose that the gradual 'thinning' of national cultures in the New World was solely due to immigration. This sort of thinning has been a response, not only to the demands of immigrant groups, but also to the demands of various non-ethnic forms of diversity within the dominant national group—for example, feminists, gays, religious minorities and atheists, and political dissidents. The 'thick' WASP-based national identity and culture promoted by old models of Americanization was not only unjust to immigrants, but also to many subgroups within the historically dominant Anglo-Saxon society, such as women or gays.[81]

So immigrant multiculturalism is just one part of a much broader movement for greater openness, tolerance, and pluralism in our conceptions of nationhood and national identity. Any liberal society will face this broader movement to thin its national culture, regardless of its rate of immigration.[82] This, I believe, is an inescapable part of the liberalization of modern societies.[83] In so far as ECE countries wish to become liberal states, they will have to move towards a thinner conception of their state-promoted national cultures.[84]

However, let's accept that it is indeed legitimate for ECE states to adopt thicker forms of nation-building. This then raises my second objection. Walzer's theory requires that countries with thicker notions of national culture be *more* generous to minorities than those with thin notions. It follows that ECE states must be more generous towards immigrant groups than those in the West or the New World. But this is an unrealistic expectation—much more unrealistic than my own rather optimistic proposal.

So far as I can tell, the thicker the form of nation-building, the more unlikely the majority is to accord significant rights to immigrants and other minorities.[85] As a general rule, those countries with a thinner conception of nation-building are also more generous in their treatment of groups which do not belong to the dominant nationality. This suggests that tolerance of diversity within the national group goes hand in hand with tolerance of groups outside the dominant group. The combination that Walzer envisages of thick nation-building combined with generous minority rights seems chimerical. As I've noted, states in ECE have generally only adopted significant minority rights under external pressure or when faced with civil war. Given this reality, I think it is more realistic to ask majorities to liberalize their national culture than to ask them to grant corporatist rights to minorities that exceed those offered in the West. The former is optimistic, the latter is utopian.[86]

However, let's assume that Walzer's proposal is both feasible and desirable, and that we can expect ECE states to adopt a different model of nation-building and minority rights. If true, some of the specific models I described in my paper may not be appropriate in ECE—for example, the model of immigrant multiculturalism. However, at another level, Walzer's argument supports and illustrates my more general claim that minority rights must be seen in the context of, and as a response to, state nation-building. Even on Walzer's view, our goal should be to come up with a package of minority rights that protects minorities from the disadvantages they would otherwise suffer as a result of nation-building. As Walzer himself emphasizes, different forms of nation-building are only acceptable if they are accompanied by the appropriate sorts of minority rights to protect minorities from the barriers, burdens, and exclusions implicit in each form of nation-building.

There are many ways of carving up the world into different types of countries: East vs West; Catholic vs Orthodox vs Muslim; New vs Old. All of these distinctions are useful for some purposes, and all provide some insight into the nature of ethnic relations in particular countries. But all of these states are now integrated into a global system of nation-building sovereign states. Minorities face certain structural vulnerabilities within this system of nation-building states, whether they are in New or Old states, Catholic or Orthodox states, Eastern or Western states. In all of these contexts we need to think about the sorts of minority rights that will protect minorities from the vulnerabilities created by state nation-building.

Indeed, I believe that this will remain true even in an increasingly postnational world, such as that envisaged by Kis. According to Kis, justice for ethnocultural groups not only requires moving from a model of the nation-state to that of a multination-state. It also requires moving from the model of exclusive jurisdiction to a model of overlapping jurisdiction, and requires creating new political institutions that link co-ethnics across borders. He complains that my approach focuses too narrowly on achieving ethnocultural justice within a single sovereign state, and ignores the need and potential for new transnational forms of minority rights.

I agree with Kis that it will become increasingly feasible to create political institutions that link co-ethnics across state borders. And I agree that this development has great potential in the long-term. In my paper, I took for granted that we are living within a system of sovereign states, and that our aim should be to achieve ethnocultural justice within the boundaries and institutions of each state. Kis is right to challenge these assumptions. But even if we are moving beyond the era of the sovereign state, I believe we will still confront the dialectic of nation-building and minority rights. Even within Kis's own discussion of the possible future of Hungarian nationalism, it seems clear that various kinds of nation-building policies will continue to exist. The minority will use its autonomous institutions to promote its language and culture in its (trans-border) territory; the majority will use traditional state institutions to promote its language and culture within existing state boundaries. And in each case, there are clear dangers of injustice to minorities, both at the state and sub-state/transborder level. Kis's proposal complicates the story of nation-building and minority rights, and relocates the sites of this dialectic, but does not eliminate it.

Indeed, I would argue that in any plausible scenario for the future of ECE, we will face the need to balance nation-building and minority rights. No matter how complex the emerging web of transnational institutions, we will still face the problem that some circumscribed set of people will have the power to make decisions regarding issues of language, culture, education, media, mobility, citizenship and naturalization, and so on. Wherever these powers are located, we can reasonably predict they will be exercised in a way that promotes and privileges the language, culture, and identity of the dominant group within that forum. Majorities in a democratic political community, at whatever level, will use their power to privilege their language, culture, and identity, and will try to define the political community in terms of these majority characteristics. Minorities will respond by demanding the sorts of rights and powers that will protect them from the potential injustices implicit in these majoritarian nation-building policies.[87] The site of these decision-making processes may change, but the dialectic of nation-building and minority rights will continue.[88]

NOTES

1. These first three objections can be rephrased and linked this way: the first says that there is little or no real demand for Western-style minority rights in ECE; the second says that in so far as there is a demand for minority rights in ECE, it is rooted in an illiberal desire to oppress other groups, and hence is not legitimate; the third says that even if there is a demand for minority rights, and even if this demand is not intrinsically illiberal, we should not adopt such rights *now* given the fragile state of democratic institutions.

2. Other mechanisms of democratic accountability include an independent judiciary, government ombudsmen, and so on.

3. See for example the declarations of self-declared Roma leaders in Greece, funded by the Greek government, who insist that the Roma do not want minority rights, and seek only integration into Greek society. As international observers have noted, these state-sponsored Roma leaders have virtually no connection with actual Roma communities. 'Greek Roma Leaders Lash Out at International Romani Union: No to the Demand for Recognition as Nation Without a State' (*www.greekhelsinki.gr/english/articles/AIMM-Articles-Greece.html* Alternative Information Media Network on Greece Athens, 6 August 2000).

4. See Part 1 note 51 above.

5. As Ossipov rightly says, 'If a liberal theorist rejects the exclusion of groups at the nationwide level—that is, the idea that a state "belongs" to a certain ethnonation—the same conclusion should hold at the subnational level. Otherwise we have a double-standard.'

6. From a purely Hobbesian point of view, decentralizing tyranny might be a worthwhile goal. An autonomous government dominated by Albanians in Kosovo is likely to be as intolerant of minorities as the central Serbian state has been intolerant of the Kosovar Albanians. However, there is an enormous difference in scale here: the Serbian state was oppressing 1.5 million Albanians in Kosovo, whereas the Albanians are oppressing 'only' 200,000 Serbs and Roma. From a purely numerical point of view, this is a significant reduction in oppression. But liberal pluralists are not Hobbesians, and are not satisfied with this sort of decentralizing of tyranny.

7. This seems to be Doroszewska's position.

8. The crude version of this view is that the majority Russians are civilized and 'Western', whereas national minorities in Russia tend to be Eastern/Asian/Muslim and hence assumed to be incapable of democracy.

9. See the works of Ignatieff, Franck, and Hollinger discussed in Kymlicka 2001: chs. 13–15.

10. See Kymlicka 2001: chs. 11–16.

11. Note that no one makes the reverse assumption that minorities should have a right to secede unless and until majorities have proven that they have the capacity for liberal governance. Why then should minorities only have self-government if and when they have proven their liberal credentials?

12. Consider Turkey's rejection of Kurdish autonomy on the grounds that their leadership is illiberal, conveniently forgetting that it is Turkish repression which had caused the radicalization of the Kurdish leadership.

13. This again is suggested in Ossipov's commentary.

14. Ossipov argues that not all disadvantages facing national minorities were inten-

tionally created by the majority, and hence are not injustices. I agree that not all disadvantages are intentionally created, but where they can be remedied without violating people's rights, the refusal to remedy such disadvantages is indeed an injustice. The idea that only intentionally-created disadvantages create injustices is inconsistent with the norms and practices of modern Western welfare states, which seek to create equal life-chances for citizens regardless of whether the inequality is intentional or not.

15. As the OCSE puts it, 'questions relating to national minorities can only be satisfactorily resolved in a democratic political framework based on the rule of law, with a functioning independent judiciary'.

16. See Holmes 1999 on the importance of building state capacity in ECE states. See also Schöpflin's comments on the need for enhanced state capacity to deal with the complexity inherent in modernity.

17. Hence it was, and remains, a serious mistake to suppose that removing Milošević is sufficient to resolve the crisis in Kosovo. Some people argue that if Albanians in Kosovo had not boycotted the December 1992 election, and supported the main opposition party, they could have helped defeat Milošević. But the main opposition to Milošević was equally hostile to the idea of territorial autonomy for Kosovo (Guzina 2000).

18. Similarly, the Roma do not benefit from the fact that ECE states show little interest in investigating discrimination or hate-crimes against them.

19. MINELRES, 17 October 1999. This bias is heightened by the fact that private minority-language TV and radio is prohibited in Latvia. So if Russians are to be served, it has to be through public media, regulated by this National Council.

20. For example, while most Albanians in Macedonia live in the western part of the country, where they form a majority, the largest single concentration is in the capital Skopje, where they are 150,000 or 25% of the population. An even more extreme case concerns the ethnic Tatars, 75% of whom live outside Tatarstan.

21. Anglophones within Quebec have the same non-territorial rights.

22. It is sometimes said that if TA were adopted, the minority diaspora would be subject to increased persecution, prejudice, and discrimination by the majority. The majority would tell the minority diaspora that they should 'go home' to their self-governing region. If so, this is an argument for the firm upholding of anti-discrimination laws, not an argument for pandering to such illiberal majority prejudices.

23. On this trend in Belgium, see Lejeune 1994; Senelle 1989; in Switzerland, see Mansour 1993. For a more general theoretical account of the 'territorial imperative' in multilingual societies, see Laponce 1987, 1993.

24. See Dorff 1994: 113; Kalin 1997: 178–82. The commentators in this volume express a range of views on this question. Some argue that while TA is not appropriate now due to existing levels of distrust, it may be a viable option later on, once this distrust is lessened. On this view, it is premature to implement federalism—or even for minorities to claim it—but it could be a long-term development—see for example, Fesenko on Ukraine; Andreescu on Romania; Pettai and Tsilevich on the Baltics. Dimitras and Papanikolatos argue the opposite: namely, that while TA is necessary now in some cases of overt distrust, it ideally will be replaced with non-territorial forms of autonomy once this distrust is lessened.

25. When a coalition of Romanian and Hungarian intellectuals from Transylvania in June 1999 proposed federalization, the President said that the whole country had

to 'watch so that constitutional provisions regarding national, sovereign, independent, unitary, and indivisible state' were not attacked either from inside or outside the state (MINELRES 9 June 1999). In Kazakhstan, it is illegal to press for territorial autonomy.

26. For example, the Albanians in Macedonia boycotted the vote on the Macedonian constitution because it did not recognize them as a 'state-founding people', co-equal with the Macedonian Slavs. While none of the ECE states are consociational, some of the republics in Russia are. In particular, Dagestan has a consociational system, and some people think this has helped it avoid the serious ethnic violence plaguing other republics in the Caucuses (Ware and Kisriev 1999). However, as elsewhere in the Caucuses or the former Soviet Union in general, it is difficult to determine when political arrangements are the result of consensual negotiations amongst the various groups, and when it is the result of manipulation and coercion by Russia.

27. Belarus is the only country with two official languages—Belarus and Russian. But this is the exception that proves the rule, since Belarus is not democratic; and Lukashenka, the dictatorial president of Belarus, wants to reunify with Russia in a new Slavic federation, and actually suppresses the use of Belarus in many contexts.

28. James Headlam-Morley, the key British drafter of the League of Nations' minority treaties, argued that minorities should have mother-tongue primary schools, but not higher education, since 'this is the system which exists in Wales and applies to those countries where the minority language is one with inferior cultural value' (quoted in Cornwall 1996: 17). This, he argued, would lead to gradual assimilation into the majority national community. On the often explicitly assimilationist aims of the League's minority protection scheme, see Kovacs 2000.

29. She uses this phrase to describe the old Soviet policy toward the Latvian language. I think it is also a fair description of the current Latvian policy toward the Russian-speaking community, although she would disagree.

30. As Vàrady notes, there were various minority rights provisions in the early-twentieth century and the inter-war period in ECE, which some people point to as a source for a more tolerant approach today. But most of them were imposed by undemocratic multination empires (Walzer 1997), or by international pressure as part of the League of Nations. There were few democratically endorsed minority rights regimes in inter-war ECE, just as there were few in the West at the time.

31. Hungary appears to be an exception, since it has adopted a seemingly generous system of local autonomy for its minorities. But this is an exception that proves the rule, for the purpose of this system of minority autonomy was not to help the minorities within Hungary. Most of these minorities are too small and dispersed to take advantage of their new legal rights, and indeed few of them had asked for a system of local self-government. The purpose of this law was not to respond to the demands of Hungary's internal minorities, but rather to put pressure on Slovakia and Romania to adopt local autonomy for Hungarian minorities in those countries.

32. Why did Russia, alone of ECE countries, voluntarily adopt multination federalism? Several reasons may explain this anomaly: (a) Russia is simply too large to govern as a unitary state; (b) the national minorities accorded self-government in Russia do not have kin-states, and so do not raise the prospect of irredentism; (c)

the central government in Russia was very weak in 1991–2, and in mortal combat with the Communist leadership of the old Soviet Union. Yeltsin needed to rely on the co-operation of regional leaders in his struggle against the Soviet Communist leadership; (d) many Russians have traditionally viewed Russia as the embodiment of a supranational empire or civilization, rather than a nation-state, and so the presence of national minorities is part of the very idea of Russia. These factors may explain the greater willingness to consider multination federalism. However, I also suspect that many Russian leaders simply didn't realize what they were in fact agreeing to. They didn't consider the possibility that federalism would enable some national minorities to engage in the sort of substate nation-building that would challenge the hegemony of Russian language and culture throughout the territory of the state. After all, a similar system of ostensibly self-governing territories had existed within Russia under the Soviet Union, and yet Russian was the hegemonic language within all of these 'autonomous' territories, and national minorities were gradually assimilating into the russophone community. I think that many Russians assumed that these trends would continue under the renewed form of Russian federalism. They assumed that federalism would not challenge the hegemony of Russian throughout Russia, or the long-term assimilation of national minorities. In fact, however, some of the 'ethnic republics' are now seriously attempting to establish the hegemony of their own language and culture in their public institutions, and Russian-speakers in these republics increasingly find that they must learn the titular language in order to advance and succeed—just as anglophones in Quebec must learn French to succeed, or as Castilians must learn Catalan to succeed in Catalonia. This has surprised and even shocked many Russian leaders. And, as a result, support for multination federalism is in fact very low amongst most Russians. Although it is unlikely that the system of multination federalism could be eliminated in the foreseeable future, most liberals in Russia do not like what they call 'ethnic federalism', and several proposals have been made to replace it with a form of administrative/territorial federalism disconnected from any principle of minority self-government. Their acceptance of the current system of multination federalism is purely transitional and strategic. So many Russians share the same hostility to minority nationalism and multination federalism as other ECE countries. See Smith 1996; Stepan 2000; Ilishev 1998; Vasilyeva 1995; Teague 1994; Hughes 1999; Solnick 1998; Lynn and Novikov 1997; Tolz 1998; and Opalski's commentary at 2.14 in this volume.

33. And even these exceptions are under pressure. Many commentators think that enhanced autonomy for Corsica is in the cards. If and when France adopts a stronger form of autonomy, it will start to more closely fit the usual Western pattern. And as I've noted, multination federalism is widely disliked by Russian leaders, and there have been several plans to replace with a more purely administrative/territorial form of federalism. If and when one of these plans is adopted, Russia will more closely fit the usual ECE pattern.

34. The extreme case is the use of military power, such as the NATO bombing of Serbia to force the granting of autonomy to Kosovo. However, I doubt that sort of intervention will occur again in the foreseeable future, so I will focus on economic and political pressures, particularly those related to accession to Western organizations.

35. For examples of the power of this inducement, see Järve 2000; Daftary and Gal 2000, and Kis's and Andreescu's commentaries at 2.9 and 2.12 in this volume.

36. Brett 1993: 157–8. For a detailed discussion of the way various countries try to deny the existence of minorities, see Greek Helsinki Monitor 2000.
37. Indeed, Western countries 'had no conception of how to apply such policies in relation to their own minorities or of accepting such a level of international regulation in their affairs of state' (Chandler 1999: 66).
38. This has led some commentators to say that Recommendation 1201, adopted just two years earlier, is now void (Dunay 1997: 223–4).
39. Countries are required to submit reports to the Council of Europe discussing their compliance with the Convention, but there are no judicial remedies for violations.
40. See the Hague Recommendations on Linguistic Rights of National Minorities (1996); Oslo Recommendations on Education Rights of National Minorities (1998); Lund Recommendations on Effective Participation Rights of National Minorities (1999). These recommendations are all posted on the HCNM's website: www.osce.org/hcnm/documents.
41. The European Commission on Human Rights has twice declared that there is no right of national minorities to self-determination (European Commission for Democracy through Law 1996). Autonomy is recommended more strongly in the UN Draft Declaration on the Rights of Indigenous Peoples, but is not yet legally binding, and won't apply to substate nations. In short, international conventions view autonomy as entirely a matter of the discretion and good will of states, most of whom reject it. As Heintz puts it, 'Despite the possible positive effects of autonomy on the protection of minorities, State practice has shown no willingness to regard it as a general model for the resolution of minority conflicts. Delegating State competence to minority bodies of self-government is often suspected to be a step toward secession'(1998: 13; cf. Heintz 1997: 88).
42. Indeed, the office of the HCNM is located within the 'security basket' of the OSCE, not the 'human dimension basket', concerned with human rights.
43. Moreover, the HCNM is expressly forbidden from dealing with terrorist groups, a clause which was added on the insistence of Great Britain, Spain, and Turkey precisely to ensure that the HCNM did not get involved in their serious ethnic conflicts.
44. As John Packer puts it, the fact that the HCNM is 'the principal mechanism by which the situation of minorities in candidate countries is measured' allows the HCNM to 'dangle the carrot of EU membership to encourage compliance' (Packer 2000: 719).
45. See section 3.1 in Part 1 of this volume.
46. For example, while the OSCE supported autonomy in Crimea—once the Russians seized it—this was not defended in terms of any right of self-government, since 'the Ukrainian SSR had declared its independence as a unitary State including the Crimean peninsula and it had been recognized as such by other states and, on this basis, was a participating state of the OSCE. To accept a constitutive premise [of minority self-government] would be to accept that there were in fact two distinct and separate sovereignties at play: that of Ukraine and that of Crimea. . . . the OSCE principles of territorial integrity and inviolability of international borders as recognized by OSCE participating states prevailed over expressed or implied references to the self-determination of a part of the population' (Packer 1998: 312).
47. Even in Kosovo, the OSCE was very 'passive' in its promotion of autonomy. According to some commentators, 'by not pushing for a meaningful autonomy

at an earlier stage the escalation of the conflict has undermined the credibility of the OSCE's preferred solution, namely autonomy' (Cohen 1998: 83). Moreover, the OSCE insisted that autonomy for Kosovo operate within the boundaries of Serbia, rather than as a federal republic within Yugoslavia, with the same status as Montenegro. Many commentators think that allowing Kosovo to secede from Serbia while remaining within Yugoslavia was the only or best solution for Kosovo, and that the OSCE's refusal to consider this option reinforced Milošević's brutality (Troebst 1998: 105).

48. The OSCE sometimes encourages a more general form of decentralization, but insists that this should be defended on the grounds that it satisfies the aspirations of all citizens, not just minority citizens, and not because of any principle of minority self-government. This is said to be more 'fruitful' since less 'controversial' (Zaagman 1997: 254; cf. van der Stoel 1999: 112).

49. For a comprehensive review, see Cohen 1998; Ratner 2000.

50. Although even interpreted this way, one might expect OSCE intervention in Turkey or Cyprus. For reasons of geopolitics, the West is unwilling to challenge Turkey's treatment of minorities, yet the problem of Kurdistan is clearly more of a threat to international security than the problem of Hungarians in Slovakia.

51. As Schöpflin notes, ECE countries remain aggrieved at the continuing double standard. See also Cohen 1998: 52, 86–7; Ratner 2000: 662; and the RFE/RL report on 'OSCE: Countries Supervised and Not', posted on MINELRES 20 July 1999.

52. For the conflicts in Slovakia, see the Hungarian Coalition in Slovakia 1997: 12, 22, 37 re territorial autonomy, and 24–6 re education, including university. For the OSCE's approach to Slovakia, see Mihalikova 1998.

53. For the OSCE's approach to Kosovo, see Troebst 1998.

54. 'Who is to say, and how are "we" to measure, when Slovakia, for example, had "done enough" for their Hungarian minority, to satisfy European institutions? It is revealing that the constant criticism of the country is rarely accompanied by a list of specific and attainable objectives, only that "more must be done". The moving goal posts of "demonstrate democratic behaviour or be damned" are ultimately impossible to fulfil' (Burgess 1999: 59).

55. On the double standard in the way Russia is treated—for example, regarding Chechnya or Dagestan—see Cohen 1998: 80, 86.

56. For other examples of Western selectivity and double standards in the way minority rights norms are applied in ECE, see Burgess 1999: 54, 57.

57. Chandler 1999: 68. Compare with Alfredsson and Turk: 'Minorities should not be confronted with the situation that the international community will only respond to their concerns if there is a conflict. Such an approach could easily backfire and generate more conflicts than it resolves. An objective, impartial and non-selective approach to minorities, involving the application of minority standards across the board, must therefore remain a crucial part' (1993: 176–7).

58. In all of these cases except Crimea, the minority seized power through an armed uprising. In the case of Crimea, the Ukrainian state barely existed on Crimean territory, and so the Russians did not have to take up arms to overthrow the existing state structure. They simply held an (illegal) referendum on autonomy and then started governing themselves.

59. See Ratner 2000: 640–7 for a discussion of the HCNM's innovative activities in developing new norms of minority rights.

60. Wheatley is discussing the Council of Europe's Framework Convention, rather than the OSCE guidelines, but I think the same sentiment applies to the OSCE's efforts.

61. Several ECE countries view the continued presence of OSCE missions in their country as 'stigma', and have pushed for them to be closed (Cohen 1998: 76).

62. Here I am agreeing with Chandler that 'The OSCE-led international consensus on national minority rights protection would appear to be much weaker than the conference agreements and public declarations from leading statesmen might suggest' (Chandler 1999: 71).

63. As I just noted, the OSCE often attempts to provide arguments of justice for the recommendations which emerge from its security-track activities. However, it is considerations of security which determine which minority issues are scrutinized, and which recommendations are advanced.

64. Burgess argues that this is true of all attempts at intervention: 'Historical evidence suggests that the politicisation which follows external involvement is more likely to escalate domestic stand-offs into wider conflicts, and local rivalries into broader questions of the international pecking order, than bring peace and harmony. No matter how difficult, internal problems can only be resolved by internal actors—without the "disciplining" force of external powers looming over them' (Burgess 1999: 59). Burgess offers no evidence for this claim, which I think is probably false as a generalization. But it may be true of interventions founded solely on considerations of power politics, unsupported by a clear rationale in terms of universal and impartially-administered principles.

65. Posted on MINELRES, 26 November 1999.

66. Similarly, the Romanian government has said that claims for autonomy are 'anachronistic', as if 'mature' democracies do not adopt such means.

67. See also the Resolution of the Slovak Republic on the ratification of its treaty with Hungary (28 March 1996), which states that Slovakia 'similarly to the whole international community' rejects on principle 'the conception of collective rights of minorities as well as any kind of attempt to establish autonomous structures with special status based on ethnic principles' (quoted in Thornberry 1998: 115). Similarly, when Moldova offered territorial autonomy to Gaugazia, Romania criticized them for 'setting up special-status regions instead of applying internationally accepted standards', and of encouraging a 'possible federalization' of the country that fails to defend 'the rights of the majority population'—meaning presumably the 'right' of the ethnic Moldovans that every important decision be made in a forum where they form a majority. See Socor 1994.

68. Compared to other Balkan countries, Macedonia is indeed a model of ethnic coexistence, but Albanians in Macedonia have nowhere near the sorts of rights accorded many Western national minorities, in terms of official language status, tertiary education—Macedonia bulldozed a privately-funded Albanian-language university in Tetovo—or regional autonomy.

69. Estimates of the Albanian population in Macedonia are notoriously difficult, and very politicized. The official estimates are around 30%, but many think it is closer to 40%, and because of the differential birth rates, it is widely expected that Albanians will in fact become the majority in a few decades—it is no surprise, therefore, that Macedonia was reluctant to accept Albanian refugees from Kosovo. To try to hide the reality of this growing Albanian population, the Macedonian government has avoided an accurate count of the population, and indeed at one point was making it difficult for Albanians to register births.

70. Part of the problem here is that majority nationalists in ECE often invoke the Western language of civic nationalism, common citizenship, and constitutional patriotism to justify removing self-governing minority institutions. Hence we have the odd situation in which authoritarian nationalists in ECE are invoking the language of civic nationalism, and the OSCE doesn't know how to respond, since it doesn't want to be seen as defending 'ethnic' minority nationalism. This is one of the pernicious consequences of the popularity of the myth of the 'neutral' state amongst Western political theorists. As both Vàrady and Tsilevich note, the language of civic nationalism and common citizenship is in fact more easily used and abused by defenders of homogenous nation-states than by defenders of multination federations—for similar observations, see Hughes 1999: 6; Kymlicka 2001: ch. 15.

71. Power-sharing takes many forms in the West, and it will surely do so in ECE as well. There are undoubtedly some circumstances where consociational models— based on minority veto rights within common institutions—are preferable to federal models—based on minority self-government over separate institutions. Note that the same choice between self-government or consociational veto rights can emerge at lower levels. In Romania, for example, there is currently a debate about whether Hungarians should have a separate Hungarian-language university, or whether there should be a bilingual Hungarian-Romanian university in which Hungarians would have a veto right over important changes to the university's rules. However, in this debate, as in the debate about federalism or consociationalism at the level of the state, the majority shows little enthusiasm for either model of power-sharing.

72. In general, the sorts of minority rights which the OSCE is currently promoting— primarily linguistic, education, and participation rights—do not challenge the majority's commitment to a unitary nation-state, or challenge the majority's belief that a multination federation is abnormal and dangerous. In the short-term, this decision to limit the range of minority rights being pursued may indeed be the most pragmatic approach to take. But it's important to realize that this is not a healthy long-term scenario for many ECE countries. It may be sufficient in relatively homogenous ECE countries like Poland, Hungary, or Slovenia, but it is a mistake in countries like Slovakia, Macedonia, Georgia, Moldova, Bulgaria, and Romania. Any stable long-term solution in these countries will require directly challenging the principle that a normal state is a centralized, unitary state with majoritarian democratic procedures. It would be helpful, therefore, for the OSCE to more sharply distinguish questions of short-term pragmatism from long-term justice. Paradoxically, part of the problem here, I believe, is the HCNM's attempt to always provide a cover of justice for his security recommendations. He continually tries to merge, rather than clearly distinguish, issues of security and justice. While the OSCE may have to acknowledge the concerns of ECE states about their short-term security, he should not endorse the views of ECE states about long-term justice. On the need to distinguish short-term pragmatic reasons from enduring principles in minority rights debates, see Kovács 2000.

73. My suspicion is that, if there were such an open and informed debate, at least some ECE countries would adopt federalism. For as Crawford Young puts it, the main justification for federalism is simply that 'no other formula could work' for many ethnically diverse societies with territorially-concentrated minorities (1994: 12; cf. Stepan 1999). And as I noted earlier, Russia and Ukraine are almost certainly better off today for having granted TA. However, my main goal is

not to promote TA claims in particular, but rather to promote an environment in which these and other minority claims can be freely discussed and fairly evaluated.

74. The HCNM has in fact been actively engaged in the elaboration of new international norms, reflected in its recent recommendations on education, linguistic, and participation rights—see note 40 above—but these still avoid the difficult issues of autonomy, veto rights, official language status, and higher education, and in any event are not legally binding. And most people assume that they will only be invoked to pressure ECE states, not Western states.

75. Hence my disagreement with the current OSCE strategy is not the modesty of its short-term goals, but rather the fact that the OSCE is pretending as if these modest goals are sufficient to fairly accommodate diversity, and is tacitly—and sometimes explicitly—endorsing the view that minority demands for more substantial rights are 'radical'. We should be modest in our short-term pragmatic aims, but clear about the long-term requirements of justice.

76. For a discussion of the role of bilateral treaties, see Gal 1999.

77. This is one reason why federalism in India has failed to reduce Kashmiri secessionist sentiments. In the name of national security, the central government intervenes constantly to replace elected state governments, repeal state laws, and so on. Federalism only works to reduce secessionist sentiments if it allows for genuine self-government.

78. Rawls argues that a liberal-democratic theory of justice should be premised on the idea that people are bound to a state 'in perpetuity'. I believe that this is an unrealistic and inappropriate goal, particularly in multination states. See Kymlicka 2001: ch. 5.

79. 'In Western and Northern Europe the political rise or decline of one's country, the growth or diminution of its role as a great power, and the gaining or losing of colonial empires could have been mere episodes, distant adventures, beautiful or sad memories; in the long run, however, countries could survive these without fundamental trauma, because they had something that could not be taken away or questioned'. In Eastern Europe, by contrast, there was 'an existential fear for one's community' (Bibo 1991: 39).

80. This distinction is emphasized by Walzer and Schöpflin, and endorsed as well by Barša, although he attaches less normative significance to it. The commentators do not all agree on this point, however. Andreescu, for example, thinks I *overstate* the difference between East and West. And Djumeav suggests that the fundamental cleavage is not between New World and Old World, but between Christian states and Muslim states.

81. And unlike immigrants, there is no way to avoid this injustice by granting corporatist rights to such subgroups so that they can exist outside of the dominant society. Justice for these subgroups must involve equality within the institutions of the dominant nation, not self-government outside them.

82. For example, the thinning of Québécois national culture and identity in the 1950s and 1960s predated the influx of immigrants in the late 1960s and 1970s. The increasing presence of immigrants has reinforced this process of liberalization, but was not the initial cause.

83. This shows the importance of situating issues of ethnocultural minorities within the broader context of issues of diversity and pluralism. In this Part, I have restricted my focus to the claims of ethnocultural groups, but this is an artificial limitation, and a more thorough discussion would have to explore the links with,

for example, feminism, gay rights, the growth of alternative religious communities, and so on.

84. Walzer might deny that thicker forms of nation-building are unjust to subgroups within the dominant nation. Or perhaps he would agree that it is unjust on liberal grounds, but that Old World countries need not be liberal. In other writings, he has indeed emphasized that not all states should be liberal. It would take us too far afield to enter that debate here. So let me rephrase my argument: I believe that any *liberal* country should thin its conception of national culture—although of course individual citizens will have and nurture various and sometimes competing thicker notions of this culture. This is needed, not only to accommodate immigrant diversity, but also to accommodate diversity within the dominant national group.

85. Compare Romania and Hungary, or Greece and Italy, or France and Britain.

86. In any event, it's important to note that this issue about the thickness of the national culture is only relevant to the claims of immigrants or dispersed groups, not to sizeable national minorities. Walzer's view endorses the same principle of self-government for national minorities as my approach.

87. Perhaps the term 'nation-building' would no longer be appropriate when discussing the majority-privileging policies adopted in such transnational institutions. We could instead call them 'political-community-building' policies. If so, we could then say that the traditional 'nation-building/minority rights' dialectic within sovereign states is just one particular form of a more general dialectic that can arise at various levels in a postnational order: namely, the dialectic between 'political-community-building' and minority rights. The terminology may differ in a postnational context, but the problem is structurally similar.

88. There are many other points in the commentaries that deserve a response. Let me mention just three of them: (a) Ossipov chastises me for using the rhetoric of 'hosts and guests'. In fact, I have never used these terms, and firmly reject any notion of hosts and guests. As I explained in Part 1, all permanent residents should be seen as equally citizens of the state, and of their substate government. All permanent residents equally 'belong' there, and the state equally belongs to them. So any notion of 'guests' is out of place for permanent residents. But this doesn't yet tell us where the boundaries of states and substate units should be drawn, or how powers should be distributed amongst and between levels of government. Nor does it tell us anything about the languages of public institutions at either the state or substate level. My answer to these questions is that these decisions should be made in such a way as to enable national minorities to maintain themselves as distinct societal cultures if they so desire. I still think that is the principle most consistent with liberal equality; (b) Ossipov also claims that the very distinction between immigrants and national minorities cannot be made, and that the usage of these labels is merely a matter of power politics. I certainly agree that there are grey areas and hard cases, and that the application of these terms will often be politically contested. This is well illustrated in the commentaries by Pettai and Tsilevich. This is not however a reason to abandon the concepts. Almost all political concepts—including that of 'person' or 'citizen' or 'democracy'—generate hard cases and grey areas. As with all concepts, we have to distinguish between good-faith disagreements over how to apply a contested term from cynical manipulation of the term to serve self-interested motives. I don't see that the terms immigrants and national minorities are any more subject to misuse than other political categories and concepts, and various theorists in

the ECE region agree that it is a useful and necessary distinction—see, for example, Vàrady 1997: 14–15; Kaklins 1994: 7; cf. Kymlicka 2001: ch. 3). There are some clear-cut cases where the concepts work well to guide us; and there are hard cases where we need to discuss in good faith how to deal with the anomalies and complexities. (c) Andreescu and Doroszewska both mention the question of the costs of minority rights under conditions of economic hardship. This is an important question, but it cannot be invoked as a blanket justification or explanation for the hostility to minority rights in ECE. On the contrary, many states have scrapped minority rights even when this has increased costs to the state—for example, changing the names of streets or cities or toponyms; replacing existing bilingual signs with unilingual signs; forbidding private minority-language schools or media. Moreover, some ECE countries have actually turned down offers of financial assistance from other countries to fund minority rights provisions. Concerns about costs are often a smokescreen to obscure much deeper sources of opposition to minority rights.

REFERENCES

Alexanderson, Martin (1997) 'The Need for a Generalised Application of the minorities regime in Europe', *Helsinki Monitor*, 4, 47–58.

Alfredsson, Gudmundur and Turk, Danilo (1993) 'International Mechanisms for the Monitoring and Protection of Minority Rights: Their Advantages, Disadvantages and Interrelationships', in Arie Bloed (ed) *Monitoring Human Rights in Europe: Comparing International Procedures and Mechanisms* (Kluwer, Norwell, MA), 169–86.

Barcz, Jan (1992) 'European Standards for the Protection of National Minorities', in Arie Bloed and Wilco de Jonge (eds) *Legal Aspects of a New European Infrastructure* (Europa Instituut, Utrecht), 87–99.

Bibo, Istvan (1991) 'The Distress of East European Small States', [1946] in Karoly Nagy (ed) *Democracy, Revolution, Self-Determination* (Social Science Monographs, Boulder, CO), 13–86.

Brett, Rachel (1993) 'The Human Dimension of the CSCE and the CSCE Response to Minorities', in Michael Lucas (ed) *The CSCE in the 1990s: Constructing European Security and Cooperation* (Nomos Verlagsgesellschaft, Baden-Baden), 143–60.

Bunce, Valerie (1999) *Subversive Institutions: The Design and the Destruction of Socialism and the State* (Cambridge University Press, Cambridge).

Burgess, Adam (1999) 'Critical Reflections on the Return of National Minority Rights to East/West European Affairs', in Karl Cordell (ed) *Ethnicity and Democratisation in the New Europe* (Routledge, London), 49–60.

Chandler, David (1999) 'The OSCE and the internationalisation of national minority rights', in Karl Cordell (ed) *Ethnicity and Democratisation in the New Europe* (Routledge, London), 61–76.

Cohen, Jonathan (1998) *Conflict Prevention Instruments in the Organiza-
tion for Security and Cooperation in Europe* (Netherlands Institute of
International Relations, The Hague).
Coppieters, Bruno *et al.* (eds) (2000) *Federal Practice: Exploring Alternatives
for Georgia and Abkhazia* (VUB University Press, Brussels).
Cornwall, Mark (1996) 'Minority Rights and Wrongs in Eastern Europe in
the Twentieth Century', *The Historian*, 50, 16–20.
Daftary, Farimah and Kinga Gal (2000) *The New Slovak Language Law:
Internal or External Politics* (European Centre for Minority Issues,
Working Paper 7, Flensburg).
Dimitras, Panayote (1998) 'The Minority Rights Paradox', *War Report*, 58
(February–March 1998).
Dorff, Robert (1994) 'Federalism in Eastern Europe: Part of the Solution or
Part of the Problem?' *Publius*, 24, 99–114.
Druviete, Ina (1997) 'Linguistic Human Rights in the Baltic States', *Inter-
national Journal of the Sociology of Language*, 127, 161–85.
Dunay, Pal (1997) 'Concerns and Opportunities: The Development of
Romanian-Hungarian Relations and National Minorities', in Gunther
Bachler (ed) *Federalism Against Ethnicity: Institutional, Legal and Demo-
cratic Instruments to Prevent Violent Minority Conflicts* (Verlag Ruegger,
Zurich), 215–27.
Erk, Can (1999) 'Anarchic Subsystems, Security Dilemma and Federalism:
Kurdish Nationalism in Turkey', paper presented at Association for the
Study of Nationalities Annual Convention, New York, May 1999.
Estebanez, Maria (1997) 'The High Commissioner on National Minorities:
Development of the Mandate', in Michael Brohe, Natalia Rozitli, and
Allan Rosas (eds) *The OSCE in the Maintenance of Peace and Security*
(Kluwer, The Hague, 1997).
European Commission for Democracy through Law (1996) 'Opinion of the
Venice Commission on the Interpretation of Article 11 of the draft
protocol to the European Convention on Human Rights appended to
Recommendation 1201' (Council of Europe, Strasbourg).
Ford, Stuart (1999) 'OSCE National Minority Rights in the United States:
The Limits of Conflict Resolution', *Suffolk Transnational Law Review*,
23/1, 1–55.
Gal, Kinga (1999) *Bilateral Agreements in Central and Eastern Europe: A
New Inter-State Framework for Minority Protection* (European Centre
for Minority Issues, Working Paper 4, Flensburg).
Greek Helsinki Monitor (2000) 'Statement at the OSCE on (Partly or Fully)
Unrecognized Minorities in Albania, Bulgaria, France, Greece, Macedo-
nia, Slovenia and Turkey', (24 October 2000, posted on MINELRES, 27
October 2000).
Guzina, Dejan (2000) *Nationalism in the Context of an Illiberal Multination
State: The Case of Serbia* (Ph.D. thesis, Department of Political Science,
Carleton University, Ottawa).

Hamilton, Paul (1999) 'The Scottish National Paradox: The Scottish National Party's Lack of Ethnic Character', *Canadian Review of Studies in Nationalism*, 26, 17–36.

Heintz, Hans-Joachim (1997) 'Autonomy and Protection of Minorities under International Law', in Gunther Bachler (ed) *Federalism Against Ethnicity: Institutional, Legal and Democratic Instruments to Prevent Violent Minority Conflicts* (Verlag Ruegger, Zurich), 81–92.

——(1998) 'On the Legal Understanding of Autonomy', in Markku Suksi (ed) *Autonomy: Applications and Implications* (Kluwer, The Hague), 7–32.

Holmes, Stephen (1999) 'Can Weak-State Liberalism Survive?', in Dan Avnon and Arner de-Shalit (eds) *Liberalism and Its Practice* (Routledge, London), 31–49.

Horowitz, Donald (1985) *Ethnic Groups in Conflict* (University of California Press, Berkeley).

Hughes, James (1999) 'Institutional Responses to Separatism: Federalism and Transition to Democracy in Russia', paper presented to Association for the Study of Nationalities Annual Convention, New York, May 1999.

Hungarian Coalition in Slovakia (1997) *The Hungarians in Slovakia* (Information Centre of the Hungarian Coalition in Slovakia, Bratislava).

Ilishev, Ildus (1998) 'Russian Federalism: Political, Legal and Ethnolingual Aspects: A View from the Republic of Bashkortostan', *Nationalities Papers*, 26/4, 723–39.

Järve, Priit (2000) "Language Legislation in the Baltic States. Changes of Rationale", presented to the annual meeting of the Association for the Study of Nationalities, New York.

Kalin, Walter (1997) 'Federalism and the Resolution of Minority Conflicts', in Gunther Bachler (ed) *Federalism Against Ethnicity: Institutional, Legal and Democratic Instruments to Prevent Violent Minority Conflicts* (Verlag Ruegger, Zurich), 169–83.

Karklins, Rasma (1994) *Ethnopolitics and Transition to Democracy: The Collapse of the USSR and Latvia* (Woodrow Wilson Center Press, Washington D.C.).

——(2000) 'Ethnopluralism: Panacea for East Central Europe?', *Nationalities Papers*, 28/2: 219–41.

Kovács, Mária (2000) 'Standards of Self-Determination and Minority Rights in the Post-Soviet Era: A Historical Perspective', forthcoming in *CEU Nationalism Studies Yearbook*, (CEU Press, Budapest, 2001).

Kymlicka, Will (2001) *Politics in the Vernacular: Nationalism, Multiculturalism and Citizenship* (Oxford University Press, Oxford).

Laponce, Jean (1987) *Languages and their Territories* (University of Toronto Press, Toronto).

——(1993) 'The Case for Ethnic Federalism in Multilingual Societies: Canada's Regional Imperative', *Regional Politics and Policy*, 3/1, 23–43.

Lejeune, Yves (1994) 'Le Fédéralisme en Belgique', in Leslie Seidle (ed) *Seeking a New Canadian Partnership: Asymmetrical and Confederal Options* (Institute for Research on Public Policy, Montreal), 171–86.

Will Kymlicka 411

Lewis-Anthony, Sian (1998) 'Autonomy and the Council of Europe—With Special Reference to the Application of Article 3 of the First Protocol of the European Convention on Human Rights', in Markku Suksi (ed) *Autonomy: Applications and Implications* (Kluwer, The Hague), 317–42.
Liebich, André (1995) 'Nations, States and Minorities: Why is Eastern Europe Different?', *Dissent*, Summer 1995, 313–17.
——(1998) *Ethnic Minorities and Long-Term Implications of EU Enlargement'* (Robert Schuman Centre, Working Paper RSC 98/49, European University Institute, Florence).
Lynn, Nicholas and Novikov, Alexei (1997) 'Refederalizing Russia: Debates on the idea of federalism in Russia', *Publius*, 27/2, 187–203.
Mansour, Gerda (1993) *Multilingualism and Nation Building* (Multilingual Matters, Clevedon).
Mihalikova, Silvia (1998) 'The Hungarian Minority in Slovakia: Conflict Over Autonomy', in Magda Opalski (ed) *Managing Diversity in Plural Societies: Minorities, Migration and Nation-Building in Post-Communist Europe* (Forum Eastern Europe, Ottawa), 148–64.
MINELRES (Electronic Resources of Minority Rights in Eastern Europe): daily messages are archived at http://www.riga.lv/minelres
Nelson, Daniel (1998) 'Hungary and its Neighbours: Security and Ethnic Minorities', *Nationalities Papers*, 26/2, 314–30.
Offe, Claus (1993) 'Ethnic Politics in East European Transitions', in Jody Jensen and Ferenc Miszlivetz (eds) *Paradoxes of Transition* (Savaria University Press, Szombathely), 11–40.
Packer, John (1996) 'The OSCE and international guarantees of local self-government', in *Local Self-Government, Territorial Integrity, and protection of minorities* (European Commission for Democracy Through Law, Council of Europe Publishing, Strasbourg), 250–72.
——(1998) 'Autonomy within the OSCE: The Case of Crimea', in Markku Suksi (ed) *Autonomy: Applications and Implications* (Kluwer, The Hague), 295–316.
——(2000) 'Making International Law Matter in Preventing Ethnic Conflicts', *New York University Journal of International Law and Politics*, 32/3, 715–24.
Poulton, Hugh (1998) *Minorities in Southeast Europe: Inclusion and Exclusion* (Minority Rights Group, London).
Pritchard, Eleonar (2000) 'A University of Their Own', *Central Europe Review*, 2/24, 19 June 2000. Available at: groups.yahoo.com/group/multiethnic/message/682
Ramet, Sabrina (1997) *Whose Democracy? Nationalism, Religion, and the Doctrine of Collective Rights in Post-1989 Eastern Europe* (Rowman and Littlefield, London).
Ratner, Steven (2000) 'Does International Law Matter in Preventing Ethnic Conflicts?', *New York University Journal of International Law and Politics*, 32/3, 591–698.

412   *Reply and Conclusion*

Reaume, Denise (1995) 'Justice between Cultures: Autonomy and the Protection of Cultural Affiliation', *UBC Law Review*, 29/1, 117–41.

Resler, Tamara (1997) 'Dilemmas of Democratisation: Safeguarding Minorities in Russia, Ukraine and Lithuania', *Europe-Asia Studies*, 49/1, 89–106.

Senelle, Robert (1989) 'Constitutional Reform in Belgium: From Unitarism towards Federalism', in Murray Forsyth (ed) *Federalism and Nationalism* (Leicester University Press, Leicester), 51–95.

Smith, Graham (1996) 'Russia, ethnoregionalism and the politics of federation', *Ethnic and Racial Studies*, 19/2, 391–410.

Socor, Vladimir (1994) 'Gagauz Autonomy in Moldova: A Precedent for Eastern Europe?', *RFE/RL Research Report*, 3/33, 20–8.

Solnick, Steven (1998) 'Will Russia Survive? Center and Periphery in the Russian Federation', in Barnett Rubin and Jack Snyder (eds) *Post-Soviet Political Order: Conflict and State-Building* (Routledge, London), 58–80.

Stepan, Alfred (1999) 'Federalism and Democracy: Beyond the US Model', *Journal of Democracy*, 10/4, 19–34.

——(2000) 'Russian Federalism in Comparative Perspective', *Post-Soviet Affairs*, 16/2, 133–76.

Teague, Elizabeth (1994) 'Center-Periphery Relations in the Russian Federation', in Roman Szporluk (ed) *National Identity and Ethnicity in Russia and the New States of Eurasia* (M. E. Sharpe, Armonk), 21–57.

Thompson, Paula (1998) 'The Gagauz in Moldova and Their Road to Autonomy', in Magda Opalski (ed) *Managing Diversity in Plural Societies: Minorities, Migration and Nation-Building in Post-Communist Europe* (Forum Eastern Europe, Ottawa), 128–47.

Thornberry, Patrick (1998) 'Images of Autonomy and Individual and Collective Rights in International Instruments on the Rights of Minorities', in Markku Suksi (ed) *Autonomy: Applications and Implications* (Kluwer, The Hague), 97–124.

Tolz, Vera (1998) 'Forging the Nation: National Identity and Nation Building in Post-Communist Russia', *Europe-Asia Studies*, 50/6, 993–1022.

Troebst, Stefan (1998) *Conflict in Kosovo: Failure of Prevention* (European Centre for Minority Issues, Flensburg).

van der Stoel, Max (1999) *Peace and Stability through Human and Minority Rights: Speeches by the OSCE High Commissioner on National Minorities* (Nomos Verlagsgesellschaft, Baden-Baden).

Várady, Tibor (1997) 'Majorities, Minorities, Law and Ethnicity: Reflections on the Yugoslav Case', *Human Rights Quarterly*, 19, 9–54.

Varennes, Fernand de (1997) 'Ethnic Conflicts and Language in Eastern Europe and Central Asian States: Can Human Rights Help Prevent Them?', *International Journal on Minority and Group Rights*, 5, 153–74.

Vasilyeva, Olga (1995) 'Has Ethnic Federalism a Future in Russia?', *New Times*, March 1995, 34–7.

Waever, Ole (1995) 'Securitization and Desecuritization', in Ronnie

Lipschutz (ed) *On Security* (Columbia University Press, New York, NY), 46–86.

Walzer, Michael (1997) *On Toleration* (Yale University Press, New Haven, CT).

Ware, Robert Bruce and Kisriev, Enver (1999) 'Ethnic Parity and Democratic Pluralism in Dagestan: A Consociational Approach', paper delivered at Association for the Study of Nationalities annual meeting, New York.

Wheatley, Steven (1997) 'Minority Rights and Political Accommodation in the "New" Europe', *European Law Review*, 22 Supplement, HRC63-HRC81.

Young, Crawford (1994) *Ethnic Diversity and Public Policy: An Overview* (UNRISD, Occasional Paper 8).

Zaagman, Rob (1997) 'Commentary', in Wolfgang Danspeckgruber and Arthur Watts (eds) *Self-Determination and Self-Administration: A Sourcebook* (Lynne Rienner, Boulder, CO), 248–54.

——(1999) *Conflict Prevention in the Baltic States: The OSCE High Commissioner on National Minorities in Estonia, Latvia and Lithuania* (ECMI Monograph 1, European Centre for Minority Issues, Flensburg).

INDEX

428   *Index*